GOD'S
New Testament
ECONOMY

☺

W I T N E S S   L E E

Living Stream Ministry
Anaheim, CA • www.lsm.org

First Edition, March 1986.

Library of Congress Catalog
Card Number: 86-80370

ISBN 978-0-87083-199-7

Published by

Living Stream Ministry
2431 W. La Palma Ave., Anaheim, CA 92801 U.S.A.
P. O. Box 2121, Anaheim, CA 92814 U.S.A.

Printed in the United States of America

16 17 18 19 20 21 / 16 15 14 13 12 11

CONTENTS

FOREWORD

Fifty-one messages given by Brother Witness Lee during 1984 in Stuttgart, Germany and several localities in the United States constitute the content of this book of forty-four chapters. Brother Lee has told us that what is presented in this volume is the consummation of what the Lord has shown us in His recovery and that the chart on pages 12 and 13 is the extract and final reaping of his fifty-nine years of studying the New Testament.

Through the ministry of our brother as he has opened the Word to us in the United States since 1962, we have been helped to realize that the one thing that should be focused on, stressed, and ministered in the Lord's recovery is God's New Testament economy. We have seen that God's *oikonomia,* economy (1 Tim. 1:4), is God's household administration, His household management, His plan to distribute or dispense Himself into His chosen, redeemed, and regenerated people as their life and everything to produce a unique thing in the universe, the Body of Christ, which is His corporate expression as the golden lampstands in this age and ultimately as the New Jerusalem for eternity. The Triune God dispenses Himself in His entirety into us, His Body, by the Father being embodied in the Son and the Son being realized and consummated as the Spirit, reaching us through seven major steps, for our experience, enjoyment, and building up. The content of this divine economy is a wonderful, all-inclusive Person. This Person is the processed and consummated Triune God— the Father, the Son, and the Spirit. The New Testament is a full record of the marvelous revelation of God's New Testament economy.

May the Lord richly supply us with His grace that we might see, possess, and minister such a revelation. May the Lord also preserve us from any teachings or practices, however "scriptural," that might distract us from this basic, crucial, and central matter—the New Testament economy of God.

February 1986   Benson Phillips
Irving, Texas

CHAPTER ONE

AN INTRODUCTORY WORD

Scripture Reading: Eph. 1:9-10; 3:9-11, 2; Col. 1:25-27

The entire revelation of the entire Bible shows us God's dispensing. The Bible shows us that God wants to dispense Himself into His chosen people. No other point is so crucial or so central as this one. God chose us, predestinated us, redeemed us, saved us, and regenerated us for the purpose of dispensing and working Himself into us. God's intention is shown in the Old Testament, but it was not fully revealed. The full development of the revelation concerning God's intention to dispense Himself into us is in the New Testament. In the New Testament this matter is the main subject and the focus of God's economy.

GOD'S ECONOMY

God's economy is God's plan, and this plan is a kind of arrangement. This arrangement is His administrative dispensation. God has a plan, a divine arrangement, an administration, to distribute Himself into His chosen people. Ephesians 1:9-10 and 3:9-11 fully reveal this matter. The word dispensation in these verses refers to God's economy, God's plan, God's arrangement, God's administrative dispensation. This arrangement, this plan, this dispensation, is for God to dispense Himself as the processed Triune God into His chosen people. The Divine Trinity is for the divine dispensing. The matter of dispensing is revealed in Ephesians 3:2 and Colossians 1:25-27. In these verses the word stewardship means dispensing. A stewardship is a dispensing. A waiter in a restaurant has a stewardship to serve food to others. To serve food, to dispense food to people, is the stewardship of

the waiter. Paul told us that God had given him a stewardship. His stewardship was his dispensing duty to dispense
Christ as the embodiment of the Triune God into God's chosen
people. Today our preaching the gospel and ministering the
Word must be a dispensing of the Triune God into people.

The New Testament Revealing the Triune God
for Dispensing

We must realize that the entire New Testament is a dispensing book. It opens the veil to show us God's desire to
dispense Himself into His people. Many Christians would say
that the Bible is a book of salvation. The Bible, however, is
something more than this—it is a book that reveals the dispensing of the Father, the Son, and the Spirit, embodied in
Christ, consummated in the Spirit, and intensified in the
seven Spirits, into His chosen and redeemed people.

The New Testament Unveiling a Wonderful Person

There are twenty-seven books in the New Testament.
When I was young, I was taught that the New Testament
could be divided into three sections. The first section was the
five books from Matthew through Acts, the historical books.
The second section was comprised of the Epistles, the letters
written by the apostles from Romans through Jude. The last
section was comprised of the book of Revelation, a book of
prophecy. I would not say that this interpretation is wrong,
but it is superficial.

The New Testament unveils to us a wonderful Person.
This wonderful Person was first the Son of God unveiled in
the four Gospels. Then this Person became the life-giving
Spirit, unveiled in a full and detailed way in the twenty-two
books from Acts through Jude. Then in Revelation this
life-giving Spirit is intensified into the seven Spirits. By this
we can see that the New Testament shows us a Person as the
Son of God, as the Spirit, and eventually as the seven Spirits.

I have been studying the Bible nearly every day since
1925. The chart on pages 12 and 13 is the consummation,
final reaping, and extract of my fifty-nine years of studying
the New Testament. This chart shows us that the content of

God's New Testament economy is a Person. To say that this Person is Jesus Christ is right, but not absolutely, perfectly, and completely right. The content of the New Testament economy of God is a Person, and this Person is the Triune God. God's *oikonomia,* God's household administration, is to distribute Himself as the Triune God—the Father, the Son, and the Spirit—into all His chosen people. The twenty-seven books of the New Testament are a full revelation of one great Person—the Triune God. No one is greater than the Triune God. His greatness reaches to an extent which is far beyond our apprehension.

The Son, with the Father, by the Spirit— the Embodiment of the Triune God

In the first section, the four Gospels, this wonderful Person was revealed as the Son of God coming with the Father by the Spirit to be the embodiment of the Triune God in Jesus Christ as God's tabernacle and God's temple, living the life of God to develop into the kingdom of God. This is in the Gospels as the initiation.

The Triune God is first revealed in the New Testament as the Son of God in His humanity—Jesus Christ. We must realize, however, that when the Son came, He did not come alone and leave the Father on the throne. This is a wrong thought in the teaching of tritheism. The ones who have this concept use Matthew 3:16-17 as a basis for their belief. In these verses, the Son went up from the water, the Spirit descended upon the Son, and the Father spoke concerning the Son. These verses do prove that the Father, the Son, and the Spirit exist simultaneously. The tritheists, however, press the side of the three in the Godhead too far, and they consider the Father as a God, the Son as another God, and the Spirit as a third God. Many of us have held or even now hold this concept, unconsciously or subconsciously, that there are three Gods.

The New Testament reveals that when the Son of God came, He came with the Father (John 8:29; 16:32). The Son said that He was never alone on this earth because the Father was with Him all the time. The Son was with the Father and by

GOD'S NEW TEST

| 1. | 2. |

Matthew ⟵⟶ John   Acts ⟵

       The Son   The

With the Father   By the Spirit   As the Son

The Embodiment   The Consum

of   of

The Triune God   The Triune

in   in

Jesus Christ   The

as   as

God's Tabernacle   God's Temple   The Body of Christ

The Kingdom of God

Living the Life of God   Living

To Develop into   un

The Kingdom of God   The Fullness

Gospels   (Initiation)   22 Books

AMENT ECONOMY

	3.
⟶ Jude	Revelation

Spirit ↘	The Seven Spirits
With the Father	Out from the Eternal One ↙ ↘ Of the Redeemer
mation	The Intensification
	of
God	The Triune God
	in
Church	The Overcoming Church
	Consummating in
The Temple of God	(1) The Golden Lampstands
The House of God	(2) The New Jerusalem
Christ	
to	
of God	
(Development)	Revelation (Finalization)

the Spirit. Matthew 1:18 and 20 tells us that Mary "was found having in womb out of the Holy Spirit" (lit.) and "the thing begotten [generated] in her is out of the Holy Spirit" (lit.). The Holy Spirit was the very divine essence that constituted Jesus' conception. The One who was born of the virgin Mary and named Jesus had the divine essence in His being; this was the reason that He was born not merely as a man but as the God-man. He was the complete God and the perfect Man because the divine essence was His very constitution. Therefore, the Son came in the flesh with the Father and by the Spirit.

Also, the Son with the Father by the Spirit came to be the embodiment of the Triune God (Col. 2:9). This One is the Triune God embodied. Do not consider that the Son could be alone, separated from the Father or from the Spirit. According to the entire revelation of the Bible, the Father, the Son, and the Spirit are coexisting and coinhering from eternity past to eternity future. Coexisting means to exist together at the same time, but coinhering means to exist within one another, to abide in each other. When the Lord Jesus told Philip that He was in the Father and that the Father was in Him, this is coinhering. It is easy to demonstrate the coexistence of three items. It is more than difficult, however, to demonstrate the coinherence of three items. How marvelous it is that the three of the Godhead coexist and coinhere from eternity to eternity!

When Jesus was walking on this earth, He was not separate from the Father, leaving the Father in heaven, and He was not separate from the Spirit, leaving the Spirit as a dove soaring in the sky. He was the Son living in His humanity with the Father and by the Spirit. The Son with the Father and by the Spirit is the embodiment of the Triune God in Jesus Christ. This is fully confirmed by Colossians 2:9 which says, "For in Him dwells all the fullness of the Godhead bodily." The Godhead is the Father, the Son, and the Spirit. All of the fullness of the Triune Godhead dwelt in this Man Jesus Christ bodily, so this Man was the embodiment of the Triune God as the Son, with the Father, and by the Spirit.

This embodiment of the Triune God is God's tabernacle

and also God's temple. In the Old Testament, both the tabernacle and the temple were types of Jesus Christ. John 1:14 tells us that the Word became flesh and tabernacled among us. This indicates that the humanity of Jesus was a tabernacle to embody God. Furthermore, in John 2:19 and 21 the Lord told us that His body was God's temple. This embodiment of the Triune God also lived the life of God. He did not live the life of anything else. He did not live the life of an angel or of a good man. He lived the life of God because He was the embodiment of God. He could not live any other life, and He should not have lived any other life. He had to live the unique life of God for the expression of God to develop into the kingdom of God. The four Gospels reveal to us the Person of the Son of God, Jesus Christ, and they also reveal to us that the life lived by this Person was the life of God. The four Gospels also refer us frequently to the kingdom of God. Many of us do not realize thoroughly what the kingdom is. The kingdom of God is a Person (Luke 17:21), and the development of this wonderful Person (Mark 4:3, 26).

All of this is in the four Gospels as the initiation. The word initiation means to have a start that will usher the entire situation into a new realm. In the four Gospels there is a new start, a new age, and a new dispensation. The Gospels are an initiation to usher the entire situation into a new realm. The Gospels talk about the Son with the Father by the Spirit to be the embodiment of the Triune God in Jesus Christ as God's tabernacle and God's temple, living the life of God to develop into the kingdom of God.

The Spirit, as the Son, with the Father— the Consummation of the Triune God

The second section is from Acts through Jude. What is revealed here is the Spirit. The Son who became flesh died and resurrected and became the life-giving Spirit (1 Cor. 15:45b). In these twenty-two books this life-giving Spirit is as the Son with the Father. In the four Gospels the Trinity was the Son with the Father by the Spirit, but in these twenty-two books the Trinity is the Spirit as the Son with the Father. This is the consummation of the Triune God in the church as the Body of Christ, the temple of God, the kingdom of God, and the house of God, living Christ unto the fullness of God. The fullness of God means the expression of God in full. After His death and resurrection the Lord Jesus became the Spirit as the Son with the Father to be the consummation of the Triune God, not only in one Person, Jesus Christ, but in the church as the Body of Christ, the temple of God, the kingdom of God, and the house of God. This is a corporate Person, and this corporate Person lives Christ unto the fullness of God, the expression of God in full. This is the development in the twenty-two books from Acts to Jude of the initiation in the Gospels. Today we are in this development.

The second section of the New Testament still talks about the same Person, but in a further stage. In the four Gospels we can see how God, the Triune, became incarnated, manifested in the flesh. The complete God, the God of the Trinity, became flesh and lived on this earth for thirty-three and a half years. He died on the cross for our sins to accomplish a full redemption for us, and He was resurrected. First Corinthians 15:45b tells us clearly that the last Adam, Jesus Christ, became a life-giving Spirit through death and resurrection. On the day of His resurrection, He came back to His disciples as the Spirit, the "pneumatic Christ."

The Lord came with a resurrected body (Luke 24:37-40; 1 Cor. 15:44) into the room where the disciples were with the door shut. He was there with a resurrected body because He showed them His hands and His side. He was there in a pneumatic way. Then He breathed into His disciples and said to them, "Receive the Holy Spirit" (John 20:22). The Greek word for Spirit is *pneuma* which can be translated into either spirit, breath, or wind. Actually, the Holy Spirit in this verse should be translated into the Holy Breath, the Holy Pneuma. The Holy Spirit is not a separate Person from the Son, Jesus Christ. How could your breath be breathed out of your being to become a second person? This is not logical. The breath is the very release of the intrinsic essence of someone's being. Breath is the intrinsic essence of the breather. The pneumatic Christ, the very Christ who is pneuma, came back on the day of resurrection to His disciples and breathed out the intrinsic essence of His being into them. On that day, the pneumatic Christ entered into His disciples.

From that day onward, He was not only among His disciples but also within them in order to train them to get accustomed to His invisible presence. For the three and a half years of His earthly ministry, Peter, John, James, and the other disciples were used to His visible presence, but then His presence became invisible. The disciples were not used to this invisible presence so the Lord trained them for forty days. In these forty days, He appeared to them unexpectedly without their realization (John 21:4; Luke 24:15-16). When the two disciples on the road to Emmaus realized that it was Jesus who was with them, He disappeared from them (Luke 24:31). Many times we may not have much realization that Jesus the Lord is with us. However, many saints have experienced the Lord's appearing to them when they were going somewhere or doing something against His wishes. For example, in John 21 we see that Peter returned to his old occupation, backsliding from the Lord's call (Matt. 4:19-20; Luke 5:3-11), due to the trial of the need of his living. It was then that the Lord appeared to them on the shore. He appears to us many times in order to restrict us and enlighten us to keep us on the way that leads to life.

Since His resurrection, the Lord's presence is invisible in the Spirit. His manifestation or appearings after His resurrection were to train the disciples to realize, to enjoy, and to practice His invisible presence, which is more available, prevailing, precious, rich, and real than His visible presence. This dear presence of His was just "the Spirit" in His resurrection, whom He had breathed into them and who would be with them all the time.

In the twenty-two books of the Bible from Acts to Jude we see the Spirit as the Son. First Corinthians 15:45b tells us that the last Adam, Jesus Christ, became a life-giving Spirit, and 2 Corinthians 3:17 tells us, "the Lord is the Spirit." In these twenty-two books, the main figure is the Spirit—the Spirit as the Son with the Father. John 14:23 says, "Jesus answered and said to him, If anyone loves Me, he will keep

My word, and My Father will love him, and We will come to him and make an abode with him." This means that when the Son comes, He always comes with the Father. The Epistles tell us clearly that the Spirit is the Son; He is also with the Father because the Father is always with the Son. The Spirit as the Son with the Father is the consummation of the Triune God in the church.

The embodiment of the Triune God was in Jesus Christ, and the consummation of the Triune God is in the church as the Body of Christ and the temple of God. The Body of Christ is the kingdom of God, and the temple of God is the house of God living Christ. The church today is living Christ. We all are living Christ every day unto the fullness of God, which is the very expression of God, the Triune God. This is in the twenty-two books of the Bible from Acts to Jude as the development. Christ was the initiation to develop into His enlargement which is the church, the fullness of the Triune God.

The Seven Spirits, Out from the Eternal One, of the Redeemer—the Intensification of the Triune God

In the third section, Revelation, we see the seven Spirits out from the Eternal One, the One who was, who is, and who is coming. The seven Spirits are out from the Eternal One and of the Redeemer (Rev. 1:4-5) to be the intensification of the Triune God in the overcoming church, consummating in the golden lampstands and in the New Jerusalem. This is the finalization in the book of Revelation. The intensification of the Triune God in the overcoming church consummates in the golden lampstands in this age and in the New Jerusalem in the new heaven and new earth in eternity.

The Eternal One, the One who is, who was, and who is to come, is Jehovah in the Old Testament. Jehovah in the Old Testament is revealed in Exodus 3 as the Triune God, the God of Abraham, the God of Isaac, and the God of Jacob (vv. 14-15). In Revelation 1:4-5 "Him who is and who was and who is coming" is God the eternal Father. "The seven Spirits" who are before God's throne are the operating Spirit of God, God the Spirit. "Jesus Christ," to God "the faithful Witness," to the church "the Firstborn of the dead," and to the world "the Ruler of the kings of the earth" (v. 5), is God the Son. This is the Triune God. However, this record of the Trinity is totally different from the record revealed in Matthew 28:19—the Father, the Son, and the Spirit. Only the word Spirit is used in Revelation 1:4-5 and it is used in plural—the seven Spirits. Also, the first of the Trinity is not the Father but the Eternal One, the One who was, who is, and who is coming. Furthermore, the Spirit is not the third of the Trinity but the second of the Trinity. God the Son is revealed as the faithful Witness, the Firstborn of the dead, and the Ruler of the kings of the earth.

The book of Revelation reveals that there is not only one divine Spirit but seven. Both the Catholic and Protestant churches highly regard the Nicene Creed. They often recite this creed in their Sunday service. The Nicene Creed, however, does not include this point of the seven Spirits because when the Nicene Creed was made (A.D. 325) the book of Revelation was not yet formally recognized. (Revelation was formally recognized at the council of Carthage in A.D. 397).

The seven Spirits are unveiled in the book of Revelation as the seven eyes of the Lamb (5:6). The Lamb is our Savior, Christ, and the seven Spirits are the Spirit of God. Thus, the seven Spirits, are the seven eyes of Christ. Can you say that your eyes are one person and that you are another person? This shows that the Spirit cannot be separated from Christ. Revelation reveals to us an observing Christ who has seven eyes watching over all the churches. The seven eyes, the seven Spirits of God, are Christ Himself watching over all the churches on this earth and observing their real situation. For the church to overcome today's dark age and the decline in today's Christendom, we need the seven-fold intensified Spirit of God.

The seven Spirits are not only out from the Eternal One, but they also belong to the Redeemer because the seven Spirits come out of the throne of the Eternal One and the seven Spirits are the seven eyes of the Lamb. In Revelation the Trinity is the seven Spirits out from the Eternal One and of the Redeemer. This is the intensification of the Triune God. Now we have three words to describe the Triune God in the New Testament—embodiment, consummation, and intensification. In the four Gospels is the Triune God embodied in Jesus Christ; in Acts through Jude is the Triune God consummated in the church; finally, in Revelation is the Triune God intensified in the overcoming church consummating in the golden lampstands in this age and in the New Jerusalem in eternity. This is the book of Revelation, and this is the finalization of God's economy.

The Depths of the New Testament

The New Testament unveils to us how the Triune God became flesh in the Son with the Father by the Spirit to be a Man. As this Man, He lived on this earth for thirty-three and a half years, yet He did not live a human life; He lived *in* the human life. He lived a divine life, the life of God, in the human life. Then He died on the cross as seven items to terminate all the negative things in the universe and to release all the positive things: as the Lamb of God He died to deal with our sin and sins (John 1:29; 1 Cor. 15:3); as a Man in the flesh (John 1:14), He died in the form of fallen man, in the likeness of the flesh of sin (Rom. 8:3), to deal with the fallen flesh; as a man in the old creation, He died to crucify our old man (Rom. 6:6); He also died as a serpent (John 3:14) to bruise the serpent's head (Gen. 3:15) and to destroy him (Heb. 2:14) along with his satanic world (John 12:31), that all His believers may have eternal life (John 3:15-16); as the Firstborn of all creation (Col. 1:15) He died on the cross as part of the old creation to terminate the entire old creation; He also died as the peacemaker (Eph. 2:14-15) to abolish all the ordinances and differences in living, customs, and habits between all kinds of people; on the positive side He died as a grain of wheat to release the divine life (John 12:24). He died such an all-inclusive death on the cross, through which He cleared up the entire universe and released the divine life for us to receive. Then He was buried and He was resurrected. He entered into a new realm, a new universe, a new sphere. In this sphere He was no longer in the flesh, but He became pneumatic. He became the life-giving Spirit. At the end of the four Gospels such a One in His resurrection breathed Himself as the pneumatic One into His disciples. Thus, He became the very intrinsic life and essence of His disciples. This is the very depths of what is revealed in the four Gospels.

In Acts through Jude this pneumatic One is always with His church. He is the Spirit, as the Son, with the Father—the very consummation of the Triune God. Before His resurrection, the title "the Father, the Son, and the Spirit" in Matthew 28:19 had never been revealed or used. Such a title indicates that the Triune God has been completed and consummated, and this consummation is the all-inclusive, compound, life-giving, indwelling Spirit. The Spirit, as the Son, with the Father is within us to make the church the Body of Christ as God's kingdom and the temple of God as the house of God.

Finally, due to the degradation of the church, this Spirit has been intensified sevenfold. Therefore, in Revelation this One becomes the seven Spirits out from the eternal One and of the Redeemer to be the intensification of the Triune God in the overcoming church consummating in the golden lampstands in this age and in the New Jerusalem in the coming eternity for God's finalization of His economy that He may have a corporate expression for eternity. These are the depths of the revelation of the New Testament. We all should dive into these depths; otherwise, we will remain superficial in our understanding of the central revelation of the New Testament.

CHAPTER TWO

THE WORD'S INCARNATION AND
THE SON'S LIVING ON THE EARTH

Scripture Reading: John 1:1, 14; 7:29; 6:46; 17:8; Matt. 1:18, 20; 1 Tim. 3:16; Col. 2:9; John 16:15a; 1:14a; 2:21; 14:10a, 11a; 17:21; 10:30; 17:22; 8:29; 16:32; 6:57a, 5:17, 19; 10:25; 5:30; 6:38; 14:24; 7:16-17; 12:49-50; 7:18; 14:7-9; Matt. 3:16-17; Luke 4:18a; Matt. 4:1; 12:28

THE WORD'S INCARNATION

The first crucial item of God's New Testament economy is the incarnation of the Word. Strictly speaking, the incarnation is the incarnation of the Word. John 1:14 says that the Word became flesh. It does not say that Christ became flesh or that God became flesh. The Bible tells us that the Word, who was God (John 1:1), became flesh. The Word is God's definition, and since it is God's definition it is God's embodiment. God is abstract and invisible since God is Spirit (John 4:24). Our thought is abstract and invisible, but when we put our thought into words, these words become the definition of our thought, the very embodiment of our thought. The word is the definition, the expression, and the embodiment of our thought. If I spoke to you for one hour, you would know what my thought was because my thought is embodied in my word.

The Word Becoming Flesh

The Word as God's definition, God's expression, and God's embodiment, became flesh. The Word, which was God's definition and God's embodiment, needed to be embodied further in a Person, and this Person was God the Son. When the

Word became flesh, the very embodiment of God became a Person by the name of Jesus Christ. This Person is the embodiment of the Word, which Word was the embodiment of God. In this way we may say that God has been embodied twice. God was embodied in the Word before His incarnation (John 1:1), and the Word was embodied in a living Person who was the Man, Jesus Christ (Col. 2:9).

Sent by the Father and with the Father

When the Word became flesh, He was sent by God and with God (John 7:29). When the sent One came, He came with the sending One. When the Son came by becoming a man, He came with the Father. According to John 6:46 and 17:8, the Son came from God the Father. The Greek preposition translated "from" is *para* which means "by the side of." Therefore, the sense here in the Greek is "from with." Darby has a note in his *New Translation* on John 6:46 which also indicates that the sense in the Greek is "from with." The Son came not only from the Father, but also with the Father. While He is from the Father, He is still with the Father (John 8:16, 29; 16:32). In John 8:29 the Lord says, "He who sent me is with me," which indicates that the Father sent the Son "from with" Him. When the Son came, He did not leave the Father in the heavens on the throne. This is why the Bible tells us that "everyone who denies the Son does not have the Father either; he who confesses the Son has the Father also" (1 John 2:23).

Even in our experience today, when we call "Lord Jesus," we have the deep sensation that the Father is right in us (Eph. 4:6). As a young believer I was taught to address my prayer to the heavenly Father, and that sometimes I might address my prayer to the Lord. I was also told never to address my prayer to the Spirit. I could only pray to the Father and sometimes to the Lord through the means, the instrument, of the Spirit. Based on this teaching, whenever I knelt down to pray, I had to think about whom I was going to address my prayer to. When we initially received the Lord Jesus, though, we had the sensation that He was near to us (Phil. 4:5; James 4:8). We spontaneously addressed Him in our prayer in an

intimate way. We may have said, "Lord Jesus, I love You.
You are so dear, precious, sweet, and real to me. Thank You,
Lord Jesus, that You died for me. Hallelujah! I love You, Lord
Jesus." It was not until we received some "theological help"
that we began to address the "Father on the throne" in
heaven. However, when we pray in a spontaneous and intimate way to our dear Lord Jesus, we have a deep sensation
that the Father is in us. We pray to the Lord Jesus, yet we
have the sensation that the Father is here.

Our concept has been that when the Son came to the
earth, He left the Father sitting on the throne. We all must
see that when the Father sent the Son, He sent the Son with
Himself. The Son indwells us (2 Cor. 13:5) and the Father
does also (Eph. 4:6). The Lord Jesus told Philip in John 14:9,
"He who has seen Me has seen the Father." While the Lord
Jesus was speaking to Philip, He furthermore declared that
the Father was in Him and that He was in the Father (14:10).
This shows that when we have the Son, we have the Father
also. Even the Son is the Father (Isa. 9:6).

We must also realize that while the Father is with the
Son and in the Son, He is also on the throne. The two are distinct, yet not separate. This is a divine mystery which we
cannot fathom. On the one hand, the three in the Godhead
coexist and on the other hand, they coinhere. They mutually
indwell each other and interpenetrate one another. Electricity provides us with a good example of such a mystery. The
electricity which we are enjoying in our room is the same
electricity in the power plant. It is simultaneously at the
power plant and also in our room. In like manner, God the
Father was within Jesus on the earth and at the same time
He was on the throne. We should not be bothered by this. We
need to realize that with the infinite God there is no element
of time or space. Because He is the eternal God, He is above
time and space and not limited by them.

By the Spirit

Luke 1:35 and Matthew 1:18 and 20 also show us that the
Son came by the Spirit. He was conceived of the Holy Spirit.
This Spirit was the very Spirit of God the Father, the very

essence of God the Father. When the Spirit entered into the womb of Mary, that was the essence of God the Father entering into the virgin. This was a divine conception accomplished in a human virgin's womb. The divine essence was mingled with the human essence to produce a child born as a God-man. This shows how the Son came with the Father's essence and by the Spirit.

When I was younger, I could not understand why the Lord needed to do things by the Spirit since He was almighty. The Lord Jesus told the Pharisees that He cast out demons by the Spirit of God (Matt. 12:28). When the Son came, He came with the Father. When He worked, He worked by the Spirit. The Triune God is a mystery. It is a mystery that the Son of God is almighty, yet He still needed to do things by the Spirit. In the four Gospels we do not see the Son alone, but we see the Son, with the Father, by the Spirit.

God Manifest in the Flesh

The Trinity was mingled with the human nature. This one conceived in the womb of Mary was the complete God and the perfect Man. The Son came with the Father by the Spirit to be mingled with humanity, thus becoming a God-man. This is God manifest in the flesh (1 Tim. 3:16). This is the incarnation of the Word and this is our Savior, Jesus Christ, who is the Triune God mingled with man. In Him we see the Father, the Son, and the Spirit, and in Him we see a perfect Man. He is the very God-man, the embodiment of the Triune God in the Man, Jesus Christ.

The Initiation of God's New Testament Economy

The Word's incarnation was the Triune God's incarnation—the Son of God, with the Father, by the Spirit became flesh. This was God, the Triune, becoming a man; therefore, this Man is the very embodiment of the Triune God in Jesus Christ as God's dwelling place, the tabernacle and the temple, living the life of God to develop into the kingdom of God. This was the initiation of God's New Testament economy. Initiation does not only convey the thought of beginning, but it also conveys the thought of beginning by creation. It denotes something new that has never before existed. The Triune God's incarnation created a new thing, and this new thing created by the Triune God's incarnation was an initiation. A new realm, a new sphere, with a new embodiment came into existence. In this new realm or new sphere, God became one with man. There had never been such a thing. This was something absolutely new. God's incarnation brought in a new creation. Eventually, this new creation will consummate in the New Jerusalem, the center of the new heaven and new earth (Rev. 21:1-2).

A Wonderful Person

This Person is universal, excellent, marvelous, wonderful, and unique. Before the incarnation, there was not such a Person. In the age to come, this Person will be developed, enlarged, and increased to the uttermost. That will be the New Jerusalem as the center of the new universe, the new heaven and the new earth. That will be the ultimate consummation of the development of such a wonderful, excellent Person.

The entire New Testament is an unveiling of such a unique Person who is the embodiment of the Triune God in a Man. This Man is Jesus Christ. In this perfect Man, Jesus Christ, is the Father, the Son, the Spirit—the complete God. This perfect Man is the container, the holder, of the Triune God. He is the embodiment of the Son, with the Father, by the Spirit.

Some teachers of the Bible told people that in the Old Testament is God the Father, in the Gospels is God the Son, and in the rest of the Bible is God the Spirit. I received this teaching sixty years ago, but after my personal study of the Bible, I discovered that the Father, the Son, and the Spirit were all in the Old Testament. Isaiah 9:6 refers to the eternal Father. Genesis 1:2 tells us that the Spirit of God brooded upon the face of the waters. Also in Genesis 18, the Lord Jesus came as a real man to Abraham, and Abraham prepared water for Him to wash His feet and fed Him. Before the incarnation, God had already appeared to Abraham as a man. This man's name in Genesis 18 was Jehovah (v. 1). The

Lord Jesus walked with Abraham as a friend in Genesis 18.
This is why James tells us that Abraham was the friend of
God (2:23). This again shows us the mystery of the Divine
Trinity. The Old Testament, the Gospels, Acts through Jude,
and Revelation reveal to us the same wonderful Triune
God-man.

Many of us Christians believe in Christ, yet we do not
know Him in His Person. His Person is so excellent, so wonderful, and so marvelous. He is the embodiment of the Triune
God who mingled Himself with humanity to be born a God-
man, in whom we see the Father, the Son, and the Spirit—the
complete God and a perfect man for the purpose of dispensing
the Triune God into us. We must learn to know this Person, to
describe this wonderful Person, and to present this excellent
Person to others.

THE SON'S LIVING ON THE EARTH

The first item of God's New Testament economy is the
Word's incarnation. The second item in God's New Testament
economy is the Son's living on this earth, which is the continuation of the Word's incarnation. In the New Testament, the
first thing seen is the Word, who was God, becoming flesh.
This is the Triune God embodied in a Man. Now this Man continues to live on the earth. He was the embodiment of the
Triune God living the life of God. His living is marvelous and
needs thousands of words to describe.

The Highest Life

God created different lives in His creation. God's creation
began from the lowest life, which is the vegetable life. Flow-
ers, trees, and vegetables are living things, but their life is
the lowest. Their life does not have any personality. They do
not have any feeling, and thought, or any love or hatred.
Then God created the animal life which is higher than the
vegetable life. Dogs can like you or dislike you, and sometimes they get mad and bark at you, but this is still not the
highest life. The third level of life created by God is on
a higher plane. This is the human life. Without the vegetable
life, the animal life, and the human life, the earth would be

desolate. This earth is quite pleasant and interesting due to these three lives. The highest life in this universe, however, is the life of the tree of life. In Genesis 1 are the vegetables, the animals, and the man created by God. After the creation of man, God brought this man to the tree of life, showing that there was still a life that was higher than the human life (Gen. 2:8-9). This life is the divine life.

The Mingling of the Divine Life with the Human Life

In the New Testament a marvelous thing happened—the mingling of the divine life with the human life! When we say that the very embodiment of the Triune God lives the life of the Triune God, we mean this is a living of a combined life, a living of a mingled life. It is a life both human and divine. The human life is wonderful and the divine life is marvelous, but now these two lives are married. The divine life is the husband and the human life is the wife—a wonderful couple! This is the mingling of the divine life with the human life. Jesus Christ is the embodiment of such a mingling, and He lived a life, a particular life, an extraordinary life, a life that is a mingling of the divine life with the human life. In this life, in this living of such a life, we can see all the divine attributes and all the human virtues. This was the life lived by this embodiment of the Triune God in the Man, Jesus. Such a living will develop into the kingdom of God. The kingdom of God is just the living of the divine life mingled with the human life. Today the kingdom of God should be the church life—the development of that wonderful living of two mingled lives.

Living a Combined Life

We who are regenerated, who love the Lord, who seek after the Lord, and who are under God's transformation, must ask ourselves what kind of life we live. We should not merely live a human, ethical life. We must live a combined life—a life that is a combination of the divine life with the human life. Such a life is the church life. Jesus Christ, as the very embodiment of the Triune God, lived such a life.

His living sets up a model of the church life, and this life
is one that lives God in humanity. The church life should
be exactly the same as His living. He was Jesus the Man,
yet He lived the Triune God. He was a Nazarene, yet He lived
the divine life. When He was twelve, He went to Jerusalem
and He behaved, acted, and lived in a way that showed
the divine life in a young human being. He was a Galilean
human being, but the divine life was lived out of Him. Luke 2
shows us a young, human boy only twelve years old living a
life on the highest plane. In that young life we can see
the human virtues and the divine attributes. This is the
model of the church life. When that young boy lived, the Son,
the Father, and the Spirit all lived there with Him. Apart
from the Bible, there is no human record of such a life. Such
a life is the result of the divine dispensing. The incarnation
of the Word was a dispensing that dispensed the Son with
the Father by the Spirit into humanity. Then out of this incarnation the life of the Triune God was lived out in a young
human being. The four Gospels firstly show us the incarnation of the Word and then present the Son's living, which was
a combination of the divine life with the human life.

The Embodiment of the Triune God

The Son's living on the earth was as the embodiment
of the Triune God. Colossians 2:9 refers to "the fullness of
the Godhead." It does not say the riches of the Godhead,
but the fullness of the Godhead. The difference between the
riches and the fullness can be illustrated by a cup of water.
A cup which contains water has the riches of water. It may
have the riches of water, but these riches cannot be seen until
the water fills the cup to overflowing. Now the riches have
become the fullness, which is the expression of the riches.
Colossians 2:9 says that the fullness of the Godhead dwells
in Him bodily. This means the riches of the Godhead are fully
expressed in Him. When this Man Jesus lived on the earth,
He lived in a way that all the ones around Him saw the
fullness of the Godhead. The Godhead in its fullness just
flowed out of Him. The fullness of the Godhead not only
dwelt in Him, but flowed out of Him. When He lived in that

carpenter's home in Nazareth, He was the embodiment of the fullness of the Godhead. He was the very embodiment of the Godhead in its fullness, possessing all that the Father had. In John 16:15 He told us that all that God the Father had was His. He inherited all that God the Father had because He lived as the embodiment of the Father, the Son, and the Spirit. Even when He was twelve years old He lived in a way that every one saw the fullness of the Godhead flowing out of Him. That was not merely His work or His ministry but His living. He lived out the fullness of the Godhead; therefore, He could say, "He who has seen Me has seen the Father" (John 14:9).

God's Tabernacle and God's Temple

The Son lived as the tabernacle of God, as the temple of God (John 1:14a; 2:21). He was God's dwelling place. Every Christian's life must be like this. When we live, we must live as God's dwelling. We must live in a way that people can see God dwelling in our living. Our daily life should be God's tabernacle. When we work at school or in the office people should be able to see God in our daily life.

Coinhering with the Father

The Son was also coinhering with the Father. Coinhering simply means indwelling one another. The Father dwells in the Son, and the Son dwells in the Father (John 14:10a, 11a; 17:21). When the Son was living on this earth, His living was a mutual abiding. He was abiding in the Father and the Father was abiding in Him.

One with the Father

The Son was one with the Father (John 10:30; 17:22). The Son, when He was living on this earth, lived a life that showed people that He and the Father were one. We all must live a life that shows people we and Christ are one. We must be one with Jesus.

Having the Father with Him

In the Son's living He had the Father with Him, so He told

us He was never alone (John 8:29; 16:32). He had the Father with Him all the time. We also should live a life in which the Lord is with us all the time.

Living Because of the Father

The Son lived because of the Father (John 6:57). He did not live His own life, but the Father's life. We also can live a life that is not ourselves, but Christ. We should live a life that is not us, but Christ. Paul said, "I have been crucified with Christ, and it is no longer I who live, but Christ lives in me" (Gal. 2:20). We all can live because of Christ (John 6:57b). The Lord Jesus was the Son living the Father; now we should live Christ (Phil. 1:21a).

Anointed by the Father with the Spirit

The Son was also anointed by the Father with the Spirit (Matt. 3:16-17; Luke 4:18a). Whatever the Son does, He does it with the Father by the Spirit. When the Father anointed the Son, the Father did not go back to the heavens. The Father remained with the Son all the time, and He anointed the Son with the Spirit. Then one day the Son said the Spirit of the Lord was upon Him and that He was sent to proclaim the glad tidings (Luke 4:18a). He proclaimed the glad tidings with the Father and by the Spirit.

A Model of the Christian Life and the Church Life

We must see a vision concerning the Triune God embodied in Man, a Man who lived the life of the Triune God. The incarnation was the dispensing of the Triune God into humanity, and the Son's living was the result of such a dispensing. The Man Jesus was a model confirming to us that the dispensing of the Triune God into humanity works! In human history there was at least one Person who was the result of God's dispensing and who lived a life of the divine nature mingled with the life of the human nature.

When I was younger I wondered why our God needed to become a Man to live on this earth for thirty-three and a half years. For thirty years He lived in a carpenter's home.

Seemingly He did not do anything; He just lived there. To me there was no need of that. We need a Savior, and a Redeemer, but why did our Lord need to live on this earth for thirty years, seemingly doing nothing? Even the Lord Jesus' work for three and a half years did not involve much; He traveled mainly in Palestine, a narrow strip of land about three hundred miles from north to south and about one hundred miles from east to west. Eventually He only gathered one hundred twenty (Acts 1:15). Among these one hundred twenty there was not one with a doctor's degree. Most were unlearned, some were fishermen, and then there were a group of women, one of whom was possessed by seven demons. Seemingly, Jesus did not do much in the way of work. Actually, He did something quite significant. He lived a life which is a model, a pattern, of the Christian life and the church life. This shows that God does not treasure that much what we do. God treasures His dispensing and how much of the divine dispensing has been imparted into our being. Jesus was altogether the aggregate of the divine dispensing, the embodiment of the divine dispensing. He lived a life as a Man saturated with the Triune God. His living was the expression of the divine dispensing. He lived in Nazareth for thirty years doing no work because His burden and His intention was not to work, but to live a life that was the result of the divine dispensing. In every page of the four Gospels we can see a picture of the divine dispensing lived out by this Man Jesus.

Working with the Father

Most young boys do not like to work with their father because he may restrict them with rebukings. But Jesus never did any work without the Father. He always worked with the Father (John 14:10b; 5:17, 19). To work with the Father requires an absolute denial of the self. Christ denied Himself to work with the Father. In today's church life we always need to work with the Father.

Working in the Name of the Father

The Son worked in the name of the Father (John 10:25). To work in the name of the Father means it is not I that work but I work as the Father. When this Man lived on this earth, He was the Son with the Father by the Spirit, living to set up a pattern so that man can live a life mingled with the Triune God. At least one Man among mankind succeeded in living such a life. Thousands of men possessing the divine life should follow this Man to live a life which is the result of the divine dispensing.

Doing the Father's Will

The Son put His will aside and took the Father's will, so He did the Father's will (John 5:30; 6:38). In John 6:38 the Lord says, "For I have come down from heaven, not to do My own will, but the will of Him Who sent Me."

Speaking the Father's Word

The Son never spoke His own word. Whatever the Son spoke was the Father's speaking (John 14:24; 7:16-17; 12:49-50).

Seeking the Father's Glory

With Christ there was no ground for the self. He did not seek His own glory, but the Father's (John 7:18).

Expressing the Father

Finally, the Son expressed the Father (John 14:7-9). No wonder He said, "He who has seen Me has seen the Father" (14:9). He was one with the Father. He had no work, no will, no word, no glory, and no ambition for Himself. He only expressed the Father. The Triune God was expressed in this Man. This was the result of the divine dispensing in the first man of the new creation. This was the first man in human history who was the result of the divine dispensing. This result will develop and this dispensing will go on in thousands of God's chosen people. All of them will live a life which is the result of the divine dispensing. This is the Son's living on earth.

CHAPTER THREE

THE SON'S DEATH
IN HIS HUMANITY WITH HIS DIVINITY
THROUGH THE SPIRIT

Scripture Reading: Col. 1:22; John 3:14; Rom. 8:3; Eph. 2:15; Luke 1:35; John 1:14; Rom. 9:5; Matt. 27:45-46; 1 John 1:7; John 12:24, 31-33; Heb. 9:14, 12; 1 Pet. 1:19-20; Rev. 13:8

THE SON'S CONCEPTION AND BIRTH

We must be deeply impressed that the New Testament reveals to us a wonderful Person for the divine dispensing. This Person is the Triune God incarnated to be a man (John 1:14). The Gospels show us this Person's conception and birth. His conception was carried out by the Triune God. All three of the Godhead, the Father, the Son, and the Spirit, joined and participated in this conception. Many of us have an inadequate concept about His conception. We used to think that this conception was merely the Son of God's conception, yet we have to realize that both the Father and the Spirit joined in that conception. The Father's divine essence was mingled with the human essence by the Spirit (Matt. 1:18, 20; Luke 1:35). Therefore, all three of the Godhead participated in that conception which was carried out in the womb of a human virgin. This brought forth a child with two natures—the divine nature and the human nature. He was born as a God-man. From His birth He was the complete God (Rom. 9:5) and the perfect Man. From such a conception and birth we see the three of the Godhead in humanity. No human word can explain such a mysterious, excellent, and marvelous conception and birth. The Person that was produced by such a conception is also mysterious, excellent, and marvelous. In human history there has never been such a Person.

THE SON'S LIVING

The New Testament then tells us that such an excellent and marvelous Person lived a life which was so mysterious, so excellent, and so marvelous. This life combined and mingled the human life with the divine life. In this life we can see all the divine attributes and all the human virtues, in this life we cannot find any trace of sin, and in this life there is no room left for Satan and no element of the world. This life is not only a mysterious, excellent, and marvelous life, but also a victorious life, a life of victory to the uttermost. Such a life accomplishes God's eternal purpose and has been set up as a pattern, a model, for all the Christians to live. It is a full model for the church life.

THE SON'S DEATH

In the previous chapters we have seen two basic items of God's New Testament economy: the incarnation of the Word and the living of the Son. Now we come to the third item of God's New Testament economy, the Son's death. Whether or not a death is honorable, whether or not a death is dignified, depends on the source of this death. A mosquito's death does not bear any significance, but the death of a king has a great significance. In the New Testament there is a death which is full of significance. It is mysterious, excellent, marvelous, and wonderful because it is the death of a mysterious, excellent, marvelous, and wonderful Person. This is the death of the God-man. This is the death of a Man who had God wrought into His intrinsic nature, a Man mingled with the Triune God. The Triune God, the Father, the Son, and the Spirit, is all wrapped up with this Man, so this Man was a Triune God-man. Such a Man died a wonderful, excellent, mysterious, marvelous, and victorious death.

THE FACTORS REQUIRING THE SON'S DEATH

Now we need to see all the factors that required the death of this wonderful Person. The first factor was sin (John 1:29).

In this universe sin came in (Rom. 5:12) between God and man. Out of sin came many sins (1 Pet. 2:24). Besides these two factors, another factor is that there was an enemy, who is not only the enemy of God, but also the enemy of man. This enemy is the Devil, Satan (Heb. 2:14). Satan produced a system called the world, which usurped the man whom God created for His purpose (John 12:31). The world is another factor that required the death of the God-man, Jesus. When this wonderful Man lived on this earth, He confronted the satanic system, the world. In addition to these factors, there is the old creation. Whatever God had created became old. When the Bible says old it denotes corruption. God's creation became corrupted because the factor of death invaded and corrupted the creation. All the items in the universe became deteriorated through the invasion of death, causing everything to become old. The universe was created by God, but it was ruined by Satan and made old by death. This old creation included mankind (Rom. 6:6). We belong to the old creation. Another factor requiring the wonderful death of Christ is the religious regulations, rituals, and ordinances (Eph. 2:15). The religious ordinances became a separating factor between men. The Jews had many ordinances which separated them from the Gentiles.

The last factor requiring the death of Christ is a positive factor. He died in order to release the divine life (John 12:24). If His death had only taken away the six negative factors, it would have cleared up the entire universe, but the result would have just been emptiness. If sin and sins are gone, Satan is over, the world is finished, the old creation is terminated, and all religious ordinances are taken away, all that is left is emptiness. However, there is a wonderful, positive factor. The death of Christ released the divine life for the divine dispensing. If the divine life had never been released, it could never have been dispensed. Once the divine life is released, it is good for the divine dispensing. Sin, sins, Satan, the world, the old creation, the religious ordinances, and the release of the divine life are the seven factors requiring the wonderful death of Christ.

IN HIS HUMANITY

In human history there was only one Person who was qualified to die such a death—the Son of God, Jesus Christ. He died such a death in His humanity. He was the Son of God, having the divine life (John 1:4; 14:6). He was God (John 1:1), even the embodiment of the Triune God (Col. 2:9), the aggregate of the Father, of the Son, and of the Spirit. In Him was life, and this life was released through His death. However, if He were only the complete God and not a man, He could not die for man. To die for man, to accomplish redemption for man, He had to be a man with a man's blood (Eph. 1:7; Heb. 9:22) since only a man's blood can redeem men. Therefore, He was not only the Son of God, but the man, Jesus Christ. God has the divine life, but He does not have the human blood. God, by Himself, is qualified for everything, but He is not qualified by Himself for man's redemption. Man's redemption needs the genuine blood of a genuine man.

Praise the Lord that there was such a mysterious, excellent, marvelous, and wonderful One who was both God and man. He had the divine life and He had the human blood. Our Savior, our Redeemer, was the complete God and the perfect Man. As the complete God, He had the divine life, and as the perfect Man, He had the human blood. Because He had the divine life, He could release the divine life for the divine dispensing, and His human blood qualified Him to be our Redeemer, to die a vicarious death for us. This God-man's death takes away our sin and sins (John 1:29; 1 Cor. 15:3), and His blood cleanses us from all sin (1 John 1:7). He accomplished His redemption for us, the sinful man, in His humanity, that is, in His flesh (Col. 1:22).

The Word Becoming Flesh

When God became a man, He did not become a new man. John 1:14 does not say the Word became a man, but it says the Word became flesh. When the Son of God became a man, man had become old and man had become flesh. In the Bible, especially in the New Testament, flesh denotes the fallen

man. The Bible tells us that God created man, but God did
not create the flesh. Genesis 1 tells us that after God created man, He "saw everything that He had made, and,
behold, it was very good" (v. 31), indicating that the man
God created was very good. In Genesis 3, however, this
God-created man fell and in Genesis 6 this fallen man became
the corrupted, fallen flesh through sin (v. 3). Romans 3:20
says that by the works of the law "no flesh shall be justified
before Him." Flesh here refers to fallen man. In the eyes of
God, fallen mankind is simply flesh.

Although John 1:14 says the Word became flesh, in our
understanding, we always say the Word became a man. There
is a big difference between the God-created man and the
flesh, which denotes the fallen man. The reason God sent the
flood in Noah's time was because man had become flesh.
Because the God-created man had become flesh, God's will
was to destroy him (Gen. 6:7).

The Likeness of the Flesh of Sin

Romans 8:3 says, "For, the law being impossible in that it
was weak through the flesh, God sending His own Son in the
likeness of the flesh of sin and concerning sin, condemned sin
in the flesh." God sent His Son in the likeness of the flesh of
sin. Even though Christ was only in the likeness of the flesh
of sin, we still must realize that this flesh was something
related to sin. In John 1:14 only the flesh is mentioned. John
does not give us any modifier for the flesh. Paul, however,
uses the term "the likeness of the flesh of sin." Three items
are here in Romans 8:3—the likeness, flesh, and sin. If Paul
said that God sent His Son to come in the likeness of an
angel, this would not give anyone a problem. But God sent
His Son to come in the likeness of the flesh of sin.

The Brass Serpent

In John 1:14 we see the flesh and in John 3:14 we see the
serpent. John 3:14 says, "And as Moses lifted up the serpent
in the wilderness, even so must the Son of Man be lifted up."

In this verse, Christ is typified as a serpent. Verse 15 says, "That everyone who believes in Him may have eternal life." The Bible likens Christ to a serpent. In John 1:29 Christ is typified as the Lamb of God that takes away the sin of the world. The Lamb is a type of Christ and the serpent is also a type of Christ. Numbers 21 tells us that Moses did not lift up a real serpent with poison, but he lifted up a brass serpent (vv. 4-9).

If there were a serpent in our bedroom, I do not think most of us would be able to sleep so well. Even if you gave me a golden serpent, I still would not put it in my room. Gold is precious, but I do not care for gold in the form of a snake. Have you ever realized that the Bible likens Christ to a serpent? The very flesh which Christ became is related to this serpent. The old serpent is in our flesh. Christ became flesh, and Satan, the serpent, is related to this flesh. In the eyes of God, when Christ was crucified on the cross, He was like a serpent only in form, in likeness, without the poisonous, sinful nature. For Christ to be in the form of the serpent is the same as saying that He is in the likeness of the flesh of sin.

Christ came in the likeness of the flesh of sin, and in this flesh was Satan. To say that Christ became flesh, and in His flesh was Satan is heretical. However, to say Christ became flesh, and in the flesh (not Christ's flesh) was Satan is correct. To teach the truth we must learn of the attorneys. They use many modifiers in their speech, and they are very careful, cautious, and detailed. For example, the Bible says that the Word became flesh, but this does not mean the Word became something sinful. The Bible also likens Christ to a serpent, but it does not mean that the Bible likens Christ to something having the poisonous nature. In Romans 8:3 Paul modifies the flesh. He says that God sent His Son in the likeness of the flesh of sin. Also, the serpent in John 3:14 is defined in Numbers 21. The very serpent lifted up by Moses was a brass serpent. It only had the form, the likeness, of the serpent, without the poisonous nature.

Christ as the Son of God became a man in the likeness of

the flesh of sin. The fallen man had sin, but Christ did not
have sin (2 Cor. 5:21; 1 Pet. 2:21-22). He was in the likeness
of the fallen man, but He did not have the fallen nature of
the fallen man. When He became flesh, He became a part
of the old creation since flesh is a part of the old creation. As
a result, His death was the death of the old creation.

This wonderful One was qualified in three ways to die
a marvelous, all-inclusive death. As the Son of God, He was
qualified to release the divine life, as a man He was qualified to shed the genuine human blood, and as the flesh,
the last Adam (1 Cor. 15:45) of the old creation, He was qualified to terminate the old creation including the old man
(Rom. 6:6).

We also must realize that God's enemy, Satan, got into
man's fallen flesh through the fall. In the fallen flesh of man
there was Satan, and with Satan was the satanic system, the
world. It was in the likeness of this fallen flesh that Christ
died on the cross as a Man. Hence, through His death in the
flesh He destroyed the Devil, Satan (Heb. 2:14), and judged
his world (John 12:31-33).

Satan as Sin Being in the Flesh

We have already said that Christ became flesh (John
1:14), and in the flesh (not Christ's flesh) was Satan. If we
said that Satan was in the flesh of Christ, this would be
heretical. However, some of us may still have a problem
regarding the statement that Christ became flesh and in the
flesh was Satan. The diagram on page 42 showing the sphere
of the flesh with Satan as personified Sin in it according to
Romans 7 may help us.

Based upon Romans 7, we say that Satan and sin are in
the flesh. Romans 7 tells us that sin is in our flesh, and
in Romans 7 sin is personified. This chapter shows us that
sin can deceive and kill people (v. 11), and that it can dwell in
people and do things against their will (vv. 17, 20). It is quite
alive (v. 9) and exceedingly active; so it must be the evil
nature of Satan, the evil one, dwelling, acting, and working in
fallen mankind. Sin in Romans 7 is a person. This person is
the source of sin, the origin of sin. This Sin who is Satan still

remains in our flesh where he lives, works, and moves, even after we have been saved. The sin in our flesh is a person, just as the divine life in our spirit is a Person. This Person who is our life is Christ (Col. 3:4), the embodiment of the Triune God. The Triune God as life is in our spirit, and Satan as sin is in our flesh. If we saved ones are not on the alert, and do not watch and pray, this evil one can instigate us to do sinful things. In our flesh there is lust (Gal. 5:16), and this lust is related to Satan in our flesh.

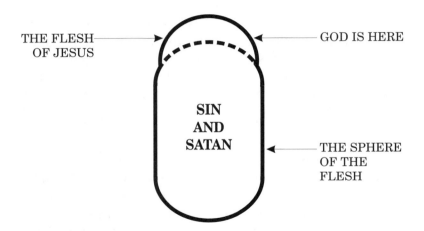

Christ Joining Himself to the Sinful Flesh, yet without Sin

One day the Word became flesh. Remember that Jesus was not born of a human father, but of a human mother (Matt. 1:18). His humanity is flesh; however, His humanity is not of the male, but of the female. Our flesh is a sinful flesh because it is of the male with the female. But the flesh of Jesus is only of the female, not of the male; therefore, His flesh is not sinful. Our flesh is not only flesh but sinful flesh, but the flesh of Christ, having nothing to do with the male, is not sinful flesh. Jesus' flesh is surely joined to the sinful flesh as the diagram on page 42 indicates. However, the element of sin is in the sphere of the flesh below the dotted line, but not in the spot above the dotted line. Within the part above the dotted line is God! In the sphere of the flesh below the dotted line is Satan, but in the sphere of the flesh above the dotted line is God!

The diagram shows that these two spheres are joined together with a dotted line separating them. Since God was in the sphere of the flesh above the dotted line, sin could not penetrate through this line because God is too strong for His enemy, Satan. Satan was restricted within the realm, the sphere, of the flesh below the dotted line. Satan tried again and again to enter into the flesh of Jesus, but he could not get through. The Spirit even led Jesus into the wilderness to be tempted by the Devil. After having fasted forty days and forty nights, He was tempted by the Devil three times (Matt. 4:1-11). Satan tried three times to enter into the flesh of Jesus, but he could not get through.

The diagram on page 42 illustrates the two parts of the flesh. The main part is sinful, and the small part is not sinful. In the main part is Satan; in the small part is God. During the thirty-three and a half years of the life of Jesus, Satan was fighting to get through the border line into the flesh of Jesus. However, he could never get through because God was always resisting him, and God is stronger than he is. When the Word became flesh, He joined Himself to the flesh. Then when Christ went to the cross, He put the entire sphere of the flesh to death, which included Satan and sin, by injecting death into it. When Jesus brought His flesh to the cross, He brought Satan and sin which are in the flesh to the cross also, and He injected death into the flesh which included Satan and sin, the flesh to which He had been joined. Satan had no way to reject this death. Hebrews 2:14 tells us that the death of Jesus on the cross destroyed the Devil who had the might of death. This marvelous, wonderful, all-inclusive, victorious death killed the flesh in which Satan and sin were residing.

Taking Away Sin, Releasing the Divine Life, and Destroying the Devil

Christ died on the cross not only as the Lamb of God to take away our sin, but also as a grain of wheat to release the divine life from within Him (John 12:24). He also died as the serpent to destroy the old serpent, the Devil (Heb. 2:14). He destroyed Satan by dying in the flesh. Within the flesh was Satan, so when He died in the flesh His death destroyed Satan. His death is all-inclusive.

Being Made Sin on Our Behalf

Second Corinthians 5:21 says, "Him (Christ) who did not know sin He (God) made sin on our behalf." It should have been in the last three hours, from twelve noon to three o'clock in the afternoon (Matt. 27:45), while He was dying the vicarious death for us sinners who are flesh, that God made Christ sin on our behalf, and through His death in His flesh condemned sin (Rom. 8:3) which is in man's flesh. When God condemned Christ on the cross in His flesh, God condemned sin in the flesh. When His flesh was condemned, Satan who was in man's flesh was also destroyed.

WITH HIS DIVINITY

When Jesus the man was crucified on the cross, the Triune God, the Father, the Son, and the Spirit were all involved. The Son's death was with the Father and by the Spirit. Yes, it was in His humanity, in the flesh, that Christ died on the cross. However, He also died with His divinity. When Christ was dying on the cross, He was not only the Son of Man, but also the Son of God. We must remember that He was one Person with two natures—the human nature and the divine nature. We cannot say that when Christ was dying on the cross the divine nature was taken away, because the very Person who was dying on the cross, as both the Son of Man and the Son of God, still possessed the divine nature and the human nature. This was His very being and this is related to His intrinsic nature.

For example, a person may take away the jacket I am wearing, but he cannot take away my intrinsic nature. The intrinsic nature of Jesus was the nature of both the Son of Man and the Son of God. Jesus as a Person was both the Son of Man and the Son of God. When He was walking on the earth, living on the earth, when He was arrested, when He was judged, when He was crucified on the cross, He was always both the Son of Man and the Son of God. On the cross He was dying as both the Son of Man and the Son of God.

The Son of God

He was the Son of God through the conceiving of the Holy Spirit essentially (Luke 1:35). Essentially means intrinsically. A person's intrinsic nature cannot be changed. Just because a German puts on a Japanese kimono does not make him Japanese; he is still a German. Essentially he is German. Economically he is wearing Japanese clothing. Jesus was born to be the Son of God essentially because He was conceived of the Spirit of God. Nothing can change His essential nature.

His Conception Being God's Incarnation

His conception was God's incarnation (John 1:14); hence, He was God (Rom. 9:5). Jesus was God when He was in the manger as a little babe. Isaiah 9:6 tells us that a Child is born unto us and His name shall be called the mighty God. The little babe in the manger was God essentially. Can we say that when He was put on the cross He was no longer God? To say He was no longer God on the cross is not logical since nothing can change His essence. He was always with the Father and by the Spirit.

God Leaving Him Economically
While He Was Dying

Essentially, on the cross Christ was God. Economically, God left Him while He was dying His vicarious death for sinners (Matt. 27:45-46). Many Christians have never seen the difference between the essential and economical aspects of the Trinity. Jesus was conceived of the Holy Spirit and the divine element of the Holy Spirit became His very essence. From His birth the Holy Spirit was all the time in His being, but when He was thirty, after His baptism, the Holy Spirit descended upon Him as a dove (Matt. 3:16). Before the Holy Spirit descended upon Him, He had the Holy Spirit as His intrinsic essence essentially (Matt. 1:18, 20). Why then did the Holy Spirit still need to come down upon Him? The reason is that essentially Jesus already had the Spirit of life for His existence, but economically for His ministry He did not have the Spirit of power yet. He had the Holy Spirit as His life essence already, but He did not have the Holy Spirit as His power. At the time of His baptism the Holy Spirit came upon Him economically, and this economical Spirit remained with Him for three and a half years until the time He was crucified to die for us, the sinners. At this juncture, God left Him economically (Matt. 27:45-46), just as God came to Him by the Spirit as power economically three and a half years previously.

Whether God came economically or whether God left Him economically did not change His intrinsic essence or nature. Whether I put on a jacket or take off a jacket does not change my essence. God came upon Him at His baptism economically and God also left Him on the cross economically. This did not change His essence. When He was standing in the water of baptism, He was the Son of Man and the Son of God. When He was crucified on the cross, He was still both the Son of Man and the Son of God. Essentially there was no change, but economically there was some change. At His baptism God came upon Him, and on the cross God left Him. But this economical coming and this economical leaving did not change His essence. When Jesus was dying on the cross, God was dying there. One line from a famous hymn by Charles Wesley says, "Amazing love! How can it be that Thou, my God, shouldst die for me?" (see *Hymns*, #296). Jesus was God, and He died on the cross not only as a Man but also as God. Therefore, even when He was on the cross He was still the Son, with the Father, and by the Spirit.

The Triune God was there at the conception of Jesus. The Triune God lived on the earth, and the Triune God was also dying on the cross. The Triune God was involved with the conception of Jesus, with the living of Jesus on this earth, and with the death of Jesus on the cross. The Triune God was altogether wrapped up with Jesus.

The Eternal Efficacy of His Death

The death of Jesus on the cross as a man provides the human blood necessary for our forgiveness in redemption. But if He died merely as a man the effectiveness of His death would not be eternal. The efficacy of Jesus' death is eternal, without limit in space and without limit in time. His efficacious death can cover millions of believers. His humanity qualifies Him to die for us, and His divinity secures the eternal efficacy of His death.

AN ETERNAL REDEMPTION

An eternal redemption was accomplished by the blood of the Son of God through the eternal Spirit (Heb. 9:12, 14; 1 John 1:7). The blood He shed on the cross was not only the blood of Jesus the Man, but also of the Son of God. First John 1:7 tells us that the blood of Jesus the Son of God cleanses us from all sin. The blood of Jesus the Man qualifies His redemption for us as men. He was a genuine man who died for us and shed genuine blood for us. But the efficacy of His redemption has to be secured by His divinity and it has been secured for eternity by Him as the Son of God. Therefore, His redemption is the eternal redemption (Heb. 9:12) because this redemption was accomplished not only by the blood of Jesus the Man but also by the blood of Jesus the Son of God, which the Apostle Paul even called "God's own blood" (Acts 20:28). This is marvelous!

THROUGH THE SPIRIT

The Son's death was also through the Spirit (Heb. 9:14). He offered Himself to God for His death through the eternal Spirit. He died with the Father in the nature of the Triune God, and He offered Himself to death through the Spirit. Again, this indicates that even in His death as the Son of God, He was with the Father and by the Spirit. Hence, His death accomplished an eternal redemption by the blood of the Son of God and through the eternal Spirit. This eternal redemption has no time element. As the redeeming Lamb, He was foreknown before the foundation of the world (1 Pet. 1:19-20), and was slain from the foundation of the world (Rev. 13:8). In our eyes Christ died two thousand years ago, but in the eyes of God He was slain from the foundation of the world. His death is eternal without any element of time.

THE DEATH OF CHRIST
BEING OUR INHERITANCE

Such an all-inclusive death has been compounded into the all-inclusive Spirit (Phil. 1:19). Our intention is to see, to know, and to realize the compound Spirit because the elements of Christ's conception, of Christ's human living, and of Christ's death are all compounded in this Spirit. When we apply the all-inclusive Spirit to ourselves, this all-inclusive death is ours. This death was not merely a human death, but also a divine death. This was the death of the Father, the Son, the Spirit, and the Man. In this death, sin is condemned, Satan is destroyed, the world is judged, and man with the flesh of sin is crucified. This is a mysterious, excellent, marvelous, wonderful, and victorious death. We must treasure this death since it is a great inheritance to us. It is one of the great bequests of the New Testament. God the Father has bequeathed to us the treasure of Christ (2 Cor. 4:7) with His unsearchable riches (Eph. 3:8). Among these unsearchable riches is His wonderful death. May the Lord grant us a proper view and a proper knowledge of this marvelous, all-inclusive, wonderful death, so that we may be able to be brought into the enjoyment of our New Testament inheritance.

CHAPTER FOUR

THE SON'S RESURRECTION
IN HIS DIVINITY WITH HIS HUMANITY

(1)

Scripture Reading: 1 Pet. 3:18; Rom. 1:4; 1 Cor. 15:44a; John 10:17-18; 1 Thes. 4:14; Rom. 10:9; 8:11; Acts 13:33; Rom. 8:29; 1 Pet. 1:3; Heb. 2:11-12; John 12:24; 1 Cor. 15:45b

Thus far, we have seen the Word's incarnation, the Son's living on this earth, and the Son's death on the cross. The Son's death is all-inclusive, excellent, and mysterious. After death there is resurrection. The Son's resurrection, which is the fourth item in God's New Testament economy, is even more mysterious than His death.

A PROOF OF RESURRECTION

In 1936 I was speaking to a group of university students in the old capital of China, Peking. Their university was one of the top universities in China. After I spoke, a young student came to me and told me that the thing that bothered him about the Christian faith was the teaching of resurrection. He could not understand how a man could die and be resurrected. In front of the window where we were standing was a wheat field. Pointing to the wheat field, I told him that it was full of resurrection. Then, I explained to him that when a grain of wheat is sown into the earth, it dies. Then after it dies, it grows up in resurrection. I told him that we could see resurrection everywhere in nature. I pointed out to him strongly that a grain of wheat dies, but it does not stop at death because through its death it grows; thus, its growth is by its death. Actually, a grain of wheat grows by its death. As a

result of this fellowship, this young student was caught by
the Lord.

RESURRECTION FOLLOWING DEATH

If we sowed a little rock into the earth, that little rock
would never die and neither would it grow. The reason for
this is that there is no life in the rock. Anything that does not
have life can never die. A chair or a statue does not die because
neither of them has life. The death of anything is a proof that
that very thing has life. Death, however, is followed by resurrection. The New Testament tells us that Christ has resurrected
(1 Cor. 15:4) and that we Christians all will be resurrected
(1 Thes. 4:16-17). After the millennium, even the unbelievers
will be resurrected (John 5:29; Rev. 20:5, 12). Because every
man has life, every man will die and be resurrected. According to the Scriptures, there are different resurrections. The
resurrection of Christ was the firstfruit (1 Cor. 15:20). Then
at His coming back there will be another resurrection—the
resurrection of the believers. After the millennium of a thousand years, there will be the third kind of resurrection—the
resurrection of the dead and perished ones.

LIVING TO DIE

In John 12:24 the Lord Jesus told us that He was a grain
of wheat who came to this earth not to live but to die. The
Lord Jesus came to die and He lived to die. Christ was born to
live and He lived to die. In Luke 12:50 the Lord told us that
He was pressed until His death would be accomplished. This
shows that He expected to die and that His goal was to die.
The Word became flesh to die and His death was not an end
but an initiation. His death ushered in resurrection. Peter,
James, and John treasured the Lord as a grain of wheat, and
when the Lord Jesus told them that He was going to die, they
were bothered. They were disappointed to the uttermost.
After the Lord told the disciples that He was going to be
killed, Peter said, "God be merciful to You, Lord; this shall by
no means happen to You!" (Matt. 16:22). Peter was satisfied
to have the Lord merely as a grain of wheat, but Jesus was
not satisfied with this. He wanted to die. Death was His

initiation since through death He entered into resurrection. Death brings in resurrection and resurrection is the issue of life. If the grain of wheat did not have life and if it did not die, it would never resurrect. Because a grain of wheat has life, it dies and this death releases the life in resurrection.

THE TRIUNE GOD-MAN

We must see that Jesus Christ was the Triune God-man. He was not only the God-man, but also the Triune God-man. The constituents of this God-man were the Father, the Son, the Spirit, and the Man Jesus. He was the Father-the Son-the Spirit-man. This Man Jesus, who was likened to a grain of wheat, embodied God the Father, God the Son, and God the Spirit. When the Man Jesus was put to death, the Father, the Son, and the Spirit with this Man rose up from death. The Man Jesus was the shell of the grain and within this Man, this shell, were the Father, the Son, and the Spirit. While He was dying, the Father, the Son, and the Spirit were growing to rise up. What can restrict the Father, the Son, and the Spirit? What can put the Father, the Son, and the Spirit down? Nothing! Hallelujah! This wonderful Triune God-man died on the cross and resurrected.

PASSING THROUGH DEATH

After this fellowship, some may ask how God could die. Actually, God only passed through death. Scientifically speaking, none of us will die. What dies is only our body. Our spirit and our soul never die. When I die, it does not mean that my entire being dies. It means that only one of the three parts of my being dies. After our body dies, our spirit and our soul go to Paradise to await the resurrection of our body. Even when the unbelievers die, their body dies, and their spirit and their soul go to Hades. Luke 16 shows that with the poor man Lazarus and the rich man their body died, but their spirit and their soul went to Hades (vv. 22-26). In Hades there are two sections—a pleasant section called Paradise and a section of torment. This section of torment is like a jail where criminals are retained temporarily.

When Christ died on the cross, the part of Him that died

was His human body. The divine essence was not in His body but in His Spirit. When He was crucified on the cross, His entire being suffered death, but only His body died, not His Spirit. His Spirit only suffered death and passed through death. Strictly speaking, His Spirit never died. First Peter 3:18 says, "For Christ also has suffered once for sins, the Righteous on behalf of the unrighteous, that He might bring you to God, on the one hand being put to death in the flesh, but on the other, made alive in the Spirit." He was put to death in His flesh, in His body, but He was being made alive in His Spirit.

When Christ was dying on the cross, He was being put to death not in His entire being, but only in His flesh. In His Spirit He was made alive! Man put Him to death in His flesh, but when the Roman soldiers were putting Jesus to death in His flesh, the Triune God was making Jesus alive in His Spirit!

Concerning the expression *the Spirit* in 1 Peter 3:18, footnote 3 in the Recovery Version says:

> Not the Holy Spirit but the Spirit as the essence of Christ's divinity (Rom. 1:4; cf. John 4:24a). The crucifixion put Christ to death only in His flesh—which He received through His incarnation (John 1:14)—not in His Spirit as His divinity. His Spirit as His divinity did not die at the cross when His flesh died; rather, His Spirit as His divinity was made alive, enlivened, with new power of life, so that in this empowered Spirit as His divinity He made a proclamation to the fallen angels after His death in the flesh and before His resurrection.

First Peter 3:19-20 tells us that immediately after the death of His body, Christ was strong and active in His Spirit and went to proclaim His victory to those disobedient ones at Noah's time. "In the Spirit" (v. 18) does not refer to the Holy Spirit, but to the Spirit which is Christ's spiritual nature (Mark 2:8; Luke 23:46). After He died, Christ in the Spirit went to proclaim something to the spirits in prison, to those once disobedient at Noah's time. Throughout the centuries, great teachers of different schools have had varying interpretations of these verses. The most acceptable interpretation of these verses according to the Scriptures is as follows:

The spirits here refer not to the disembodied spirits of dead human beings held in Hades but to the angels (angels are spirits—Heb. 1:14) who fell through disobedience at Noah's time (v. 20 and *Life-study of Genesis* Message 27, pp. 363-364) and are imprisoned in pits of gloom, awaiting the judgment of the great day (2 Pet. 2:4-5; Jude 6). After His death in the flesh, Christ in His living Spirit as His divinity went (probably to the abyss—Rom. 10:7) to these rebellious angels to proclaim, perhaps, God's victory, through His incarnation in Christ and Christ's death in the flesh, over Satan's scheme to derange the divine plan (note 19[3] in 1 Peter 3—Recovery Version).

Based on this interpretation, I realized that the Spirit in verse 18 does not refer to the Holy Spirit. It refers to the Spirit as His divinity. While Christ was being crucified on the cross, the Roman soldiers were putting Him to death in His flesh, and the Triune God, the Father, the Son, and the Spirit, was making Him alive, strengthening Him, and empowering Him in His Spirit. In the conception of Christ, in the human living of Christ, and in the death of Christ, the Triune God was fully involved. The Lord must grant us a clear view of how the Triune God, the Father, the Son, and the Spirit, was fully involved not only in Christ's conception and His human living on this earth but also in His death. The One dying on the cross was the Triune God-man. The Father, the Son, and the Spirit passed through the death of the Man Jesus on the cross.

The crucifixion put Christ to death only in His flesh, which He received through incarnation (John 1:14), not in His Spirit. His Spirit did not die at the cross when His flesh did; rather, His Spirit was made alive, enlivened with new power of life, so that in this empowered Spirit He made a proclamation to the fallen angels after His death in the flesh and before His resurrection. Death never put the Lord Jesus down in His Spirit. Death only put His body down.

DYING OUTWARDLY, RISING UP INWARDLY

While the Roman soldiers were killing Him, His resurrection was going on. While a grain of wheat is dying under the earth, the life inside is growing. On the one hand, the grain dies outwardly. On the other hand, the inner life of the grain rises inwardly. Two things are going on simultaneously in two directions. Death is taking place in the shell of the grain and life is growing within the shell. At the same time that a grain of wheat is dying, resurrection is taking place. First Peter 3:18 is a crucial verse in the New Testament unveiling to us what was happening when Christ was dying on the cross. When He was dying in the flesh on the cross, at the same time He was rising up in His Spirit. This rising up was the beginning of His resurrection. His resurrection did not take place suddenly early in the morning on the third day after His death. It began when He was on the cross, when He was under the killing.

When Jesus as the grain of wheat was dying outwardly on the cross, inwardly He was rising up! The killing was carried out by the Roman soldiers, and the rising up was carried out by the Triune God. Two things were going on at the same time. All the people standing by, viewing the crucifixion, saw the soldiers killing Jesus outwardly, but they did not have the inner sight to see that while the Roman soldiers were killing Him outwardly, the Father, the Son, and the Spirit were inwardly making His Spirit to rise up. While a team of Roman soldiers was killing Him, another team, a team of the Father, the Son, and the Spirit, was rising up from within Him. This was the beginning of the resurrection.

IN HIS DIVINITY WITH HIS HUMANITY

In the previous chapter we saw the Son's death in His humanity with His divinity. In this chapter we are seeing His resurrection in His divinity with His humanity. He resurrected first in His Spirit, and to be in His Spirit means to be in His divinity. Then He resurrected in His body with His humanity. He resurrected first in His Spirit as His divinity and then in His body with His humanity.

The Two Natures of Christ

Romans 1:3-4 says, "Concerning His Son, Jesus Christ our Lord, who came out of the seed of David according to the flesh, and was designated the Son of God in power according

to the Spirit of holiness out of the resurrection of the dead."
Notice that in these two verses "according to" is used twice.
Verse 3 talks about Christ as the seed of David according to
the flesh, while verse 4 talks about Him as the Son of God
according to the Spirit of holiness. According to the flesh, He
was the Son of Man out of the seed of David, a descendant of
David. This is His human nature, His humanity. However,
according to the Spirit of holiness, He was the Son of
God. This is His divine nature, His divinity. In the flesh He
was the Son of Man. In the Spirit He was the Son of God. His
humanity is in His flesh, and His divinity, the Spirit, as
His divine essence, is in His spirit. In His flesh was man, and
in His spirit were the Father, the Son and the Spirit, the
Triune God.

The subject in Romans 1:3-4 is the Son of God, Jesus
Christ; these verses tell us that this One is constituted with
two natures—humanity and divinity. One nature is according
to flesh, and the other nature is according to the Spirit. The
Spirit of holiness is in contrast with the flesh in verse 3. As
the flesh in verse 3 refers to the human essence of Christ, so
the Spirit in this verse does not refer to the Holy Spirit of God
but to the divine essence of Christ, which is "the fullness of
the Godhead" (Col. 2:9). This divine essence of Christ, being
God the Spirit Himself (John 4:24) is of holiness, full of the
nature and quality of being holy.

The Son of Man and the Son of God

We must realize that when Christ was dying on the cross,
He was dying as both the Son of Man and the Son of God.
This wonderful Person was both the Son of Man and the Son
of God. In His flesh He was the Son of Man. In His spirit with
the Spirit He was the Son of God. He had two natures with
two essences—the human and the divine. On the cross the
Man Jesus was dying. And at the same time the Triune God,
the Father, the Son, and the Spirit, was dying. The Son of
Man was the Man Jesus, and the Son of God was the embodiment of the Triune God. All the fullness of the Godhead
dwells in Him bodily (Col. 2:9). If we say that the Son of God
was dying on the cross, this implies that the entire God, the

Father, the Son, and the Spirit, was dying on the cross. Remember that Christ has these two parts: the flesh and His spirit with the Spirit, humanity and divinity. According to the flesh He was out of the seed of David, the Son of Man. According to the Spirit who was in His spirit, He was the Son of God. The Spirit in Romans 1:4 is related to the Spirit in 1 Peter 3:18. Christ had a body which was His flesh, and Christ had a spirit with the Spirit as His divine essence, which was the divine part of His being. His flesh was His human part with His human essence, and His spirit had the Spirit as His divine part with His divine essence.

Designated the Son of God

First Peter 3:18 shows us that while Jesus was being killed on the cross, the Triune God as His divine essence was rising up in His spirit. This happened before His body was resurrected. In this way His resurrection was going on until the morning of the third day when His entire body was resurrected (1 Cor. 15:4). By this time the inward moving of His resurrection by the Triune God was manifested. This was His designation in power according to the Spirit of holiness out of the resurrection of the dead (Rom. 1:4). His resurrection began from His spirit and was accomplished in His body. While He was being killed on the cross, His resurrection began in His spirit. His resurrection was a process that lasted for about three days, beginning from the time when He was being killed on the cross and fully accomplished at the time of His body's resurrection. When His body was resurrected, He was fully designated and manifested to be the Son of God.

There was no need for Christ to be designated as the Son of Man because when people saw Him they immediately recognized that He was a man. However, there was a need for Him to be designated the Son of God because the Son of God was concealed in Him as the Son of Man. His divinity was concealed in His humanity. People could easily recognize His humanity, but not His divinity. This concealed divinity needed to be designated, and made manifest by the resurrection. His resurrection was a designation, a making manifest.

When Christ was resurrected, even in His body He was designated or manifested to be the Son of God.

When I was young I used to think that when the Lord Jesus was crucified on the cross the Father was sitting in the heavens and the Spirit was standing by waiting for some orders. Then when He was killed He was taken down from the cross and buried. Eventually, He was raised from among the dead on the third day. This concept, however, is not according to the revelation of the Scriptures. While Jesus was being killed on the cross, the Triune God, the Father, the Son, and the Spirit, was making His Spirit alive and strengthened. When His body was buried in the earth, His Spirit went to proclaim God's victory over His enemy to the spirits in prison. Eventually this resurrection saturated His body and "invaded" His body to raise it up. Then His resurrection was completed. By this He was fully designated the Son of God in power according to the divine Spirit out of the resurrection of the dead. Hallelujah! This was the procedure, the process, of the Son's resurrection in His divinity with His humanity.

CHAPTER FIVE

THE SON'S RESURRECTION IN HIS DIVINITY WITH HIS HUMANITY

(2)

Scripture Reading: Rom. 1:4; 1 Pet. 3:18; 1 Cor. 15:44a; John 10:17-18; 1 Thes. 4:14; Rom. 10:9; 8:11; Acts 13:33; Rom. 8:29; 1 Pet. 1:3; Heb. 2:11-12; John 12:24; 1 Cor. 15:45b

In the last chapter we saw something concerning the Son's resurrection in His divinity (Rom. 1:4; 1 Pet. 3:18) with His humanity (1 Cor. 15:44a). In this chapter we will see four major items concerning His resurrection: the Son laying down His life that He might take it again in resurrection, God raising Him from among the dead, the Spirit of Him who raised Jesus from among the dead, and the marvelous issue of the Son's resurrection.

LAYING DOWN HIS LIFE THAT HE MIGHT TAKE IT AGAIN IN RESURRECTION

The Son laid down His life that He might take it again in resurrection (John 10:17-18). He died and rose (1 Thes. 4:14). To Christ, resurrection was something subjective. Christ Himself initiated the resurrection. In John 11:25 He said He was not only the life but also the resurrection. Resurrection is something living and rising up. If resurrection is put down, it rises up. Christ is not only life, but also resurrection. He is living all the time; He is rising up all the time. The New Testament tells us that the Roman soldiers killed Him, but it also tells us that He Himself laid down His life. When the soldiers came to arrest Him, He asked them whom they were seeking. When they said they were seeking Jesus of

Nazareth, He answered, "I Am," indicating He was Jehovah (John 18:3-6; cf. Exo. 3:13-15). He was Jehovah, and if He had not been willing to give Himself to them, who could have arrested Him? If He had not been willing to lay down His life, who could have killed Him? Even the entire Roman army could not have killed Him (cf. Matt. 26:53). Apparently the Roman soldiers killed Him. Actually, He laid down His life which means that He died.

In the three days after His death He was taking His life back again. He had the ability to lay down His life and He also had the ability to take His life back again because He was the resurrection, and resurrection always rises up. When the soldiers were killing Him, the life within Him, the resurrection within Him, was rising up. This rising up of the resurrection made His Spirit powerful with His divinity. It empowered His Spirit and strengthened His Spirit. After His body was buried, His Spirit with His divinity went to the abyss to proclaim God's victory over Satan to the disobedient spirits. After that proclamation, He came to His killed and buried body and His resurrection invaded and raised up His body. This was the process of His resurrection.

GOD HAVING RAISED HIM FROM AMONG THE DEAD

God has raised Jesus from among the dead (Rom. 10:9). The New Testament tells us that Jesus Himself rose from among the dead, and it also says that God raised Him up. Jesus and God are one. When Jesus rose up, that was God within Him rising up. The Triune God was fully involved in the resurrection of Jesus. While Jesus was rising up, God was within Him. Because Jesus was born of the divine essence intrinsically, God was in His nature. In the conception of Jesus, God became His very essence. Therefore, when He was a babe in the manger He was the mighty God (Isa. 9:6). The Mighty God was His intrinsic essence. When He was twelve years old, He was the mighty God; God was His essence. When He was standing in the water after baptism, He was the Mighty God; the Mighty God was the essence of His being. When He was nailed to the cross, that was the Mighty God being put to death since God was His intrinsic essence.

When He was being raised from among the dead, He was God rising up; the very God Himself was the intrinsic essence of this rising up One. Therefore, His rising up was God's rising up.

Jesus could never be separated from God since God was His intrinsic essence. Death could not hold Him because He was the resurrection. This resurrection is the Triune God Himself, the Father, the Son, and the Spirit. Life is the Triune God and resurrection is the Triune God. Since the Triune God was the intrinsic essence of Jesus, the intrinsic essence of Jesus was also resurrection itself. Death cannot overcome resurrection, but it is so easy for resurrection to overcome death. Hallelujah, He arose! He arose because He was God intrinsically, essentially, and He was resurrection itself.

THE SPIRIT OF HIM
WHO RAISED JESUS FROM AMONG THE DEAD

Romans 8:11 says, "But if the Spirit of Him who raised Jesus from among the dead dwells in you, He who raised Christ Jesus from among the dead will also give life to your mortal bodies through His Spirit who indwells you." "Him" in the phrase "the Spirit of Him" refers to the Triune God Who raised up Jesus. This resurrection is ours through the Spirit of the One who raised up Jesus. In the all-inclusive, life-giving Spirit, there is the element of resurrection. Through this all-inclusive Spirit the resurrection of Christ, which is an accomplished fact, is applied to us subjectively and becomes our experience.

From the conception of Jesus through His resurrection the Triune God was fully involved. Essentially, God was involved in the conception of Jesus; essentially, God was involved in Jesus' living on this earth; essentially, God was involved in Jesus' death on the cross; and essentially, God was involved in His resurrection. His conception, His living, His death, and His resurrection were all by, with, and of the Triune God. His conception, His living, His death, and His resurrection were not merely of a man, but of God also. The Triune God was there in His conception, His living, His death, and His resurrection, and these elements have all been compounded into the life-giving Spirit for us to experience.

Now we want to see the wonderful result of the resurrection of the Son of God. Through His resurrection Jesus was born as the Firstborn of God (Acts 13:33; Rom. 8:29), through His resurrection He brought forth many brothers (John 12:24; 1 Pet. 1:3; Rom. 8:29; Heb. 2:11-12), through His resurrection a new child was born (John 16:20-22), and through His resurrection He became a life-giving Spirit (1 Cor. 15:45b). These were four new items in the history of the entire universe as the issue of the Son's resurrection.

Being Born as the Firstborn of God

God's only begotten Son is eternal (Heb. 1:8, 10-12; 7:3). From eternity He was the only begotten Son of God (John 1:18; 3:16). God never had more than one son. His only begotten Son was unique. In resurrection, however, the only begotten Son of God became the Firstborn. Romans 8:29 tells us that He was the Firstborn among many brothers. We as the many sons of God are the Firstborn's brothers. How wonderful it is that the Son of God has many brothers. Today He is not merely the only begotten Son of God, but He is also the Firstborn of God, and we are His many brothers.

From eternity Christ was the only begotten Son of God. In incarnation He was born of a human virgin to be the Son of Man (Gal. 4:4). Then in His resurrection, as the Son of Man, He was born of God, that is, divinely sonized to be the firstborn Son of God among many brothers. Christ was born twice. The first time He was born to be the Son of Man as the Firstborn of all creation (Col. 1:15). The second time He was born to be the Son of God as the Firstborn from among the dead (Col. 1:18).

Since Jesus was already the Son of God, why did He need to be born as the Son of God? To answer this question we must first see the verse which tells us that Jesus Christ was born to be the Son of God. Acts 13:33 says, "That God has fully fulfilled this promise to us their children in raising up

Jesus, as it is also written in the second psalm, You are My Son; today I have begotten You." "Today" refers to the day of resurrection. On the day of resurrection God said to Him, "You are My Son; today I have begotten You." On the day of resurrection God had begotten Jesus to be His Son. Before this day, Jesus was the Son of God already. However, He still needed to be born in resurrection to be the Son of God.

Jesus was the Son of God in His Spirit. According to His divinity He was the Son of God, but according to His humanity He was the Son of Man. A part of Jesus Christ, His flesh, was altogether human. It was not divine, not the Son of God. To make Him the firstborn Son, Jesus' humanity had to be divinely sonized by God. His humanity was not a part of the Son of God but a part of the Son of Man. This part had to be made divine, to be made the Son of God, by God bringing this part into death and resurrecting it. By such a process, He was divinely sonized by God in His humanity. His human part was divinely sonized by God in His resurrection.

In Acts 13:33 we saw that on the day of resurrection God said that He had begotten Jesus as His Son. To beget means to impart life. To say I have begotten you means that I have imparted my life into you. In the human part of Jesus there was no divine life. However, through His death and resurrection the Triune God imparted His divine life into the human part of Jesus. While the resurrection was taking place, the Triune God was making Jesus alive in His Spirit (1 Pet. 3:18). The Triune God was energizing Him from within to stir up His life to invade the humanity of Jesus. To invade the humanity of Jesus with life means to impart the divine life into His human part. This was to sonize the humanity of Jesus, and this sonizing was the begetting. Through His death and resurrection, Jesus, in His human part, was sonized to be the Son of God. Through such a process He became the firstborn Son of God. As the only begotten Son of God He merely had the divine element, but now as the firstborn Son of God He has both the divine and the human elements.

This One who has both the divine and human elements as the firstborn Son of God brought forth many brothers. Today we are the sons of God who also have both the human and the divine elements. We are human beings, yet we are divine sons of God. This is wonderful! Human beings can be divine sons and as the sons of God we possess the divine element and the human element. Jesus Christ is the firstborn Son of God possessing the divine and human elements, and His human element has been divinely sonized. He is not merely the only begotten Son of God, but also the firstborn Son of God. According to His deity, He is still the only begotten Son of God. Deity refers to His Godhead, but divinity refers to His divine Being. We can participate in His divinity, but we can never participate in His deity. If we say that we partake of His deity, this is heresy. But the Bible tells us that we are partakers of His divine nature (2 Pet. 1:4). To partake of His divine nature means to partake of His divinity. As the sons of God we can say that we are both human and divine. Praise the Lord! Today He is the firstborn Son of God, and we are the many sons of God. We are His many brothers produced through His resurrection.

Bringing Forth Many Brothers

First Peter 1:3 tells us that God has regenerated us through the resurrection of Jesus Christ from among the dead. We must realize that when Christ was resurrected we were regenerated. When He was resurrected, we were resurrected in Him also (Eph. 2:5-6). We, as human beings, were all divinely sonized through His resurrection to be many sons of God to participate in His divine sonship. We were regenerated before we were born since His resurrection was our regeneration. Before we came into existence, God the Father had regenerated us already. From God's point of view we were regenerated about two thousand years ago. According to our physical life we do not have that many years, but according to our spiritual life we were regenerated that many years ago. Every child of God was begotten of God nearly two thousand years ago through the resurrection of Jesus Christ. Before we became part of the old creation, we were already a part of the new creation through Christ's resurrection, so we are the many brothers of the firstborn Son of God in His resurrection (Rom. 8:29). God is our Father and the Firstborn of God is our

Brother. This is marvelous! Christ, the only begotten Son of God, as the unique grain of wheat, fell into the earth to die. Through His life-releasing death, His divine life within Him grew and rose up to produce many grains to be God's many sons and His many brothers.

A New Child Being Born

In John 16:20-22 the Lord told the disciples that they would be sorrowful, but that their sorrow would be turned into joy because He as "the child" (v. 21) would be brought forth in His resurrection (Acts 13:33; Heb. 1:5; Rom. 1:4). The Lord's death and resurrection were the process of delivery. A new child was delivered through His death and resurrection. This was a universal delivery, not of a single child, but of a corporate child, which included the Son of God as the Head and His many brothers as the Body. This was the birth of a new corporate child comprising Christ and us, the believers. Actually, this was the birth of the new man (Eph. 2:15). The old man was created by God in Genesis 1 and 2, but the new man was born through the death and resurrection of Christ referred to in John 16. We were born into the old man, but we were regenerated into the new man.

Remember that before we were born into the old man, we were already regenerated into the new man, since we were regenerated before we were born according to 1 Peter 1:3. This is a divine mystery which our human mentality cannot solve, but the fact is that we were regenerated as the new man before we were born as the old man. We do not need to try, struggle, or endeavor to be a new man. We are already a new man. We were a new man two thousand years ago. All of us should declare, "Hallelujah! I am a part of the new man!" Do not look at yourself. When you look at yourself, you will be disappointed. When you look at yourself, you will see the old man. We do not need to look at ourselves, but we need to say amen to God's word. All of us should declare, "I am a part of the new man through the wonderful death and resurrection of the Son of God!" Through His resurrection, He as the only begotten Son of God became God's Firstborn, and through His resurrection, His many brothers were brought forth. Also, through His resurrection, a new child was born, and this new child comprises all of us.

Becoming a Life-giving Spirit

After accomplishing incarnation, human living, death, and resurrection, He became the life-giving Spirit (1 Cor. 15:45b) to apply whatever He had accomplished to us. He accomplished incarnation, human living, crucifixion, and resurrection. He became the firstborn Son of God, He brought forth His many brothers, and a new child was born through His resurrection. Now He wants to apply all this to us, His many brothers. He can apply all this to us since He has become a life-giving Spirit. As the life-giving Spirit He has come into us to apply to us all that He has achieved, accomplished, attained, and obtained. All of His accomplishments now become ours! His incarnation becomes ours, His human living becomes ours, His crucifixion becomes ours, and His resurrection becomes ours. His being the firstborn Son of God becomes ours, His producing many brothers becomes ours, and even the birth of the new child becomes ours. Whatever He has achieved, accomplished, attained, and obtained have become ours because this life-giving Spirit is the totality of His wonderful Person, including all His wonderful accomplishments.

This all-inclusive, life-giving Spirit is the ultimate consummation of the Triune God. All that the Triune God is and all that the Triune God has achieved, accomplished, attained, and obtained are compounded together into the life-giving Spirit. After His resurrection, the Lord Jesus became such a Spirit and breathed this Spirit into His disciples (John 20:22). Then after His ascension, He poured out this Spirit upon His disciples (Acts 2:1-4, 16-17). On the day of resurrection He breathed this all-inclusive Spirit into His disciples essentially. Then after 50 days, on the day of Pentecost, He poured out this Spirit upon His disciples economically. Essentially, the Spirit was breathed into His disciples, and economically, such a Spirit was poured out upon His disciples. Now within His disciples is the Spirit of life essentially, and upon His disciples is the Spirit of power economically.

We are now persons with the Spirit within us essentially and with the Spirit upon us economically. Therefore, we are persons of the Spirit. You may not feel that you are a person of the Spirit, but your feeling means nothing. The Word of God means everything. We should not forget that the Word of God is a testament, a will. We must learn to say amen to the bequests of this will. We should say amen to every item. Amen to the Spirit of life bequeathed to me! Amen to the Spirit of power bequeathed to me! Amen to the Spirit in me and amen to the Spirit upon me! Amen that I have the Spirit essentially and amen that I have the Spirit economically! Amen! I am a man of Spirit! If we amen the Word of God, we will be filled with the Spirit. As believers in Christ we should follow the New Testament. Hallelujah for the testament and hallelujah for all the bequests in this testament! Amen to every item of the New Testament.

CHAPTER SIX

THE SON'S SENDING OF THE SPIRIT

Scripture Reading: John 14:16-20, 26; 15:26; 16:7, 11, 13-15;
20:19-22

THE INITIATION OF THE SECOND SECTION
OF GOD'S NEW TESTAMENT ECONOMY

The Son's sending of the Spirit is the initial item of the
second section of God's New Testament economy (see chart on
pages 12 and 13). The verses included in the Scripture reading at the beginning of this chapter from John 14, 15, and 16
were prophecies or promises when they were spoken by the
Lord. The fulfillment of these promises is in John 20. Thus,
the disciples' breathing in of the Spirit in John 20 was the initiation of the second section of God's New Testament economy
from Acts through Jude. In the first section of the four Gospels the disciples were with the Son. In the second section
they began to be with the Spirit. The central Person in the
four Gospels was the Son, who was with the Father and by
the Spirit. After the disciples had received the Holy Spirit
intrinsically as their essence, they began to be with the
Spirit, as the Son, with the Father.

John 14, 15, and 16 are the contents of the last message
given by the Lord while He was on this earth. These three
chapters are profound, mysterious, and divine. No Bible student can exhaust the understanding of these chapters. All of
the verses quoted from these chapters in the Scripture reading are concerning the Spirit. Also, these three chapters are
structured with the Divine Trinity, the Father, the Son, and
the Spirit.

THE SON AND THE FATHER BEING ONE

In John 14 the Lord Jesus revealed to His disciples that He and the Father are one (vv. 8-11). He as the Son was present with them. They all saw Him, they all were with Him, and they all could touch Him. However, they wanted to know the Father. Philip said to the Lord, "Show us the Father and it suffices us" (v. 8). Then the Lord unveiled to them that He and the Father were one. He was in the Father and the Father was in Him. He and the Father lived together, worked together, and spoke together. When the Son spoke outwardly, the Father worked inwardly (v. 10). There is no way to divide the Son from the Father. When you see the Son, you see the Father (v. 9).

ANOTHER COMFORTER

Following this in 14:16, the Lord said, "And I will ask the Father, and He will give you another Comforter, that He may be with you forever." "Another Comforter" means that the Son was already there as the first Comforter. The Son was a Comforter, but the Son asked the Father to give the disciples another Comforter. This may sound like there are two Comforters. Actually, 14:16-20 show us that the other Comforter to be given was the reality of the Comforter who was asking the Father. The Comforter was there talking to the disciples and was there asking the Father to give them another Comforter. This other Comforter is the Spirit of reality. Verse 17 says, "Even the Spirit of reality, whom the world cannot receive, because it does not behold Him or know Him; but you know Him, because He abides with you and shall be in you." This verse reveals a great advancement because the original Comforter was only abiding with the disciples, but not in the disciples. By that time the Son was only able to be with the disciples, but He was unable to be in them. The other Comforter, however, would not only be with the disciples but would also be in the disciples.

In verse 18 the Lord continues, "I will not leave you orphans; I am coming to you." While the Lord was speaking, He was coming. His going was His coming. He had come to the disciples to be among them, but He could not be within them. He had come already to be with them, but He could not get into them, so He had to have a further coming to enter into them. Actually, the Lord's going was really His coming into the disciples.

Verse 19 says, "Yet a little while and the world beholds Me no longer, but you behold Me; because I live, you shall live also." This verse shows us that when the Lord would come further into the disciples, He would live in them to make them live in Him. In this verse the Lord was telling the disciples that they will behold Him because He will live in them to make them live in Him. Only the believers would have this privilege, but the world would not have it. The Lord would come into the disciples and live in the disciples that they might be in Him and live in Him. In verse 20 the Lord continues, "In that day you shall know that I am in My Father, and you in Me, and I in you." "That day" was the day of resurrection. On the day of resurrection the disciples would know that the Lord was in the Father, that they were in Him, and that He was in them. This is coinherence.

These verses also tell us that the Son of the Trinity was asking the Father of the Trinity to send the Spirit of the Trinity to be another Comforter that He could enter into the disciples. The disciples could live in Him as He could live within the disciples. Eventually, the disciples would realize that this other Comforter is just the original Comforter. They would also realize that they were in the Son, the Son was in the Father, and the Son with the Father was in them. These three parties are within one another and they all coinhere one with the other.

THE SON BEING THE FATHER AND THE SPIRIT

John 14:26 says, "But the Comforter, the Holy Spirit, whom the Father will send in My name, He will teach you all things, and remind you of all things which I said to you." In this verse it is hard to say what the phrase "in My name" modifies. Does the Father in the Son's name send the Spirit, or does the Father send the Spirit in the Son's name? Is the sending One in the Son's name or the sent One in the Son's name? This is not only ambiguous in English, but also in the Greek text. "In the Son's name" means "as the Son." Did the Father as the Son send the Holy Spirit, or did the Father send the Holy Spirit as the Son? Which denotation should we take? If the Father in the Son's name sent the Spirit, this means that the sending Father and the Son are one. If the Father sent the Spirit in the Son's name, then this means that the Spirit and the Son are one.

The Father sending the Spirit in the Son's name must be the first denotation. This means that the Spirit and the Son are one. Because the Spirit and the Son are one, the Spirit can be sent by the Father as the Son. This interpretation indicates strongly that the Spirit is the Son. The Father sending the Spirit in the Son's name means that the Father sent the Spirit as the Son. This verse could also mean that when the Father was sending the Holy Spirit, He was doing the sending as the Son. In other words, the Father, in the Son's name, sent the Spirit. This indicates that the Son and the Father are one, and this is the second denotation. This sentence is full of ambiguity. Despite this ambiguity, both interpretations are correct. This verse first denotes that the Father sent the Spirit as the Son. Second, it denotes that the Father as the Son sent the Spirit.

The Father sending the Spirit as the Son indicates that the Son is the Spirit. The Father as the Son sending the Spirit indicates that the Son is the Father. Therefore, the ambiguity of this verse denotes that the Son is both the Father and the Spirit. At least two verses in the Bible confirm this interpretation. Isaiah 9:6 says, "For unto us a child is born, unto us a son is given: and the government shall be upon His shoulder: and His name shall be called Wonderful, Counselor, The mighty God, The everlasting Father, The Prince of Peace." This verse shows us that the Son given to us is called the everlasting Father. Isaiah 9:6 shows us that the Son is the Father. Also, 2 Corinthians 3:17 says, "And the Lord is the Spirit." This verse denotes that the Son is the Spirit. The ambiguity of John 14:26 shows us that the Son is both the Father as the Sender and the Spirit as the Sent One.

Hallelujah! The Son is both the Sender and the Sent One (Zech. 2:8-11), the Father and the Spirit.

John 14:26 shows us that the Son is both the Sender, the Father, and the Sent One, the Spirit. When the Lord Jesus spoke this word He uttered it in such a way to indicate that He was the Sender, the Father, and that He was also the Sent One, the Spirit. The Son is all-inclusive. He is the Son as the Father and as the Spirit. He is the Father as the Son, and He is the Spirit as the Son. The asking One is the Son, the Sender is the Son, and the Sent One is also the Son. The Asker, the Sender, and the Sent One are all one. This is wonderful! This One is the Son as the Father and as the Spirit. We all need to go back over these two portions of the Word: John 14:16-20 and verse 26. We need to eat these verses (Jer. 15:16) and make them our spiritual food (1 Cor. 10:3).

THE SPIRIT AS THE CONSUMMATION
OF THE TRIUNE GOD REACHING THE BELIEVERS

John 14:26 says, "But the Comforter, the Holy Spirit, whom the Father will send in My name, He will teach you all things, and remind you of all things which I said to you." In this verse the Father is the Sender of the Spirit. John 15:26 says, "But when the Comforter comes, whom I will send to you *from with* the Father, the Spirit of reality who proceeds *from with* the Father, He will testify concerning Me." In this verse the Son sends the Spirit "from with" the Father. The Greek word which we have translated "from with" is *para*, which means "by the side of." The sense here is from with. In 14:26, the Sender was the Father, but in 15:26, the Sender is the Son. Also, in 14:16 the Son was the Asker, and in 15:26 the Son is the Sender. These verses indicate that the Father and the Son are one. When the Father was the Sender, that was the Son's sending. When the Son was the Sender, that was the Father's sending.

In 15:26 the Son will send the Spirit from with the Father. This means that the Son will send the Spirit and the Father also. Therefore, the Sent One was not only the Spirit but also the Father because the Sent One will come from with the Father. The Son sent the Spirit not only from the Father, but

also with the Father. Also in both 14:26 and 15:26 the Spirit
as the Comforter was to be sent. In 14:26 the Spirit will be
sent in the name of the Son, which means that the Spirit will
be sent as the Son. In 15:26 the Spirit will come with the
Father as the Sent One. The main point in these verses is
this: the Spirit will be sent as the Son, and the Spirit will
come with the Father. This is why the second section of
the chart on God's New Testament economy (see pages 12
and 13) shows the Spirit as the Son with the Father. When
the Spirit comes, He comes as the Son with the Father. These
two verses show us that the Sender is both the Father and
the Son, and the Sent One is the Spirit as the Son with the
Father. The Father and the Son are both the Sender and the
Sent One. The Spirit is only the Sent One as the Son with
the Father; thus, He is the consummation of the Divine Trinity. When He comes, the Triune God comes. When the Triune
God comes, He comes firstly as the Spirit, then as the Son,
then with the Father. Thus, the Spirit comes to us as the Son
with the Father, and this is the Triune God reaching us.
When the Triune God reaches us, He reaches us as the Spirit.
He comes as the Spirit, and this Spirit is as the Son with the
Father.

In the first section of God's New Testament economy,
we saw the Son with the Father by the Spirit, who was
the embodiment of the Triune God. This embodiment of the
Triune God was in one Person, Jesus Christ. In the second
section of God's New Testament economy, we see the Spirit.
The Spirit is as the Son with the Father to be the consummation of the Triune God in the church. The embodiment of the
Triune God was in Jesus Christ. The consummation of
the Triune God is now in the church. This indicates that
now the Triune God does not only reach us, but He is also
in us, in the church. The One who is in the church is the
wonderful Spirit as the Son with the Father to be the consummation of the Triune God. The Father is in the Son (John
14:10) who is the Spirit in us (2 Cor. 3:17; John 14:17; 2 Tim.
4:22). After the Son's resurrection, He became the Spirit as
the Son with the Father to be the consummation of the processed Triune God to live in the church in the divine oneness.

THE SPIRIT INCLUDING THE SON'S ACCOMPLISHMENTS, ATTAINMENTS, AND OBTAINMENTS

When this Spirit comes to us as the Son, He comes with all that the Son has accomplished, attained, and obtained. The first item of the Son's accomplishments is His incarnation. Then the Son accomplished human living. Many Christians neglect this item, but we all must realize that for God to live on this earth for thirty-three and a half years was a great thing. The very Creator of the universe, which includes the heavens, the earth, and billions of items, lived on this earth as a man among men, even in a poor family. This is marvelous that God the Creator would live as a man on this earth for thirty-three and a half years. He experienced the human life, the human sufferings, all the human sorrows, all the human problems and troubles, and all the trials and temptations. He experienced all these things, and He passed through all these things. Such a human living was accomplished by Jesus. He also accomplished an all-inclusive death, an excellent and marvelous resurrection, and an exalting ascension. Thus, the accomplishments of Christ include His incarnation, human living, death, resurrection, and ascension. These are all included in and attached to the Person of Christ.

The attainments of Christ include His ascension "far above all the heavens" (Eph. 4:10). The visible clouds may be considered the first heaven, and the sky, the second heaven. The third heaven must refer to the heaven of the heavens (2 Cor. 12:2), the highest heaven (Deut. 10:14; Psa. 148:4), where the Lord Jesus and God are today (Eph. 4:10; Heb. 4:14; 1:3). His ascension to the third heavens means that He attained to the highest place in the universe. He ascended on high, and nothing is higher than Him (Eph. 1:21). This is spacewise; according to space, He is the highest. Christ also attained to the height of all the virtues. He attained to the height of all morality. His attainments include Him being a mingling of the divine attributes with the human virtues, issuing in a life in the highest standard of morality. Ephesians 1:21 also tells us that His attainments include His being "far above all rule and authority and power and lordship, and every name that is named." His attainments also include His being crowned with glory and honor in ascension (Heb. 2:9). Glory is the splendor related to Jesus' Person; honor is the preciousness related to Jesus' worth, value (1 Pet. 2:7, "precious" in Gk. is the same word as "honor" here), and dignity which is related to His position (2 Pet. 1:17; cf. 1 Pet. 2:17; Rom. 13:7).

In addition to His attainments, Christ obtained the kingship, the lordship, and the headship, including all authority. This embodiment of the Triune God is not only a wonderful Person, but a wonderful Person with the highest accomplishments, attainments, and obtainments. We must remember that when the Spirit comes into us as the Son, this includes all the Son's accomplishments, attainments, and obtainments.

THE SPIRIT COMING INTO US WITH THE FATHER

The Spirit does not only come into us as the Son, but also with the Father, including the Father's plan, the Father's choosing (Eph. 1:4), the Father's predestination (Eph. 1:5), and the Father's glory (John 17:22). The divine title of the Father, especially in the New Testament, comprises His plan, His selection, His predestination, and His glory. The Spirit comes into us as the Son with the Father, which includes all that the Son has accomplished, attained, and obtained and all of the Father's plan, selection, predestination, and glory.

THE SPIRIT BEING ALL-INCLUSIVE

This is why we say that the Spirit we have received is the all-inclusive Spirit. According to the type in Exodus 30 this Spirit is a compound Spirit (vv. 22-25). The compound ointment in Exodus 30 was comprised of various spices compounded together with olive oil. This compound ointment is a picture, a type, of the all-inclusive compounded Spirit as the consummation of the Triune God. We must praise the Lord that this Spirit is in the church, in you and in me!

CONVICTING THE WORLD
CONCERNING SIN, RIGHTEOUSNESS, AND JUDGMENT

In John 16:7-11 the Lord Jesus told the disciples, "But I

tell you the truth, it is expedient for you that I go away; for if I do not go away, the Comforter will not come to you; but if I go, I will send Him to you. And having come, He will convict the world concerning sin, and concerning righteousness, and concerning judgment; concerning sin, because they do not believe in Me; and concerning righteousness, because I go to the Father and you no longer behold Me; and concerning judgment, because the ruler of this world has been judged." These verses tell us that when the Comforter, the Spirit of truth, comes, He will convict the fallen sinners of three things: of sin, of righteousness, and of judgment. These three things are related to three persons: sin is related to Adam, righteousness is related to Christ, and judgment is related to Satan. We fallen human beings were all born of sin in Adam. In Adam we were sinful, but, praise the Lord, we can be in Christ. To be freed from sin, the only way is to believe in Christ, the Son of God (John 16:9). In Adam we inherit sin, but in Christ we inherit righteousness. If we believe in the resurrected Christ, He is righteousness to us, and we are justified in Him (Rom. 3:24; 4:25). If we do not repent of the sin in Adam and believe in the resurrected Christ, the Son of God, we will remain in sin and share the judgment of Satan for eternity (Matt. 25:41). When the Spirit comes, He convicts the unbelievers with these three things. The sinners who are born in Adam must believe in the resurrected Christ so that they may have Him as their righteousness. If they do not believe, they will be judged by God as Satan is. When the gospel is preached in a proper way those who hear would have the desire not to remain in Adam, but to be transferred into Christ. These people will be regenerated and saved. To them, the convicting Spirit will become the regenerating Spirit (John 3:6), the Spirit of life (Rom. 8:2), the Spirit of reality, dwelling within them (John 14:17).

THE TRANSMISSION OF THE DIVINE TRINITY

In John 16:13-15 the Lord says, "But when He, the Spirit of reality, comes, He will guide you into all the reality; for He will not speak from Himself, but whatever He hears He will speak; and He will disclose to you what is to come. He shall glorify Me, for He shall receive of Mine and shall disclose it to you. All that the Father has is Mine; therefore I said that He receives of Mine and shall disclose it to you." By reading the context of these verses we can see that "the reality" refers to what the Father has, what the Son has, and what the Spirit receives of the Son and of what the Father has. What the Father has is a reality, what the Son has is a reality, and what the Spirit receives is also reality.

These verses show us that what the Father has becomes the Son's, what the Son has is received by the Spirit, and what the Spirit receives is disclosed to us. The Father, the Son, the Spirit, and we, the believers, are all involved in this process. The Father has many riches. He is the source, the origin. All that the Father has becomes the Son's. The Son has the unsearchable riches (Eph. 3:8). Whatever the Father has is His, and what the Son has is all received by the Spirit. Since what the Spirit receives is disclosed or transmitted into us, we become the very destination. The Father is embodied in the Son, the Son is transfigured to be the Spirit, and the Spirit is the reaching of the Divine Trinity to us. All the riches of the Triune God reach us in the Spirit. So we are the destination of the Triune God. All that the Triune God is and has been disclosed, conveyed, transmitted into us. Because we are organically united to the Spirit, that is, organically united to the processed Triune God, whatever He is and has now is our portion as our inheritance.

We must apply these verses to our experience. Do we have all that the Father has, all that the Son has, and all that the Spirit has received? Has the Spirit disclosed all that the Father has and all that the Son has to us in our experience? Actually, we have received everything that the Triune God is and has, but we have been too veiled to see and experience what we have received. Not only do we not know this fact in our experience, but also we do not know it in the Word. For years I never realized that all that the Father has is the Son's, that all the Son has was received by the Spirit, and that the Spirit discloses to us what He receives.

These verses unveil to us the transmission of the Divine Trinity, the Father, the Son, and the Spirit into the believers.

In these verses the Lord says, "All that the Father has is mine." The Father as the source, as the origin, has a lot of riches. All that the Father has becomes the Son's. The Son not only has what the Father has, but also He has all the riches in His incarnation, human living, crucifixion, resurrection, and ascension. All that He has is in addition to what the Father has. All these riches contained in the Son are received by the Spirit and the Spirit discloses them to us. This disclosing is a transmission of all the riches of what the processed Triune God is and has into our being. This means that whatever the processed Triune God is and has is to be our element, our essence, our being, making the processed Triune God the very essence of our being. Thus, we all become God-men.

THE SPIRIT BEING NOT YET

In John 7:37-39 we are told clearly that such a Spirit of life, which is the living water, "was not yet because Jesus was not yet glorified" (v. 39). In other words, before Jesus' death and resurrection such a compound Spirit, the life-giving Spirit, the all-inclusive Spirit as the consummation of the Triune God, was not yet. The Spirit of God was there already, as was the Spirit of Jehovah, but the Spirit who gives life, the compound Spirit, the all-inclusive Spirit, was not yet until Jesus was crucified and glorified in resurrection (Luke 24:26). After His resurrection, He came back to the disciples as the Spirit because through His death and resurrection He finished the entire process to make the Spirit complete. After His death and resurrection, the Spirit was completely compounded to be the life-giving Spirit.

THE RESURRECTED CHRIST BREATHING HIMSELF INTO THE DISCIPLES AS THE SPIRIT

John 20:19-22 shows us that on the evening of the day of resurrection He came to His disciples as such a Spirit. "When therefore it was evening on that day, the first day of the week, and when the doors were shut where the disciples were for fear of the Jews, Jesus came and stood in the midst and said to them, Peace be to you. And having said this, He showed them both His hands and His side. The disciples therefore rejoiced when they saw the Lord. Then Jesus said to them again, Peace be to you; as the Father has sent Me, I also send you. And when He had said this, He breathed into them and said to them, Receive the Holy Spirit" (vv. 19-22). When the Lord came back to the disciples on the evening of the day of resurrection, He still had a body because He showed the disciples His hands and His side. The doors were shut to the room where the disciples were, yet Jesus came and stood in their midst. The Bible does not tell us how He got into the room. Our human mentality just cannot understand such a thing. His body was spiritual, yet it still could be touched. This was the resurrected Jesus, with a spiritual, resurrected body (1 Cor. 15:44).

The Lord Jesus then breathed into the disciples, and He asked the disciples to receive that breath. He called that breath the Holy Spirit. In Greek, the Holy Spirit also means the Holy Breath. The Holy Spirit is the breath of the Son. We cannot say that the breath is one person, and the breather is another person. These verses show us clearly that the Spirit is not another person, but the very breath of the Son. We should not consider that the breather is a person and the breath is another person. Actually, the breath is one person with the breather. The resurrected Christ as the life-giving Spirit is the breath. This indicates that Christ the Son coming back in resurrection is the Spirit. This is why some of the early students of the Bible called such a Christ "the pneumatic Christ." The Christ in John 20 is the very pneumatic Christ in resurrection. After He had accomplished all of His processes, He became the life-giving Spirit (1 Cor. 15:45), and this life-giving Spirit is the pneumatic Christ.

Most Christian teachers teach that the Spirit did not come until the day of Pentecost. Actually the Spirit came on the day of resurrection (John 20:1, 19, 22). He firstly came as life in a secret way, signified by the breath of the resurrected Christ. The resurrected, pneumatic Christ came back to His disciples secretly in the night in a place not open to others, and breathed Himself into His disciples. When we breathe, nobody sees what we breathe. Breathing is something secret. What we breathe cannot be seen, but it is so real. Also, the very breath breathed into our intrinsic being is very, very vital. If you do not eat for ten days, you may still live. Also, you may not drink for two days and you may still live. But try not breathing just for five minutes. If you stop breathing, even for five minutes, you would die. This shows how crucial breathing is, and this breathing did not happen on the day of Pentecost, openly, with a big loud voice. This breathing happened silently, secretly, on the evening of the day of Christ's resurrection.

We must realize that this breathing is more crucial, more vital, than the mighty wind on the day of Pentecost (Acts 2:2). Many Christians have only seen the mighty wind blowing on the day of Pentecost. They have never seen the silent, soft, secret breathing on the day of resurrection. Dear saints, consider these two things. Which is more vital? The breath or the mighty wind? If a person were dying and you put him under the mighty wind, this mighty wind would not help him. But if you give a dying person oxygen to breathe in, then this is life-saving. In like manner, the silent, soft, secret breathing on the day of resurrection is life-saving. Actually, it is more than life-saving; it is life-imparting and life-supplying. All those natural disciples, through that breathing on the day of resurrection, received the Spirit of the divine, uncreated life of God. All of them were enlivened, quickened, and filled with the Spirit. They became persons not living by themselves but by the Spirit, persons one with the Triune God intrinsically in their essence.

I believe we all have seen that the period of time from the Lord's conception to His sending of the Spirit was a complete process of what He went through while He was here on this earth. His conception brought God into man, making divinity one with humanity. This was the beginning of His incarnation. His birth carried out this wonderful incarnation that made God one with man, that brought divinity into humanity, and that even mingled God as one with man. He was a God-man who lived on this earth for thirty-three and a half years as a man living God as His life. He was fully qualified to die a death that accomplished God's full plan. After this death, He entered into resurrection and through His resurrection, man was brought into God.

His incarnation brought God into man, and His resurrection brought man into God. Through this two-way traffic, the mingling of God and man was fully accomplished. Through the incarnation, God became flesh. Through the resurrection, this God-man became a life-giving Spirit. In His resurrection He came back to His disciples as the Spirit. He was now the "pneumatic Christ." He was still the God-man, but His humanity had been resurrected and designated into the sonship of God (Rom. 1:3-4). Such a One, the pneumatic Christ as the Spirit, came back to His disciples and breathed Himself as the Spirit into them. From that day onward He became really one with His disciples. He became the very intrinsic being of His disciples essentially. This resurrected Christ, this pneumatic Christ, this Christ as the Spirit, entered into His believers to be their very essence and to be their life essentially on the day of His resurrection.

CHAPTER SEVEN

THE SON'S ASCENSION
AND THE BAPTISM IN THE SPIRIT

(1)

Scripture Reading: Acts 1:3; Luke 1:15; Acts 1:12-15; 2:1-4, 17-18; Luke 24:49

Thus far, we have seen that the Triune God became a Man who lived on this earth for thirty-three and a half years. This God-man then died a wonderful, all-inclusive death on the cross to solve all the negative problems and to release the divine life. Then He overcame death by coming out of death in resurrection. In resurrection He was born as the Firstborn of God (Acts 13:33; Rom. 8:29), and at the same time He brought forth many sons of God who are His many brothers (1 Pet. 1:3; Rom. 8:29; Heb. 2:11-12). Also, through His resurrection a new child was born (John 16:20-22), and He became the all-inclusive, life-giving Spirit (1 Cor. 15:45) to apply Himself and all that He had accomplished, attained, and obtained to this new child. Therefore, on the day of His resurrection He came back to the disciples as the pneumatic Christ and He breathed Himself into them as the Spirit of life.

This Holy Breath is all-inclusive. In this breath are all the elements of the Person of Christ and all the elements of what He has accomplished, attained, and obtained. This breath is the compound, all-inclusive Spirit which actually is the Lord Himself as the all-inclusive Christ breathed into His disciples. On the evening of the day of resurrection the Lord exhaled Himself as the breath and the disciples inhaled Him as the breath. By this exhaling and inhaling, this wonderful One got into the disciples. He entered into them to be their life, to be the essence of their new being. Their receiving of this breath was altogether a matter of life essentially. They received Him as their life, as the very intrinsic essence of their being. This is a most marvelous, excellent, and wonderful fact. We must thank the Lord that in these last days He has taken away the veil to disclose to us all these things in such a detailed way.

This wonderful One, who is the Triune God mingled with humanity, became wrapped up with human living and entered into an all-inclusive death that dealt with sin and sins, that destroyed Satan and his satanic system, the world, and that annulled all the religious ordinances, terminated the old creation, and released His divine life. All these aspects of His death became elements of His compounded Being. He has overcome Satan and death, and He has entered into resurrection. He became the Firstborn of God, and He produced many brothers to bring forth a new child. After all of this, such a wonderful Person became the all-inclusive, compound, life-giving Spirit to be breathed into His disciples as their very breath. This breath is not a small matter, but it is all-inclusive, life-giving, and indwelling. This breath, which is His indwelling presence, is life to us; it is our essential being. Now we are one with Him in the essential way of life. The believers in Christ are new beings, new persons—even divinely human persons.

THE LORD'S TRAINING OF THE DISCIPLES

Before the Lord's ascension, He spent forty days with the disciples (Acts 1:3). The number forty indicates a time of testing (Deut. 9:9, 18; 1 Kings 19:8; Heb. 3:9; Matt. 4:2). In these forty days before His ascension, He tested His disciples. He trained them to know their new being, to know that His essence had become their essence. He trained them to know that He had become them, that He had entered into them, and that He had brought them into Him. He also trained them to realize that He was in the Father, that they were in Him, and that He was in them (John 14:20). Ultimately, this kind of training was to help the disciples realize that they were mingled with the Triune God, that they were no longer merely human but divinely human, even "Jesusly human." They were no longer separate from the Triune God, but they could now live a life in which they were one with the processed Triune God. They were no longer merely men, but God-men, divine men, with the Triune God as their intrinsic essence to become their divine being.

The invisible presence of the processed Triune God was now within them. They had to be trained to practice this presence, to live and behave in this life, and to be persons in this life. The Lord was training them to be the divine persons on this earth. This is wonderful! The Lord created the entire universe in six days, but He spent forty days to train His disciples. The training of the disciples was a much bigger task than the creation of the universe. He appeared to two disciples on the road to Emmaus (Luke 24:13-35), He appeared to the disciples twice in a closed room (John 20:19, 26), and He also appeared to the disciples at the sea of Tiberias (John 21:1). His appearing and disappearing trained His disciples to know His invisible presence.

It was hard for the Lord Jesus to train the disciples to trust Him for their living. Due to the trial of the need of their living, Peter returned to his old occupation, backsliding from the Lord's call (John 21:3; Matt. 4:19-20; Luke 5:3-11), and Thomas, Nathanael, the sons of Zebedee, and two other disciples followed Him to go fishing (John 21:2-3). Peter was tested, but he could not pass the test. They all went down to the sea to return to their old profession, but they did not realize that they brought the Lord Jesus there with them because the Lord Jesus was within them all the time. No matter where they were, where they went, or what they did, they could not be separated from Him because He was mingled with them. Because they did not realize this, He needed forty days to train them.

At the sea of Tiberias, the Lord did something miraculous. Peter and the sons of Zebedee (John and James) were professional fishers, the sea of Tiberias was large and full of fish, and night was the right time for fishing, but through the entire night they caught nothing (John 21:3). It must have been that the Lord bade all the fishes stay away from their

net. Then in the morning (v. 4), which was not the right time
for fishing, they caught an abundance of fishes when they did
it at the Lord's word (v. 6). Surely this was a miracle! It must
have been that the Lord bade the fishes come into their net.
But without these fish, even on the land where the fish were
not, the Lord prepared fish and even bread for them (John
21:9). This was again a miracle! By this, the Lord trained
them to realize that without His leading, though they went to
the sea where the fish were and in the night, the right time
for fishing, they could catch nothing; but with the Lord's leading, even on the land where the fish were not, the Lord could
provide fish for them. Though they caught many fish according to the Lord's word, the Lord would not use those to feed
them. This was a real lesson to Peter. For his living he should
believe and trust in the Lord who "calls the things not being
as being" (Rom. 4:17). The disciples learned that the all-
inclusive Lord was with them, was in them, and was taking
care of them. They did not need to go fishing. They just
needed to stay with the Lord to enjoy His indwelling, blessed
presence.

From the day of His resurrection, He appeared again and
again to His disciples for forty days to train them how to realize His invisible presence. When He was with the disciples for
three and a half years, the disciples experienced His visible
presence, but that presence was terminated by His death.
After His resurrection, by His coming back as the Spirit,
another kind of presence began. This was His invisible presence, and this presence was intrinsic to His disciples. His
visible presence in those three and a half years was altogether
outward, not intrinsic. It was not life to them, but merely a
presence among them. After the resurrection, however, as the
pneumatic Christ and as the life-giving Spirit, He came back
to the disciples and entered into them. This entering in
became an invisible presence, and this presence was life to the
disciples. This presence was very inward and intrinsic, not
outward, and it brought His element into the disciples' being.

Through such an invisible presence, this invisible Christ
became His disciples' element and intrinsic essence. He was
one with His disciples intrinsically and essentially, but the

disciples were not used to such an invisible presence. They were used to visible things. Because of their weakness, He appeared to them and disappeared in order to train them to realize His invisible presence. He wanted them to know that even though they did not see Him or feel His presence, He was still there with them all the time (Matt. 28:20). His presence was always there inside their being; it even became their intrinsic essence and their thought. In Galatians 2:20 the Apostle Paul said, "It is no longer I who live, but Christ lives in me." This is the invisible presence of the pneumatic Christ. The end of the four Gospels and the beginning of Acts show how the Lord Jesus spent forty days with the disciples in order to train them to get used to His invisible presence.

The Lord had been with the disciples for three and a half years before His death, and after His resurrection He was with them in a very mysterious way for forty days. He would appear to them suddenly without their realization (Luke 24:15-16; John 20:14; 21:4). When they realized He was there, He disappeared from them (Luke 24:31). The disciples just could not trace whether He was absent or present. Eventually, however, they all were trained. Their doubts vanished, their fear was taken away, and they were fully calmed down and satisfied. They were trained to fully realize that this wonderful Person was so real and that He was with them, even within them. Whether He appeared or disappeared, He was still living within them. He was there when He appeared and He was there when He disappeared. They did not need to be troubled by His disappearing, and they did not need to be excited by His appearing. Whether He appeared or disappeared, He was still there with the disciples caring for them.

THE SON'S ASCENSION

After the Lord finished this forty day training, He had the peace to leave them, so He brought them all to the Mount of Olives where He was carried up into heaven (Luke 24:51; Acts 1:11-12). This brought Him into another new stage. Before His incarnation, He was merely God. His incarnation brought Him into a new stage, a stage for Him to live on this earth for thirty-three and a half years, a stage for Him to be a man living God. That was His second stage. Then His ascension brought Him into a third stage. This stage is that of a resurrected man living in the heavens to execute the things God determined on this earth. This resurrected One is now sitting in the heavens to execute God's administration (Heb. 12:2). This One in the heavens is the Head.

After the disciples received the life-giving Spirit breathed into them by the resurrected Christ, as life, as life-supply, and as everything related to their inner man, they all became the God-men, the men who had been mingled with God. Then they were filled with the divine life essentially, but they were not qualified to carry out God's economy. Therefore, the resurrected Christ had to ascend to the heavens to be exalted by God, and to be given by God the kingship, the lordship, and the headship over all things. He also obtained the throne, the glory, and all the authority in the universe. While the hundred and twenty were praying on the earth for ten days, God was making the exalted Christ to be the King, the Lord, and the Head of all things. God was giving the authority, the throne, and the glory to His exalted One.

THE DISCIPLES' PRAYER

In the forty days of the resurrected Lord's training, the disciples learned the lesson, so, after the Lord ascended to the heavens, they could pray together for ten days in Jerusalem in a threatening environment (Acts 1:12-15). They prayed together in a fearless way, forgetting about their eating, their drinking, and their living. Acts 1 is a wonderful record showing us how the hundred and twenty could stay together under a threatening situation for ten days, caring for nothing except the charge of the ascended Christ (vv. 14-15). Among them there was no disputation, no fighting, only oneness. Before the Lord's death, the twelve were still fighting over who was going to be greater (Luke 22:24). They were so natural, selfish, fleshly, and even sinful. Peter was very natural and very selfish. The two sons of thunder, James and John, begged the Lord Jesus to give them the two top positions when He came in His kingdom (Mark 10:35-37). They wanted to sit with Him, one on His right hand and one on His left hand. When the other ten heard this, they were indignant (v. 41). They were bothered because they were also ambitious. However, after the Lord's resurrection, His stay with them for forty days, and His ascension to the heavens, they and those of the hundred and twenty all became different. They were not only regenerated, but also transformed persons to some extent, so they could pray together in one accord for ten days. It would be difficult for even a handful of us to pray for ten hours in one accord, but they were one hundred twenty praying for ten days in a place which was full of threatening. At that time the religious leaders of Jerusalem were threatening to put the followers of Jesus to death. They were under this kind of death threatening, yet they dared to stay there and pray for ten days, and they prayed in one accord. They did not care for their safety or their peace. They cared for the Lord's commission, for the Lord's testimony, (Acts 1:8; Luke 24:48), and for the preaching in His name of the gospel (Luke 24:47; Matt. 28:19).

THE POURING OUT OF THE SPIRIT

While the hundred and twenty disciples were praying and while the exalted Christ was executing on the throne in the heavens, the day of Pentecost came (Acts 2:1-4). There was a wonderful scene in the universe which should have been seen by the angels as the spectators on the day of Pentecost. The Head was sitting on the throne in the heavens executing God's administration, and the Body, represented by the one hundred twenty, was coordinating with the Head for ten days to carry out God's move on the earth. Then on the day of Pentecost, the Holy Spirit was poured out from the Head and by the Head to the disciples and on the disciples (Acts 2:17-18). This means heaven was brought to earth, and God was poured out on man. This pouring out was not essential, but economical. It was not for life, but for power, for administration. What was needed on the day of Pentecost was not life, but power, even the mighty power to carry out God's administration. After the blowing of the mighty wind, those one hundred twenty became not only spiritual persons, but heavenly persons. They became the very joint between heaven and earth. They joined the heavens and the earth, and they were cooperating with the heavenly Head to carry out God's eternal administration. This was the pouring out of the fully consummated Spirit by the heavenly Head, the pouring out of the ultimate consummation of the processed Triune God by the resurrected and ascended Christ, to accomplish the baptism of His Body in the Spirit.

On the day of Pentecost, the exalted Christ was poured out as the Spirit, the ultimate consummation of the processed Triune God, upon the hundred and twenty prepared ones, fifty days after His resurrection. On the day of resurrection, He was the all-inclusive breath which was breathed into His disciples as the Spirit of life. But after forty days training and ten days preparation, the heaven and the earth were ready for the pouring out of this exalted One as the Spirit of power upon the believers on this earth who had been made ready.

What happened on the day of resurrection and on the day of Pentecost are landmarks in the universe. On the day of resurrection, the resurrected Christ, as the all-inclusive breath, was breathed into the disciples. On the day of Pentecost, the exalted Christ, the authorized Christ, as the mighty wind, was blown upon these ready believers. After Pentecost, within them was the all-inclusive breath and upon them was the mighty wind. On the day of resurrection the resurrected Christ was the breath to be breathed into His disciples, and on the day of Pentecost the exalted Christ was the mighty wind blown upon these ready believers. Within them they had the breath; upon them they had the wind. Within them they had the all-inclusive Christ as the resurrected One for their life, and upon them they had the ascended Christ as the exalted One for their power, for their authority, and for their uniform.

THE ALL-INCLUSIVE AND CONSUMMATED SPIRIT BEING THE BREATH AND THE WIND

The Spirit that dwells within the believers and the Spirit that descends upon the believers are not two Spirits, but one Spirit in two aspects. From His incarnation through His resurrection, He became this Spirit of breath, which is for life intrinsically and essentially. Then after His ascension, He became the Spirit of wind, which is for power. The breath is very close to the wind. When the breath is strengthened, it may become the wind. When the wind is softened or slowed down a little bit, the wind becomes the breath. Also, the Greek word *pneuma* and the Hebrew word *ruach* can be translated into Spirit, wind, or breath. In John 3 the Greek *pneuma* is translated first into Spirit (John 3:6), and then into wind (v. 8). In Ezekiel 37, the word *ruach,* which is an equivalent to the Greek *pneuma,* is translated in the English version into three words: Spirit (v. 14), wind (v. 9), and breath (vv. 6, 8). We should not consider the breath as something separate from the wind. After being strengthened, the breath becomes the wind. After being softened, the wind becomes the breath. The wind and the breath are two aspects of one matter. Also, the wind brings us the fresh air to breathe. The fresh air for our breathing depends upon the proper, strong wind. The wind is for power, and the breath is for life. Praise the Lord for the breathing of the Spirit, and praise the Lord for the blowing of the Spirit! The Spirit is the breath and also the wind. The breath comes into us, and the wind comes upon us. In the Pentecostal movement, the breath has been neglected, and the wind has been misunderstood.

THE INDWELLING SPIRIT AND THE MANTLE SPIRIT

In the past century, the Brethren teachers in England saw these two aspects to some extent. They called the Spirit on the day of resurrection the indwelling Spirit. Then they called the Spirit on the day of Pentecost "the mantle Spirit." The mantle Spirit is the Spirit as the outer clothing, the uniform. The British Brethren teachers saw from Luke 24:49 that the disciples were to wait in Jerusalem until they were clothed with power from on high. The word clothed reminded them of the mantle of Elijah, which was a symbol of the power of the Spirit (2 Kings 2:13-14). The aspect of the mantle Spirit, which is outward, is different from the indwelling Spirit, which is inward. Their teaching has greatly helped us, but by the Lord's mercy, standing on their shoulders, we have gone a little bit higher to see that this indwelling Spirit as the breath of life is the resurrected Christ Himself. The Brethren teachers did not see this in full.

The life-giving Spirit, who is still God's Spirit, the Holy Spirit, is the pneumatic Christ, the resurrected Christ. This Christ, who is the embodiment of God mingled with man, comprising all His processes, is the all-inclusive, life-giving Spirit. The Lord has also shown us that the mantle Spirit is the very exalted Christ. The indwelling Spirit is the resurrected Christ, and the outpoured Spirit is the exalted Christ. This Christ in exaltation is the mantle Spirit, which is the Spirit of power and the Spirit of authority. Both the resurrected Christ and the exalted Christ are the all-inclusive Spirit with these two aspects: the indwelling aspect and the mantle aspect.

CLOTHED WITH POWER FROM ON HIGH

Even though these hundred and twenty had received the Lord as life essentially, they still had not been equipped and qualified to carry out God's economy. They still needed to be clothed with power from on high (Luke 24:49). After we wake up in the morning, our eating of breakfast fills us with life essentially. Even though we have been filled with life essentially, we still are not qualified to come to the meeting to speak something for the Lord. We need to wash, comb our hair, and put on the proper clothing. Now we are not only constituted intrinsically, essentially, but we are also equipped economically. If a policeman did not have a uniform, no one would respect him or recognize him. When a person is driving his car and he sees a man with a police uniform, he becomes very careful in his driving. The uniform means a lot to the policeman because it represents the government for which he is working. It is his authority which qualifies him to carry out the administration of his state or government.

After the Lord had breathed Himself as the all-inclusive, life-giving Spirit into the disciples on the evening of the day of His resurrection, the disciples were filled inwardly with the Spirit, but they still had not received their uniform. They did not have the proper clothing to carry out God's administration, God's economy. In Luke 24:49 the Lord told the disciples, "And behold, I am sending forth the promise of My Father upon you; but you, stay in the city until you are clothed with power from on high." After their forty-day training, the hundred and twenty still needed the uniform, so the Lord charged them to wait in Jerusalem until they were clothed with power from on high. This power from on high was the outpoured Spirit who is the ascended, pneumatic Christ. This power from on high was the heavenly uniform to be put on God's chosen and prepared people for their qualification to carry out God's administration.

THE SPIRIT AS THE MANTLE

Elijah was a man who received authority from God to control the weather (1 Kings 17:1; 18:41-45). The book of James tells us that Elijah prayed that it should not rain and it did not rain on the earth for three and a half years. Then Elijah prayed again and it rained (James 5:17-18). Elijah had a mantle, and that piece of clothing was his uniform, his authority, to control the heavens for God's administration. He had the power from God, and that power was in his mantle. Elisha realized that he needed the mantle of Elijah to carry out God's administration. When Elijah ascended to the heavens, his mantle was transferred to Elisha (2 Kings 2:12-15). Therefore, Elisha inherited the power and the authority which was in the uniform of Elijah.

If a man puts on a police uniform, we all must respect him. Actually, our respect is for his uniform. His uniform is his power and his authority because it represents his government's administration. The disciples were charged by the Lord to wait in Jerusalem until such a mantle, such a uniform, would descend upon them. Then they would all be clothed with the heavenly uniform, which is the power from on high. After they prayed for ten days, this mantle came down from heaven and they all received the uniform. This mantle, this power from on high, was the ascended, exalted Christ poured down upon them.

THE AUTHORITY OF THE EXALTED CHRIST

The Bible tells us that Christ ascended into heaven (Eph. 4:8-9; Heb. 9:24), but it also says that he was taken up and exalted by God (Mark 16:19; Luke 24:51; Phil. 2:9). After God exalted Him, the Holy Spirit was poured out on the disciples. The Son ascended, the Father exalted Him, and the Spirit was poured out. The Triune God, the Father, the Son, and the Spirit, was fully involved with the ascension and the pouring out of the Spirit. In the Son's death the Triune God was involved, in the Son's resurrection the Triune God was involved, and in the Son's ascension and exaltation the Triune God is also involved. The Father, the Son, and the Spirit are wrapped up with the Son's ascension and the pouring out of the Spirit.

In the Son's ascension God exalted Him, and His exaltation includes the highest attainment. In His ascension He obtained the kingship (Acts 5:31; Rev. 17:14), the lordship (Acts 2:36), the enthronement (Heb. 12:2), the headship (Eph. 1:22), and the glory and honor (Heb. 2:9). All authority has been given to Him in heaven and on earth (Matt. 28:18; Eph. 1:20-21). All these attainments of Christ are not essential for us and have nothing to do with us intrinsically, but these attainments have everything to do with us economically. If a government is weak and disorderly, the policeman's uniform does not mean that much. But if the government is strong, proper, full of power, and orderly, the uniform of the policeman means a lot. If Jesus had never been exalted and had never received the kingship, lordship, headship, the enthronement, the glory and honor, and all the authority, nothing could have been carried out economically. Even though He succeeded in incarnation, human living, death, and resurrection, He still needed to be inaugurated into His heavenly office with all its attainments.

We should praise the Lord that our Christ has ascended and that God has exalted Him. He is the top One in the whole universe sitting on the unique throne in the universe. He is the King of kings, the Lord of lords, and the Head of all things. He has received all the authority, and He has a name above every name (Phil. 2:9). After His ascension, His exaltation, He poured out Himself as authority on His disciples. This poured out, exalted Christ is the authority of the entire universe, and this poured out, exalted Christ has become our clothing, our uniform. Now we not only have His life essentially, but we also are equipped and qualified economically with His authority to carry out God's economy, God's administration.

THE SPIRIT BEING OUR LIFE AND OUR AUTHORITY

The very Spirit of life (Rom. 8:2) as the breath breathed into us is absolutely for life. We have the Triune God in His humanity with His human living, His all-inclusive death, and His excellent resurrection within us as our life. This is satisfying to the uttermost, but we still need the equipment, the power, the authority, the heavenly uniform. After ten days of prayer, the exalted, pneumatic Christ was poured out upon the disciples. He was breathed into them on the evening of the day of the resurrection as their life essentially, and He was poured out upon them on the day of Pentecost as their authority, as their mantle, as their clothing, as their heavenly uniform economically. Our friends, colleagues, neighbors, and family may not realize that we are wearing the exalted, pneumatic Christ as our uniform, but every demon and evil spirit knows this. They know that we are authorized, and that we are part of the ascended Christ.

ESSENTIAL AND ECONOMICAL

Thus far, in our definition of the Divine Trinity and of our experience of the Divine Trinity, we have used two new words in our spiritual vocabulary: "essential" refers to the existence, to the being, and to the life for existence; "economical" refers to economy, work, and function. When we say the essential Trinity, we mean the Divine Trinity in His existence, referring to His Being. When we say the economical Trinity, we mean the Divine Trinity in His economy, referring to His move, work, and function. To experience the Triune God as our life for our spiritual being, spiritual existence, is essential. To experience the Triune God as power for our spiritual work and spiritual function, is economical. To feed on the Lord as food, to drink Him as water, and to breathe Him as air is essential because it is related to the inner life for our spiritual existence. To put on the Lord as our clothing, to be clothed with the outpoured Spirit as power from on high, is economical because it is related to the outward move and work. On the day of resurrection, the Lord breathed the Spirit of life into the disciples. That is essential. On the day of Pentecost, the Lord poured out the Spirit of power upon the disciples. This is economical. On the one hand, they received the Spirit of life into their being essentially, and on the other hand, they received the Spirit of power upon them economically. Eventually, they became persons of the all-inclusive Spirit as the ultimate consummation of the processed Triune God.

CHAPTER EIGHT

THE SON'S ASCENSION
AND THE BAPTISM IN THE SPIRIT

(2)

Scripture Reading: 1 Cor. 12:13; Matt. 28:19; Eph. 1:22-23; Rev. 1:4; 3:1; 4:5; 5:6; Matt. 28:18-19; Mark 16:17-18

BAPTIZED INTO THE BODY OF CHRIST
TO CARRY OUT THE DIVINE ADMINISTRATION
BY THE AUTHORITY OF THE EXALTED CHRIST

According to His New Testament economy the Triune God, after passing through all the processes of incarnation, human living, crucifixion, and resurrection, was consummated to be the all-inclusive, compound Spirit. In His ascension this Spirit was poured out to accomplish the baptism of the Body of Christ. Hence, for the believers to be baptized in this Spirit is to be baptized into one Body that, as His Body, we may be joined to Him as the Head to receive His authority for the carrying out of the divine governmental administration.

The breath breathed into us makes us the members of Christ who are so living and full of life. But all the members of Christ need to be put together to form one Body. This needed another step; therefore, the pneumatic Christ also must be the ascended, exalted Christ. After being exalted, He became the authority of this universe and He poured Himself out upon all the members to authorize them and to put them together to form them into one Body. This Body is the universal government because this Body is united to the Head. Although Christ as the Head of all things is the authority and the government of this universe, He needs a Body to execute

His orders. Therefore, the Head and the Body become the authority and government of the entire universe.

Every member of the Body has the authority of the Head. Every member of this Body is a part of the universal government. In this Body and joined to our ascended Head, we have the power, the authority, and the entire universe must respect us. All of the demons and the evil spirits have to fear us. As the resurrected, pneumatic Christ, the Lord dealt with all the negative items in the universe and released Himself into us as our life. He imparted Himself into us essentially as our life to make us His living members. Another step was needed for Him to be exalted to be the authority of the universe, to be the ascended, exalted Christ. Then He poured Himself out as the exalted Christ upon us as authority to make us His Body, the executing organ of the Head. This Body connected to the Head is the government, the administration of this universe. In the Body every member is a part of the universal authority. We are qualified and equipped to carry out the divine administration on this earth. With the pneumatic, ascended, exalted Christ as our heavenly uniform, we have the power and the authority to move and to work to accomplish God's eternal plan.

The baptism in the Holy Spirit is the outpouring of the Triune God, consummated in the all-inclusive compound Spirit, by the heavenly Head upon His Body on this earth, not for life, but for administration, not as life essentially, but as power economically to carry out God's economy. This baptism in the Spirit was prophesied by John the Baptist. John told his followers that he was sent to baptize people in water. To baptize people in water is to terminate people in their old realm of life, the world, and bury them. He also told his disciples that One was coming after him who would baptize people in the Spirit (Matt. 3:11). To baptize people in the Spirit is to bring people into a new realm of life, the kingdom of God. For the processed Triune God to be given into us as the Spirit of life is for our germination. Then for the processed Triune God to be poured upon us as the Spirit of power is to bring us into a new kingdom. These two things should be put together since they are both carried out by the same one Spirit (1 Cor.

12:13). The same one Spirit as the Spirit of life germinates us, and as the Spirit of power brings us into a new kingdom. Therefore, all the believers of Christ are Spirit germinated persons, and also persons brought into a new kingdom by the Spirit.

This kind of person is altogether a person of the Spirit, who is the ultimate consummation of the processed Triune God. Such persons are germinated by the Spirit as life, and also brought into a new kingdom by the Spirit as power. These persons are not only germinated, enlivened, and quickened in life, but they are equipped to carry out God's administration in His kingdom for the fulfillment of His eternal plan. I hope that we all would receive a clear vision of this. The Spirit is the ultimate consummation of the processed Triune God, first, to be breathed into our being, to germinate us, to enliven us, to quicken us, that we may have the processed Triune God as our life essentially. We then become the God-men, living God's life. Then the Spirit as the ultimate consummation of the processed Triune God brings us into a new kingdom by baptizing us with the power from on high to make us qualified persons in God's kingdom to carry out His eternal plan.

From Acts 2 these one hundred twenty, including the twelve, all became persons who were enlivened, quickened, and regenerated by the Spirit of life breathed into them by the resurrected Christ in His resurrection to be God-men, living God, expressing God, and also brought into God's kingdom by the Spirit of power poured upon them by the ascended Christ in His ascension to execute God's administration. These are the kind of persons we have to be today. We have to be germinated by the Spirit of life essentially, and we have to be empowered by the Spirit of power economically. Then we live God, and we carry out God's plan. The resurrected Christ's breathing of the Spirit of life germinates us, making us the members of Christ, and the ascended Christ's baptizing in the Spirit of power, putting us into the Triune God, makes all the members of Christ one Body. Germinating makes us the members of Christ, but there is another step— the step of baptizing. Baptizing makes us, all His members, one Body. First Corinthians 12:13 says that we all were baptized in one Spirit into one Body. As long as we have been first germinated and then baptized, we become members of Christ and are composed into the one Body of Christ. It is by the breathing Spirit that we are made members of Christ, and it is by the baptizing Spirit that all the members of Christ are made one Body of Christ. Now in this universe, there is the Head in the heavens, and there is the Body on this earth, cooperating together to carry out God's administration for His eternal plan. Even though we are still in the old heaven and the old earth, we are already in the new heaven and the new earth through the germination of the Spirit of life and the baptism in the Spirit of power.

BAPTIZED IN ONE SPIRIT
AND GIVEN TO DRINK ONE SPIRIT

To be baptized in the all-inclusive consummated Spirit does not only put us, the believers, all together to be the Body of Christ, but also positions us to drink Him to receive the all-bountiful supply (Phil. 1:19) of the processed and transmitted Triune God, that we may be nourished to be the strong and active members of the Body of Christ for the carrying out of God's eternal plan. When the Lord poured Himself out as this all-inclusive consummated Spirit upon His disciples, He accomplished the baptism in the Spirit. He passed through incarnation, human living, crucifixion, resurrection, and ascension. Then He poured Himself out. For Peter, James, and John, the early disciples who were with the Lord throughout His earthly ministry, to be baptized in the Spirit was the last step they went through. However, for the house of Cornelius (Acts 10) to be baptized in the Spirit was the first step. Today we are just like the house of Cornelius. Our beginning is from the baptism in the Holy Spirit. When the house of Cornelius received the baptism in the Spirit, they began their spiritual life. They began to drink of the Spirit. This is why 1 Corinthians 12:13 tells us that "in one Spirit we were all baptized into one body...and were all given to drink one Spirit." After we were baptized, we began to drink. To be baptized is to be put into Christ and to put Christ upon us (Gal. 3:27); then we begin to drink of Christ and to take Him in.

First, we are put into Christ; then we receive Christ into us. This corresponds to the Lord's word in John 15:4 where He says, "Abide in Me and I in you." He also said in John 14:20 that He was in the Father, that we are in Him, and that He is in us. We must firstly be in Him; then He will be in us. We are in Him by being baptized into Him, and we have Him in us by drinking of Him. To baptize people into water is a demonstration of the baptism of the Spirit. One who believes in the Lord is baptized into the Triune God. Then we demonstrate this by putting this one into water, signifying that he has been baptized into the Triune God, into Christ, into the all-inclusive Spirit. From this time onward, this baptized one begins to drink of the Spirit so the Lord can abide in Him.

Today the Lord has accomplished everything. The breathing of Himself into the believers has been accomplished, and His baptizing the believers in the Spirit has also been accomplished. Once we believe in Him, we receive His breathing and we receive His baptizing. He breathed once for all and He baptized once for all. In the book of Acts thousands of people believed in the Lord in many instances; there is no record that every time new believers came in, the Lord breathed again and the Lord baptized again. Breathing was accomplished and baptizing was also accomplished. When someone believes in the Lord, he gets into His baptizing. Then he is put into Christ and begins to drink Him in. Christ begins to abide in him. This baptized one and this drinking one is a new member in the Body of Christ.

BAPTIZED INTO THE TRIUNE GOD

In Matthew 28:19 the Lord Jesus charged His disciples to go and disciple the nations, baptizing them into the name, that is, into the Person, of the Father, and of the Son, and of the Spirit. To be baptized into the Person of the Triune God is to be baptized in the all-inclusive, consummated Spirit who is the ultimate consummation of the processed Triune God (Acts 1:5, 8). This means to be baptized into the riches of the Father, into the riches of the Son, and into the riches of the Spirit. To be baptized into the Triune God means to be brought into an organic union with the Triune God. We sinners, after believing into the Lord Jesus, have been baptized into the Father, the Son, and the Spirit. This produces an organic union. Now we, the baptized ones, are in this organic union. Therefore, whatever the Father has, whatever the Son has, and whatever the Spirit receives, all become ours.

Were you baptized into the name of the Father, the Son, and the Spirit or into the name of the Lord Jesus? In Matthew 28, to be baptized is to be baptized into the Triune God. Then in Acts, to be baptized is to be baptized into the Lord Jesus (Acts 8:16; 19:5). This indicates clearly that the Lord Jesus, in Acts, is the consummation of the Triune God. He is the aggregate of the Father, the Son, and the Spirit. Then in the Epistles, the apostle defines baptism. He said to be baptized is to be baptized in the Spirit (1 Cor. 12:13). The New Testament tells us to be baptized into the Triune God, into the Lord Jesus, and in the Spirit. This indicates that the Lord Jesus is the totality of the Triune God, and the Spirit is the realization of the Lord Jesus. We all have been baptized in the Spirit, and this means to be baptized into the Lord Jesus which means to be baptized into the Father, the Son, and Spirit, into the Triune God. This baptism brings us into an organic union with the Triune God. Therefore, we become one with the Triune God, and whatever He is and has is ours because we are organically united to Him. This baptism in the Spirit is symbolized by the baptism in water (cf. Acts 9:17-18; 10:44-48). Baptism in water is a figure, the reality of which is the baptism in the Spirit. Without the Spirit as its reality, baptism in water immediately becomes an empty and dead ritual.

THE HEAD AND THE CHURCH, HIS BODY

Through the baptism in the Spirit, by being baptized into the Triune God, the believers were put together to form the Body of Christ, joined to Him as the Head. Christ is the Head and we are His Body, joined together to be the great universal man. The New Testament tells us that the exalted Christ has been given to be the Head over all things (Eph. 1:22). He is the Head over the entire universe. He is the Head over the earth, over the earthly governments, and over all the rulers. Hence, He is the King of kings, the Ruler of the rulers, and the Lord of lords (Rev. 1:5; 17:14; 19:16). He is not only the Head over all things, but He is also the Head over all things "to the church." His government is to the church that it may be carried out through the church. The Head executes His government to the church and through the church to reach every part of the earth. In God's government, His exalted Christ is the Head, and the church is the Body of this Head. The Head cannot do anything without the church because the Head executes everything through the Body. Christ as the exalted Head rules over and governs the entire world through the church.

Do not misunderstand my word to mean that the church must get involved in politics. Once the church gets involved in politics, the church loses its nature as the Body of Christ and becomes no church. History tells us that when the church became involved with politics it turned into the Roman Catholic Church, which is no church in reality. When the Bible tells us that the exalted Christ as the Head is executing His governmental administration through the church which is His Body, it means that the church stands with Him. He is executing the divine administration on the throne in the heavens, and His Body is standing on this earth as a universal man, cooperating with Him, executing the divine administration throughout the entire world. This is above all the politics. This is to rule over the earth with the Head in the heavenlies with the divine power.

The history of the world throughout the past twenty centuries shows us that actually there was an invisible ruler above the scene. (See *The World Situation and God's Move* published by Living Stream Ministry.) This invisible Ruler above the scene actually is ruling over the entire earth. Who was ruling over the earth during the period of the Roman Empire? Jesus Christ. This ascended Christ was ruling over all the Caesars, and later over Napoleon, and over all the rulers of the earth. Today He still is the Ruler of the kings of the earth. All the presidents, kings, and prime ministers are under this unique Ruler. He is executing His government through the church, His Body. His ruling is not merely behind the scene, but above the scene. The worldly people and even the worldly historians do not realize this. Their eyes are only on the world rulers and the world political situation. They do not have the spiritual view to see that the world situation is under the Head with His Body. The church should not be involved with any politics, but the church as the Body of the Head is used by the Head to carry out His heavenly ministry on this earth. The direction of the situation of the world today depends upon how the genuine church, the proper church, is proceeding on this earth.

THE SEVEN SPIRITS
BEING THE SEVEN LAMPS OF FIRE
TO CARRY OUT GOD'S ADMINISTRATION

In Revelation, the all-inclusive and consummated Spirit, who was likened to the breath for life and to the wind for power, becomes the seven Spirits (Rev. 1:4; 3:1; 4:5; 5:6), which are the seven lamps of fire burning before the throne of God (Rev. 4:5) to carry out God's administration. These seven Spirits are the lamps on the seven lampstands. The seven lampstands are the seven churches holding the lamps, which are the seven Spirits as the lamps of fire burning before the throne to carry out God's administration. Such a picture shows us that the exalted Christ on the throne as the Head is executing God's government through the church by the seven Spirits. When Christ ascended to the heavens, He was authorized to be the Ruler of this universe. In Revelation He is revealed as the One Who has the authority to open the seals so that God's administration in its entirety can be carried out on this earth (5:2-5, 9; 6:1, 3, 5, 7, 9, 12; 8:1). The ascended, exalted Christ carries out His administration by the seven Spirits as the lamps of fire through the churches as the lampstands.

Whenever the saints on this earth, representing the Body of Christ, pray about the situation of this earth, the throne in the heavens immediately takes action to perform the things on this earth to carry out God's administration (Rev. 8:3-5). Christ as the Head sitting on the throne is executing, and the churches are standing on this earth holding the seven Spirits to carry out God's administration. In the Gospels the Spirit is likened to breath, in Acts the same Spirit is likened to wind, and in Revelation the same Spirit is likened to fire. On this earth today nearly everything is carried out by fire. Electricity is for burning and gas is for burning. Airplanes and automobiles cannot move if they do not burn some type of fuel. Even atomic power involves a type of burning. If there were no burning, the moving on this earth would be severely limited. The all-inclusive Spirit is breath to us for life, wind to us for power, and He is also the fire for us to carry out God's administration in God's move.

PREACHING THE GOSPEL
TO CARRY OUT GOD'S ADMINISTRATION

In resurrection Christ is life to us and in His exaltation He is power to us, not merely for preaching the gospel, but also for carrying out God's administration. We must realize that preaching the gospel is a part of the carrying out of God's administration. We preach the gospel to carry out God's administration to spread the kingdom of God. To usher in the kingdom of God is to carry out God's administration. Preaching the gospel effectively does not depend upon our eloquence. It depends upon our power. We may not be so eloquent in speaking, but if we are a people full of the breath within, and filled with the wind without, our speaking will be full of power and authority. Preaching the gospel is not only to let sinners hear our voice, but also to let all the demons and evil spirits hear the voice of the divine power.

After the ascension and exaltation of the Savior the disciples went out to preach the gospel to the whole creation (Mark 16:15). This corresponds with Matthew 28:18-19 where the Lord tells the disciples, "All authority has been given to Me in heaven and on earth. Go therefore and disciple all the nations." The disciples went and discipled the nations not merely by preaching the Word, but even more by exercising the authority of the Head. This kind of preaching is always followed by the authority of the ascended Christ. This is the reason why Mark 16:17-18 mentions five kinds of miracles following the preaching of the gospel by the disciples: "And these signs will accompany those who believe: in My name they will cast out demons; they will speak with new tongues; they will pick up serpents; and if they drink anything deadly, it shall by no means harm them; they will lay hands on the sick, and they will be well." To cast out demons is not a matter of preaching, but a matter of authority. If you do not have the authority, you cannot deal with demons. To speak with new tongues is to solve the problem of the nations which came in at Babel to divide all mankind (Gen. 11:6-9). To overcome the dividing factor of different languages, the new tongue is needed. With the new tongue, the oneness of mankind is recovered. The genuine tongue speaking is the issue of the power and authority of the ascended Christ to overcome the divisions of mankind. In the Lord's salvation, by the exalted Head, tongue speaking overcomes the divisions of mankind caused by different dialects. This is the main principle.

From His incarnation to His ascension the all-inclusive Christ accomplished many things, He attained many things, and He obtained many things. First, He breathed Himself as the breath of life into His believers. Then He poured Himself out as the Spirit of power upon these believers. By breathing Himself into them, He made them members of His Body. By pouring Himself upon them, He formed them into His Body. Now in this universe there is a universal man. The Head is in the heavens, and the Body is on this earth. The Head and the Body are corresponding and coordinating one with another to carry out God's eternal plan. Today we have Him within us as life essentially, and we have Him upon us as power economically. Now we are living a life which is the processed Triune God, and we are carrying out His economy which is the accomplishment of God's eternal plan. This is the church life.

Once He poured Himself out upon His believers, they were put together to be His Body, and this brought His believers into the foretaste of the works of power of the coming age. Today we are still living in the old age which is full of demons, sickness, death, division, and problems and troubles. Yet among mankind, there is a group of people who believe in such a wonderful One, having received this wonderful One into them as life essentially, and having had this wonderful One poured upon them as power economically. These are new persons of mankind who have been brought into a new realm, a new kingdom, which is the kingdom of God. In this new realm they enjoy a foretaste of the coming age, the age of the kingdom.

In the coming age there will be no more divisions among mankind, Satan will be bound, all his demons and evil spirits will be dealt with, sicknesses will be healed, death will be swallowed up, and all the problems among mankind will be solved. That will be the time of the "restoration of all things" referred to in Acts 3:21, the kingdom of peace and righteousness on this earth. That age has not yet come, but we believers who are the new persons and who have been brought into a new realm, the kingdom of God, have a fore-taste of the coming age. Therefore, we can speak the new tongues which unify us, we can cast out demons who recognize us and fear us, we can overcome death, we can heal diseases, and we can solve all the problems. This is the fore-taste of the coming age.

THE REALITY OF
GOD'S GOVERNMENTAL ADMINISTRATION

In 1969 five brothers who meet with us went to a Pente-costal, charismatic meeting where there was much "speaking in tongues." When these five brothers went into their meet-ing, the pastor and his helpers were attempting to cast out a demon. The demon-possessed man laughed at them and the demon within him said, "You cannot cast me out." Then he said, "In this room there are only five genuine Christians." This shows that if we are truly one with the Lord, even the demons will know it (Acts 19:13-17). Within we are intrinsi-cally, essentially one with the Lord, and without we are economically one with Him in His governmental administra-tion. Even though the people around us do not realize this, the demons know. This is related to God's governmental administration.

God has an exalted Head, and this Head has a Body which is the church. The genuine church, the church that is one with this ascended Head, is one with Him in the inner life and one with Him in the outer economy. If we are people of the Spirit, filled with Him inwardly as our inner life and clothed with Him outwardly for His administration, all the demons will know us. The evil spirits know that we have the authority because the heavenly uniform is upon us.

The proper understanding of the casting out of demons and of the speaking of new tongues is to realize that they are related to God's governmental administration. All of the items listed in Mark 16:17-18 are the display of the governmental authority of Christ's administration.

THE NEED OF AN APPROPRIATE
UNDERSTANDING AND APPLICATION

We must realize that not all the things mentioned in Mark 16 happened at the same time or happened to everyone. Even the things mentioned in Acts 2 do not all necessarily happen to one person. Since the Lord poured Himself out as the Spirit of economy upon His believers, a new age began. History tells us that in this new age, from the ascension of Christ up until today, here and there, now and then, new tongues were spoken, illnesses were healed, demons were cast out, and dead people were raised up. This does not mean that all these things happened at the same time on one person or at the same time on one group.

Furthermore, at the time of Pentecost and in Peter's ministry there were miracles of healing and even of resurrection (Acts 3:6-8; 9:32-42). In the earlier stage of the Apostle Paul's ministry there were also healing miracles. But in the later stage of Paul's ministry he charged his intimate co-worker, Timothy, to use a little wine for the sake of his stomach and frequent weaknesses (1 Tim. 5:23). Why did not Paul execute his healing gift to cure Timothy of his stomach sickness, rather than instruct him to take the natural way for healing?

Acts 19:12 tells us that God wrought special miracles by

the hands of Paul so that even handkerchiefs from him could heal people. Some people in today's Pentecostalism like to imitate the age of the apostles in the matter of healing. They would even try to imitate Paul by putting their hands on a handkerchief while praying for their sick friend. They believe that if they would mail this handkerchief to their sick friend, he could receive divine healing. Why did not Paul do this with Timothy? Paul rather told Timothy to take the natural way to be healed. He told him to drink a little wine for his stomach's sake.

We must thank the Lord for such a record in the Bible. Paul and his co-workers were under the exercise of the inner life in this time of suffering rather than under the power of the outward gift. The former is of grace in life; the latter of gift in power—miraculous power. In the decline of the church and in suffering for the church, the gift of power is not as much needed as the grace in life. I hope this kind of word rescues us from our natural concepts. Actually, the Lord did not have any trust in miracle-seeking people. John 2:23-24 says, "When He was in Jerusalem at the Passover, during the feast, many believed in His name, when they saw the signs which He did. But Jesus Himself did not entrust Himself to them." Too much miraculous healing distracts people from the inner life.

Chapter Nine

THE SON'S ASCENSION
AND THE BAPTISM IN THE SPIRIT

(3)

Scripture Reading: Heb. 6:4-5; Mark 16:17-18; John 3:3, 6; 1 Pet. 1:23; 1 John 5:11-12; 2 Pet. 1:4; Rom. 8:9, 11, 16; Eph. 4:6; 2 Cor. 13:5; 3:18; 1 Cor. 6:17; 1 John 3:2; 1 Pet. 5:10

THE TASTE OF THE WORKS OF POWER
OF THE COMING AGE

The Enjoyment of Christ

Hebrews 6:4-5 says, "Who have tasted of the heavenly gift, and have become partakers of the Holy Spirit, and have tasted the good word of God, and the works of power of the coming age." In this verse we can clearly see that the believers, after tasting the heavenly gift and becoming partakers of the Holy Spirit, have tasted two categories of things: the good word of God and the works of power of the coming age. In Hebrews the word of God is in two categories. "The good word" mentioned in 6:5 is "the word of the beginning of Christ" (6:1). The word of righteousness (5:13), however, embodies the deeper truth of God's justice and righteousness in His dispensational and governmental dealings with His people. In the entire book of Hebrews, the good word refers to Christ in His earthly ministry, including His incarnation, His human living, His crucifixion, and His resurrection; and the word of righteousness refers to Christ in His heavenly ministry, including His ascension, His exaltation, and all His attainments and obtainments in His exaltation. The purpose of the book of Hebrews was to help the Hebrew believers to go on from the good word to the word of righteousness, to go on from the enjoyment of Christ in His earthly ministry to the enjoyment of Christ in His heavenly ministry; thus, to enjoy the all-inclusive, all-embracing Christ.

The book of Hebrews stresses the heavenly Christ in the heavens (1:3). The word of righteousness concerning such a Christ is for the mature ones (5:13-14). This kind of word is considered as solid food, but the good word, which is considered as milk, is for the children. Both the milk and the solid food refer to the all-inclusive Christ. Our primary enjoyment that we have in the all-inclusive Christ in the New Testament age is as the milk and as the solid food. In the Lord's recovery the main thing is to recover the lost enjoyment of the all-inclusive Christ. We enjoy Him in His earthly ministry, and we also enjoy Him in His heavenly ministry—we enjoy Him as the all-inclusive Christ in His all-inclusive Person and in His all-inclusive work. We see Him in His earthly work, and we see Him also in His heavenly work. This is the divine enjoyment, the spiritual enjoyment, the main enjoyment, and the top enjoyment of the New Testament age.

A Secondary Enjoyment

For God to carry out His New Testament economy, there is also the need of the miraculous works, miracles, such as healing the diseases, casting out the demons, swallowing up the death poison, controlling the Devil, which is signified in the picking up of the serpents, and speaking in tongues to diminish the differences, the separations, and the divisions of mankind. These are miraculous, supernatural things which will be fully manifested in the coming millennium, the age to come. Isaiah 11 and 65 and Revelation 20 give us a clear view of the coming millennium. During those one thousand years, the people living on this earth will not be saved in the regeneration way, but they will all be restored back to their original, God-created condition.

Due to the fall of man, the entire creation became old. Everything began to go down hill, to decay, and sickness and death came in. Due to the fall, the demons began to work among mankind, and all the dividing languages came in at

Babel. The entire human race was damaged and ruined, and the entire old creation became corrupted. The principle of the old creation and the fallen human race is to go down, to be decayed, to be ruined, to be corrupted, and to be sick and to die. All the bad things are prevailing. When the millennium comes, however, everything will be restored. Diseases will be healed, death will be swallowed up, demons will be dealt with, Satan will be bound, and the dividing languages will be taken away. This will be an age of restoration, an age of restitution, as prophesied by the Lord Jesus in Matthew 19:28. Acts 3:21 also refers to this time of restoration. The believers, after being baptized in the Spirit of power into a new realm, are ushered, with the power and authority of the exalted Head, into the foretaste of this coming restoration, so we can cast out demons, speak new tongues, pick up serpents, defeat the death poison, and heal diseases. This is revealed in Mark 16:15-20. Today in the church life we can have such a foretaste. Satan and the demons have no ground among us, and the language barrier is no longer a problem. It has been overcome by all speaking the same word of Christ—the word concerning Christ. Also, we are being healed, and the death poison is being removed. All the other peoples are still remaining in the old age, but we, the believers, who are genuinely one with the exalted Christ, have been brought into a foretaste of the coming age. This kind of taste of the power of the coming age, however, is secondary to the enjoyment of the all-inclusive Christ, which is the believers' primary enjoyment in the New Testament age.

THE NEW TESTAMENT BLESSINGS

Due to our natural understanding and our natural desire, we treasure this kind of taste of the miraculous things more than the New Testament blessings. We must differentiate between the New Testament blessings and the miraculous things of the coming age. The first item of the blessings of the New Testament is regeneration (John 3:3, 6; 1 Pet. 1:23). Regeneration is to have a new birth, not merely a restoration or restitution. The second blessing we enjoy in the New Testament is the divine life (1 John 5:11-12) and the divine

nature (2 Pet. 1:4). We must praise and worship the Lord that
we have received the life and nature of God. The indwelling
Spirit is another New Testament blessing (Rom. 8:9, 16). The
Spirit as the ultimate consummation of the processed Triune
God lives in us (Eph. 4:6; 2 Cor. 13:5; Rom. 8:11). Transformation, which is the metabolic change of our being, is the fourth
blessing of the New Testament (2 Cor. 3:18). Our natural
being is being transformed into a divine being not by outward
change, but by an inward, metabolic change by the divine life.
Another New Testament blessing is that we human beings
can be mingled with God and can join to Him as one. First
Corinthians 6:17 says, "He who is joined to the Lord is one
spirit." Finally, we shall be like God and have the same image
as God (1 John 3:2), being changed from glory to glory (2 Cor.
3:18) to enter into God's glory (1 Pet. 5:10). Regeneration, the
divine life and nature, the Triune God living in us, transformation, the mingling of God with man, the image of God and
the likeness of God, and the glory of God are the New Testament blessings. All these New Testament blessings are the
issues of the marvelous earthly ministry and the excellent
heavenly ministry of the all-inclusive Christ for our enjoyment today.

In contrast to the New Testament blessings we can enjoy in
this age, there are the works of power of the coming age. The
blessings of miracles of the coming age include the casting out
of demons, speaking in new tongues, handling the serpents,
healing diseases, and overcoming the death poison. We must
ask ourselves which category of blessings we prefer today—the
New Testament blessings or the blessings of the coming age?

The tragedy today is that many Christians have never
received any kind of vision of the marvelous New Testament
blessings we can enjoy in this age. They do not have a view of
the value of regeneration or of God's life and nature. They
do not know anything about the Triune God living in them,
transformation, the mingling of God with man, the image of
God, the likeness of God, or the glory of God. When many
Christians read Mark 16, however, they get excited. All the
outward miracles such as casting out demons, speaking in
tongues, picking up serpents, drinking the poison and still

being able to live, and healing the diseases, have become the attractive things to many Christians. Many Christians have no realization of the New Testament blessings but are seeking after the miraculous, outward signs. But the Lord would not entrust Himself to the miracle seekers (John 2:23-25). In John 3, however, Nicodemus, who was a man of the Pharisees, came to the Lord Jesus. The Lord Jesus did not heal him and did not perform any miracles, but He told him that he needed to be regenerated, to be born again (v. 3). What is more precious—outward, physical healing or the inward regeneration? Which do you treasure? Thousands may be healed, yet never receive any spiritual blessing.

THE CONTENT OF GOD'S NEW TESTAMENT ECONOMY—A PERSON

We need a clear vision that the content of God's New Testament economy is not any kind of "ism," not any kind of religion, and not any kind of movement. The content of God's New Testament economy is a Person who is both divine and human, a Person who is both God and man, who has passed through incarnation, human living, crucifixion, resurrection, and ascension and has consummated in the all-inclusive, processed, compound, life-giving, and indwelling Spirit imparted into us in His resurrection as life to us, and poured out upon us in His ascension as power to us that we may live the divine life to express God and move with the divine power, economically, to carry out God's economy. Through this Person, we all have been regenerated to receive the divine life and partake of the divine nature. Through Him we even have the processed Triune God as the all-inclusive Spirit living in us to transform us and mingle Himself with us that we may bear His image and participate in His divine glory. What a marvelous blessing! This is much higher than healings, much higher than tongue speaking, and much higher than any kind of miracle. May we be thus blessed!

ENJOYING AND FOCUSING ON THE NEW TESTAMENT BLESSINGS

We must praise the Lord for all the visions we have seen

concerning Christ in His incarnation, in His human living, in His crucifixion, in His resurrection, and in His ascension. We must learn how to enjoy Him in the Spirit and how to speak Him with the Spirit. We must speak Him forth to others. We must be those enjoying the New Testament blessings and, if the Lord wills, we will also enjoy the subsidiary blessings which are the works of power of the age to come. We should not, though, focus on the subsidiary blessings which we enjoy as a foretaste of the blessings of the age to come; we should focus on the New Testament blessings, which are the main blessings.

CHAPTER TEN

THE SON'S ASCENSION
AND THE BAPTISM IN THE SPIRIT

(4)

Scripture Reading: Luke 24:49; Acts 1:5, 8; 2:4; 10:44, 46; 4:8, 31; 13:9; 8:14-17; 9:13-17; 19:1-7; 6:3, 5; 7:55; 11:24; 13:52; 8:29, 39; 13:2; 15:28; 16:6-7; 20:23, 28; 21:4, 11

GOD'S NEW TESTAMENT ECONOMY
CONCERNING THE SPIRIT IN THE ACTS

In this chapter, we want to see God's New Testament economy concerning the Spirit in the book of Acts.

The Baptism in the Spirit

The first thing accomplished in God's New Testament economy concerning the Spirit in the book of Acts was the baptism in the Spirit. This was accomplished by two instances. One happened on the day of Pentecost when the one hundred twenty were baptized (Acts 2:1-4), and the other was in the house of Cornelius (Acts 10:24, 44-46). By these two instances, the Head, Christ, accomplished the baptism in the Spirit on His entire Body. On the day of Pentecost, He baptized the Jewish side of the Body, and in the house of Cornelius He baptized the Gentile side since the Body of Christ is composed of the Jews and the Gentiles. All the Jewish believers need to realize that they were baptized in the Spirit on the day of Pentecost with Peter and the one hundred twenty. The Gentile believers must realize that they were all baptized in the house of Cornelius.

On the day of Pentecost, the one hundred twenty disciples

were filled with the Holy Spirit and began to speak in other tongues (Acts 2:4). At that time many Jews from the dispersion had come back to Jerusalem (Acts 2:5). Most of these Jews could not speak Hebrew so well; therefore, there was the need for the speaking in tongues. Acts 2:7-11 shows us that these Jews spoke many different languages. The speaking in tongues on the day of Pentecost was economical because it was needed to unify the people by language so they all could understand each other.

Also, the Holy Spirit fell on the house of Cornelius and they spoke in tongues (Acts 10:44, 46). Because the house of Cornelius was Gentile, there was the need for them to speak in tongues. The Jewish believers thought that the Lord's salvation was only for Israel. Even Peter thought this way until the Lord revealed otherwise (Acts 10:28-29). To receive the Gentiles was a great thing for the Jews. The Jews would never be one with the Gentiles. They would not eat and communicate with the Gentiles nor contact the Gentiles. They even condemned the Roman rulers and viewed them as robbing ones. Cornelius was a Roman ruler (Acts 10:1), a ruler of the ancient Roman imperialism. Therefore, the Lord had to do something to cause the house of Cornelius to speak in tongues to show Peter and the other Jewish brothers that all these Gentiles had received the same gift and the same grace that they had on the day of Pentecost (Acts 10:44-48). After they heard the house of Cornelius speak in tongues and magnify God Peter said, "Can anyone forbid water that these should not be baptized who have received the Holy Spirit even as we?" (10:47). The speaking in tongues in this instance was for the unifying of the believers into one Body. The speaking in tongues in today's Pentecostalism, however, does not unite people but divides them.

The Outward Filling with the Spirit for Power

Being filled (Gk. *pletho*) with the Spirit outwardly for power is the experience of the baptism in the Spirit (Luke 24:49; Acts 1:5, 8). In Acts 2:2 a rushing mighty wind filled all the house where the disciples were sitting. In this verse there is another Greek word for filled—*pleroo*. This Greek word means the inner filling, to fill something within. At the same time the wind filled the house, it also filled the one hundred twenty. For the wind to fill the house is an inner filling, but to the one hundred twenty, it was an outward filling (*pletho*—Acts 2:4). When water fills a baptistry, that is an inner filling (*pleroo*). When the persons who are being baptized enter into the water, the water fills them outwardly. This is the outer filling (*pletho*).

Peter's Experience

Peter was filled (*pletho*) with the Holy Spirit again and spoke the word in Acts 4:8. On the day of Pentecost, Peter was filled once. That was his initial experience of the baptism, and Acts 4:8 is the following experience. This does not mean that he was baptized in the Spirit twice, but that he applied the experience of the baptism in the Spirit a second time.

In Acts 4:31 Peter and his company were filled (*pletho*) again with the Holy Spirit and spoke the word of God with boldness. This was the third time for Peter to experience the baptism in the Spirit. This was not the third time for him to be baptized, but for him to experience the baptism. In this verse it does not say that Peter was filled with the Holy Spirit and he spoke in tongues. Rather it says that he and the other disciples spoke the word of God with boldness. Today in some Pentecostal groups, however, every time they come together they speak in tongues. It was different, however, with Peter and the other disciples. Peter repeated the speaking of the word with boldness again and again, not the speaking in tongues. He spoke forth Christ; he prophesied in this way again and again. When there was the need, though, of speaking in tongues, God did it through them.

Paul's Experience

Paul experienced the baptism in the Holy Spirit for the first time when he was filled (*pletho*) with the Holy Spirit right after his conversion (Acts 9:17). Then, he had the same experience again when he was filled (*pletho*) with the Holy Spirit in his ministry (Acts 13:9). According to the record of

Acts, this was Paul's second time to be filled outwardly, economically, with the Holy Spirit.

Three Extraordinary Cases

There are three extraordinary cases of believers being filled with the Spirit outwardly which we must investigate. First, the Holy Spirit fell upon the Samaritans through Peter and John laying their hands on them (Acts 8:14-17). In the two instances that constitute the baptism in the Spirit (on the day of Pentecost and in the house of Cornelius) there was no laying on of hands because the Head baptized His Body in the Spirit directly. With the Samaritans, however, with Saul of Tarsus (Acts 9:13-17), and with the twelve disciples in Ephesus (Acts 19:1-7), there was the need for the members of the Body to lay hands upon them. The one laying on the hands is a member of the Body and the baptism is upon the Body. When a member of the Body lays hands on another, this means to impart what is on the Body to a new member.

A number of the Samaritans in Acts 8 believed in the Lord Jesus through Philip's preaching (v. 12). The Samaritans were despised by the Jews and the Jews had no dealings with them (John 4:9). Now some of them believed in the Lord Jesus through some Jewish believers' preaching of the gospel. The news went to Jerusalem and the church sent Peter and John to come to Samaria to visit them (v. 14). After praying for these believers, Peter and John laid their hands upon them and the Spirit came upon them. This was the outward filling with the Spirit economically. Peter and John's laying on of hands upon these Samaritan believers confirms that they were added to and accepted by the Body of Christ. Peter and John, who represented the Body of Christ, identified them with the Body of Christ and imparted what the Body of Christ had to them.

Saul of Tarsus was also filled with the Holy Spirit outwardly through Ananias laying his hands on him (Acts 9:13-17). Saul of Tarsus was a Jew who was opposing the church to the uttermost. All of the church people were afraid of him, but the Lord met him on the road to Damascus and saved him directly (Acts 9:3-6). The Lord, however,

appeared to Ananias in a vision and told him to go into the
street which is called Straight and inquire in the house of
Judas for a man named Saul. Ananias, a little member of the
Body of Christ, went and told Saul what the Lord had told
him. Then he laid his hands upon Saul, whom the Holy Spirit
then fell upon. This was a strong confirmation that Saul, the
opposer of the church, was saved and received by the Lord
into His Body. This was another extraordinary case that
needed the laying on of hands to identify Saul as a member of
the Body of Christ and to impart to him what was on the
Body of Christ.

The third extraordinary case was with the twelve disciples
in Ephesus, who received the preaching of John the Baptist's
teaching, which was not a complete gospel. After they
received the complete gospel, Paul laid his hands upon them,
and they spoke in tongues and prophesied (Acts 19:1-7). Paul
laid his hands upon these Gentile believers in Ephesus to
impart what was on the Body of Christ to them. They also
spoke in tongues because they were Gentiles. They needed
this sign so that the Jewish believers would realize that they
had been received by the Lord. All three of these extraordinary cases needed the laying on of hands. All of these
believers received the Spirit upon them, not directly from the
Head, but indirectly through the Body.

Being Full of the Spirit Inwardly for Life

Those who were filled with the Spirit outwardly for power,
being baptized into one Body, began to drink of one Spirit
(1 Cor. 12:13). When they began to drink of the Spirit, they
became full of the Spirit within. This is inwardly and essentially for life. To be baptized into the Spirit is to be filled with
the Spirit outwardly for power, but to drink of the Spirit is to
be full (Gk. *pleres* from *pleroo*) of the Spirit inwardly for life.
After we have been baptized into the Spirit outwardly, we
keep drinking of the Spirit and become full of the Spirit
inwardly.

There are four cases in Acts which illustrate this matter of
being full of the Spirit inwardly for life. In Acts 6:3 seven
were chosen who were full of the Holy Spirit and wisdom.

Acts 6:5 tells us that Stephen was a man full of faith and the Holy Spirit. Acts 7:55 tells us again that Stephen was full of the Holy Spirit. Finally, Acts 11:24 tells us that Barnabas was a good man, full of the Holy Spirit and faith. Being full of the Spirit in these verses is not for the outward power, but for the inward life.

The Inward Filling of the Spirit for Life

Acts 13:52 tells us that the disciples were made full of joy and of the Holy Spirit. This is to be filled (Gk. *pleroo* from *pleres*) with the Spirit inwardly for life. After being baptized in the Spirit, the disciples began to drink of the Spirit and become full of the Spirit. They were filled with the Spirit again and again inwardly until they were made full of the Holy Spirit. The word *joy* in this verse indicates that this kind of inward filling of the Spirit is for the inner life and not for work.

The Guidance of the Spirit

In Acts in addition to the outward filling of the Spirit, being full of the Spirit inwardly, and the inward filling of the Spirit, there is also the guidance of the Spirit. In Acts 8:29 and 39 Philip, the evangelist, enjoyed the guidance of the Spirit: "The Spirit said to Philip, Approach and join this chariot," and "when they came up out of the water, the Spirit of the Lord caught away Philip." In 13:2 the brothers in Antioch enjoyed the guidance of the Spirit in separating Barnabas and Saul for the work: "As they were ministering to the Lord and fasting, the Holy Spirit said, Set apart for Me now Barnabas and Saul for the work to which I have called them." In 15:28 the brothers in Jerusalem sent a letter to the Gentile churches, which also reveals something of the guidance of the Spirit: "For it seemed good to the Holy Spirit and to us to lay upon you no greater burden than these necessary things."

In 16:6 Paul and Timothy were forbidden of the Holy Spirit to preach the word in Asia. Furthermore, "When they had come down to Mysia, they tried to go into Bithynia, and the Spirit of Jesus did not allow them" (v. 7). Paul and Timothy were guided by the Spirit of Jesus. "The Spirit of Jesus" is a special term. Its meaning differs from that of "the Spirit of God." Since Jesus was a man, and is still a man, "the Spirit of Jesus" is the Spirit of the man, Jesus. Because the Spirit of Jesus possesses humanity, He could give guidance to the apostles who were carrying out the propagation of the resurrected and ascended Christ in their humanity among the human race.

In 20:23 Paul said, "The Holy Spirit solemnly testifies to me in city after city, saying that bonds and afflictions await me." Although this was the Holy Spirit's testifying to Paul it bore some indication as a guidance to him. In verse 28 of the same chapter Paul said to the elders of the church in Ephesus, "The Holy Spirit has placed you as overseers, to shepherd the church of God." The elders of the churches were appointed by the apostles (14:23). But Paul said here that the Holy Spirit had placed the elders as overseers to shepherd the church. This indicates that the apostles' appointment of the elders was under the guidance of the Holy Spirit. In 21:4 the disciples in Tyre "told Paul through the Spirit not to set foot in Jerusalem." This was a direct guidance of the Spirit given to Paul through some disciples. In verse 11 of the same chapter, Agabus the prophet, having bound his own feet and hands with Paul's girdle, said, "Thus says the Holy Spirit, In this way shall the Jews in Jerusalem bind the man whose girdle this is and deliver him into the hands of the Gentiles." This was a foretelling bearing some indication of the Holy Spirit's guidance to Paul. All these cases show us that the apostles and the disciples in Acts were people living, moving, working, laboring, traveling, and doing everything by the guidance of the Spirit, who is not only the Holy Spirit of God but also the Spirit of Jesus. Outwardly they were filled with the Spirit of power economically for them to carry out the work of God's New Testament economy, and inwardly they were filled with the Spirit of life essentially for them to live a life of the processed God. As a result, they moved, walked, worked, acted, traveled, and did everything by the Spirit as men of the Spirit. These are the members of the Body of Christ, living and moving on this earth for the testimony of the resurrected and exalted Christ and the fulfillment of

God's plan according to His eternal economy. Now we have the Head in the heavens and the Body on this earth living and cooperating together to live the life of God to carry out God's economy.

CHAPTER ELEVEN

THE SPIRIT OF LIFE

Scripture Reading: Rom. 8:2, 4, 6, 9-11, 14, 16, 23, 26-27; 15:16

MATTHEW THROUGH THE ACTS

In the first five books of the New Testament we have seen that Christ, the God-man, after entering into His resurrection, became the Spirit of life as the breath breathed into His disciples (John 20:22). Then after His ascension, as the Spirit of power, as the wind, He poured out Himself upon His disciples. In the Acts we see a group of people on this earth filled with the Spirit inwardly for life and outwardly for power. They were persons of the Spirit, having the divine life within essentially and possessing the divine power economically. They walked, lived, worked, moved, and did everything as persons of the Spirit. They were persons living God to accomplish and carry out God's economy. They were persons enjoying the seven basic items of the New Testament blessings. They were regenerated, having God's life and possessing God's nature. They had the Triune God living in them. By these basic elements, they were being transformed and mingled with the Triune God to have His divine image and to enter into His divine glory.

THE BOOK OF ROMANS

The remaining twenty-two books of the New Testament show us the details of how this wonderful Spirit makes sinners the sons of God, including the book of Romans, which mainly reveals that the Spirit who transforms sinners into sons of God is the Spirit of life. The term, "the Spirit of life," is used only once in the entire New Testament—in Romans 8:2. The all-inclusive, compound Spirit in Romans is the Spirit of life. Romans tells us how the Triune God, in His consummation as the Spirit of life, makes sinners the sons of God who become the living members of the Body of Christ. These members, who form the Body of Christ, have been regenerated and possess God's divine life and God's divine nature. Every member is wrapped up with the Divine Trinity, who is being wrought into their tripartite being. Thus, they are being transformed, renewed, and even conformed to the image of the Firstborn Son of God. Even their mortal bodies are being supplied with the divine life (Rom. 8:11) to make them living members of Christ. These members are put together into a Body to express Christ, and this Body is manifested in many localities as the local churches. Romans, then, gives us the details of how the Spirit of life works in the tripartite man with the Triune God. This is the message, the revelation, and the vision that is carried out in this book.

THE SPIRIT OF LIFE

The Spirit of God Dwelling in Us

The Spirit of life is the Spirit of God who dwells in the believers. Romans 8:9a says, "the Spirit of God dwells in you." The Spirit of God in this verse is not the same as the Spirit of God in Genesis 1:2 where He was brooding upon the face of the waters. The Spirit of God in Romans 8:9 now dwells in the tripartite man and is now the Spirit of Christ who possesses humanity as well as divinity. In Genesis 1 the Spirit of God had not yet gone through the processes of incarnation, human living, crucifixion, resurrection, and ascension. The Spirit of God in Romans 8, however, is the Spirit of life who in Christ has gone through incarnation, lived a human life on this earth, died an all-inclusive death, entered into an excellent resurrection, and is now in His exalting ascension. All these elements are compounded with the Spirit of God, who is no longer outside of us but inside of us to dwell in us. This is the consummation of the Triune God living in us.

The Spirit of Christ—
the Pledge That We Are of Christ

When many Christians hear the term "the Spirit of God," they think this is the Spirit of the Creator. According to the human concept, the term God mainly denotes the Creator. The Spirit of Christ (Rom. 8:9b), however, denotes a great deal. Christ is the Son of God, even God Himself. Christ is also a man. He is Jesus, the Redeemer, our Savior, our sanctification, righteousness, holiness, life, light, and everything. The title "the Spirit of Christ" conveys the all-inclusiveness of the One who is living in us. This title includes not only God the Creator but also Christ the Redeemer with all His divine and human elements and all the items of His achievements, attainments, and obtainments. All these are compounded in the Spirit of Christ.

Many Christians have not seen such a compound Spirit as the Spirit of Christ. This Spirit is compounded with divinity, humanity, incarnation, human living, death, resurrection, and ascension. Even though I was in organized Christianity for years, I never heard a message concerning the Spirit of Christ. As a young man, I read through Romans again and again, but I was not impressed with the Spirit of Christ. It was not until I read Andrew Murray's book *The Spirit of Christ* that the Lord really impressed me with this divine title. I treasured this book to the uttermost. Over fifty years ago, Brother Nee told me that he would pay the publication expenses if someone would translate Andrew Murray's book into Chinese. A few years later, he repeated the same thing to me. This gave me a deep impression concerning this book. As a result, I myself read this book, and I arranged for some young ones to help me translate. When we were working on this book, I was deeply impressed with chapter five which covers "The Spirit of the Glorified Jesus." This chapter indicates that in the Spirit of Christ, there is the human element. From that time, I began to see the all-inclusiveness of the Spirit.

Some of us may have read this book in the past, but we still did not have much spiritual apprehension or impression concerning the Spirit of Christ. However, if Andrew Murray had taught concerning Mark 16:17-18 where it talks about casting out demons, speaking with new tongues, picking up serpents, drinking something deadly without being harmed, and healing diseases, we would have immediately been impressed with this book. There would be no need to read it two or three times since you would immediately be impressed with these miraculous things. The reason for this is because even without reading such a book, all these things are already in our natural mentality. Many Indian magicians cannot only pick up things, but they can also wrap snakes around their arms and neck. In the matter of picking up serpents, their "foretaste of the millennium" may be much better.

Most readers of Andrew Murray's book of thirty-one messages, one message for each day of the month, have retained nothing in their memory concerning it because in this book, he is talking about something which is far, far beyond our limited, natural comprehension. There is nothing in the natural concept concerning the Spirit of Christ. Many Christians may know something concerning the "Holy Ghost" or the Spirit of God. The Spirit of Christ, however, is something foreign to their understanding. After many years, one day when I was studying Romans 8 these three words, "the Spirit of Christ," impressed me deeply. This caused me to study Romans 8 again and again. I have spent much time studying Romans 8 and have given many, many messages on this chapter. There are many riches here. In this chapter we can see the Triune God working Himself, in His Trinity, into the tripartite man. In Romans 8:9 the Spirit of God and the Spirit of Christ are synonyms which are interchangeably used with a particular significance. The Spirit of Christ is the pledge that we are of Christ. Romans 8:9 says, "but if anyone has not the Spirit of Christ, he is not of Him." We know that we are of Christ because the Spirit of Christ is in us. Also, this Spirit of Christ in us is the very Spirit of God as the Spirit of life.

Christ in Us

In Romans 8:9 we see the Spirit of God and the Spirit of

Christ. Then in verse 10 we see Christ. The Spirit of God, the Spirit of Christ, and Christ are not three separate entities. These three are one. The Spirit of God is the Spirit of Christ, and the Spirit of Christ is Christ. These are different titles denoting one Person. You may call this Person Christ; you may call Him the Spirit of Christ; and you may call Him the Spirit of God. This one divine Person, who is all-inclusive, has three titles here: the Spirit of God, the Spirit of Christ, and Christ. These three titles are interchangeably used to bear a particular significance.

The Spirit of the One

Thus far, we have seen the Spirit of life, the Spirit of God, the Spirit of Christ, and now we come to the Spirit of Him (Rom. 8:11). In Greek this actually means "the Spirit of the One." After Paul referred to the Spirit of Christ and the Spirit of God, he referred to the Spirit of the One who raised Jesus from among the dead. This One who raised up Jesus is the Father, the Son, and the Spirit, the Triune God. This Triune God is the resurrecting One. When the Sadducees asked the Lord concerning resurrection in Matthew 22 the Lord referred them to Exodus 3:6 and 16 where God unveils Himself as the God of Abraham, the God of Isaac, and the God of Jacob—the Triune God. This divine title indicates resurrection because God could never be the God of the dead ones. He is the God of the living ones (Matt. 22:32). The Triune God, the God of Abraham, the God of Isaac, and the God of Jacob, is the resurrecting God. In Romans 8:11 we see the resurrecting God, the Triune God. It is wonderful and marvelous that in Romans 8:11 we can see the Spirit of the resurrecting Triune God.

It is easy to realize that the Spirit of God refers to God the Creator and that the Spirit of Christ refers to the Spirit of the Savior, but it is not easy for us to gain a deeper understanding of these terms. Thus, to apprehend the title "the Spirit of the One who raised Jesus from among the dead" requires much understanding. We must realize who dwells in us. The Spirit of God, the Spirit of Christ, Christ Himself, and the Spirit of the One who raised Jesus from among the dead dwell in us. These are not four, but one. The one who is the Spirit of God, the Spirit of Christ, and Christ Himself is the One that raised Jesus from among the dead. This kind of speaking indicates that this One is all-inclusive.

This One is now in us to dwell in us to do a wonderful work. The Spirit of Him who raised Jesus from among the dead dwells in us to make our spirit life (8:10b), to make our mind life (8:6b), and to give life to our mortal body (8:11b). The first thing He does is to make our spirit life. When Christ is in us, our spirit is life. Before Christ came into us, our spirit was dead. Now that Christ is in us, however, our spirit is not only living but life. This wonderful One who is so all-inclusive as the Spirit of life, the Spirit of God, the Spirit of Christ, Christ Himself, and the Spirit of the resurrecting One, who is the Triune God, dwells in us firstly to make our dead spirit life. This is regeneration.

Following this, this indwelling Spirit makes our mind life. The mind set on the spirit is life. This is the renewing of our mind, which is transformation. To make our spirit life is to regenerate us. To make our mind life is to renew our mind and to transform us.

In addition, such a wonderful One dwells in us to give life to our mortal body. This is not the outward healing but the inward life impartation. Day after day the divine life is spreading into our body until that day when our body will be redeemed (8:23) and transfigured (Phil. 3:21).

This is the Triune God dispensing Himself into the tripartite man. Man is of three parts—the human spirit, the human soul, and the human body. As believers our spirit has been regenerated, and our soul with its leading part, the mind, is now under renewing which is our transformation. The day will come when our body will be transfigured, conformed to the body of His glory. This will be the redemption of our body. Our regeneration has already been accomplished, our transformation is an ongoing process, and our transfiguration, the redemption of our body, will be accomplished at Christ's coming back. This all-inclusive One as the consummation of the Triune God is working the Triune God into our three parts—into our spirit, into our soul, and into our body. This is the Triune God working Himself into the tripartite man by His divine dispensing.

The Spirit of the Divine Sonship

Such an all-inclusive Spirit to work the Triune God into our tripartite being is to make us the sons of God. We were enemies of God, but such a wonderful, divine work by the consummation of the Triune God is making us sons of God. Romans 8:14 says, "For as many as are led by the Spirit of God, these are sons of God." This all-inclusive Spirit is making us the sons of God by accomplishing the divine sonship in our being. The Spirit is divinely "sonizing" us. We are sinners and we were God's enemies, yet this all-inclusive Spirit is not merely making us spiritual, holy, or victorious, but divinely sonizing us, making us the sons of God. This is a great matter.

The Witnessing Spirit in Our Spirit

The witnessing Spirit witnesses in our spirit all the time that we are the children of God (Rom. 8:16). The Spirit is making us sons of God and at the same time He is witnessing that we are the children of God. Many sisters have the experience that even while they are shopping in the department store, within there is a witnessing, reminding them that they are children of God. Sometimes the young people would go to the movies. While they were on their way to the movies, there was something within witnessing and saying, "Don't forget that you are a child of God." Sometimes while a husband is losing his temper with his wife there is also a witnessing— "Don't forget that you are a child of God." Nothing stops a person's temper as fast as saying amen to this kind of witnessing in their spirit. This is the witnessing Spirit within our spirit who witnesses that we are the children of God.

The Spirit as the Firstfruit

Romans 8:23 tells us that we have the firstfruit of the Spirit. This is not the foretaste of the coming age, but the firstfruit of the rich God to be our portion. The foretaste of the coming age is the taste of the outward things, but the firstfruit is the foretaste of the processed Triune God Himself. What we have enjoyed and what we are still enjoying of God Himself is just a foretaste. The full taste is coming. The Holy Spirit, the all-inclusive Spirit, is the firstfruit of all the riches of God's being for our enjoyment. We are tasting just a foretaste of God and the full taste of God will come. We will enjoy the full taste of God in eternity.

The Interceding Spirit

The interceding Spirit helps us, sympathizes with us, sustains us, comforts us, and supports us by interceding for us (Rom. 8:26-27). Many times we felt that we were weak and depressed, but within us even at that time there was something sustaining, supporting, encouraging, and comforting us. There was something within us telling us that we should not be disappointed. Although we are weak, there is some sustaining and support within us. There is even a kind of prayer going on within us and for us. When we got disappointed before we were saved, we remained disappointed. But after being saved, quite often, when we were disappointed, something within us was still supporting us, comforting us, and sympathizing with us in a sweet way. This is the interceding Spirit and this is the intercession of the helping Spirit. He helps us in any kind of situation.

No one fully understands us, but the interceding Spirit understands us thoroughly. We can tell anyone that they do not understand us, but we cannot say to the interceding Spirit, "Dear Spirit, You misunderstood me and You do not understand me." If you would say this, the Spirit would say, "I understand you much more than you understand yourself. I know your need, your problems, your weakness, and your shortcomings. No one else knows and even you do not know. But I know so I sympathize with you, I support you, and I even sustain you. I am your helper. As long as you have Me, you are alright. You do not need to worry about yourself." It is so easy, however, for us to neglect this One. Despite this, He is within us, so soft, so tender, so sympathizing, and so loving. This is wonderful! This is much better than any material thing. The witnessing Spirit plus His interceding is so sweet. He tempers us and makes us to be the proper persons.

The Sanctifying Holy Spirit

This One is sanctifying us all the time (Rom. 15:16). This is not objective, positional sanctification but subjective, dispositional sanctification. This sanctification is to renew us, to transform us, and to conform us to the image of God's first-born Son that we may be so fitting to be a living member of the Body of Christ.

The Mingled Spirit

Eventually, such a Spirit becomes a mingled spirit, the Spirit mingled with our spirit (cf. Rom. 8:4; 1 Cor. 6:17), according to whom we walk. We do have such a mingled spirit within us and what we should do now is to behave, to act, to live, to walk, and to have our being according to this mingled spirit. If we walk according to this mingled spirit, we will be a son of God in full, and as such a son we will be a living member of Christ, living in the church life which is the kingdom of God. This kingdom is mentioned in Romans 14:17 and is not mainly of power or ruling or government. The kingdom of God, which is today's church life, is of righteousness with ourselves, peace toward others, and joy with God in the Holy Spirit. Do not think that the kingdom of God is for you to be a king to rule over others and to execute God's government. You have to forget these thoughts. The kingdom of God today in the church life is not for ruling or for governing but is for living—a righteous living, a peaceful living, and a joyful living. The church life as the kingdom of God today is a kingdom of righteousness, peace, and joy in the Holy Spirit. This is the Lord's recovery.

CHAPTER TWELVE

THE LIFE-GIVING SPIRIT

Scripture Reading: 1 Cor. 15:45b; 2:10, 12, 14; 3:16-17; 6:11, 17, 19-20; 7:40; 12:13, 4, 7-11

THE SAME PERSON IN DIFFERENT ASPECTS

In this chapter, we come to the second Epistle of the New Testament, 1 Corinthians. In the first Epistle, the Epistle to the Romans, is the Spirit of life. In this first Epistle to the Corinthians is the life-giving Spirit. The very Christ we see in the four Gospels is now the "pneumatic Christ," the all-inclusive Spirit, in the Epistles. First Corinthians 15:45 says, "The last Adam became a life-giving Spirit." The last Adam is seen in the four Gospels, and the life-giving Spirit is seen in all the Epistles. Therefore, the very Christ as the last Adam in the Gospels is now the pneumatic Christ as the all-inclusive Spirit.

In the two sections of the Gospels and the Epistles in the New Testament, we see the same Person in different aspects. In the four Gospels we see this Person as the Son, with the Father, by the Spirit. In the Epistles is the same Person becoming the Spirit, as the Son, with the Father. In every book of the New Testament, we see the same Person. We do not have two Saviors, two Redeemers, two life-giving Spirits, two Masters, or two Lords. Our God is uniquely one. We only have one Redeemer, one Savior, one life-giving Spirit, one Master, and one Lord. What we see in the twenty-seven books of the New Testament is altogether just one wonderful, all-inclusive, excellent, marvelous Person.

Do not think that in the four Gospels is Christ and in the Epistles is the Spirit who is separate from Christ. We must realize that essentially Christ and the Spirit are one, but economically they are two. Eventually they are a wonderful, unique, and excellent Person; economically this Person was the Christ, the last Adam in the four Gospels, and He is now the pneumatic Christ, the Spirit, in the Epistles. As Christ in the four Gospels, He accomplished incarnation, He passed through human living, He died the all-inclusive death, and He entered into resurrection. By all these steps, He accomplished an all-inclusive redemption in God's economy. After accomplishing the redemption of God, He became the life-giving Spirit, not to remain on the cross, but to come into our being, to stay with us, remain in us, and mingle Himself with our being to be our life, our life-supply, and our everything to make us humanly divine and divinely human, thoroughly mingled with the Triune God in God's economy.

THE SPIRIT OF LIFE
TO BE THE LIFE-GIVING SPIRIT

We have seen that the Spirit of life is unique. This title is only used once in the New Testament in Romans 8:2. The life-giving Spirit is also unique. This same type of expression, of course, is used a few times in the New Testament. John 6:63 refers to "the Spirit who gives life." Second Corinthians 3:6 says, "the Spirit gives life." First Corinthians 15:45, however, is the only place in the New Testament which specifically says the "life-giving Spirit." The One in Romans who is the Spirit of life is the life-giving Spirit in 1 Corinthians. The title of the Spirit of life does not convey any thought that He is moving and working. The title of the life-giving Spirit, though, indicates that the Spirit of life is moving, working, and imparting life.

In John 6 there are two expressions concerning Christ— He is the bread of life (v. 35) and He is the living bread (v. 51). When I was young, I was very much bothered by these two expressions and asked myself what the difference was between them. The bread of life refers to the nature of the bread, which is life; the living bread refers to the condition of the bread, which is living. For example, the physical bread in a bread basket is not the living bread. This is the bread of life.

However, when we eat some of this bread and it gets into our stomach, immediately the bread is living in our stomach to nourish us, to impart the life element into us, and to distribute all kinds of vitamins into our being through our blood vessels. After being eaten, the bread of life becomes the living bread that lives, moves, and works in us.

The Spirit of life denotes that the element of the Spirit is life. On the other hand, the life-giving Spirit denotes the same Spirit moving, working, and living in us to impart life into us. This does not mean that in Romans the Spirit of life does not work, but the stress in Romans is different. The stress in 1 Corinthians is that the Spirit of life is now working within every member of Christ. The Spirit of life is working and moving in the being of the believers; it is the life-imparting Spirit, and its work is to give life into your being.

SEARCHING CHRIST AS THE DEPTHS OF GOD

The life-giving Spirit is searching Christ as the depths of God (2:10, 12, 14). When anything is searched, that thing is stirred up and cannot remain calm. Without the life-giving Spirit, Christ is everything to you, but in a calm situation. You may have the all-inclusive Christ, but the Christ in you may be nearly nothing to you because He is so "calm" within you. There is the need of someone who is so active and so living to come to search, to stir up the Christ within you. This someone is the life-giving Spirit.

First Corinthians unveils to us that the very Christ, who is the portion of all believers, and into whose fellowship we all have been called, is all-inclusive. He is firstly our portion, our fellowship (1:2, 9). He is God's power and God's wisdom as righteousness, sanctification, and redemption to us (1:24, 30). He is our glory for our glorification (2:7; Rom. 8:30), hence, the Lord of glory (2:8). He is the depths (deep things) of God (2:10). God is mysterious enough, yet with this God, there are the depths. Christ is the depths of this most mysterious God. He is the unique foundation of God's building (3:11). He is our Passover (5:7), the unleavened bread (5:8), the spiritual food, the spiritual drink, and the spiritual rock (10:3-4). Christ is the moving rock, the following rock, which followed

the children of Israel. He is the Head (11:3) and the Body
(12:12). In chapter fifteen of 1 Corinthians we see that Christ
is the firstfruit (vv. 20-23), the second Man (v. 47), and the
last Adam (v. 45). Because Christ is the first, the second, and
the last, He is everything. As such a one, Christ became the
life-giving Spirit (15:45), the aggregate of all the foregoing
items. The all-inclusive Christ, with the riches of at least
nineteen items, is totaled in the life-giving Spirit. God has
given such a One to us as our portion for our enjoyment.

The main work of the life-giving Spirit is to search Christ,
to stir up Christ within us concerning these nineteen items.
Christ is our wonderful portion for us to enjoy. The Spirit that
gives life is searching Christ to stir up this Christ in our love,
pursuit, and experience of Him. This searching is still going
on to show us and to bring us into the realization of Christ as
our portion, our wisdom, our power, our righteousness, our
sanctification, and our redemption. The Spirit would do some
further searching to show you that Christ is the Lord of glory,
the depths of God, the foundation, the Passover, the unleavened bread, the spiritual food, the spiritual drink as the
living water flowing out of the cleft rock, and the spiritual
rock following us all the time. This searching is still going on
to further show us that Christ is the Head, the Body, the
firstfruit, the second Man, and the last Adam. Christ is the
first, the second, and the last, indicating that He is everything to us. This is the searching by the life-giving Spirit to
stir up Christ in our realization of Him and to show us every
item of what He is.

The best way to study the Word is to search. Do not merely
read or study the Bible but search the depths of God, Christ.
Today this Christ is hinged on the life-giving Spirit. The
life-giving Spirit is the hinge, and Christ is altogether
wrapped up with this Spirit. He is the life-giving Spirit
moving and searching within us. By this searching, He
imparts the riches of Christ into our being.

DWELLING IN THE BELIEVERS, THE TEMPLE OF GOD

Christ as the life-giving Spirit is dwelling in the believers,
who are the temple of God (3:16-17). This is altogether

heavenly language. On this earth there is not a religion which tells people that their God dwells in them. Even the Jewish religion, which was founded according to the Old Testament, never tells others that God dwells in His people. Only the New Testament, God's New Testament economy, tells us that our God as the consummation of the Triune God, the all-inclusive, life-giving Spirit, dwells in us. In the entire universe only One can dwell in us in a positive sense and He does dwell in us in this sense—as the life-giving Spirit, the consummation of the Triune God. This is marvelous! Nothing can compare with the indwelling God. We should all boldly declare that we are the richest people on earth! Nothing in this entire universe can dwell in us in the way that He does. The consummation of the Triune God, who is the life-giving Spirit, dwells in us and counts us as His temple. Christ as the life-giving Spirit is our indwelling treasure (2 Cor. 4:7).

WASHING AND SANCTIFYING THE BELIEVERS

The life-giving Spirit is also washing and sanctifying the believers (1 Cor. 6:11). Every house, every building, needs some washing and needs some cleaning. All the peoples on this earth practice cleaning their houses to some degree. Even the church as the temple of God today needs the washing, and the life-giving Spirit does this washing.

The beginning of our church life experience was a honeymoon. After the honeymoon, some "dirt" began to accumulate little by little, requiring the need of some cleaning. When we first came to the church life, this was our honeymoon and everything was so pleasant. The church life was wonderful to us. After a while, though, when our church life honeymoon was over, we began to consider that the church life was not really that good. We might have said, "I considered the elders as the top angels when I came into the church life but now— aha." This kind of thought shows that now you need the cleaning and you need the washing. When we turn to the Spirit, the Spirit cleanses and washes away our "aha." If you do not turn to your spirit for one week, many "ahas" will pile up inside you. This will cause you to be unable to pray. You may even think that you should not go to the meetings. You may not want to go to the meetings because in the meeting you will see a certain brother whom you feel unpleasant about. All of this is dirt. Therefore, you need the washing and you need the cleaning. If you would turn to your spirit and pray for half an hour, you would jump and run to the church meeting. This shows us that the temple of God today needs the washing. The life-giving Spirit does this washing.

JOINING THE BELIEVER TO THE LORD
AS ONE SPIRIT

Also, the life-giving Spirit joins the believer to the Lord as one spirit (6:17). In this matter of joining, the life-giving Spirit joins us individually to the Lord as one spirit. This is a great blessing. After the washing comes the joining. Every time we are washed by the Spirit, we immediately have the sensation that we are one with the Lord. If I stay in a certain locality for only two weeks, I may feel that the leading ones in the church there are very good. If I stayed there for over half a year, however, the "aha" would begin. This "aha" separates me from the Lord. When I turn to the Spirit and stay in the Spirit, the life-giving Spirit washes me. Immediately after the washing, I begin to have the sensation that I am one with the Lord. The joining follows the washing. We need the washing all the time.

We must realize that there is not one elder who is so perfect that he can stand the "sharp watching" and observing of the saints. The leading ones in the church life are under a strict, thorough, and sharp watching and observing. People may look to see what kind of tie, jacket, or shoes the leading ones are wearing. All the saints are watching over the elders. Who can stand this kind of watching and observing? In the entire human race, only one man is so perfect who can stand the test of people's watching and observing. This man is Jesus Christ. None of us can pass such a thorough and strict inspection. We cannot stand the watching, but we can enjoy the washing. The washing cleanses us, and the washing by the life-giving Spirit always brings us back to being joined to the Lord as one Spirit.

OCCUPYING THE BODY OF THE BELIEVERS
AS THE TEMPLE OF GOD FOR GOD'S GLORIFICATION

The life-giving Spirit is occupying the body of the believers, which is the temple of God, for God's glorification (6:19-20). This means that the life-giving Spirit does not only remain in our spirit, but even indwells and occupies our body. Many Christians do things to shame the Lord, mainly by their body. For instance, if you gamble by playing cards, you are using your body to gamble. If you go to a gambling place, you use your two feet to go there. Most of the things that are done which are a shame to the Lord are done through the body. Your body, however, should be occupied by the indwelling, life-giving Spirit. We should not let our feet and our legs take us to sinful places, but they should always take us to the meetings of the church. If this is the case, our feet would always be occupied by the life-giving Spirit. This is a glory to God. Even when we gossip, we are using our mouth, a part of our body. Gossip does not glorify God. The Spirit has to occupy our mouth; then whatever comes out of our mouth would be a glory to God. This is the life-giving Spirit's work.

SATURATING THE BELIEVERS' OPINION

The life-giving Spirit can also saturate the believers' opinion (7:40). As brothers and sisters pursuing the Lord, I believe we all hate opinion. If I were to tell you that you were full of opinions, you would be offended. Paul, however, said he had an opinion in 1 Corinthians. In 7:25 Paul said that he had no commandment of the Lord, but he still gave his opinion. After telling us his opinion in 7:40 he says, "I think that I also have the Spirit of God." This shows that the Spirit of God was in Paul's opinion. This is the real spirituality. To have the Spirit of God should not merely be in our praying, singing, and speaking for God. Even in our opinion there must be the saturation of the life-giving Spirit. Paul was so saturated by the life-giving Spirit that even his opinion had the Spirit of God within it. The Spirit of God had penetrated and saturated his opinion. All of us can be like this.

THE BELIEVERS BEING BAPTIZED
IN THIS SPIRIT INTO ONE BODY

The believers were baptized in this Spirit into one Body (1 Cor. 12:13a). As the Spirit is the sphere and element of our spiritual baptism and in such a Spirit we were all baptized into one organic entity, the Body of Christ, so we should all, regardless of our races, nationalities, and social ranks, be this one Body. Christ is the life and constituent of this Body, and the Spirit is the reality of Christ. It is in this one Spirit that we were all baptized into this one living Body to express Christ.

THE BELIEVERS BEING GIVEN TO DRINK
THIS ONE SPIRIT

The believers were also given to drink this one Spirit (12:13b). After being baptized, we need to drink of one Spirit. Let us all be immersed in this Spirit. We need to be saturated, permeated, and soaked in this Spirit. We should always live in this reality—whatever is outside of us is the Spirit and whatever is inside of us is the Spirit. We should all be wrapped up with the Spirit. This is the work of the life-giving Spirit.

THE GIFTS, THE MANIFESTATION OF THIS SPIRIT

In 1 Corinthians 12 we see the gifts, the manifestation, of this Spirit in the Body of Christ (vv. 4, 7-11). The gifts are not mentioned until chapter twelve of 1 Corinthians to show us that to exercise them there is the need of the adequate growth in life and the full development of the growth of life. In this full development of life we can have the manifestation of the Spirit, the different gifts. In 1 Corinthians 12 Paul lists nine gifts as the manifestation of the Spirit: the word of wisdom, the word of knowledge, faith, gifts of healing, works of power, prophecy, discerning of spirits, tongues, and interpretation of tongues. The last manifestation of the Spirit is tongues and interpretation of tongues. The topmost manifestation of the Spirit is the word of wisdom and next to this is the word of knowledge. Among the nine gifts of the manifestation of the Spirit, five are related to speaking—the word of wisdom, the word of knowledge, prophecy, tongues, and interpretation of tongues. The other four gifts that are mentioned are miraculous items—faith that can move mountains, gifts of healing, works of power (miracles), and the discerning of spirits. (See the notes in the Recovery Version of 1 Corinthians on verses 4 through 11 of chapter twelve.) Of the nine gifts mentioned by the Apostle Paul here, speaking in tongues and interpretation of tongues are listed as the last two, because they are not as profitable as the other items for the building up of the church (14:2-6, 18, 19). This is the life-giving Spirit working within us to make us the proper, functioning members in the Body.

Chapter Thirteen

THE TRANSFORMING SPIRIT

Scripture Reading: 2 Cor. 3:18; 1:21-22; 3:3, 6, 17, 18; 13:14

GROWTH IN LIFE AND TRANSFORMATION

Thus far, we have seen that the first Epistle, Romans, is on the Spirit of life, and the second Epistle, 1 Corinthians, is on the life-giving Spirit. The third Epistle, 2 Corinthians, is on the transforming Spirit. This shows us that under the sovereignty of the Lord, the arrangement of the New Testament books is in a good sequence. In 1 Corinthians what is stressed is the matter of the growth in life. Paul says, "I planted, Apollos watered, but God made to grow" (3:6). Transformation is emphasized in 2 Corinthians. In the first Epistle to the Corinthians we see the growth in life, with the indication that this growth is for transformation. The more we grow, the more we will be transformed. However, to grow is one thing and to be transformed is another thing. Growth needs life and transformation needs the elements of life.

In 1 Corinthians 3 we see the growth in life for transformation. The word transformation is not used in that chapter, but the issue of the growth in life is there indicating transformation. As God's farm (3:9) with planting, watering, and growing, the church should produce plants; but the proper materials for the building up of the church are gold, silver, and precious stones (3:12), all of which are minerals. Hence, the thought of transformation is implied there. We need not only to grow in life but also to be transformed in life that we may become the precious materials for God's building.

Paul continued in his second Epistle to the Corinthians from the growth in life to transformation. In his first Epistle there are many points referring to the growth in life, but in the second Epistle there are not any points regarding the growth in life but a number of points referring to transformation. This is why we say that the Spirit in the first Epistle is the life-giving Spirit, the Spirit that always gives life for the growth in life. In the second Epistle, however, Paul always points out to us the things related to transformation. This is why we say that in 2 Corinthians we see the transforming Spirit. The one Spirit is first life-giving and then transforming.

The word transformation is not mentioned in the first Epistle, but the indication of transformation is there. Both the Spirit that gives life and the transforming Spirit are mentioned in 2 Corinthians 3. Verse 6 tells us that "the letter kills, but the Spirit gives life," and verse 18 says that we are being transformed "even as from the Lord Spirit." The life-giving in verse 6 leads to the transforming in verse 18. In the first Epistle growth in life issues in transformation, and in the second Epistle transformation is the result of the growth in life. Growth in life needs the life supply, but transformation needs the elements of life.

THE ANOINTING, SEALING, AND PLEDGING SPIRIT

Second Corinthians 1:21-22 shows us that this transforming Spirit is the anointing, the sealing, and the pledging Spirit. Anointing, sealing, and pledging are different from life-giving. To give life is to impart life into us. To anoint someone there is the need of some ointment, and the ointment is full of elements. The ointment may be likened to paint. Paint is a composition of elements. Without the elements, there could not be paint. The more I paint a table, the more elements are put on the table.

In the Old Testament, the holy anointing oil is the compound ointment. It is compounded with four kinds of spices into one oil (Exo. 30:23-25). This holy anointing oil is no longer merely oil, but a compound ointment composed of five elements. The more anointing there is, the more these elements are being added on. In 2 Corinthians, the Spirit is the transforming Spirit, and this transforming Spirit is anointing us. To anoint is to put more elements on. With transformation there is the need of elements.

The petrification of wood is another good example of transformation. As the current of water flows through a piece of driftwood it carries away the old elements and brings in the new elements of minerals. Eventually, the minerals entirely replace the cell structure of the wood. This transforms the wood into a piece of stone by the continual addition of new elements. In like manner, the Spirit transforms us by adding more and more of the divine elements into our being. The transforming Spirit flowing through our being adds into us the divinity of Christ, the humanity of Christ, His human living, His all-inclusive death, and His excellent resurrection. All these elements are carried into our being by the transforming Spirit, and these elements become the factors of our transformation. Therefore, such a flowing Spirit is a transforming Spirit. The Spirit transforms us by putting into us more and more of the divine elements. This is the Spirit anointing us.

The sealing is also a matter of imparting some elements. If I were to stamp a piece of paper with a seal and the seal did not have any element of ink on it, we would not see anything on the paper. Suppose, however, that the seal is saturated and full of the element of ink. When I seal the paper, a mark or an impression is left on it. The mark is constituted with the element of ink. Without any ink element, there is no mark. Sealing is a marking. The Holy Spirit, who is the transforming Spirit, is sealing us all the time, and this sealing makes a mark which people can read. When a new convert who has just believed in the Lord Jesus is happy and full of joy in the Lord, his cousins, in-laws, relatives, and friends recognize and know that he is now a Christian. However, they do not know and they cannot see what kind of Christian he is. After two years of growing in life and allowing the transforming Spirit to seal him every day, this sealing is always putting some elements upon him. After two years, all of his acquaintances will be able to read some mark upon him. They will testify that he is so extraordinary, fine, and excellent in his living and character. This is a mark built up by the sealing of the transforming Spirit. Anointing imparts God's elements into us. The sealing does the same thing, but it also forms the divine elements into an impression, a mark, to express God's image.

The pledge of the Spirit is the Spirit Himself as the pledge. The pledge is a sample, a foretaste. In ancient times, the Greek word for pledge was used in the purchase of land. The seller gave the buyer a sample of the soil from the land being purchased. Hence, a pledge, according to the ancient Greek usage, was also a sample. The Holy Spirit is the sample of what we shall inherit of God in full. By enjoying the sample we have a foretaste of what is coming. The anointing Spirit, the transforming Spirit, pledged Himself into us as a foretaste. The foretaste gives us a taste of God; this is also a pledge, a security, a guarantee of the full taste to come.

By the anointing, sealing, and pledging, all the elements of the Triune God, including the wonderful process He went through, are imparted into our being. The title "the life-giving Spirit" indicates the giving of life in a general way. The transforming Spirit, however, involves the anointing, the sealing, and the pledging of the elements of Christ into our being. As we enjoy Him and open our being to Him, the divine elements are being added to us all day long. Since I received the Lord over fifty years ago, I can testify that every day, through the anointing, sealing, and pledging, I have received more of the divine elements into my being. I believe that now a distinct and strong mark is upon me, and I must testify that I am enjoying many riches of Christ. I am also enjoying more of the pledge of God being my portion in Christ. This is all for transformation. In 2 Corinthians 1:21-22 we see that through the anointing, sealing, and pledging, the believers are receiving more and more of the divine elements into their being.

THE SPIRIT OF THE LIVING GOD
AS THE INSCRIBING INK

In 2 Corinthians 3:3 we see the Spirit of the living God as the inscribing ink. Before ball-point pens were invented, people who wrote with ink had to refill their fountain pens frequently. At that time in using a fountain pen, I sometimes forgot to refill it. When I began to use it to write something, nothing was there because the pen did not have the element of ink. Actually, the transforming Spirit is the inscribing ink. God is inscribing Christ into our being, which is like a piece of parchment. In ancient times they did not have paper so they used parchment. You must realize that you are like a piece of parchment and God is inscribing Christ into your being. This inscribing, however, needs some element and this element is the transforming Spirit. The transforming Spirit is the inscribing ink used by God as an element to write Christ into your being. God is writing Christ, yet He needs the transforming Spirit as the writing element. Actually and in reality this inscribing ink is just Christ Himself.

The more I write with a pen, the more ink gets onto the paper. What I have written may be a composition, but the element of this composition is ink. God is also writing Christ into our being. The element of His writing is the Spirit of the living God as the inscribing ink. The transforming Spirit is the element, the reality, of Christ. God is writing Christ into us with the transforming Spirit. The transforming Spirit is the element for God to compose Christ, for God to write Christ. Therefore, the composition of Christ is altogether done with the Spirit, and the Spirit is the element of the composition of Christ.

What is on the paper after the writing? Elementary speaking, it is the ink—the Spirit of the living God. Composition wise, it tells us something—Christ. Therefore, the writing ink is the element of Christ. Second Corinthians 3:17 indicates that Christ is the Spirit. Every day the transforming Spirit is being written upon our being as the element, and it manifests Christ. The ink is Christ and the ink is also the element of Christ. Therefore, the inscribing Spirit, who is the transforming Spirit, is the very element of Christ, even Christ Himself. This is all for transformation. While God is writing with the inscribing Spirit, we are being transformed.

THE SPIRIT OF THE NEW COVENANT MINISTRY
THAT GIVES LIFE

Also, the transforming Spirit is the Spirit of the new covenant ministry that gives life (2 Cor. 3:6). Within life, there are many elements. The transforming Spirit not only transforms us, but also constitutes the New Testament ministry. We must realize that the New Testament ministry is one with the transforming Spirit, and that this ministry is a transforming ministry. Paul's ministry was constituted by and with the transforming Spirit. When Paul was ministering, the transforming Spirit was transforming the saints. When we are listening to a person whose speaking is the New Testament ministry, the transforming Spirit is transforming us. When we are under this speaking, this ministry, many divine elements are being ministered and imparted into our being by the transforming Spirit. Therefore, the New Testament ministry is working with the transforming work of the Spirit. These two actually work together as one to impart more and more divine elements into us for our transformation. When we are under such a ministry, we are being transformed.

THE LORD BEING THE SPIRIT, THE SPIRIT
OF THE LORD, FOR OUR FREEDOM

Second Corinthians 3:17 shows us that the Lord is the Spirit, the Spirit of the Lord, for our freedom. The Lord is the Spirit, and the Lord being the Spirit is to free us from regulations, from rituals, from religious teachings, and from the traditional doctrines. At Paul's time, the Old Testament law was a great bondage. The Lord as the Spirit frees us from the bondage of the law. The Jews were under the bondage of circumcision, under the bondage of dietary regulations such as not eating certain things and not eating with Gentiles, and under the bondage of the Sabbath and other Old Testament regulations. Even though one was diseased or hungry, nothing could be done for him on the Sabbath, nor could he do anything for himself. This was a bondage.

Today, however, is not the age of Moses and the law in letters but the age of the Lord Jesus being the "pneumatic Christ." The Lord today is the pneuma, the Spirit. Moses,

with the letter of the law, put all the people under bondage—
the bondage of keeping the Sabbath, the bondage of circumcision, the bondage of dietary regulations, the bondage of not
contacting Gentiles, and many other bondages. Man had been
bound with bondage after bondage, but then Jesus came. He
is the wonderful One and He is the Lord. He is also the
pneuma, the Spirit. He is not the letter of the law. With Him
there is no more bondage, no more Sabbath, no more circumcision, no more dietary regulations, but there is full freedom.

The Lord being the Spirit is freedom to us. We have been
freed. Formerly, we were under bondage just like the Jews,
and every bondage is a veil. All the bondages are layers of
veils. This means bondage, blindness, and darkness, even
death. But hallelujah! Jesus came! He is the Spirit and He is
the Freedom. When the heart turns to the Lord, the veil is
taken away (2 Cor. 3:16). Furthermore, the Lord is the Spirit
who would give us freedom. Since the Lord is the Spirit, when
the heart turns to Him, the veil is taken away, and the heart
is freed from the bondage of the letter of the law. We have
been freed!

THE BELIEVERS BEING TRANSFORMED
AS FROM THE LORD SPIRIT

We "are being transformed into the same image from glory
to glory, even as from the Lord Spirit" (2 Cor. 3:18). This verse
also tells us that we are beholding the glory of the Lord with
unveiled face. Formerly our face was veiled and we could not
see anything, but the Spirit took away all the veils. Now with
an unveiled face we are beholding and reflecting as a mirror.
While we are beholding Him, we are being transformed into
His image from glory to glory. Beholding is to see the Lord by
ourselves; reflecting is for others to see Him through us.
When we turn our heart to the Lord, the veils are taken away,
we see Christ directly, and we reflect Him. He is the life-
giving Spirit. When we see Him in such a direct, open, and
transparent way, He as the Spirit infuses Himself into our
being, adding more of Himself as the divine element into
our being and we reflect Him to others. This transforms us.
This changes us metabolically. We could never be the same as

we were in the past. We are being transformed into His image from one degree of glory to another degree of glory, from glory to glory. This is as from the Lord Spirit. Now we see a compound, divine title—the Lord Spirit. This is transformation.

THE FELLOWSHIP OF THE SPIRIT

Second Corinthians has a marvelous concluding verse— "The grace of the Lord Jesus Christ, and the love of God, and the fellowship of the Holy Spirit be with you all" (13:14). Some denominations in Christianity use this verse as a benediction. Many times the pastor will quote this verse at the end of the service. At the end of his quoting, the congregation says amen and they are dismissed to go home. However, do they really know or have an idea of what this verse really means? Actually, the quoting of this verse is mostly a ritualistic, traditional benediction. The pastor repeats this every Sunday and the congregation says amen again and again with little realization of the actual contents of this verse. Actually, if we do not know what transformation is, we cannot understand this verse adequately.

The grace of Christ is the rich element of Christ, the love of God is the rich element of God, and the fellowship of the Holy Spirit is the aggregate of the rich element of Christ and God transmitted into our being practically for our spiritual enjoyment. In this fellowship we are enjoying the rich elements of the Triune God, which are the elements for our transformation. Day after day, more and more, the rich elements of the Triune God are being added into our being and we are being transformed.

This concludes the vision of God's New Testament economy in 2 Corinthians. Second Corinthians shows us that the consummation of the Triune God is the transforming Spirit who is transmitting the rich element of the Triune God into our being to transform us into His image, making us His very expression. This is the transforming Spirit revealed in 2 Corinthians.

CHAPTER FOURTEEN

THE SPIRIT AS THE BLESSING OF THE GOSPEL

Scripture Reading: Gal. 3:14, 2-3, 5; 4:6, 29; 5:16-18, 22-25;
6:8

It is not so easy for us to see the aspect of the Spirit mentioned in the book of Galatians. We have seen that the book of Romans talks about the Spirit of life. By studying 1 Corinthians diligently we all can see that the Spirit there is the life-giving Spirit. It is easier to see that in 2 Corinthians there is the transforming Spirit; however, it is not so easy to see what is the aspect of the Spirit mentioned in Galatians.

THE BACKGROUND OF GALATIANS

During the time that Paul wrote this book, the Christians were being bothered, troubled, and distracted by the law keepers, the Judaizers. These law keepers or Judaizers, on the one hand, pretended to be Christians, but they still remained so faithful to Moses. They treasured the law much more than the gospel. They not only kept the law by themselves but they also did their best to Judaize the Gentile believers, misleading them to keep the law rather than hearing the faith. To hear the faith means to receive the gospel.

We realize today that the law was absolutely an Old Testament matter. It was something in letter and at best it was something in promise, in types, and in prophecies. Nothing was a reality and everything was in letters and in shadows. The Judaizers, however, did not realize this and treasured these shadows, and they forced the Gentile believers to follow them in treasuring these shadows. The stress in their teaching distracted and even misled the believers. Those believers who had been distracted were missing the blessing of the gospel. Under such a background, Paul wrote this short Epistle to the Galatians.

GALATIANS 1—3

In the first two chapters Paul presented the Galatians with a clear view that God's intention is to work Christ into us as everything. God had no intention for His chosen people to keep the law. His intention was only to use the law as a custodian, a guardian, a child-conductor, to watch over His chosen people before Christ came, and to escort and conduct them to Christ when He did come (3:24-25). The law is also likened to a sheepfold (John 10:1), in which God's chosen people were kept and guarded in custody and ward until Christ came. When the day of Christ's coming dawned, God wanted His chosen people to come out of the fold, to come out of custody, to receive Christ directly as their life and life-supply.

In chapter one Paul showed that God's intention is to reveal His Son, Jesus Christ, into His chosen people (v. 16). God did not have any intention of revealing the law in His chosen people. God's desire is that His chosen people would receive His Son into them. This is the gospel. In chapter two Paul goes on to show us that Christ replaces the law and that God did not want us to keep the law. Rather, God put us on the cross with Christ, and we have died to law that we might live to God (2:19). We have been crucified with Christ on the cross, and it is no longer we who live but Christ lives in us (v. 20). Christ lives in us not to the law, but to God. We do not live to the law, but we live to God. We do not live a life to keep the law, but we live a life to express God. We have nothing to do with the law since the obligation under the law, the relationship to the law, was terminated in Christ's death. Not only were we crucified, but even the law of the commandments in ordinances was nailed to the cross (Col. 2:14).

In chapter three Paul was very frank in his writing to the Galatians. He called them "foolish Galatians" (v. 1). When Paul wrote the Galatians, they had all been misled to be blind and veiled, to be foolish. Therefore, Paul called them foolish Galatians and he asked them, "Did you receive the Spirit by the works of law or by the hearing of faith?" (3:2). By receiving the gospel, the Galatians received the consummation of the Triune God which is the living, all-inclusive Spirit. He is so living, so real, so availing, and so prevailing, and much higher than the law. Paul wanted to show the Galatians how foolish it is to neglect the Spirit and drift back to the law. Paul told them that since they had begun their Christian life in a good way by the Spirit, they should run the race to be perfected by the Spirit. However, they were distracted, trying to take the way of the law. So Paul asked them, "Are you so foolish? Having begun by the Spirit, are you now being perfected by the flesh?" (3:3). To begin by the Spirit is by faith in Christ; to be perfected by the flesh is by works of law (3:2).

THE BLESSING OF THE GOSPEL

Paul then goes on to present to them a clear picture concerning the gospel preached beforehand to Abraham (Gal. 3:8). God did not give Abraham the law but the promise, which was not only concerning Abraham and his descendants but also concerning all the nations on this earth. This promise was initially given to Abraham in Genesis 12:1-3 where God told Abraham—"in thee shall all families of the earth be blessed" (v. 3). In Galatians 3:16 Paul shows us that Christ is the unique seed of Abraham that brings the blessing to all the nations. In Genesis we can see the blessing, but we cannot find the Spirit. Paul was a marvelous writer. When he was talking about the seed of Abraham and the blessing to all the nations, he mentions the Spirit as the blessing promised by God to Abraham for all the nations (3:14).

Galatians 3:13 says, "Christ has redeemed us out of the curse of the law, having become a curse on our behalf; because it is written, Cursed is everyone hanging on a tree." Paul was telling the Galatians that the law did not bring any blessing to them but it only put them under a curse. Then Christ came and died on the cross to redeem us out of the curse of the law, having become a curse on our behalf. Christ Himself became a curse on the cross. While Christ was being crucified on the cross, there was a sign of curse upon Him—a crown of thorns. Genesis 3 shows us that after man fell, sin entered and with it the curse. The curse was that the earth would bring forth thorns and thistles (Gen. 3:18). Thorns were a sign of the curse and on the cross Jesus bore this curse. When He was hanging on the cross wearing a crown of thorns, this indicated that He was made a curse on our behalf.

The sentence in verse 13 continues in verse 14—"In order that the blessing of Abraham might come to the nations in Jesus Christ, that we might receive the promise of the Spirit through faith." The nations means all Gentiles, all the nations of this earth. When Paul said, "that we might receive the promise of the Spirit through faith," he changed the nations to "we." Therefore, the nations include the Jews.

Galatians 3:14 does not say that all the nations on this earth might receive the promise of going to heaven. The natural, religious mentality believes that the blessing of the gospel is to go to heaven. Many Christians believe that the goodness of believing in Jesus Christ is having a happy life in this age and then after we die we go to heaven. To them this is the top blessing, even the everlasting blessing of the gospel. From my youth I heard frequently that if a person did not believe in Jesus Christ, he would go to hell and that if he did believe in Jesus Christ, he would go to heaven. I heard the gospel preached in this way time after time. Sixty years ago in China many preachers would warn people about going to hell and would tell them that God prepared a heavenly mansion with golden streets and pearly gates. They preached in this way to motivate their listeners to believe in the Lord Jesus. The "going to heaven" gospel never stirred me up. I always wondered what kind of religion would always talk about hell and heaven again and again. In 1925, however, when I was still under twenty, I heard the genuine gospel and got caught by the Lord.

The blessing of the gospel is that we might receive the promise of the Spirit, who is the consummation of the processed Triune God. This is not merely the God who created the heavens and the earth. This is the Triune God who has gone through all these processes: incarnation, human living, crucifixion, resurrection, and ascension. After passing through all these processes, He was consummated to be the Spirit, the extract of the Triune God. The blessing of the gospel is the Spirit, who is the sum total and the aggregate of the Triune God, the processed Triune God. Because our natural mind cannot comprehend this, we need a vision. What a blessing this is! An expensive car, even the so-called heavenly mansion, cannot be compared with the Triune God. Even the entire universe cannot compare with our Triune God. The blessing of the gospel is the Spirit, who is the ultimate realization of the processed Triune God.

We should not forget that we receive such a wonderful Spirit through faith. There is the need to believe. God is prepared. He is fully ready to give Himself to you. He has been processed; He is not a "raw God." He is the processed God consummated in the all-inclusive Spirit, ready for you to receive and enjoy, but you have to believe. You may wonder how you can believe, but you do not need to try to believe. Just look at the promise. Look at the Triune God. Look at Jesus Christ. Look at the Son of God who died on the cross for you. If you would look at Him, faith would rise up within you (Heb. 12:2). In Hong Kong, a city famous for selling jewels, the salesmen have a special art of showing someone these precious things. After their presentation of these precious things and after you see them, "faith" rises up in your heart. You may even sell everything to buy those jewels. A good preacher is one who presents "the jewels" in such a way. When this preacher gives you a look at the Triune God, faith rises up in you to receive such a One. This One is the blessing of the gospel.

I hope that today all of us would thank the Lord for such a blessing, which is nothing less than Himself. This blessing is nothing less than the Triune God who became a man in the flesh, who lived on this earth for thirty-three and a half years, passing through the entire human life. He went to the cross to terminate all the negative things for us, He released the divine life for us, He arose from among the dead, entered into resurrection, became the life-giving Spirit, and breathed Himself into us. He ascended into heaven and poured Himself out upon us. Now we have Him as our life essentially, and we have

Him upon us as our power economically. We can live such a universal man, a wonderful man, a man of the Spirit, a man of God. We should all declare—"I am now a God-man." This is the blessing of the gospel.

THE SPIRIT BEING SUPPLIED TO THE BELIEVERS BY THE HEARING OF FAITH

The Spirit is being supplied to the believers by the hearing of faith (Gal. 3:5). Whenever we are under the speaking of the New Testament ministry, we are hearing the faith. The more we hear the faith, the more we receive the supply of the Spirit. After we have been under the speaking of the ministry we all can declare, "Now I have more Spirit within me." Also, when we review what we have seen when we were under the speaking of the ministry, that review will supply us with more Spirit. The Spirit is being supplied to the believers to make what they heard real.

THE BELIEVERS BEING BORN OF THE SPIRIT

The believers were born of the Spirit (Gal. 4:29). Galatians reminds us that we were born of the Spirit. We are sons born of God. We were born firstly of Adam, but we were reborn of God, of the Spirit, the consummation of the Triune God.

THE SPIRIT OF GOD'S SON TO MAKE THE BELIEVERS' DIVINE SONSHIP REAL

The Spirit, who is the consummation of the Triune God, is particularly the Spirit of the Son of God who makes the believers' divine sonship real (Gal. 4:6). Today we are sons of God not only in name but also in life. In our practical daily life we are sons of God. Who makes us the real sons of God? The Spirit of the Son of God. The very divine Spirit within us today is the Spirit of the divine Son, so He is the reality of our divine sonship. When we walk and live by Him, we walk and live as a real son of God.

THE BELIEVERS LIVING AND WALKING BY THE SPIRIT

The believers should live and walk by the Spirit (Gal. 5:16-18, 22-25). We must be deeply impressed that the New

Testament does not charge us to keep the letter of the Bible. Rather, the New Testament charges us to live and walk by the Spirit. Now we must ask what the difference is between living and walking. To live means to have life and it also means to exist. A Christian is a believer in Christ, born of God. He has the Spirit of sonship in his being. He has the life of this Spirit and he exists by this Spirit. To live by the Spirit is to have life and to exist by the Spirit. To walk means to move, to act, to speak, and to do things by the Spirit. All of our living and walking should be by the Spirit who is in us.

This Spirit is the consummation, the totality of the Triune God. He is living, real, practical, and present in you all the time. You do not need to seek after Him since He is right in you. You do not need to pray, "Lord, be with me the whole day." In the past, I liked to pray such a prayer. I followed Moses to ask the Lord that His presence would go with me (Exo. 33:15). One day when I prayed this way, however, I became condemned. I said to myself, "Foolish man, the Lord is with you every day, and He says clearly that He will never leave you. But in your daily life, you still ask the Lord to be with you." I also taught people that the Lord was within them and would never leave them. That day, though, the Spirit within asked me why I prayed that the Lord would be with me when He was with me all the time. As a result, I stopped praying in this kind of way.

We do not need to pray in this way. The Lord is here with us right now. Even if you would go to a movie, He is still within you. However, do not be encouraged by this word to go to a movie. He is within you and you need to walk by the Spirit. When you are going to a movie, He goes with you, but He goes with you indicating that you should not go further. You know this, but you may still say, "Let me go just for today and I will not go anymore." The Spirit, though, is still within you telling you to turn and walk by Him. When He indicates within you that you should turn to Him and you respond by saying, "Lord Jesus, I will go by You," you will not go to the movie theater, but to the church meeting. When we are going with the Lord and by the Lord, our mouth will be full of praise.

According to what I have observed, I have never seen a married couple who have never argued with each other. The real situation of every marriage life is that there is always the tendency and the temptation to exchange words with each other. I must confess that I wanted to exchange words with my wife many times. As soon as I began to speak something to her, the Lord was there indicating that I should stop. At that moment I did not try to stop, but I went with the Lord and I went by Him. That practice stopped my speaking. This is an example of walking by the Spirit. If we try to stop our bad habits by ourselves, we could never make it. We must walk by the Spirit.

Do not try to walk by the Spirit merely in great things, but walk by the Spirit in small things. Some of the saints may be trying to walk by the Spirit in great things. They may be praying, "Lord, You need a recovery in Athens, Greece. Should I go there or not? Lord, I've been praying for three months. I surely would like to go by the Spirit." However, do not go by the Spirit in great things first, but go or walk by the Spirit in small things first, such as talking on the telephone. When many saints, especially the sisters, talk on the telephone, it seems as if they do not have the Lord Jesus or the Spirit within them. Quite often their talk on the telephone is vain talk or gossip. If we mean business to walk by the Spirit, we should firstly practice walking by the Spirit in the small things, such as talking on the telephone. If you try this, you will find out how rebellious and how stubborn you are. Maybe during one phone call the Lord Jesus would tell you to stop your talk many times but you would tell Him—"just one more sentence." You would not stop your talk on the telephone. We should walk by the Spirit when we receive a phone call or when we make a phone call. Practice to walk by the Spirit in small things. Walk by the Spirit when you are going to buy a tie. You will see that you are not so obedient or so faithful to walk by the Spirit. The believers should live and walk by the Spirit.

THE BELIEVERS SOWING UNTO THE SPIRIT

Also, the believers should sow unto the Spirit that they

may reap of the Spirit eternal life (Gal. 6:8). Paul says that if you sow unto the flesh you shall reap corruption of the flesh. The word "unto" means "with a view to" or "for." To sow unto the flesh is to sow for the flesh, with the purpose of the flesh in view, fulfilling what the flesh covets. To sow unto the Spirit is to sow for the Spirit, with the aim of the Spirit, accomplishing what the Spirit desires. We must realize that whatever we do and whatever we say is a kind of sowing. With sowing there is always a result, a reaping. Whatever we say and do is a kind of sowing and some result will come out. When you do things and say things, you must have a proper view. Do not sow anything, do anything, say anything, unto the flesh, but unto the Spirit. Have this in your view. This will stop you from doing many things which you should not do. Sow everything with a view to the Spirit. Eventually, you will reap of the Spirit eternal life. When I talk to a brother, I should talk in view of the Spirit. I should not talk in view of the flesh. If I sow something unto the flesh, one day corruption will come. I will reap corruption. This is the last word in this book concerning the Spirit.

Hallelujah, we do have such a blessing within us! However, we must always live and walk by this living blessing, by this Spirit. Then whatever we do and whatever we say will be said and done in view of this Spirit. If we sow unto the Spirit, a reaping of eternal life would always be our portion. The eternal life in Galatians 6:8 does not refer to the eternal life in the future. If we sow unto the Spirit, we will reap of the Spirit eternal life today. Otherwise, a result of corruption will be our portion. This word should encourage us to live and walk by the Spirit. To live and walk by the Spirit is to enjoy the blessing of the gospel.

CHAPTER FIFTEEN

THE SPIRIT OF THE BODY AND
THE BOUNTIFUL SPIRIT OF JESUS CHRIST

Scripture Reading: Eph. 4:4; 1:13-14; 2:18; 3:14-19; 4:3, 30;
6:11-12, 17; Phil. 1:19-21a; 2:12-16; 3:8-9; 4:13

In the Epistles of Ephesians and Philippians we see the
Spirit, as the Son, with the Father, being the consummation
of the Triune God. The Spirit is the consummation of the
Triune God or the Triune God consummated. After the Triune
God had gone through a marvelous process, the consummation came out, that is, the all-inclusive, processed, compound
Spirit. In the Epistles the Spirit is not something "raw," but
something processed. The Triune God has passed through all
the processes, consummating in the Spirit.

THE SPIRIT OF THE BODY

In Ephesians such a compound Spirit is the Spirit of the
Body (4:4). In Ephesians the main topic is the Body of Christ,
the church, so in this book the aggregate Spirit, the compound Spirit, is the Spirit for the Body and the Spirit of the
Body. If there is no Spirit, there is no Body, no church. When
people talk about the Body of Christ, the church, they mostly
neglect the Spirit. Actually, the Spirit is the intrinsic reality
of the Body of Christ. The reality of the church is this compound, aggregate Spirit.

The Members of the Body Being Sealed
with the Spirit as the Pledge of Their Inheritance

Ephesians 1:13 tells us that we believers, who are the
components, the members of the Body, have all been sealed
with the Holy Spirit. A good example of a seal is a rubber

stamp. When a piece of paper is stamped or sealed it receives some element of ink. Now it is no longer purely a piece of paper, but a piece of paper with the element of ink. This shows us that, firstly, to be sealed is to be impressed with some element. Ephesians 1:13-14 tells us that when we heard the Word and believed in the Lord Jesus, we were sealed with this compound Spirit. This sealing put the divine element into our being. This is just like the stamping of the ink on a piece of paper. It is very easy to erase something written with pencil. However, when the best ink is used, it is very hard to erase. Sometimes it cannot be erased unless you rub through the paper. This means that the ink element has become one with the paper and that the two elements are mingled as one. In like manner, the divine element has become one with us. The divine Spirit dwells in our human spirit and these two are mingled together as one spirit (2 Tim. 4:22; Rom. 8:16; 1 Cor. 6:17).

In addition, sealing something gives it a mark. To be sealed with the Holy Spirit means to be marked with the Holy Spirit as a living seal. If we had a seal with someone's name on it, the stamping of this seal on a piece of paper would leave the mark of this person's name on the paper. The mark looks exactly the same as the stamp. After we believed in the Lord Jesus, the Holy Spirit sealed us. It not only brought the divine element into our being, but it also put a mark upon us, causing us to bear God's image signified by the seal, thus making us like God.

Sealing also denotes ownership. When a person buys a new book and stamps or seals it with his name, this seal denotes that the book belongs to him. The Holy Spirit put the divine element into our being as a seal to mark us out, indicating that we belong to God. The divine element added into our being, the mark made in us, and the indication of the divine ownership, when added together, become a pledge. A pledge is a guarantee that something is yours. The Holy Spirit sealed upon our being is the pledge that God is ours. It guarantees that God is our inheritance. The members of the church are the sealed ones. All the members have received the Holy Spirit as the divine element, as the divine mark, as the divine ownership, and eventually as a pledge that God is their inheritance. From the day of our salvation we may enjoy God every day as our portion.

The Members of the One Body
Having Access through Christ in the One Spirit
unto the Father

In Ephesians 2:18 we are told that through Christ both the Jewish and Gentile members of the Body have access in the one Spirit unto the Father. Our access "unto the Father" means for us to contact God for our enjoyment. Whenever we come to God to contact Him, we enjoy Him. There is no enjoyment better than this. When we contact God, we come to Him through Christ in the Spirit to the Father. This is the Divine Trinity in our experience of God as our enjoyment. We all have been sealed with the Spirit as a pledge that God is our inheritance for us to enjoy. Now through the Son in the Spirit we come to the Father to enjoy Him. According to the context, this verse also indicates that through Christ all the Jewish and Gentile believers, who were once at enmity, have access to the Father in one Spirit for their enjoyment. Regardless of whether we are Jewish or Gentile believers, all of us are coming to the Father, through the Son, in the one Spirit, to enjoy the Father as our inheritance.

The Father Strengthening
the Members of the Body through the Spirit
for Christ to Make His Home in Their Heart

In Ephesians 3:14-19 Paul prayed that through the Spirit the Father would strengthen the members of the Body into their inner man, that Christ may make His home in their hearts, that they may be strong to apprehend with all the members the breadth, length, height, and depth of Christ, that they may be filled unto all the fullness of God. Again, this is the Triune God. Ephesians 2:18 tells us that we have access unto the Father, through the Son, in the Spirit. Ephesians 3:14-19 indicates that Christ comes to make home in our hearts from the Father through the Spirit. This is two-way traffic. In one Spirit, through Christ, we go unto

the Father, which means we come to Him and enjoy Him.
On the other hand, through the Spirit, Christ comes from
God to make His home in our hearts. He is making His
home in our hearts that we may know His breadth, length,
height, and depth, His unlimited dimensions, that we may
be filled unto all the fullness of God. This God is the Triune
God.

Paul prayed that the Father through the Spirit would
strengthen us into the inner man, that Christ may make His
home in our heart, that we may be filled unto the fullness of
God. In Paul's prayer we see four divine titles: the Father, the
Spirit, Christ, and God. These four titles do not refer to four
different persons but to the same One, the same complete
Triune God. Paul had such a vision of God's New Testament
economy that even in his prayer he had the Triune God in
view. All the members need to be strengthened by the Father,
through the Spirit, into the inner man, in order that Christ
may make His home in their hearts. This will enable all the
members to apprehend this wonderful Person together. Our
goal is to apprehend together this wonderful Person in His
unlimited dimensions that we may be filled with the Triune
God unto His full expression.

In Colossians 2:9 we are told that in Christ dwells all the
fullness of the Godhead bodily. When this Christ comes to
make His home in our heart, He comes with all the fullness of
God, and He imparts to us all the fullness of God to such an
extent that we become the fullness of God, the expression of
God. Christ wants to make home in our hearts, to fill us with
His riches to such an extent that we, the church, may become
the full expression of God. This is to be filled unto all the fullness of God. When the riches are in God Himself they are His
riches, but when the riches of God are expressed they become
His fullness.

To apprehend the breadth, length, height, and depth, the
unlimited dimensions of Christ, requires all the saints, not
individually but corporately. No one can tell how broad is the
breadth, how long is the length, how high is the height, and
how deep is the depth. These are the universal dimensions
of Christ. Our Christ is immeasurable and unlimited. All

the saints must work together to apprehend the universal, unlimited dimensions of Christ, that they may be filled unto all the fullness of the Triune God. "Unto" in Greek means resulting in. We are filled resulting in the fullness of God. It is wrong to translate this word into "with" or "by." It is not with or by the fullness of God, but unto the fullness of God, resulting in the fullness of God. When Christ makes His home in your heart, occupying your entire inner being, this means that Christ is filling you with all His riches. Every corner, every avenue of our mind, our emotion, our will, and every inward part of our being is being occupied by this unsearchably rich Christ until we are filled resulting in the fullness, the expression, of the Godhead.

A cup may contain some water and it may be rich in water, but there is no expression of the water because the cup is not completely full of water. If the cup is filled with water until it is overflowing, this is the fullness, the expression, of the water. If you only have the riches without the fullness, there is no expression. We all need to let Christ with all His riches make His home in our hearts. The heart is a composition of our inner being, consisting of the mind, the will, the emotion, and the conscience. The heart, therefore, is composed of all the parts of the soul plus one part of the spirit, the conscience. When Christ with all His unsearchable riches makes home in our heart, this means that He is occupying every part of our inward being. His filling us from within with all His riches results in one thing—the full expression of God.

The Members of the Body
Keeping the Oneness of the Spirit

Ephesians 4:3 tells us that the members of the Body should keep the oneness of the Spirit. The Spirit is the oneness of the Body. We should not act, move, work, or speak without the Spirit. We must be people living, moving, walking, and having our being in the Spirit. Then we keep the oneness. If a husband and wife are not moving, living, and acting in the Spirit, there is no way that they can be one. When the husband and wife move, act, live, and even breathe in the Spirit, they are one. I have learned a secret in marriage life—that it is better for the couple not to talk if they are not in the Spirit. If a couple is not in the Spirit, when the husband says "west" the wife will say "east." When I was not in the Spirit, I was fearful of talking to my wife. When I was in the Spirit and she was in the Spirit we had the full freedom to talk and we were one. We must remember that we are one only when we are in the Spirit. When we are outside the Spirit it is better not to talk to keep the peace. The only way to keep the oneness of the Spirit is to be in the Spirit. There is no other way.

The Members of the Body
Not Grieving the Spirit

Ephesians 4:30 tells us that the members should not grieve the Spirit, in whom they were sealed unto the day of redemption. Once the Spirit gets into us, He is always with us and will never leave us. Even if we offend Him or insult Him, He remains within us. We cannot be divorced from the Spirit, but we can surely grieve Him. We have been sealed with the Holy Spirit and this sealing is going on continually unto the day of redemption. Since the day of our salvation, unto the day of the redemption of our body, this sealing is always taking place. Do not forget that this sealing brings us the divine element. Day after day the divine element is being added into our being and the divine mark within us is being made more striking, more evident, and God's ownership of us is strengthened more and more. This sealing brings us into the transfiguration of our body, which will be the redemption of our body. We should not be those who grieve the sealing Spirit.

The Spirit as the Word of God
Being the Sword for the Body
to Fight the Battle

We must realize that actually the Spirit *is* the Word of God. Ephesians 6:17 charges us to receive "the sword of the Spirit which is the word of God." The antecedent of which is Spirit, not sword, indicating that the Spirit is the Word of God, both of which are Christ (2 Cor. 3:17; Rev. 19:13). The

Bible is the Word of God, yet if we do not have the Spirit with us when we come to the Word of God in the Bible, the Bible is merely dead letters to us. When we have the Spirit with us, the Spirit with us makes the black and white dead letters the living Word of God. Therefore, the Spirit is the Word of God and such a Spirit is a sword, a weapon, for us to fight the battle against God's enemy to bring in His kingdom, which is the church. In Ephesians we see such a wonderful Person— the Triune God consummated in the Spirit to produce, to build up, to strengthen, and to enrich the church to live Christ, to express God, and to fight the battle for God's children to bring in His kingdom.

THE BOUNTIFUL SPIRIT OF JESUS CHRIST

In Philippians 1:19 the Apostle Paul uses a special expression—"the bountiful supply of the Spirit of Jesus Christ." The first mention of the Spirit is in Genesis 1:2 which tells us that the Spirit of God brooded upon the death waters. Philippians, however, refers to the Spirit of Jesus Christ. We must realize that these are not two Spirits. In creation the Spirit was the Spirit of God. However, after creation, incarnation, crucifixion, and resurrection, the Spirit of God is the Spirit of Jesus Christ. In our Christian experience the Spirit of God is no longer merely the Spirit of God, but He is now the enriched, compounded, processed, all-inclusive, life-giving Spirit—the Spirit of Jesus Christ.

The Spirit of Jesus and the Spirit of Christ

The Spirit of Jesus (Acts 16:7) includes Jesus' incarnation, humanity, human living, suffering, and crucifixion. The Spirit of Christ (Rom. 8:9) includes Christ's divinity, victory over death, resurrection, and power of resurrection. All these items added together issue in a compound. This is why we say that today the aggregate Spirit is a compound Spirit. It is compounded with the divine nature, the human nature, human living, human suffering, the all-inclusive death, Christ's victory over death, His resurrection, and the power of His resurrection. These are the elements of the compound, processed, all-inclusive Spirit. The Spirit of God in Genesis 1 was like a glass of plain water. Through the marvelous processes which the Triune God has gone through, many elements were added to this "water." Through the Triune God's incarnation, crucifixion, and resurrection, the Spirit of God has been compounded with divinity, humanity, human living, human suffering, crucifixion, resurrection, and the power of resurrection. Today the Spirit of Jesus Christ is the all-inclusive, processed, compound, life-giving, indwelling Spirit. In Him there is a bountiful supply! Do you need anything? Whatever you need, He is! He is the bountiful Spirit of Jesus Christ.

The Believers Living Christ and Magnifying Him

This bountiful Spirit of Jesus Christ is for the believers to live Christ and magnify Him (Phil. 1:20-21a). Nothing is as hard as living Christ. A person may get a Ph.D., but no one can graduate from living Christ. In order to live Christ, you are not adequate, you are not able, and you are not capable. To live Christ you need the bountiful supply of the Spirit of Jesus Christ. Every morning of every day you must learn to give yourself to this bountiful supply. You must trust in this bountiful supply and you must rely on this bountiful supply. The bountiful supply of the Spirit of Jesus Christ sustains you to live Christ.

In marriage life, if either the husband or the wife gives the other a long face, the other party forgets about Christ. The wife may have been enjoying Christ and living Christ all day until the husband gets home at 5:30 P.M. When the husband walks in the door he may not say anything; he only gives his wife a long face. Immediately the wife is bothered and Christ is gone. In this case, the wife did not live Christ, but she lived herself by reacting to her husband's long face. She reacted to her husband by giving him a longer face. Do not think that this is a small thing. It takes the strongest power, the bountiful supply of the Spirit of Jesus Christ, to deal with this small thing. To overcome the long face of your spouse is not easy, so we need the bountiful supply. The bountiful supply of the Spirit of Jesus Christ is for us to live Christ and to manifest Him in death or in life, in prison or in freedom. To make

Christ great in His expression we need the bountiful supply of the Spirit of Jesus Christ.

God Operating in the Believers
Both the Willing and Working

Philippians 2:12-16 shows us the bountiful Spirit of Jesus Christ as God operating in the believers both the willing and working, for them as luminaries to shine forth the word of life in the world, that they may work out their own salvation. It is God who operates in you the willing and the working. This is the Triune God, the processed God, not merely the God in creation. For God to create the universe was somewhat easy. When He said, "Let there be light," there was light. In creating the universe God did not operate, He only spoke things into being. In our Christian life, however, God needs to operate, to energize. A young Christian may have the thought of going to a movie. The Triune God, who is this aggregate Spirit, operates and struggles within him to keep him from going and to operate in him both the willing and working to carry out his salvation, to bring it to its ultimate conclusion.

Every day the processed Triune God suffers this struggling within us. To create the universe God spoke it into being. But if God says, "Let there be no movie," many believers still desire to go to the movie, so God has to operate within them. The only thing we need to do is to obey the inner operating God. He has to exercise His divine, everlasting patience. Some have said that the patience of the Chinese is endless. However, everlasting patience does not belong to the Chinese but to God. God surely exercises His everlasting patience with His chosen and redeemed people. This operating God operates in us both the inner willing and the outer working for His good pleasure. This God is the Spirit, as the Son, with the Father, the consummation of the Triune God, for the believers as luminaries to shine forth the word of life in this world that they may work out their own salvation.

We must realize that God's salvation is full of many sections. The initial section was our salvation from hell, from eternal perdition. Today, however, we need a practical, present salvation to save us from our temper, our "long face," our gossiping, and our going to the movies. We need to be saved from many things. We have to work out such a present, daily, and practical salvation for ourselves but not by our own strength. For a husband to overcome his wife's long face he needs the bountiful supply of the processed Triune God. This processed Triune God is operating in us for the inner willing and the outer working that we may be luminaries shining forth the word of God to work out our own daily, present, and practical salvation.

The Believers Gaining Christ and Being Found in Him

The bountiful Spirit of Jesus Christ is for the believers to gain Christ and be found in Him, having Him as the righteousness of God for the expression of God (Phil. 3:8-9). This is not to gain Christ positionally. Positionally, we have gained Christ already. Christ is ours, but now we have to gain Christ dispositionally, experientially. To gain Christ means to experience and enjoy Christ. We have to experience and enjoy Christ and be found, be seen, and be discovered by others that we are living in Christ. We should be those not having our own righteousness but having Christ as God's righteousness expressed from within us.

Empowering the Believers to Do All Things in Christ

Finally, the bountiful Spirit of Jesus Christ is to empower the believers to do all things in Christ (Phil 4:13). In this Triune, processed God as the life-giving Spirit, we are empowered to do all things for expressing Christ. The wonderful Person revealed in Ephesians and in Philippians is not merely Christ but the pneumatic Christ. He is not merely the Spirit of God but also the bountiful Spirit of Jesus Christ. He is the Spirit, as the Son, with the Father, being the consummation of the Triune God today in the church. Hallelujah for such a Person!

CHAPTER SIXTEEN

THE SPIRIT OF
THE PRACTICAL CHRISTIAN LIFE

Scripture Reading: Col. 1:8, 4; 1 Thes. 1:5-6; 4:3-8; 5:19; 2 Thes. 2:13-14; 1 Tim. 3:16; 4:1-3; Titus 3:5

The Spirit revealed in the seven books of the Bible from Colossians through Philemon is the all-inclusive, compound, processed, life-giving, indwelling Spirit as the consummation of the Triune God. It is difficult to arrive at a subject or a topic which can cover these seven books. Colossians reveals to us the all-inclusive Christ as the Head of the Body. The theme of 1 and 2 Thessalonians is a holy life for the church life. The subject of 1 Timothy is God's dispensation concerning the church, and the subject of 2 Timothy is the inoculation against the decline of the church. In Titus we see the maintenance of the order of the church, and Philemon is an illustration of the believers' equal status in the new man. The sum total subject of these seven books, however, is "the Spirit of the practical Christian life."

In the twenty-two books from Acts through Jude we see a full definition and explanation of a wonderful Person. This wonderful Person is the Triune God, the Father, the Son, and the Spirit, becoming a man in the likeness of the flesh of sin. After going through the process of incarnation, human living, crucifixion, and resurrection, this One became the all-inclusive, life-giving Spirit. He is defined and presented to us in Romans as the Spirit of life, in 1 Corinthians as the life-giving Spirit, in 2 Corinthians as the transforming Spirit, and in Galatians as the blessing of the gospel. The main blessing of the gospel is the all-inclusive, processed, compound, life-giving, indwelling Spirit. Ephesians is a book on the Spirit of the Body, and Philippians is a book on the bountiful Spirit of Jesus Christ. Now we want to see the all-inclusive Spirit in Colossians through Philemon for the practical Christian life.

THE SOURCE AND ELEMENT OF THE BELIEVERS' LOVE

The Spirit in Colossians is revealed as the source, the element, and the sphere of the believers' love toward all the saints in Christ the Head (1:4, 8). According to our natural understanding the matter of love is common, but according to the divine fact it is not common. Colossians 1:4 refers to the love which the saints in Colossae had unto all the saints; verse 8 reveals that their love to all the saints was the love in the Spirit. We would never imagine that in Colossians, which is a book on the all-inclusive Christ as the Head of the Body, the all-inclusive Spirit is defined and presented in such a "common way." According to our natural understanding it may be common, but actually it is very particular. For us to experience Christ as the Head of the Body we must have a love that is toward all the saints. The Greek word in verse 4 is *pan*. In America there is an airline called Pan American. *Pan* means covering everything. To experience Christ as the Head of the Body we need to have a love that is toward all the saints.

In my lifetime, I have traveled to many countries and I have contacted many different peoples. All of the peoples of the world have their distinctive characteristics. Our Lord has redeemed men out of every tribe and tongue and people and nation (Rev. 5:9). We must ask ourselves whether or not we can love all these people whom God has redeemed. When I was a young boy, the young people of China were infused with a hatred toward Japan since Japan invaded, damaged, and subdued our country. Now that I am a Christian, however, I have to love my Japanese brothers. History also tells us that in Europe, Germany, Britain, and France were always fighting. How can the redeemed peoples from these three countries love one another? You must even ask yourself if you love everyone and feel happy about everyone in the church at your locality.

In ourselves we can never have a love which is toward all the saints. This love is in the Spirit. Many secular historians have said that Christianity is a religion of love. Surely God's people should be a people of love, but of what kind of love? Should we love others with our human and natural love? We need a love that will love all kinds of peoples from all kinds of cultures. Our love is not this kind of love. It has to be the love in the Spirit. The Spirit is the source, the element, the very essence and sphere of such a love. After being a Christian for over fifty-nine years, by the Lord's mercy, I can testify that I love all the saints from all the different countries. This love, however, is not my love but the love in the Spirit.

The church is the Body of Christ, which is also the new man. For this new man the basic need is unique—His love. For people to stay together without love is very difficult. How could a husband and wife remain together without love? Neither of them could endure such a marriage. For human society, the basic need is love. How can different peoples with different tongues of different races and of different colors be one Body and be one new man? It is impossible without love. Only love unites and only love makes all of us one new man.

Many would say that Christianity is a religion of universal love, but actually our human and natural love is not universal. There is a love, however, that we Christians have in the Spirit which loves all the different members of the Lord's Body. We love all the brothers in the Lord from all cultures, from all races, and from all countries. This is not possible by our natural love, but there is the love in the Spirit, who is a wonderful Person. The New Testament is not a book of doctrine or a book teaching us universal love. What the New Testament reveals to us is a Person. This love is a Person who is the all-inclusive Spirit; in Him there is such a love. He is the source, the element, and the sphere of this love. If you live in Him, He is the universal love that causes you, makes you, and stirs you up to love all the unlovable saints.

THE REALITY OF THE GOSPEL

In 1 Thessalonians 1:5-6 we are told that the gospel preached by the apostle was not only preached in word but also in power and in the Holy Spirit. The Spirit in 1 Thessalonians is revealed as the reality of the gospel preached by the apostles. Verse 6 tells us that the believers accepted the gospel with joy of the Holy Spirit. The gospel was in the Spirit, and the joy with which the believers accepted the gospel was of the Holy Spirit. On the preacher's side the gospel was in the Spirit, and on the receivers' side the joy was of the Spirit. If there were no Spirit, there would be no reality of the gospel and no real joy to receive the gospel. If I did not have the assurance that my ministry of the Word was in the Spirit, I would not do it. If I minister the Word outside the Spirit, my ministry is in vain. When I speak in the Spirit, however, it can never be in vain because the Spirit is the reality of my speaking.

GIVEN BY GOD TO THE BELIEVERS
FOR SANCTIFICATION

In 1 Thessalonians 4:3-8 we see that the Spirit is given by God to the believers for sanctification versus fornication. This sanctification is in the Spirit. We may say that the sanctification is to make us holy. We also have to realize, however, what it is to be holy. You may be very moral, very ethical, very pure, very clean, and living for others, but you still may not be holy. To be holy is to be absolutely for God. You may be good, moral, ethical, pure, and kind, but if you are not for God you are not holy; instead you are common. You must be absolutely for God to be holy.

Fornication is to use the body for something other than God, while sanctification is to use the body absolutely for God. Sanctification is versus fornication. No one could commit fornication if they were using their body absolutely for God. We may not commit fornication physically, but spiritually speaking every one of us has committed fornication. The reason for this is because we do not use our being for God but for something else. Spiritual fornication is not using yourself for God. You use yourself for things other than God.

How could we be a person who is not for anything else other than God? Seemingly, this is impossible, but we can do this in the Spirit. When you exchange words with your wife or husband, you have to realize that in principle this is committing spiritual fornication. Your lips, your tongue, and your entire mouth should be absolutely for God. It should not be used for exchanging words with the other party in the marriage life. If you use your mouth for something else other than God, this is spiritual fornication. Your mouth should be absolutely for God and not for anything else. To gossip is a kind of spiritual fornication. The only way to escape this kind of spiritual fornication is to be in the Spirit. When we are in the Spirit, we would never use our mouth to gossip and we would never let our mouth exchange words with the other party in our marriage.

First Thessalonians 4:3-8 is a strong portion of the Word telling us that sanctification in the Spirit is versus fornication. To use our entire being for God is only possible by being in the Spirit. When we are in our mentality, we have many things to gossip about. When we are in our emotions, we are impelled to speak about things other than God. To use our mouth for something other than God is a kind of spiritual fornication, and the only way to be sanctified unto God absolutely is by being in the Spirit.

THE BELIEVERS NOT QUENCHING THE SPIRIT

First Thessalonians 5:19 says, "Do not quench the Spirit." Before we were saved, we did not have any kind of feeling that someone was moving in us. Since we have been saved, however, it seems that we have someone else within us all the time. Sometimes it may seem that someone is watching over you or "tailing" you. Wherever you go He goes, just like a shadow. Before you were saved you were really alone and nobody was with you. Since you have been saved, though, One is with you all the time. You may like to go to a movie, but someone within you says, "Don't go." It seems as if there is always someone around you, above you, behind you, or within you speaking to you. This is the wonderful One, the Savior, the Redeemer, Jesus Christ, the Son, as the embodiment of the Triune God, including the Father, the Son, and the Spirit, in His humanity and with His human living as the all-inclusive Spirit. This One is the best detective; He knows every detail of your life. Even before you speak a word He knows what you will speak. The Apostle Paul told us not to quench this Spirit. This Spirit makes our spirit burning (Rom. 12:11) and our gifts flaming (2 Tim. 1:6), so we should not quench Him. We need to go along with this Spirit.

SALVATION IN SANCTIFICATION OF THE SPIRIT

In 2 Thessalonians 2:13-14 we see salvation in sanctification of the Spirit unto the obtaining of the glory of Christ to express God. God chose us unto salvation, but the salvation referred to here is not the salvation from perdition or from God's condemnation. God has chosen us unto a particular kind of salvation, and this salvation is in the sanctification of the Spirit. This is to be saved by being sanctified by this all-inclusive Spirit all the time. When we are going shopping, we need the salvation which is in the sanctification of the Spirit. When we go shopping, most of the time we are "going downhill." Many times while we are going up in the elevators or escalators in the department stores, actually we are going downhill. Sometimes when we want to purchase something, there is One within us telling us not to buy it and even telling us to go home. The only One who can save us from purchasing things according to our lusts is the sanctifying Spirit.

Also, who can save us from the temptation of exchanging words with our spouse? It must be Jesus Christ, the Son of God, as the embodiment of the Triune God, consummating in the Spirit. This Spirit separates you from your habit and desire to exchange words, and this is the sanctifying. We daily need this kind of sanctifying salvation. We need to be saved from losing our temper and from the desire to gossip on the telephone. To many sisters the telephone is very "sticky." Once these sisters pick up the telephone, it is hard for them to put it down. The only One who can save us from this is the sanctifying Spirit. We need a daily, practical, and present salvation, not by mighty power or miracles, but by the quiet, gentle, mild, sanctifying Spirit. He does not fight us nor does He force us not to do certain things. He is like a dove within us. We need such a salvation, and God has chosen us unto this salvation in the sanctifying grace of the Spirit.

The result of such a salvation is the obtaining of the glory of Christ to express God. When we are saved by the sanctifying Spirit, we are people under glory, and this glory is for the expression of God. Many of us really love the Lord, but in our daily lives when we go shopping, when we gossip, and when we argue there is no obtaining of the glory of Christ. The glory of Christ is to be God's sons, possessing God's life and nature to express Him. If we would be saved by the sanctifying Spirit daily, we will surely bear the glory of Christ to express God as sons of God, possessing His life and partaking of His nature.

VINDICATING THE MANIFESTATION OF GOD IN THE FLESH

According to 1 Timothy 3:16 the Spirit is vindicating the manifestation of God in the flesh. This transpired in Christ while He was on this earth. He was God manifested in the flesh and this was vindicated and verified by this Spirit. The same principle applies to us, the church, today. God is manifested in our flesh, but this has to be verified, justified, and vindicated by the all-inclusive Spirit. This means that only when we live in the all-inclusive Spirit, do we have a kind of vindication, justification, and verification that God is manifested in us, the church.

WARNING THE BELIEVERS OF APOSTASY

In 1 Timothy 4:1-3 the Spirit speaks to the believers, warning them of apostasy in later times. This is the Spirit who dwells in our spirit and speaks to us there (Romans 8:9-11, 16). We need to exercise our spirit that it may become keen and clear to listen to the Spirit's speaking and be kept from the deceiving spirits and teachings of demons.

DWELLING IN THE BELIEVERS THROUGH WHOM
THEY GUARD THE GOOD DEPOSIT

In 2 Timothy 1:14 the Spirit is also dwelling in the believers through whom they guard the good deposit. Since we were saved we have received many things from God into us as a kind of deposit. This is just like a deposit in a bank. Within us and especially within our spirit, we have a divine deposit. God's life, God's Spirit, and all the precious truths we have seen in the Lord's recovery have been deposited into our being. How can we safeguard this deposit? It is only through the Holy Spirit who dwells in us. If we are a person acting, behaving, and having our life in the Spirit, all that has been deposited into our being will be guarded. If we forget about the Spirit and walk in our flesh and according to our mentality, we will immediately be the same as the nations who are apart from God (Eph. 4:17-18). If this were the case, there would be no safeguarding of the good things deposited in our being. We need to safeguard the good deposit by the Spirit.

THE RENEWING OF THE SPIRIT FOR OUR SALVATION

Finally, Titus 3:5 tells us that God saved us through the washing of regeneration and renewing of the Holy Spirit. This Spirit began to renew us from our regeneration and is renewing us continuously every day and all day to make us a new man with the divine life. Whenever we gather together for the ministry of the Word in a conference, we experience the renewing of the Spirit, and we go back to our localities as renewed persons. This is the saving work of the sanctifying Spirit. Actually, His sanctifying is His renewing.

THE SPIRIT IN COLOSSIANS THROUGH PHILEMON

Through all the points we have covered in these seven books, we can see that the Spirit in Colossians through Philemon is the Spirit of the practical Christian life. The first item of the practical Christian life is the love in the Spirit toward all the saints until we reach the last item, which is the daily renewing by the all-inclusive Spirit. This is our practical Christian life. In these seven books the all-inclusive Spirit is such a Spirit.

Chapter Seventeen

THE ETERNAL SPIRIT OF GRACE
AND THE SPIRIT OF ENVY

Scripture Reading: Heb. 1:2; 2:3-4; 3:7-8a; 6:4; 9:8, 14; 10:15, 29; John 1:14, 17; 3:16; 1 Cor. 1:2, 9; 15:45; 2 Cor. 13:14; Col. 1:12; Philem. 25; James 4:5

THE SUPERIORITY OF CHRIST

In this chapter we want to see in the book of Hebrews the New Testament economy to dispense a wonderful Person into our being. The New Testament is not composed of a number of books concerning doctrine, but it is a complete revelation of a wonderful Person. At the apostles' time, however, most of the believers were Jews who came out of Judaism, a strong, high, and profound religion. The Jewish religion had the highest doctrine and all of their basic doctrine was real. This religion was structured mainly of five crucial items: God, the angels, Moses (who gave the law), Aaron (the high priest), and the old covenant. No other religion has such crucial items, but all these items are merely doctrines in Judaism.

The Living God

Even at the time of the Lord Jesus, the Jewish leaders had all these five items as doctrine, yet they did not have the living God. In Hebrews Paul compared this wonderful Person, the Triune God Himself, with all the five crucial items of Judaism. The Jews had God in doctrine but not in Person (Heb. 1:2, 8). In Hebrews Paul presented, not the study of God or the doctrine of God, but God Himself, the Person of God. He presented "theos," not theology.

Superior to the Angels

This wonderful Person, the Son of God, Jesus Christ, who is God Himself, the Triune God, embodied in a man is much superior to the angels. How can angels who are merely servants to God (Heb. 1:7) and even servants to God's people (Heb. 1:14) compare with such a wonderful Person?

Superior to Moses

This One is also much superior to Moses (Heb. 3:3). Moses was a faithful servant in the house of God, but this wonderful Person is the Master of the house of God. Moses brought in the law, but this wonderful One, whose riches are unsearchable (Eph. 3:8), brings in grace and reality (John 1:17).

Superior to Aaron

This wonderful One is also much superior to Aaron (Heb. 4:14-15). Aaron lived and died, but this One, as the great High Priest surpassing the heavens, lived, died, and lives again forever; He is living forever to intercede for us (Heb. 7:25). Aaron was a high priest serving according to the ordinances of the law, but this One is the High Priest, who passed through the heavens, ministering by the endless life (Heb. 7:3, 16).

The Mediator of a Superior Covenant

Finally, this wonderful One has enacted the new covenant, which is much better than the old covenant. The old covenant was of dead letters, but the new covenant is of life. This One is also the Mediator, the Executor, of the better covenant of life (Heb. 8:6).

DISTRIBUTIONS OF THE HOLY SPIRIT

Hebrews 2:3-4 tells us that God bore witness to so great a salvation by distributions of the Holy Spirit. The distributions of the Holy Spirit are the things including the Spirit Himself, which the Holy Spirit distributes to those who receive salvation by believing in Christ. This also includes the imparting of the divine life into the believers. All of us who have believed in the Lord Jesus must realize that the divine life has been distributed into our being with the Holy Spirit who has been given to us. This is the first basic distribution of the Spirit. The Holy Spirit Himself is a distribution into us. A Person has been distributed into us. After we were saved, it seemed that One was always moving within us. We did not have this kind of experience before being saved, but after we were saved we had this sensation. The greatest distribution into our being is a Person. A wonderful Person has been distributed into our being.

In our experience there are also other distributions of the Holy Spirit. Many times while I am speaking, there is a distribution going on to give me the instant feeling, the instant enlightenment, the instant utterance, and the instant illustrations. These are the distributions of the Spirit to confirm the great salvation we have received. The book of Hebrews opens with the speaking of the Son but continues with the distributions of the Holy Spirit. The Son in chapter one is the Spirit in chapter two.

THE SPEAKING SPIRIT

Hebrews emphasizes that today this wonderful One is the Spirit. In the Old Testament God spoke to the fathers in the prophets, but in the New Testament God speaks to us in the Son (Heb. 1:1-2). The opening words of chapter one introduce us to the Son, but from this time onward Hebrews refers to the Spirit. Hebrews 3:7-8a says, "Wherefore, even as the Holy Spirit says, Today if you hear His voice, do not harden your hearts." This shows us again that the Son in chapter one is also the Spirit in chapter three. God speaks in the Son in chapter one, but in chapter three the Holy Spirit is speaking.

Chapter one indicates that in the New Testament age God speaks to us in the Son. In the original Greek there is no article before "Son"; therefore, we can say that in the New Testament God speaks to us in Son. Darby's New Translation of Hebrews 1:2 says that at the end of these days God "has spoken to us in [*the Person of the*] Son." To say that God speaks in the Son means that God speaks in the Person of the Son.

In the Old Testament God spoke through certain men, but

in the New Testament God Himself came to speak in the way of incarnation. John 1:14 tells us that the Word, which was God Himself, became flesh. The incarnation of God means God becoming flesh. This is the way that God came. He came to speak in a man. This man is the Son of God, Jesus Christ. God's coming to speak in this man meant God came to speak in the Son, in the Person of the Son. The Person of the Son is God Himself. The main item in a man is the person or the personality. In a man there is a person, but you cannot say that in a person is a man. This means that, in Person, God is one with the Son. In the Son there is a Person. The Person of the Son is the Father. This is what it means when we say that God speaks in the Person of the Son.

Hebrews 1:2 indicates that in the New Testament God speaks in the Person of the Son, but in the rest of the book of Hebrews, there is not one verse which tells us that the Son speaks. The introduction of the book of Hebrews is on God's speaking in the Son, but Hebrews 3:7 shows us that the Holy Spirit is speaking. Actually, in the rest of the book of Hebrews the Spirit is the One who is speaking. This indicates that God in the Son and the Son as the Spirit is the speaking One. Thus, the Divine Trinity is the speaking One as the Spirit, who is the consummation of the Divine Trinity in the book of Hebrews. The Divine Trinity is God in the Son and the Son as the Spirit. In the book of Hebrews the Father is speaking in the Son as the Spirit. We can also say that the Spirit is speaking as the Son with the Father. Hebrews tells us that God speaks in the Son, but this book also indicates that the Spirit speaks. Therefore, God speaks in the Son as the Spirit, and eventually the Spirit as the Son with the Father is speaking.

THE SPIRIT'S SPEAKING CONCERNING
THE WAY TO ENTER INTO THE HOLY OF HOLIES

The Holy Spirit shows by the Holy Place and the Holy of Holies that the way of the Holy of Holies has not been manifested while the first tabernacle still has its standing (Heb. 9:8). The Holy Spirit tells us that when the old tabernacle still remained, the way to enter the Holy of Holies was not yet opened. Also, the Spirit, by this illustration, tells us that the way to enter into the Holy of Holies has been opened and that the old tabernacle has been removed. Today we do not have the old tabernacle but the new tabernacle— Christ. In the book of Hebrews the tabernacle is Christ and the offerings today are all Christ. Christ is realized as the Spirit, so when you have the Spirit, as a partaker of the Spirit, you have the tabernacle and all the offerings. The New Testament is a book of such a wonderful, unlimited Person replacing everything of the Old Testament. This Person does not replace God because He is God Himself, but He replaces Moses, Aaron, the tabernacle, and all the offerings, and His covenant replaces the old covenant. As the eternal Spirit He is everything and everywhere and He is not objective. This Spirit is always subjective within us. This eternal Spirit as the consummation of the processed Triune God has become our eternal enjoyment.

PARTAKERS OF THE SPIRIT

Hebrews 6:4 tells us that the believers have become partakers of the Holy Spirit. This shows us that we are the partakers of a wonderful Person. The Holy Spirit is the One as the Son, with the Father, being the consummation of the Triune God. We are the partakers of such a One. We have not only received the Holy Spirit, but we are now partakers of the Holy Spirit. As long as we have the Holy Spirit, we are His partakers. He is a priceless treasure.

Hebrews was written to show the Jewish believers that the believers in Christ have this wonderful One as a treasure who is much more precious than the angels, than Moses, than Aaron, and than the old covenant. This treasure is the all-inclusive Christ. In our practical experience, however, this all-inclusive Christ is the all-inclusive Spirit. Hebrews does not tell us that we are the partakers of the all-inclusive Christ, but that we are the partakers of the Holy Spirit. The Spirit is the consummation of the Triune God, and the Spirit is the reaching to us of the Triune God. Without being the Spirit, the Father cannot reach us. Without being the Spirit, the Son, Christ, cannot reach us. The reaching of the Triune

God to us is the Spirit, the consummation of the Triune God. This Spirit is much superior to the angels, much superior to Aaron, and He is the reality of the new covenant, which is much superior to the old covenant; we are the partakers of this Spirit. As long as we are the partakers of this Spirit, we partake and enjoy the processed Triune God with all His riches.

THE ETERNAL SPIRIT

The book of Hebrews tells us that this Spirit is the eternal Spirit. Christ as the unique sacrifice offered Himself to God through the eternal Spirit (Heb. 9:14). This fact insures or secures the offering of Christ for eternity. This offering accomplished an eternal redemption because it is an eternal offering. The eternal Spirit has made the death of Christ eternally efficacious. The accomplishment of His death covers all the believing Old Testament saints and New Testament believers including you and me. Although He died on Calvary nearly two thousand years ago and many miles away from us, that death is applicable and available to us because that death was accomplished through the eternal Spirit. His death is an eternal death which is available and applicable to all persons in any place and at any time.

In Hebrews 9:14 we again see the Trinity—Christ, God, and the eternal Spirit. Christ offering Himself to God through the eternal Spirit is a great mystery. Christ, the Spirit, and God are one. Based upon this, we could say that the Triune God offered Himself as an offering through Himself to Himself.

Hebrews 9:14 does not say that the eternal Christ offered Himself to the eternal God through the Spirit, but it says Christ offered Himself to God through the eternal Spirit. This offering is eternal and real because it is offered through the Spirit. Today when we touch the Spirit we touch this offering. Since we are the partakers of the Spirit, we are also partakers of the unique offering, partakers of an eternal redemption. Once you become a partaker of the Spirit, you partake of everything which is related to the Spirit.

We must realize that the Lord labored, worked, and lived

on this earth through the eternal Spirit. Whatever the Lord accomplished and experienced in His living, labor, and work has been made eternal by the eternal Spirit. This eternal Spirit is all-inclusive and we are the partakers of such a Spirit. He is the Spirit, as the Son, with the Father being the consummation of the processed Triune God in the church.

We believers do have this eternal Spirit and we are the partakers of this Spirit. He comprises Christ, God, the eternal life, and the eternal redemption. He comprises everything because He is the eternal Spirit through whom the Triune God offered Himself to Himself as the eternal offering.

THE SPIRIT OF GRACE

This book also tells us that the Spirit is the Spirit of grace (Heb. 10:29). The Spirit of grace simply means that the Triune God in the Son as the Spirit becomes our enjoyment. The Spirit is the reaching of the Triune God to us. The Son could not get into us until He became the Spirit. He was among the disciples, but He needed to go through death and resurrection to become the life-giving Spirit (John 14:16-20; 1 Cor. 15:45). Then He was able to breathe Himself as the Holy Breath into the disciples for their enjoyment (John 20:22).

When the Bible uses expressions such as the Spirit of grace, the Spirit of life, and the Spirit of reality, this means that the Spirit is grace, life, and reality. Therefore, when we are the partakers of the Holy Spirit, this means that we are the partakers of the Holy Spirit as grace. The Holy Spirit is our possession and grace is our possession. It is always better to pray, "Thank You Lord for another day, a new day, and thank You that I have the grace to live You today." The Spirit of grace is the eternal Spirit; hence, the grace is eternal. The grace we received is the eternal grace which is the eternal, unlimited Spirit. It is inexhaustible.

THE DEFINITION OF GRACE

The Gospel of John reveals that God came in the way of incarnation. The Word, who was God, became flesh and tabernacled among us, full of grace (John 1:14). *Hymns,* #497 tells us that grace in its highest definition is God in the Son to be enjoyed by us. Grace is God in the Son for our enjoyment. Many of us enjoy eating steak. Steak is beef and beef is a small part of a big cow. The only way such a big cow could be our enjoyment is by processing it. The cow must first be killed and then cut into pieces. Cutting alone, however, is not adequate. These pieces of steak must be cooked. After such a long process, the beef is now available to you. In like manner, for God to be our enjoyment in the Son, He must be processed.

We have seen that the Word was God, and this Word became flesh, full of grace. John 1:17 tells us that the law was given through Moses, but grace came through Jesus Christ. John 3:16 tells us that "God so loved the world that He gave His only begotten Son." God has given us a unique gift, and this gift is nothing less than His only begotten Son. John 3:16 is directly related to John 1:14. God gave His Son to us by incarnation. If God had never become a man, how could He have given His Son to us? God gave His Son to us by becoming a man. Actually John 1:14 explains John 3:16, and John 3:16 defines John 1:14. By putting these two verses together we have the right understanding of the divine fact that God has given Himself in the Person of the Son by the way of incarnation. Although the Son is such a gift, before our receiving of Him He is not grace to us. When we receive Him, He immediately becomes the grace.

Someone may give you a gift of cheesecake. Cheesecake is a gift of cheese. You may say that the "person" of the cake is cheese. This cheese is given to us in the form of a cake. Jesus Christ was the form, the "cake." The Person of this cake is God. God gave Himself in the Person of the Son as a gift to us by becoming a man. The cheesecake is a wonderful gift but it cannot become our enjoyment unless we eat it. If we eat it, our eating of the cake becomes our enjoyment. God in the Son is only a gift, not grace yet. When this gift is enjoyed by you it is no longer merely a gift but grace. Before your enjoyment, the cheesecake was a gift, but after your enjoyment, the cheesecake becomes grace. After our eating, the gift becomes grace, enjoyment. The gift has been transfigured into grace.

THE GIVER, THE GIFT, AND THE ENJOYMENT

In John 1:1 we see God and in John 1:14 the Word who is God became flesh. The Son in His humanity is the flesh. In John 1:17 we see that grace came through Jesus Christ. Grace is the enjoyment of the gift. The giver was God, the gift was the Son, and the enjoyment is the grace. John 1:1, 14, and 17 unveil the Divine Trinity. The Father is the giver, the Son is the gift and the Spirit is the gift applied and enjoyed— the grace (Acts 2:38; 10:45; Heb. 10:29). John 3:16 tells us that God gave His Son. This shows us God is the giver and the Son is the gift. John 3:34 also tells us that the Son, who is the gift, gives the Spirit without measure. The giver gives the gift, and the gift gives the Spirit. This is the enjoyment. Also, in John 15:26 the Lord tells us that He will send the Comforter "from with" (lit.) the Father. The Son sends the Spirit as the Comforter from with the Father, and the Comforter proceeds from with the Father to us. In this verse we see that the Father is the source as the giver and the Son as the gift is the second giver. The Comforter, the Spirit, is the One who is our enjoyment, and this enjoyment is grace.

First Corinthians 1:2 refers to "all those who call upon the name of our Lord Jesus Christ in every place, theirs and ours." This simply means that this very Christ is yours and mine. This is wonderful! If you bought a house, you would like to tell your friends that it is yours. Perhaps you would feel glorious that such a big house is actually yours. Have you ever realized, however, that in the universe you have One that is yours? We need to call upon the name of our Lord Jesus Christ who is yours and who is mine. A little baby only cares for his mother. Babies do not care for mansions, cars, diamonds, or gold. As long as a baby has his mother, everything is all right with him. It does not even matter that much to the baby where he is just as long as his mother is there with him. As Christians we need to be like the little babes who only care for Christ.

We all need to say happily, triumphantly, and rejoicingly— "Jesus is mine!" We all know the familiar hymn that says, "Blessed assurance, Jesus is mine; Oh, what a foretaste of glory divine!" The chorus of this hymn says, "This is my story, this is my song, Praising my Savior all the day long" (*Hymns,* #308). We are not praising the Lord all the day long for a good house, for an expensive car, or for a heavenly mansion with golden streets and pearly gates. We are praising the Lord all the day long for the fact that Jesus is ours. We are those who call on the name of our Lord Jesus Christ in every place, who is both theirs and ours. To fully understand 1 Corinthians 1:2, you need John 1:1, 14, and 17, John 3:16 and 34, and John 15:26. Also, 1 Corinthians 1:9 tells us that we have been called into the fellowship of His Son, Jesus Christ our Lord. The Greek word for fellowship means joint participation, common participation. God has called us into the participation in His Son. We could even say that God has called us into the enjoyment of His Son.

In 1 Corinthians 15:45 we see that "the last Adam became a life-giving Spirit." John 1:14 tells us who the last Adam is. The Word which was God became flesh, and this flesh is the last Adam. The last Adam is the last Man in the flesh. This One who was the last Adam in the flesh became the enjoyment because He became a life-giving Spirit. This Spirit is not the giver but the gift enjoyed—the enjoyment. God is the giver, the Son is the gift, and the Spirit is the enjoyment.

The basic problem among many of today's Christians is that they only have the giver and the gift. They do not experience the Spirit as their enjoyment. We Christians may come together to worship God and to praise the Lord without the Spirit. If this is the case, we worship in deadness and we pray, not in life but in death. As Christians we believe in Jesus Christ and we worship God, but we must ask ourselves whether or not we have tasted the Triune God. For example, cheesecake is wonderful but have you eaten it? Have you tasted it and has it become your enjoyment? If you have never eaten it, you have the cheesecake in vain. All of us must see that we must come to the Spirit. The Son of God is not a separate Person from the Spirit; rather, the Spirit is the transfiguration of the Son. The Son is the embodiment of the Triune God and the Spirit is the consummation of the Triune

God. This means that the Triune God has been consummated in this Spirit for our enjoyment.

When we call on the name of the Lord Jesus we do not get the Son nor the Father directly. When we call on the name of the Lord we get the Spirit. We all can testify that whenever we call "O Lord Jesus!", we get the Spirit. Whether we repent or we praise the principle is the same. We may say, "O Lord Jesus, I repent from my sins," or "Lord Jesus, I praise You." The point is that whenever we call on Him we get the Spirit, and the Spirit is the Person of the Lord Jesus. If I call out a certain person's name, that person will come to me if he is real. When we call on the Lord Jesus, the Spirit comes because the Spirit is the Person of Jesus. Even in 1 Corinthians we can see that God gave us Christ as our portion, and we have been called by God into the enjoyment of this Person. The very enjoyment of this Person is the Spirit. This Person was the last Adam and this last Adam eventually became the life-giving Spirit.

Oranges cannot be swallowed whole by a person. The orange must first be sliced and then the slices are placed into the mouth. When the mouth chews the slices they become orange juice to get into the person who is eating them. God may be considered as a big orange and Christ may be considered as the orange slices. The juice is the Spirit. The orange juice is the extract of the orange, and the extract of the orange is the "spirit" of the orange. In like manner, the Spirit of God is the extract of God. When we have the Father, it is like having a big orange. When we believe in the Son, this is like having many orange slices which are still outside of us. When we receive these slices into us as juice, we get the enjoyment. This is the experience of the Spirit which all of us must have. The all-inclusive Christ as the portion of the saints (Col. 1:12) becomes our enjoyment as the Spirit.

We have already seen that in the book of Hebrews God speaks in the Son and eventually, the actual speaker in the book of Hebrews is the Spirit. Furthermore, there is another verse in Hebrews which is more excellent and wonderful than John 3:16 according to our experience—this verse is Hebrews 6:4. John 3:16 tells us that God loved us and gave us His only begotten Son that we may have eternal life. This is wonderful, but Hebrews 6:4 tells us that we have become partakers of the Holy Spirit. This verse does not tell us we are partakers of material blessings, such as good homes, high degrees, or high positions. We, the believers, are the partakers of the Holy Spirit. The Spirit is the totality, the sum total, the aggregate, the consummation, of the Triune God. We all need to see that we have become partakers of the Holy Spirit, who is the totality of the Triune God!

NOT INSULTING THE SPIRIT OF GRACE

Hebrews 10:29 warns us not to insult the Spirit of grace. Ephesians 4:30 tells us not to grieve the Holy Spirit of God, which means to make Him unhappy by disobeying Him. However, to insult, despise, put aside, ignore, or neglect the Spirit is more serious. None of us should do this. We all need to experience the Spirit as the totality of the Triune God for our enjoyment.

LOVE, GRACE, AND FELLOWSHIP

In 1 Corinthians we saw that Christ is ours and that we have been called into the participation in this portion, who as the last Adam became the life-giving Spirit. The conclusion to Paul's second Epistle to the Corinthians says, "The grace of the Lord Jesus Christ, and the love of God, and the fellowship of the Holy Spirit be with you all" (13:14). Love, grace, and fellowship are altogether wrapped up with the Divine Trinity. Love is the very source, the very substance or essence of grace. This is just like cheese being the essence of cheesecake. Love is the essence of the grace of Christ, and the fellowship of the Spirit is the enjoyment. The love is the essence of the grace, the grace becomes our enjoyment, and this enjoyment is the fellowship. Love is with the Father as the source, grace is with the Son as the course, and enjoyment is with the Spirit as the very consummation.

GRACE WITH OUR SPIRIT

Finally, Philemon 25 says, "The grace of the Lord Jesus Christ be with your spirit." This verse does not say that the grace of the Lord Jesus Christ is with our strong mind, our strong will, or our fluctuating emotions. The grace of the Lord Jesus Christ is with our spirit. This verse proves that the grace of the Lord must be the Spirit because it is with our spirit. God is Spirit and those who worship Him must worship in spirit (John 4:24). Only our spirit can participate in the Spirit. For example, I am not able to enjoy cheesecake by looking or even by smelling. Neither can I enjoy cheesecake by doing scientific research to find out the vitamins, the ingredients, and the elements for the cheesecake. The only way to enjoy the cheesecake is to use my mouth to eat it. In like manner, we need to use our spirit to enjoy the consummation of the Triune God. The grace of the Lord Jesus Christ be with your spirit. God is the giver, the Son is the gift, and the Spirit is the enjoyment in our spirit.

THE SPIRIT OF ENVY

James 4:5 says that "the Spirit who dwells in us longs to envy." James mentions God's indwelling Spirit negatively concerning the abolishing of the friendship of the world. This indwelling Spirit always envies when He sees us loving something other than God. When you love the world or any material thing other than God, the indwelling Spirit envies. He longs to see you loving God absolutely just like a husband. When a husband sees his wife loving someone else other than him, this husband longs to envy. God as the indwelling Spirit is our Husband and He longs to envy when He sees that we love something, someone, or some matter other than Him. This requires us to deal with whatever we love other than God. The word "dwells" in James 4:5 can also be translated "makes His home." The indwelling Spirit makes His home in us that He may occupy our entire being (cf. Eph. 3:17) for God, causing us to be wholly for our Husband.

CHAPTER EIGHTEEN

THE SPIRIT OF CHRIST

Scripture Reading: 1 Pet. 1:1-2, 10-12; 4:13-14; 2 Pet. 1:20-21

A WONDERFUL PERSON

Thus far, we have seen that the twenty-seven books of the New Testament reveal a wonderful Person. This Person is mysterious, excellent, marvelous, and wonderful. The focus of the New Testament is this living Person.

THE BELIEVERS BEING CHOSEN
IN SANCTIFICATION OF THE SPIRIT

Since we all believed in the Lord Jesus, we became members of this marvelous Person. We were chosen by God the Father in eternity past. This was done according to God the Father's foreknowledge, and is carried out in time in the sanctification of the Spirit (1 Pet. 1:1-2). All the believers in Christ were chosen "according to the foreknowledge of God the Father, in sanctification of the Spirit, unto obedience and sprinkling of the blood of Jesus Christ" (1 Pet. 1:2). God chose us before the foundation of the world, in eternity past (Eph. 1:4). The divine foreknowledge was exercised, and the sanctification of the Spirit follows unto the obedience of faith in Christ. Our believing in Christ results from the Spirit's sanctifying work. We were sanctified, separated, by the Spirit unto the obedience and sprinkling of the blood of Jesus Christ. The issue of the Spirit's sanctification is our participating in the sprinkling of the blood of Jesus Christ. Sanctification brought us to the sprinkling of the blood shed by the Savior on the cross and separates us unto this divine provision. We are now the redeemed ones. We were chosen by

God the Father, sanctified by the Spirit, and sprinkled by the blood of Jesus Christ. This is marvelous and wonderful in the full, complete, perfect, and eternal salvation of and by the Trinity. We are no longer people who were merely created by God, but we were chosen by God the Father, sanctified by God the Spirit, and sprinkled by God the Son.

THE SPIRIT OF CHRIST IN THE PROPHETS

First Peter 1:10-11, furthermore, tells us that the Spirit of Christ in the prophets made clear to them concerning Christ's sufferings and glories. The Spirit of Christ is the Spirit of God. The Spirit of God who is the Holy Spirit is also called in the New Testament age the Spirit and the Spirit of Christ. This is the same Spirit with different divine titles, and every title carries a particular denotation. The titles "the Spirit of God" and "the Spirit of Christ" denote that the Spirit conveys God and conveys Christ. For example, a cup of coffee or a glass of milk denotes that the cup conveys coffee and the glass conveys milk to the one who drinks. In like manner, the Spirit of God conveys God, and the Spirit of Christ conveys Christ. The title "the Spirit" is an all-inclusive title. This is the unique, complete, perfect, and full Spirit. Also, the Spirit of God denotes that the Spirit is God, and the Spirit of Christ denotes that the Spirit is Christ. Expressions like *the life of God* or *the love of God* denote that life is God and that love is God. The Son of God also denotes that the Son is God (John 5:18). On the one hand, the Lord Jesus was the Son of God, and on the other hand, He was God because the Son of God means the Son is God (John 5:18).

John 7:39 tells us that "the Spirit was not yet, because Jesus was not yet glorified." The Spirit of God was there from the very beginning (Gen. 1:1-2), but the Spirit as the Spirit of Christ (Rom. 8:9), the Spirit of Jesus Christ (Phil. 1:19), was not yet at the time the Lord spoke this word because He was not yet glorified. Jesus was glorified when He was resurrected (Luke 24:26). After His resurrection, the Spirit of God became the Spirit of the incarnated, crucified, and resurrected Jesus Christ, who was breathed into the disciples by Christ in the evening of the day He was resurrected (John

20:22). After His resurrection the Spirit was there because the Spirit then comprised not only the divinity of God but also the humanity of the incarnated God, Jesus Christ. Within the Spirit of Christ are the elements of incarnation, human living, crucifixion, and the resurrection of Christ. The Spirit in the New Testament is the compound, all-inclusive Spirit.

Since Jesus was not resurrected yet, how could such a compound, all-inclusive Spirit be in the Old Testament prophets? In order to answer this question we must see that in Genesis 18 the Lord appeared to Abraham as a man even before He was incarnated (vv. 1-2). Also, Revelation 13:8 tells us that the Lamb was slain from the foundation of the world. Once the creatures came into existence there was the need of redemption, so from the foundation of the world Christ was slain in the eyes of God. According to our understanding, Christ was crucified a little over nineteen hundred years ago. This understanding is in the realm of time according to our human, mental apprehension. In God's apprehension, however, there is no time element. He only recognizes the fact that the Lord's death is eternal. Constitutionally speaking, the Lord Jesus was crucified nineteen hundred years ago, but functionally speaking, He was slain from the foundation of the world. In the same way, although the constitution of the Spirit of Christ is dispensational, constituted dispensationally through and with Christ's death and resurrection in the New Testament time, His function is eternal because He is the eternal Spirit (Heb. 9:14).

This New Testament Spirit of Christ was in the Old Testament functioning to help the Old Testament prophets search out what time and in what manner of time Christ had to die and resurrect. The prophets knew that according to the prophecies and types in the Pentateuch, God's Messiah had to die, so the Old Testament prophets did their best to search out when, where, and how the Messiah would die. When they were researching, the Spirit of Christ within them made the time and the manner of time concerning Christ's death and resurrection clear. Daniel told us that the Messiah would be cut off at the end of the sixty-ninth week (9:25-26). The Spirit helped the prophets inwardly to realize when the Messiah would be cut off. Isaiah 53 tells us how the Messiah would be cut off. He was "brought as a lamb to the slaughter" (v. 7). Verses like this in the Old Testament show us that the Old Testament prophets found out the way, the time, and even the place (Dan. 9:25-26; cf. Luke 13:33) of Christ's all-inclusive death. The Spirit of Christ was there even in the Old Testament. Constitutionally speaking, He was not yet, but functionally speaking He was there.

THE APOSTLES PREACHING THE GOSPEL
BY THE HOLY SPIRIT

First Peter 1:11 refers to the Spirit of Christ and in verse 12 this same Spirit is called the Holy Spirit. This Holy Spirit is the Spirit by whom the New Testament apostles proclaimed the gospel. The Spirit of Christ helped the Old Testament prophets inwardly to search out when, where, and how Christ would die and resurrect. Then after the accomplishment of His death and resurrection, the New Testament apostles came to preach the gospel by the same Spirit, yet it is called the Holy Spirit. With the Old Testament prophets, this Spirit was the Spirit of Christ searching. Christ Himself as the Spirit of Christ was helping the Old Testament prophets to search out the time, the place, and the manner of His death and resurrection. This is why Peter called the Spirit the Spirit of Christ. With the New Testament apostles, the same Spirit becomes the Holy Spirit preaching.

After the accomplishment of His death to form the gospel, the New Testament apostles, including Peter, proclaimed the gospel to the people by the Holy Spirit. Such a divine title had never before been used in the Old Testament. Peter's thought was to indicate to the Jewish believers that the very gospel concerning Christ's death and resurrection proclaimed to them was not something common. It was not something of Judaism, something of the Old Testament, which was common to all the Jews. This gospel is something particularly separated, something holy. The apostles preached this gospel to the Jews by the Holy Spirit. To speak concerning all the items of Judaism the Holy Spirit is not needed. All that is needed are some rabbis to teach these things. The apostles, however, proclaimed to the Jewish people something particular, holy, and uncommon.

THE SPIRIT OF GLORY AND OF GOD
RESTING UPON THE SUFFERING BELIEVERS

In 1 Peter 4:13-14 we see that the Spirit of glory and of God rests upon the suffering believers in their persecution for the glorification of the resurrected and exalted Christ who is now in glory. When the believers are suffering persecution, the Spirit of God rests upon them as the Spirit of glory. Before Stephen was stoned, his persecutors saw his face as the face of an angel (Acts 6:15). Stephen was neither weeping nor pitying himself but his face was like an angel's face because the Spirit of glory was resting upon him. The face of every martyr is like an angel's face. History tells us that whenever the believers of Christ were persecuted, at the juncture when they were being killed by their persecutors, their faces were like the face of an angel. If someone were to shine a spotlight on my face, my face would glow. This is actually "the spot of electricity" resting upon me. In the same way the Spirit of glory rests upon the suffering believers. One missionary who belonged to the China Inland Mission and was killed by the Communists in the 1930s wrote a short poem before his death. This poem said that every martyr for Jesus has the face of a lion. This also shows us that the Spirit of glory rests upon every martyr.

Approximately fifty years ago, an older Christian traveling preacher came to one of our meetings in my home town; I was about twenty-nine years old at the time. After the meeting, he told me the story of how he became a Christian. He was a young apprentice in a Chinese business during the years of the Boxer Rebellion in the early 1900s. During those years many Christians were persecuted and killed by the Boxers. One day in Peking, where the place of his business was, there was a parade of Boxers in the streets with long swords, and they were about to execute a young Christian girl, only in her teens. All the stores on the street closed their doors. This preacher, however, who was a young man at the time, looked through the crack of the door. In the midst of the Boxers, this young girl was riding in an old mule wagon. She was singing, praising, and rejoicing amidst the threatening of the Boxers on her way to her execution. When the young man saw this he could not comprehend it. This young girl was fearless and full of joy. Because of this, this man said to himself that he must go to find out what it is to be a Christian. He did this, and eventually as a result of what he had seen he received the Lord Jesus, gave up his business, and made a decision to serve the Lord full time as a preacher. This story helped me to understand the Spirit of glory resting upon the persecuted one in 1 Peter 4:13-14. It is when you are persecuted for the Lord's sake, that the Spirit of God, which is also the Holy Spirit and the Spirit of Christ, becomes the Spirit of glory. The Spirit of glory means that the Spirit is glory. The Spirit of glory resting upon the persecuted ones means God's Spirit as the glory is resting upon them. Every martyr for Christ is not a pitiful one, but a glorious one. The martyrs are not full of self-pity, but full of glory.

BORNE BY THE HOLY SPIRIT

Second Peter 1:20-21 tells us that men spoke from God the prophecy of Scripture, being borne by the Holy Spirit. The Holy Spirit is also the speaking Spirit to speak forth God and to speak out Christ. No prophecy was ever carried along by the will of man. Man's will, desire, and wish, with his thought and solution, are not the source from which any prophecy came; the source is God, by whose Holy Spirit men were carried along, as a ship by the wind, to speak out the will, desire, and wish of God.

CHAPTER NINETEEN

THE ANOINTING SPIRIT

Scripture Reading: 1 John 2:20-27; 3:24; 4:2, 13; 5:5-12; Jude 20-21

First John 2:20-27 unveils to us the teaching of the divine anointing for the abiding in the Triune God.

RECEIVED BY THE BELIEVERS FROM THE HOLY ONE

John tells us that the anointing Spirit was received by the believers from the Holy One (v. 20). John also charged us to abide in the Lord by this anointing (v. 27). If we did not have this anointing, it would be impossible to abide in the Lord. The anointing is like a switch that enables us to turn on the lights. If the switch is off, everything is in darkness, but if the switch is on, everything is in the light. We all need to be full of the anointing. According to grammar, the word "anointing" is a gerund, a verbal noun. Such a noun always conveys an action with it. The anointing is the moving of the Spirit within us.

The unbelievers do not have the anointing, but as regenerated believers we possess this anointing. We have something within us which is hard to designate or entitle. Something is within us moving and acting in a gentle way. It is somewhat similar to the very comfortable, nice, sweet, and gentle sensation we experience when some soothing oil is rubbed on our hand or on our face. Some kind of moving or action is always going on within us, soothing us, comforting us, watering us, supporting us, sustaining us, and nourishing us. This is the anointing. This is the moving or acting of this wonderful Person—the Spirit, as the Son, with the Father.

This is the One who is moving, acting, and soothing your entire being from within you.

JESUS, CHRIST, THE SON, THE FATHER, AND THE ETERNAL LIFE

First John 2:20-27 also unveils to us that Jesus is Christ and Christ is the Son and the Father. The totality of Jesus, Christ, the Son, and the Father is the eternal life. Verse 22 tells us that the antichrist denies that Jesus is the Christ. The apostle John wrote such a verse because of the heresy of Cerinthus, a first century Syrian heresiarch of Jewish descent, educated at Alexandria. His heresy was a mixture of Judaism, Gnosticism, and Christianity. He distinguished the maker (creator) of the world from God, and represented that maker as a subordinate power. He taught adoptionist Christology (Adoptionism), saying that Jesus became Son of God by exaltation to a status that was not His by birth, thus denying the conception of Jesus by the Holy Spirit. In his heresy, he separated the earthly man Jesus, regarded as the son of Joseph and Mary, from the heavenly Christ, and taught that after Jesus was baptized, Christ as a dove descended upon Him, and then He announced the unknown Father and did miracles, but that at the end of His ministry Christ departed from Jesus, and Jesus suffered death on the cross and rose from the dead, while Christ remained separated as a spiritual being, and will rejoin the man Jesus at the coming of the Messianic kingdom of glory. Basically speaking, Cerinthus denied that Jesus is Christ and that Jesus is God. It is a great heresy to deny the deity, the Godhead, of Jesus.

First John 2:20 through 22 tells us that if you deny that Jesus is the Christ you are denying the Son and the Father. Then verse 23 tells us that if you deny the Son, you do not have the Father and if you confess the Son, you have the Father. Then verse 25 tells us that God promised us the eternal life. These verses show us that Jesus is Christ, that Christ is the Son, and that the Son is always with the Father. When Jesus, Christ, the Son, and the Father are added together, this is the eternal life. The eternal life is the aggregate of Jesus, Christ, the Son, and the Father. The eternal life is this wonderful Person. Jesus, Christ, the Son, the Father, and the eternal life when totaled together are the aggregate, all-inclusive Spirit.

THE MOVING AND WORKING
OF THE INDWELLING, COMPOUND SPIRIT

The anointing is the moving and working of the indwelling compound Spirit, which is fully typified by the anointing oil, the compound ointment, in Exodus 30:23-25. This compound ointment is compounded with four spices plus a hin of olive oil. Five elements were compounded together into an ointment. The great teachers among the Brethren agree that the compound ointment in Exodus 30 typifies the Holy Spirit. I was taught this, but these teachers never went further to see the ingredients of this compound ointment. Any kind of compound has different elements as the ingredients. Since the compound ointment is a type of the Holy Spirit, this indicates that the Holy Spirit is a compound Spirit. It is not merely the Spirit of God, which was typified by the olive oil. After Christ's resurrection, the Spirit of God became compounded with the divinity of the Godhead plus the humanity of the man Jesus, with His human living, with His crucifixion (the all-inclusive death), and with His resurrection. These five elements are all compounded in this all-inclusive, life-giving Spirit (see *Life-study of Exodus,* messages 157-163, and note 19[3] in Phil. 1). By reading the Life-study messages on the compound ointment you will be able to see the compound, all-inclusive, processed, aggregate, life-giving, indwelling Spirit. This is the One that moves and acts in us. His moving and His acting is the anointing which anoints us all the time.

The anointing can be exemplified by the painting of a table. The more the table is painted, the more coating it receives. After many coats of paint have been put on the table, this table becomes full of paint. We can say that the anointing Spirit is the "divine paint." This wonderful Person, the Triune God, is the heavenly, divine paint full of elements. Actually, any kind of paint is comprised of different elements compounded together. The divine paint is not a teaching or a kind of inspiration, but a wonderful Person, the Spirit as the Son with the Father who is full of elements, ingredients. We all have to say, "Lord Jesus, thank You for the painting. I am here, Lord, and I open to You for more painting. Give me another coating of the compound ointment." What kind of person would you be if you received a coating of this divine paint every day for 365 days? You would be a person full of the divine paint, a person of the Spirit, a wonderful person.

TEACHING THE BELIEVERS CONCERNING ALL THINGS PERTAINING TO THE PERSON OF CHRIST

This anointing teaches us concerning all things pertaining to the Person of Christ related to the Divine Trinity. The anointing teaches us that Jesus is Christ, that Christ is the Son, and that the Son is with the Father. If you have these four—Jesus, Christ, the Son, and the Father—you have eternal life. We all should declare, "Hallelujah! I have the eternal life!" Because the Christians have the eternal life, nothing can stop them. The Roman empire did their best to kill all the Christians, but they failed. This shows that the more the opposers try to "bury" the Christians, who are the many grains of wheat, the more these grains flourish and produce many more grains. The blood of the martyrs grows and produces. According to history, any government that persecutes Christians is unwise.

We must realize that the more we prosper outwardly, the less we grow. In this sense, sufferings are lovable and dear. None of us, however, likes to suffer. If all of our children were "straight A" students and grew up to be lawyers and doctors, would this help our growth in life? On the other hand, what if our children were naughty and not so bright? You might kneel down to pray, "Lord, have mercy upon me." When you pray in this way the Lord as the divine breath gets into you. The breath is this wonderful One. When you pray in this way you may not understand what you are praying, but as long as you pray the breath gets into you.

We all need the deep breathing of this wonderful One into our being. If a father's son graduated to be a medical doctor, he might not pray that much. He may only pray, "Lord, how good You are. Thank You for my son who is a medical doctor." He may pray this prayer without really breathing the Lord deeply into his being. If his son, however, got sick and was sent to the hospital, he probably would cry out to the Lord, "O Lord Jesus! I don't understand this situation. Have mercy upon me, Lord." This cry to the Lord is the deep breathing. This kind of desperate prayer affords the Lord a way to dispense Himself as the eternal life into our being. All the sufferings and persecution are an aid to this dispensing.

TESTIFYING THAT JESUS IS THE SON OF GOD, IN WHOM IS THE ETERNAL LIFE

We should abide in the Lord according to the anointing Spirit who is the wonderful One as the compound, processed, aggregate, all-inclusive, life-giving, indwelling Spirit. Then in the fact that God has given us of His Spirit, we know that we abide in Him and He in us (1 John 4:13; 3:24). This indwelling Spirit then becomes a reality to us, a testimony. The Spirit being the truth, the reality, testifies that Jesus is the Son of God, in whom is the eternal life (1 John 5:5-12). First John 5:7-8 tells us that there are three who testify—the Spirit, the water, and the blood. Jesus, the man of Nazareth, was testified to be the Son of God by the water He went through in His baptism (Matt. 3:16-17; John 1:31-34), by the blood He shed on the cross (John 19:31-35; Matt. 27:50-54), and also by the Spirit He gave not by measure (John 1:32-34; 3:34). By these three, God has testified that Jesus is His Son given to us (1 John 5:7-10), that in Him we may receive His eternal life by believing in His name (1 John 5:11-13; John 3:16, 36; 20:31). By thus testifying, He imparts the Son of God into us to be our life (Col. 3:4). First John 5:12 tells us that if we have the Son, we have the eternal life, and if we do not have the Son, we do not have the eternal life. We all need to praise the Lord that we have the Son and thus we have the eternal life. This eternal life, this wonderful Person, is our capital, our profit, our victory, and everything to us as Christians.

THE BELIEVERS KEEPING THEMSELVES
BY PRAYING IN THE HOLY SPIRIT

Jude 20-21 instructs us to pray in the Holy Spirit, that we may be preserved in the Triune God. We should keep ourselves in the love of God by building up ourselves in our holy faith and praying in the Holy Spirit (v. 20); thus, we await and look for the mercy of our Lord that we may not only enjoy eternal life in this age, but inherit it for eternity (Matt. 19:29). The entire blessed Divine Trinity is employed and enjoyed by the believers in their praying in the Holy Spirit, keeping themselves in the love of God, and awaiting the mercy of our Lord unto eternal life. The enjoyment and inheritance of eternal life, the life of God, is the goal of our spiritual seeking. Because we aim at this goal, we want to be kept in the love of God and await the mercy of our Lord.

Our God, our Savior, and our Redeemer is such a wonderful Person. He is the Triune God, the Father, the Son, and the Spirit, mingled with man. This Triune God-man died an all-inclusive death on the cross and resurrected to become the life-giving Spirit. This Spirit is compounded with divinity, humanity, human living, the all-inclusive death, and the marvelous resurrection. This is the wonderful One as the compounded Spirit indwelling us to move and to act within us. This moving and acting within us is the anointing to anoint the Triune God with His uplifted humanity, His human living, His all-inclusive death, and His wonderful, excellent resurrection into our being. We are receiving coating upon coating of this compound ointment. The more coating we receive, the more we grow in life. This is not merely a teaching, but a ministering of the wonderful One into all of us.

CHAPTER TWENTY

THE SEVEN SPIRITS

(1)

Scripture Reading: Rev. 1:1-8

GOD'S NEW TESTAMENT ECONOMY

We want to stress again that our fellowship is concerning God's New Testament economy. This is God's divine arrangement, divine family plan, or divine household administration. In the divine life, God has a family and this family is unique, universal, and eternal. This great, divine family is called in the New Testament the household of God (Eph. 2:19). In this household of God there is a divine arrangement, administration, or dispensation. God's family arrangement, God's household administration or dispensation, is to dispense, to distribute, and to impart Himself into His chosen and redeemed people. The Greek word for dispensation is *oikonomia,* composed of oikos meaning house and nomos meaning law. God chose His people in eternity and redeemed His people in time for the purpose of dispensing Himself into them. We have seen that God's economy is fully revealed and developed in the twenty-seven books of the New Testament, and this economy is focused on one all-inclusive Person who is excellent, marvelous, mysterious, and wonderful. This is why Isaiah 9:6 tells us that His name is called Wonderful Counselor.

THE ALL-INCLUSIVE REVELATION OF JESUS CHRIST

The book of Revelation is the conclusion of the revelation concerning Jesus Christ in the Bible. In this book of twenty-two chapters is vision after vision concerning Christ. The first vision concerning Christ shows us Christ as the High Priest walking in the midst of the seven golden lampstands. In this vision Christ is revealed and described in a very extraordinary way. In this vision Christ does not have merely two eyes but seven eyes (5:6). The disciples in the four Gospels never saw a Christ with seven eyes. John did not see such a Christ in the four Gospels but in Revelation he did.

The Christ in Revelation is a "different" Christ from that in the four Gospels. I do not believe in another Christ, but I do believe in a "different" Christ. The Christ in the four Gospels had only two eyes, but the Christ in Revelation has seven eyes. Logically speaking, this Christ in Revelation is different from the one in the Gospels. In addition, Revelation 1:16 tells us that "out of His mouth proceeded a sharp two-edged sword." In the four Gospels words of grace are proceeding out of His mouth (Luke 4:22), but in Revelation a sharp two-edged sword is proceeding out of His mouth. This is His discerning, judging, and slaying word (Heb. 4:12; Eph. 6:17) for His dealing with negative persons and things. Again, this shows us that the Christ in Revelation is different from the One revealed in the four Gospels. In the four Gospels, John was reclining on Jesus' bosom (John 13:23). In the book of Revelation, however, when John saw such a Christ he fell at His feet as dead; he was full of fear (1:17). Christ as the High Priest in Revelation 1 also holds seven stars in His right hand (v. 20) and His feet are like "shining brass, as having been fired in a furnace" (v. 15). Revelation 1:14 also tells us that "His head and hair were white as white wool, as snow." Probably in our past none of us ever heard a sermon that Christ, our Redeemer, has seven eyes and His eyes are as a flame of fire (1:14). We always heard messages telling us that Jesus is very loving, but we must realize that this One also has seven eyes for Him to observe and search for His judging by enlightening. We all need to see the vision concerning Christ in Revelation 1.

In the book of Revelation we still have the old revelation of Christ. In John 1:29 John the Baptist declared, "Behold, the Lamb of God." In Revelation, the Lamb is also mentioned many times. The revelation concerning Jesus Christ in this book is all-inclusive; it has new and old aspects. If we put all these aspects together we will have a clear view of this all-inclusive revelation of Jesus Christ (1:1), new and old, as a conclusion of the entire Scripture (2 Tim. 3:16).

THE TRINITY IN A NEW SEQUENCE

Also, the Divine Trinity in this last book of the New Testament has a new sequence (1:4-7; cf. Matt. 28:19). Matthew 28:19 refers us to the Father, the Son, and the Holy Spirit. The sequence of the Trinity in Revelation 1, however, is not only changed, but also very complicated. Revelation 1:4-7 says, "Grace to you and peace from Him who is, and who was, and who is coming, and from the seven Spirits who are before His throne, and from Jesus Christ, the faithful Witness, the Firstborn of the dead, and the Ruler of the kings of the earth. To Him who loves us and has loosed us from our sins by His blood, and made us a kingdom, priests to His God and Father, to Him be the glory and the might forever and ever. Amen. Behold, He comes with the clouds, and every eye shall see Him, those also who pierced Him, and all the tribes of the lands shall wail over Him. Yes, amen."

The Father as Him Who Is,
and Who Was, and Who Is Coming

Him who is, and who was, and who is coming is God the eternal Father. This title refers to the Old Testament title of Jehovah. Jehovah is the great I Am; He is the One who is, who was, and who shall be. In Exodus 3 the great I Am tells Moses that He is the God of Abraham, the God of Isaac, and the God of Jacob (vv. 14-15). Jehovah is the God of the grandfather, the God of the father, and the God of the grandson—the Triune God. The One who is, and who was, and who is coming is the Father, yet this One also denotes the great I Am, Jehovah, the Triune God. Some may ask, "How could the Father be the Triune God since the Triune God is the entire God and the Father is only one-third?" The thought of today's theology is that the entire God is divided into three parts—the Father, the Son, and the Spirit. Many of us subconsciously hold this concept. The description of the title given to the first of the Divine Trinity in Revelation, however, is Him who is, and who was, and who is coming. The three-fold predicate used for the first of the Divine Trinity implies and even indicates the Divine Trinity. This definitely refers to the great I Am, Jehovah, in Exodus 3. The great I Am in Exodus 3 is the Triune God, the God of Abraham, the God of Isaac, and the God of Jacob. Jehovah is the Triune God, the entire God. How could the entire God in Revelation be the first of the Triune God? This shows us the mystery of the Triune God, and it also shows us that it is not easy to study the holy Word nor to study our infinite, eternal God. Our finite minds are incapable of fully understanding Him.

The Spirit as the Seven Spirits

The seven Spirits who are before God's throne are the operating Spirit of God, God the Spirit. Now we must ask whether the Spirit of God is one or seven. He is the sevenfold intensified Spirit. For what purpose, though, is He intensified? Many Christians try to avoid studying the last book of the Bible. They say that it is too hard to understand and that we should not try to understand it. The complete Bible has been in the hands of the Lord's children since A.D. 397. As Christians we all should love this book and attempt to study it. If we are to understand the Bible, we surely have to understand the conclusion of this Bible, the conclusion of the entire divine revelation. We cannot take Revelation 1:4-7 for granted. Why has the sequence of the Divine Trinity in these verses changed and become so complicated as compared to Matthew 28:19? Even though this is hard to understand, we must find out the significance. It is not logical for us to skip over these verses by using the excuse that we are too limited to understand them.

The seven Spirits are undoubtedly the Spirit of God, because they are ranked among the Triune God in verses 4 and 5. As seven is the number for completion in God's operation, so the seven Spirits must be for God's move on the earth. In substance and existence God's Spirit is one; in the intensified function and work of God's operation God's Spirit is sevenfold. It is like the lampstand in Zechariah 4:2. In existence it is one lampstand, but in function it is seven lamps. At the time this book was written, the church had become degraded; the age was dark. Therefore, the sevenfold intensified Spirit of God was needed for God's move and work on the earth.

The seven Spirits of God are listed in the second place instead of the third. This reveals the importance of the intensified function of the sevenfold Spirit of God. This point is confirmed by the repeated emphasis on the Spirit's speaking in 2:7, 11, 17, 29; 3:6, 13, 22; 14:13; 22:17. At the opening of the other Epistles, only the Father and the Son are mentioned, from whom grace and peace are given to the receivers. Here, however, the Spirit is also included, from whom grace and peace are imparted to the churches. This also signifies the crucial need for the Spirit for God's move to counteract the degradation of the church. Verse 4 tells us that the seven Spirits are before the throne of God. This modifier, "before the throne of God," indicates why God the Spirit becomes seven and it tells you who these seven Spirits are.

The Son, Jesus Christ

Thus far, we have seen that in these verses the Father is designated as Him who is, who was, and who is coming, and the Spirit is used in plural as the seven Spirits. Furthermore, the third of the Trinity is not designated as the Son but as Jesus Christ. The two names Jesus and Christ as a compound name bear a tremendous amount of significance. Who is Jesus and who is Christ? Actually, a ten day conference would not be adequate to describe who Jesus and Christ are. To God He is the faithful Witness and to the church He is the Firstborn of the dead because it was through Him as the Firstborn from the dead that we all were resurrected and reborn to produce the church. To the world He is the Ruler of the kings of the earth. In addition, this One loves us and has accomplished redemption for us by shedding His blood which washes us and cleanses us from all our sins. He also made us a kingdom and this kingdom is the priesthood. The kingdom is for God's dominion, and the priesthood is for God's expression which fulfills the purpose of God's creation of man in Genesis 1:26. Eventually He comes with the clouds!

THE ECONOMICAL TRINITY IN REVELATION

Concerning the first of the Divine Trinity we see three modifiers—who is, who was, and who is coming. Concerning the second of the Divine Trinity in Revelation, the seven Spirits, is the modifier, "before the throne of God." For the third of the Divine Trinity, Jesus Christ, there are the modifiers: the faithful Witness, the Firstborn of the dead, the Ruler of the kings of the earth, Him who loves us, who has loosed us from our sins, who made us a kingdom and priests to His God and Father, and who comes. All these modifiers are used to modify the three of the Godhead and indicate that the Divine Trinity in Revelation is not the essential Trinity but the economical Trinity. The essential Trinity refers to God's existence. In God's existence, the Father, the Son, and the Spirit coexist and coinhere from eternity to eternity. There is no modifier needed for the essential Trinity. The book of Revelation, however, does not touch the existence of the Trinity but the economy of the Trinity. According to God's economy the Father is the One who is now, who was in the past, and who shall be in the future. These modifiers indicate economy. Also, in God's existence, the Spirit of God is one, but in God's economy the Spirit of God is seven in function. Essentially God's Spirit in existence is one, but economically God's Spirit has to be intensified to fulfill His function to carry out God's economy. In essence God the Son is just the Son, but in God's economy He is Jesus, Christ, the faithful Witness, the Firstborn of the dead, the Ruler of the kings of the earth, the One who loves us and has loosed us from our sins by His blood, the One who has made us a kingdom, priests to His God and Father, and the One who comes to execute God's final government. All these modifiers do not refer to the existence of the Son but to the Son in God's economy, in God's move, in God's actions. The sequence of every modifier of the Son in Revelation 1:5-7 is related to God's move, God's economy. Again, Revelation does not touch the divine essence of the Trinity but the divine economy of the Trinity. The throne of God in the book of Revelation is the center of God's administration. God's throne is seen in Revelation to administrate God's eternal purpose. This is altogether a matter of God's economy.

In God's essence, the Trinity is simply the Father, the Son, and the Spirit. In God's economy, though, the Trinity is complicated. Also, in God's essence the Father is first, the Son is second, and the Spirit is third. In God's economy, however, the Spirit comes before God the Son. The Spirit carries out God's administration and infuses and searches the churches. In the four Gospels, the Son was more present than the Spirit, but in Revelation the Spirit is more present than the Son, so the Spirit comes before the Son in the sequence of the economical Trinity in Revelation 1. The Trinity in Matthew 28 is the Trinity of God's existence, the essential Trinity, and the Trinity in Revelation is the Trinity in God's economy, the economical Trinity.

Some may argue, however, that the first designation of the Father refers to existence since it indicates Him who is, who was, and who shall be. To be means to exist. In Exodus 3, however, God is not referred to as the One who is, who was, and who shall be. He is referred to as "I AM THAT I AM," the great I Am. This, undoubtedly, purely denotes God's existence. God is the One that is, the great I Am. However, when it says Him who is, and who was, and who is coming, this denotes some activities. God was there in eternity past, in creation, and with Abraham, Isaac, and Jacob; He is now here with us; and He will be there in the New Jerusalem for eternity future. This does not refer to existence, but to doings, to actions. In John 5:17 the Lord Jesus said, "My Father is working until now, and I am working." The Father was working in eternity, He was working in creation, He was working in the Son for redemption, and He shall be working. This shows us that the title "Him who is, and who was, and who is coming" does not mainly refer to existence, but to the Father's working, the activities of the Father, in different times. The Father works in the past, He works today, and He will work in the future.

THE ALPHA AND THE OMEGA

Revelation 1:8 says, "I am the Alpha and the Omega, says the Lord God, He who is, and who was, and who is coming, the Almighty." This word does not refer to the existence of God the Father, but to the activities, the work of the Father. As the Alpha He is the beginning; He originated all the things of the universe. He will be the Omega, the ending for the completion of His eternal purpose. He will finalize and finish what He has initiated. God the Father worked in the past, He works in the present, and He will work in the future.

Some may think that if this is the case there is no need of the Son or of the Spirit to work. John 5:17, however, indicates that the Father works and the Son works also. The Father never works alone or by Himself. The Father always works in the Son by the Spirit. The Lord Jesus told us that when He was on the earth He was working with the Father and even in the name of the Father (John 5:43). Also, in John 14 the Lord indicated that the word He spoke was not His own word and that while He was speaking the Father was working within Him (vv. 10, 24). We must also realize that when the seven Spirits are working, this is not merely the work of the Spirit. The seven Spirits are out from the Eternal One and of the Redeemer. The seven Spirits are not working alone today, but this intensified Spirit is working out from the Father and of the Son.

Both God the Triune as the Father, and Christ as the Son, declare to be the Alpha and the Omega, indicating that God the Father and God the Son are one (Rev. 1:8; 22:12-13). Both the Son and the Father declare that They are the Alpha and Omega in the book of Revelation. This shows us, again, that the Son and the Father can never be separated.

After the fellowship in this chapter, I hope that none of us are so clear that the three of the Godhead are distinct, separate, and clear-cut persons. Even when we touch the economical Trinity in the book of Revelation none of us can be so clear that the Father, the Son, and the Spirit are three distinct, separate, and clear-cut persons. These complications involve the finalization of God's New Testament economy and the conclusion of the divine revelation.

CHAPTER TWENTY-ONE

THE SEVEN SPIRITS

(2)

Scripture Reading: Rev. 1:9-18

THE ECONOMICAL AND ESSENTIAL
ASPECTS OF THE TRINITY

In this chapter we must first see more concerning the economical and essential aspects of the Trinity. The beginning of Matthew tells us how Christ was conceived of the Holy Spirit in the womb of a virgin (1:18, 20). At the end of Matthew we see the Trinity described in a simple way as the Father, the Son, and the Holy Spirit. The Trinity in Matthew refers to the essence, the existence of the Trinity; the Father, the Son, and the Spirit are one in essence for their existence. People need to be baptized into the divine essence of the Divine Trinity. We do not need to be baptized into God's economy, His administration, His move, or His acts, but into His essence. We have been baptized "into the name." A name does not refer to a person's activity but to the very being of that person. When I call a person's name, this indicates that I desire that person. To be baptized into the name of the Father, and of the Son, and of the Holy Spirit is to be baptized into the person of the Father, the Son, and the Spirit. This is a matter of the very being, the very essence, of the Triune Godhead.

In the book of Revelation, the last book of the Bible, the Trinity is mentioned not at the end but at the beginning. The Trinity in Matthew 28 is essential and the Trinity in Revelation 1 is economical. Revelation is a book on God's administration because the center of this book is God's throne. God's throne is not related to His Person but to His administration, which is altogether a matter of God's economy. Therefore, the Trinity is mentioned in Revelation 1 not in the way of God's essence in a simple way, but in the way of God's economy in a very complicated way.

As we have seen, the first of the Trinity in Revelation 1 is Him who is, and who was, and who is coming. According to Exodus 3 this One, the great I Am, is Jehovah and also the Angel of Jehovah (v. 2). The Angel of Jehovah in the Old Testament was Christ, the One sent by God. Furthermore, in John 8:58 the Lord Jesus indicated that He was the great I Am. Therefore, Christ is also the I Am in Exodus 3, and the One who is, and who was, and who is coming refers to Christ. In Revelation 1, however, the One who is, and who was, and who is coming refers to the first of the Trinity, the Father. This shows us another divine complication in the economical Trinity.

In the previous chapter we saw the Father as Him who is, and who was, and who is coming—Jehovah, God the Triune (Exo. 3:14-15). God the Triune refers to God the Father, the Son, and the Spirit. The Father is not only God the Father, but also God the Triune, the Father, the Son, and the Spirit. The Father as the One who is, and who was, and who is coming is also Jehovah, and Jehovah is God the Triune. Jehovah is not only God the Father, but also God the Father, the Son, and the Spirit, the Triune. This is another divine complication.

In order to understand the Trinity in Revelation we must again see that the mentioning of the Trinity is not concerning the essence of the Trinity, but the economy of the Trinity. In Revelation we see the administration, the government, the activity, the motion, the move, the act, and the work of the Trinity. The Father as the One who is, and who was, and who is coming is not referred to in an essential way. Revelation 1:8, where the Father declares that He is the Alpha and the Omega, proves this. Alpha and omega are the first and last letters of the Greek alphabet. Letters are for composing words, sentences, paragraphs, and compositions. God is the divine alphabet, not for existence but for writing. God compared Himself to the alpha and omega which indicates His moving, His working, His "writing." Verse 8 continues to tell us that the Alpha and the Omega is the One who is, and who was, and who is coming. This means that He was "writing" in eternity past in choosing and predestinating us unto sonship. He is still "writing" in the present in regenerating people and in working in the believers. His coming in the future means that He is "writing" in the future. Him who is, and who was, and who is coming indicates God's moving, not God's existence.

In eternity past the Father was moving in choosing and predestinating us. The One who came to redeem us was God the Son, but the Lord Jesus told us that as He was working the Father was also working (John 5:17). This shows that the redeeming work was also the Father's work. Now the Spirit is applying to us all that God is and has done. We must realize that the applying One is also the Father because God the Father is God the Triune. God the Father is God the Triune, the Father, the Son, and the Spirit. In eternity past He was working in choosing and predestinating us, and then He came to redeem us. Do not forget that the Son is included in God the Triune, so when the Son came to redeem us that was the Father's coming and the Father's doing. Also, the Spirit does not apply Himself into us merely as the Spirit by Himself. The Spirit's application is the Father's because the Father is God the Triune. Whatever the Father does, whatever the Son does, and whatever the Spirit does is also what the Father does. The Father was doing something in the past, He is doing something now, and He will do something further in the future. All this is the Father's doing in His economy.

When the Father chose us in eternity past He was doing this with the Son. The Father chose us in Christ before the foundation of the world (Eph. 1:4). This shows us that the Father chose us in the Son. Also, 1 Peter 1:1-2 indicates that we were chosen according to the foreknowledge of God the Father, in sanctification of the Spirit, unto obedience and sprinkling of the blood of Jesus Christ. This shows us that God's choosing was something done by the Triune God and not by the

Father alone. This choosing was done in the sanctification of the Spirit. God chose us in eternity past in Christ, the Son, and also in the sanctification of the Spirit. The divine choosing in eternity past was not a matter of the Father only. Our being chosen was by the Father, in the Son, and in the sanctification of the Spirit.

According to our thinking the Son became flesh and the Son was the One who was manifested in the flesh. The Bible, however, tells us that the Word became flesh and that the Word was God. John 1:1 does not say that the Word was the Son, but that the Word was God. Do you believe that only one-third of God became flesh, one-third remained on the throne, and one-third was as a dove soaring in the heavens? The Bible does not divide God, the entire God, into thirds. Paul also tells us in 1 Timothy 3:16 that God was manifested in the flesh. This again shows us that the entire Godhead, the Triune God, became flesh. Economically speaking, God became flesh in the Son. This One who was conceived of the Holy Spirit was born to be a God-man. We cannot say that this God-man is the Son-man. This God-man is the Triune God-man. We believe that Jesus was the complete God and the perfect man. He was the Father, the Son, and the Spirit-man. He lived on this earth as the Triune God for thirty years before the beginning of His earthly ministry. In those thirty years, He was mainly a carpenter in Nazareth. While He was doing His carpentry, the Father was there with Him (John 16:32). Also, while the Father was with Him He did everything by the Spirit (Matt. 12:28). He is a wonderful Person.

When He was thirty years old, He came to be baptized. The One who was baptized in the Jordan was the Triune God-man. When He rose up out of the water the Spirit descended upon Him as a dove. The Father also spoke concerning the Son saying, "This is My beloved Son, in whom I delight." Even though the Lord Jesus was conceived of the Spirit and did things by the Spirit and even though He was with the Father, the Spirit still descended upon Him and the Father spoke well concerning Him from the heavens. We must realize that essentially, He was conceived, born, and living as the Triune God-man. Economically speaking, however, the

Spirit descended upon Him as a dove, and the Father spoke well concerning Him.

The Lord Jesus carried out His earthly ministry for three and a half years both essentially and economically. For the first thirty years of His human life the Triune God was His intrinsic essence for His being and existence. In the last three and a half years of His life while He was carrying out His ministry, He needed the economical aspect of the Trinity. He needed the anointing Spirit to be poured out upon Him, and He needed to be filled with the Spirit to carry out His ministry. The Gospels tell us that He cast out the demons by the Spirit of God (Matt. 12:28). This is all economical.

Also, Christ was crucified on the cross for us, and He was on the cross for six hours. In the first three hours, Christ was persecuted by men for doing God's will; in the last three hours, He was judged by God for the accomplishment of our redemption. It was during this time that God counted Him as our suffering substitute for sin (Isa. 53:10). Hence, darkness came over all the land (Matt. 27:45), because our sin and sins and all negative things were dealt with there. Near the end of these six hours Jesus cried out, "My God, My God, why have You forsaken Me?" (Matt. 27:46). God forsook Him because of our sin. Economically, God was judging Him as a sinner and the judging God left Him economically. Essentially, however, He was dying on the cross as the Triune God-man. This is why Charles Wesley in one of his hymns (*Hymns*, #296) says, "Amazing love! how can it be that Thou, my God, shouldst die for me?" Economically, God cannot die for us, but essentially, God within Jesus died for us. Actually, however, that was not God dying, but God passing through death.

God's sending of the Son and the Son being given to us is economical. Isaiah 9:6 tells us that a Son is given to us. This is economical. This same verse goes on to tell us that this Son is called the eternal Father. This is essential. In the economical Trinity God gives the Son and the Son is given to us. In the essential Trinity the Son is called the Father because in essence the Son and the Father are one. The Son went to the cross and was crucified and buried. After three days He resurrected and in His resurrection He became a life-giving Spirit. This is economical.

In Revelation we have seen that the first of the Trinity was moving in the past, is moving in the present, and is going to move in the future. This is economical. The second of the Trinity is the seven Spirits before the administrative throne of God. This is also economical. Finally, all the points concerning the Son as Jesus Christ, the Witness, the Firstborn of the dead, and the Ruler of the kings of the earth, do not refer to His essence but to His move and His activity. The Triune God became Jesus, and Jesus was anointed to be the Christ. Jesus Christ was the faithful Witness on this earth who died and was resurrected to be the Firstborn of God to produce many brothers that the church might be brought forth. Now He is the Ruler of the kings of the earth, He has accomplished redemption for us, and He has made us a kingdom, even the priesthood to His God and Father. Also, He will come again. All these points indicate His move and His economy. When Jesus comes again do you believe that the Father will be left in the heavens and the Spirit will be standing by in the air? Actually, when Jesus Christ comes back, the Son will come with the Father by the Spirit. The Triune God will come in the Person of the Son in His economy.

I hope that we all realize that whatever the Father did, He did in the Son by the Spirit; whatever the Son did, He did with the Father by the Spirit; and whatever the Spirit does, he does as the Son with the Father. The three in the Godhead are not separate, but they are essentially one. Economically the three in the Godhead are consecutive, yet the essential aspect still remains in the economical aspect. The Father's choosing, the Son's redeeming, and the Spirit's applying are all economical, yet in these economical aspects, the essential aspect of the Trinity is still here. When the Father was choosing, the essential Trinity was there also. When the Son came to redeem and when the Spirit comes to apply, the essential Trinity is there. As the conclusion of the sixty-six books of the Bible, Revelation is an all-inclusive revelation comprising all the essential and economical aspects of the Trinity. We have seen a wonderful Person who is both essential and economical.

THE REVELATION AND THE TESTIMONY
OF JESUS CHRIST

Two great and important terms are used in the first two verses of the book of Revelation—the revelation of Jesus Christ (v. 1) and the testimony of Jesus Christ (v. 2). The revelation of Jesus Christ is Christ Himself, and the testimony of Jesus Christ refers to the church. These two expressions refer to the revealed Christ and the testifying church and comprise the entire book of Revelation. In Revelation Christ is revealed and the church is testifying the revealed Christ. This testified Christ is actually the revealed Christ.

The Revelation of Jesus Christ

In the book of Revelation we firstly see Jesus Christ—the revelation of Jesus Christ and then the testimony of Jesus Christ. We see Him who is, and who was, and who is coming and the seven Spirits who are before His throne. We see Jesus Christ again as the Witness, the Firstborn, the Ruler, the Redeemer, the One who made us a kingdom, the priesthood to His God and Father, and the One who will come. Also, in Revelation 1 we see the Son of Man in the midst of all the lampstands as the High Priest in His priestly garments. The "garment reaching to the feet" (1:13) is the priestly robe (Exo. 28:33-35). This One in the midst of the lampstands has seven eyes as a flame of fire, a sharp two-edged sword proceeding out of His mouth, seven stars in His right hand, and two feet like shining brass having been fired in a furnace. This One is also seen as the Lord God, the Almighty, the Alpha, and the Omega.

We must remember that the book of Revelation is primarily a revelation of Jesus Christ. He is the One who is, and who was, and who is coming, and He is the seven Spirits. He is the Witness, the Firstborn, the Ruler of the kings of the earth, the Redeemer, the coming One, the Alpha, the Omega, the Lord God, the Almighty, the Son of Man, and the High Priest. This is the revelation of Jesus Christ, and this Jesus Christ is the all-inclusive, excellent, marvelous, mysterious, and wonderful One. He is marvelous in the fact that He surprises us to the uttermost. He is also mysterious in that we cannot fully understand or comprehend Him. He is Wonderful! This is our Savior, this is our God. Have you ever considered that your Savior, Jesus Christ, is so much? God's New Testament economy is focused on a Person who is all-inclusive, excellent, marvelous, mysterious, and wonderful. The revelation of Jesus Christ in the book of Revelation is all-inclusive.

The Testimony of Jesus Christ—the Church

Revelation 1:2 reveals the testimony of Jesus Christ, which is the church. The word witness refers to the person but the word testimony refers to what the person bears, his work, his doing. For example, a witness is a person in a court of law who gives his testimony. The testimony refers to his doing. The Lord Jesus was God's faithful Witness and He testified God to produce the church. The producing of the church is His testimony. In other words, the Witness refers to Himself, and His testimony refers to the church. Jesus was the Witness and what came out of Him was the church as the testimony. This church is revealed in nine aspects: the lampstands (1:11-12, 20), the great multitude of the redeemed (7:9-17), the bright woman with her man-child (12:1-17), the harvest with its firstfruits (14:4, 14-16), the overcomers on the sea of glass (15:2-4), the bride ready for marriage (19:7-9), the army of the Lamb (17:14; 19:14, 19), the co-kings of Christ in the millennium (20:4-6), and the New Jerusalem in the new heaven and the new earth (21:1-3). In no other book of the Bible are these nine items so clearly revealed, and these are the aspects of the church as the testimony of Jesus.

The Son of Man as the Priest

In Revelation 1:13-18 the Son of Man is walking in the midst of the seven golden lampstands. As the Priest He is dressing the lamps in the holy place and searching and infusing the churches, the lampstands. This One is the all-inclusive, excellent, marvelous, mysterious, and wonderful One. This One has seven eyes which are the seven Spirits of God. His eyes are as a flame of fire for searching and infusing (1:14). In the economical Trinity in Revelation, the second of the Godhead is the seven Spirits and becomes the seven eyes of the third in the Trinity. Do you consider your eyes as one person and yourself as another person? All of us realize that the eyes are of the person. The seven Spirits who are out from the eternal One are also of the Redeemer because the seven Spirits are the seven eyes of the Lamb, the Redeemer. This again is a strong point to show us that this wonderful One is all-inclusive. He is the Redeemer, but the seven Spirits are His eyes. He includes the Spirit.

This One also includes the Father, the One who is, and who was, and who is coming. Revelation 1:4 and 8 indicate that the Father is the Alpha and the Omega and the One who is, and who was, and who is coming. Revelation 22:12 and 13 show us that the Lord Jesus is the Alpha and the Omega. These portions of the Word prove that the Son includes the Father. Also, Revelation 1:18 tells us that the Lord Jesus is the living One, and that He lives forever and ever. This is the eternal One. This wonderful One in Revelation is the Son of Man in chapter one and the Son of God in chapter two. He includes the seven Spirits and the Father, and He is the everlasting One, the Almighty, the Alpha, the Omega, the First, the Last, the Beginning, and the End. He is all-inclusive.

OUR EXPERIENCE AND HIS PRESENT REVELATION

We all need to enter into the depths of the book of Revelation so that we might realize that whatever we experience, enjoy, and realize of our Lord Jesus Christ is also our experience, enjoyment, and realization of the Triune God. He is revealed to such a great extent, and we must experience and enjoy Him to such an extent. Our enjoyment then becomes His testimony, and this living testimony is the present revelation of Jesus Christ. Firstly He is revealed, then we enjoy Him and become His testimony, and eventually our testimony becomes His present revelation. He is now revealed in our experience of Him as a testimony to Him. He is revealed as the all-inclusive, excellent, marvelous, mysterious, and wonderful One. We need to experience and enjoy such a Christ in so many details that our experience can become not only His testimony but also His present revelation.

CHAPTER TWENTY-TWO

THE SEVEN SPIRITS

(3)

Scripture Reading: Rev. 2—3

THE SPEAKING ONE

Based upon what we have seen in Revelation 1, we now want to see this wonderful One in Revelation 2 and 3. In these two chapters the most striking point is that this all-inclusive, excellent, marvelous, mysterious, and wonderful One speaks. He spoke seven times to each of the seven churches. In these seven times of speaking He always declared what He was. Based upon the claim of what He was, He spoke something. At the beginning of each of the seven Epistles recorded in chapters two and three it is the Lord who speaks (2:1, 8, 12, 18; 3:1, 7, 14). At the end of all seven Epistles, however, it is the Spirit speaking to the churches (2:7, 11, 17, 29; 3:6, 13, 22). This is a strong indication that the actual speaker is the Spirit. This shows us that Christ and the Spirit are one. Firstly we see Christ speaking and then Revelation tells us that the Spirit is the One who speaks. The oneness of the Trinity here is economical based upon the essential aspect. Christ and the Spirit are one economically because they are one essentially. Because Christ, the Spirit, is speaking, this does not refer to existence. This refers to the move, the motion, the action, of the Triune God. Christ and the Spirit's being one economically depends upon their being one essentially. I hope this shows us more concerning the depth of the truth of the Divine Trinity.

At the end of the book of Revelation "the Spirit and the bride say" (22:17). In the first chapter we see many titles for this wonderful One—the One who is, and who was, and who is coming, the seven Spirits who are before the throne, Jesus Christ, the faithful Witness, the Firstborn of the dead, the Ruler of the kings of the earth, the Redeemer, the One who made us a kingdom, priests to His God and to His Father, and the One who comes. Also, in Revelation 1 we see the Son of Man appearing as the High Priest. In the last chapter of Revelation, however, in the finalization, there will only be "the Spirit." The all-inclusive, compound, sevenfold intensified, life-giving, processed, indwelling Spirit is the consummation of the processed Triune God, the Spirit, in Revelation 22:17. The word "processed" indicates all the procedures that the Triune God has gone through. In Revelation 1 are many titles for this wonderful One, but in chapter two are Christ, the all-inclusive Head, and the speaking Spirit. This means that whatever He is in chapter one has been condensed into the all-inclusive Christ and the speaking Spirit in chapter two. At the end of the book of Revelation we see "the Spirit." The all-inclusive Spirit is the consummation of the processed Triune God. The bride is the consummation of the processed tripartite man. Therefore, the processed Triune God will be the bridegroom and the processed tripartite man will be the bride. The processed God and the transformed and glorified tripartite man become a divine couple in eternity.

Revelation 2 and 3 are composed of seven epistles and are the Lord's last words written to His churches. In this chapter we want to see who the speaker is in each of these seven epistles. We want to see this speaking One's status and we also want to see what He promises to the overcoming church. We need to see all the main points of this Person and His promise. In Revelation 2 and 3 we see that the all-inclusive Christ as the Head of the church, walking in the midst of the churches and searching and infusing the churches, speaks to the churches.

THE ALL-INCLUSIVE CHRIST

Holding the Seven Stars in His Right Hand

In the epistle to the church in Ephesus we see the all-inclusive Christ as the One who holds the seven stars in His right hand (Rev. 2:1). The brothers who are taking the lead in the churches as the messengers (Gk. *angels*—Rev. 1:20) are held in this One's hand. This One is the holder of all the church leaders. However, some of the so-called church leaders may not be held by Him. He only holds those He recognizes. To be held by Him, you must be recognized by Him first. We must realize that the leading ones in the churches in the Lord's recovery are held in His hand. Revelation 2:1 also tells us that He walks in the midst of the lampstands. This is a wonderful scene! While the Lord is sitting at the right hand of God as our High Priest interceding for us, the churches (Heb. 7:25), He is holding the messengers of the churches and walking in the midst of the churches to care for them. This One who holds the leaders in His hand and who walks in the midst of the churches is the all-inclusive, excellent, marvelous, mysterious, and wonderful One.

Although we have been experiencing and enjoying One who is so rich, we did not have much realization that this One was so all-inclusive, excellent, marvelous, mysterious, and wonderful. This is why the book of Revelation is needed to unveil such a One to us. We need to realize that this One is the Spirit, the Father, the Son, Christ, Jesus, the Son of Man, the Son of God, the High Priest, and many other items. Many readers of the book of Revelation consider this as a "strange" book because of items such as the beast coming out of the sea, the scarlet beast having seven heads and ten horns, and the seven seals, seven bowls, and seven trumpets. When we come to the book of Revelation, however, we primarily need to care for this wonderful One who is holding all the church leaders in His right hand and who is walking in the midst of all the churches.

A number of times some of the saints came to me and told me that it seemed to them that I never became disappointed or discouraged. They wanted to know why this was the case. The reason for this is that by His mercy, I have seen this marvelous One and I have seen that I am in His hands. To see this strengthens me to the uttermost. I enjoy and experience the all-inclusive, excellent, marvelous, mysterious, and wonderful One. This is why the opening word in Revelation 2 says, "These things says He who holds the seven stars in His right hand, who walks in the midst of the seven golden lampstands" (v. 1). To listen to this One's words you have to see who this One is.

The First and the Last
Who Became Dead and Lived Again

In speaking to the church in Smyrna He says that He is "the First and the Last, who became dead, and lived again" (2:8). The fact that He is the First and the Last means that He never changes. Regardless of how much persecution or what kind of martyrdom the saints suffer, He is the First and He is the Last. Nothing can change Him. You may put Him to death, yet He lives again. This title is seemingly simple, but it implies the creation, the First, and the completion, the Last. This also implies the Lord's incarnation. If He had not been incarnated, He could never have been killed. This also implies His living on this earth. He was incarnated, He lived on this earth, and then He was crucified and He became dead. Then He lived again. Such a declaration implies the creation, the completion, the incarnation, the human living, the crucifixion, and the resurrection. This is a declaration to strengthen the suffering church in Smyrna. The church in Smyrna was experiencing and suffering martyrdom, and the only thing that can support the saints in their martyrdom is to see such a One who created and will complete the entire universe, who became incarnated, who lived on this earth, and who was crucified and resurrected. Such a vision sustains the martyrs to stand in their sufferings.

Having the Sharp Two-edged Sword

The third speaking is to the church in Pergamos, a fallen and worldly church. In this Epistle the speaking One has a sharp two-edged sword (2:12) proceeding out of His mouth (1:16). This sword out of the Lord's mouth is to cut, to judge, to discern, to kill, and to slay. To the degraded and worldly church, He is the One who has such a slaying and judging tongue. If you know Him as such a One, you cannot be worldly.

Having Eyes as a Flame of Fire
and Feet like Shining Brass

The One who speaks to the church in Thyatira is as
the Son of God who has eyes as a flame of fire and feet like
shining brass. The church in Thyatira is a figure of the Babylonian church. In this speaking the Lord declared Himself to
be the Son of God because this church says He is the son of
Mary. He has eyes like a flaming fire for searching and burning and He has feet like shining brass for judging. All the
people in the Babylonian church should see this vision of such
a One.

Having the Seven Spirits of God
and the Seven Stars

The One who has the seven Spirits of God and the seven
stars speaks to the church in Sardis (Rev. 3:1). The stars are
the messengers, which means that the messengers should
shine as the stars. In order to shine they must be full of the
intensified Spirit, the seven Spirits. He has the seven stars
and the seven Spirits as the supply to the stars so that the
stars can shine.

The Holy One and the True One

The sixth speaking is to the best of the seven churches,
the church in Philadelphia. He speaks to the church in Philadelphia as the holy One, the true One, who has the key of
David, and who opens and no one shall shut, and shuts and
no one shall open (3:7). To the church of brotherly love, the
Lord is the holy One, the true One, by whom and with whom
the recovered church can be holy, separated from the world,
and true, faithful, to God. Also, to the recovered church, the
Lord is the One who has the key of David, the key of the kingdom, with authority to open and to shut. Regardless of how
much opposition there is, no one can shut the door. The key is
not in the hand of the opposers, but in the hand of the One we
serve and the One in whom we trust. We have to know Him
and see the vision concerning Him. Regardless of how much

opposition there is, the doors are increasingly open and the key is in His hand. Hallelujah for this divine fact!

The Amen, the Faithful and True Witness, and the Beginning of the Creation of God

The seventh speaking is to the church in Laodicea where the Lord is revealed as the Amen, the faithful and true Witness, the beginning of the creation of God (3:14). The final speaking to the churches is done by the Amen. Amen means "that's it." Whatever He says, that's it. The Lord is also the firm, steadfast, and trustworthy One. Hence, He is the faithful and true Witness. Furthermore, He is the beginning of the creation of God. This means that the entire universe as God's creation began from Him. The Lord is the unchanging and ever-existing source of God's work. He was the beginning of God's entire creation. Without Him nothing could happen because He was the beginning.

As the Amen He is the ending. In His address to the church in Laodicea the Lord declares Himself to be the Amen first, the faithful and true Witness second, and the Beginning last. These expressions in such an order show us that He is One that we cannot explain. The order of these titles is not according to our human logic. He is the Beginning of the entire universe, the Witness to keep the things going, and the Amen, the very ending. Whatever God intended to do, this will be. Amen! God wants a New Jerusalem—amen! God wants a church in Irving—amen! God wants you to be an overcomer—amen! Just say amen; do not say you cannot make it. God wants you to be holy—amen! God wants you to be a co-king of Christ—amen! God wants to have many churches in America—amen! God wants every church to be an overcoming church—amen! To all of God's promises and to all that God desires to do He is the Amen. We should not forget that He declares Himself to be the Amen not in the first epistle but in the last epistle. He is the Amen! He is everything and He is amen to everything. We all have to see and know Him to such an extent. He is the One who is all-inclusive, excellent, marvelous, mysterious, and wonderful.

THE PROMISES TO THE OVERCOMERS

The Tree of Life and the Crown of Life

Now we must see His promises to the overcomers in the seven churches. The Lord does not promise us a big mansion, a good car, a high promotion, or good children. His sevenfold promise is much more wonderful than any of these things. To the church in Ephesus this all-inclusive, wonderful One promises to give the overcomers to eat of Himself as the tree of life. This is the divine life. To the church in Smyrna He promises to give the overcomers the crown of life. The eating of the tree of life is inward for supply and the crown of life is outward for glory. These promises are wrapped up with the divine life. This life first must be our food and then it will be our expression and our glorification as the crown of life.

Not Being Hurt of the Second Death

The Lord also promises the overcomers in the church in Smyrna that they will not be hurt of the second death (2:11). The second death is the lake of fire (20:14). This means that since you are enjoying life to such an extent, death can never touch you. The lake of fire, the second death, is the totality of death. If someone has not received the Lord, his spirit is dead and then he will die in the body. All the sinners will be thrown into the lake of fire, which means they will die in their soul. The second death, which is the lake of fire, is the totality of death. If you enjoy Christ as the tree of life, you will enjoy the crown of life and the totality of death has nothing to do with you and cannot touch you.

The Hidden Manna and the White Stone

The Lord promises to give the overcomers in the church in Pergamos to eat of Himself as the hidden manna (2:17). The hidden manna is deeper than the tree of life. The open manna was revealed in Exodus 16, but the hidden manna is something particular and specific for your enjoyment. This specific thing is still Christ Himself. When you enjoy this specific portion of the divine life, you will receive a white stone for building (2:17). This promise reveals both life and

building. Life and building are the structure of the sevenfold
promise. Life for our enjoyment and experience will result in
the building. You will be a white stone, which means a justified and acceptable stone. The color white in the Bible
signifies justification and acceptance. You will be a stone
which is so acceptable to Him and which is altogether justified in His searching eyes. This stone is for His building.

Authority over the Nations and the Morning Star

The fourth promise is to the overcomers in Thyatira. They
will be given the authority over the nations to shepherd them
with an iron rod and they will also enjoy Him as the morning
star (2:26-29). The morning star appears when the night
becomes darkest. This shows us that at the darkest time,
within us there is a star shining. This indicates that in addition to life and building we also have the light. The sevenfold
promise is wrapped up with life, building, and light. As an
overcomer the totality of death cannot touch you, you will be
full of life, you will be the precious material for God's building, and you will enjoy the particular light, the morning star.

Clothed in White Garments and Not Having
Their Names Erased out of the Book of Life

The fifth promise is to the church in Sardis where the Lord
promises to give the overcomers to be clothed in white garments and not to have their names erased out of the book of
life but confessed by Him before His Father and His angels
(3:5-6). Sardis is a figure of the reformed church, the Protestant
church. The overcomers will be clothed with white garments.
White garments signify the walk and living which is unspot-
ted by death and which will be approved by the Lord. These
white garments mean that the overcomers will be entirely
justified. Also, their names will not be erased out of the book
of life but will be confessed by Him at His second coming.

Kept out of the Great Tribulation
to Be a Pillar in the Temple

The overcomers in the church in Philadelphia will be kept
out of the hour of the great tribulation (3:10). This means

that before the great tribulation the overcomers will be raptured. While the entire earth is suffering under the great tribulation the overcomers will be taken away into the *parousia* (Gk.), the presence, of the coming One. While the other believers are suffering in the tribulation, the overcomers will be enjoying His presence. This is a reward of enjoyment to the ones who are full of life.

Also, these overcomers will be pillars in the temple of His God with the name of His God and the name of the city of His God, the New Jerusalem, which descends out of heaven from His God; also, His new name will be written upon them (3:12). Now the overcomers are not merely stones, but they are built into pillars. This means that no one can pull them out of the temple. Some of the saints came into the church life and after a couple of months they left. They left because they had never been built in. It is very hard to pull out the steel beam of a building. In the same way, the overcomers of the church in Philadelphia all have been built into the temple and are the pillars in the temple. These overcomers bear three names: the name of God, the name of the holy city, New Jerusalem, and the new name of this wonderful One. We do not know what this new name will be because it is a secret. The main point is that the overcomers experience the enjoyment of life and the building into God's temple as their reward.

Feasting with Him and Sitting on His Throne

The final promise to the overcomers in Laodicea is to feast with Him and to sit on His throne (3:20-22). The Lord promises to dine with the one who opens the door to Him. To dine is not merely to eat one food, but the riches of a meal. This may refer to the eating of the rich produce of the good land of Canaan by the children of Israel (Josh. 5:10-12). To sit with the Lord on His throne will be a prize to the overcomer that he may participate in the Lord's authority in the coming millennial kingdom.

The Essence and Issue of the Sevenfold Promise

We can see that the sevenfold promise is wrapped up with

life, with building, and with light, and the issue is the sitting on His throne and the authority to rule over the nations. Regretfully, all the aspects of the sevenfold promise are not being taught today in Christianity. Thank the Lord, however, that by His mercy we do have a burden to see such a promise. We overcome the world by such a promise. We need to be those caring for the eating of the tree of life. We should not care for riches, for position, or for a name, but for the eating of the hidden manna. We care to feast with Him, we care for the crown of life, we care to be a piece of white stone, and to be built into a pillar in God's temple. We care to sit on His throne with Him and to be rewarded with His authority to rule over the nations. Our eyes need to be opened to see this wonderful One and to see His marvelous promise. This promise is full of life, light, and building, and the issue is that we will sit on His throne to be His co-kings to rule over the nations. Today we are enjoying Him as our food—He is our tree of life and our hidden manna.

CHAPTER TWENTY-THREE

THE SEVEN SPIRITS

(4)

Scripture Reading: Rev. 4:5; 5:6b, 7-10; 7:2-8; 8:3-5; 10:1-5; 18:1; 11:15; 19:7-9, 11-21; 1:9b; 22:1-2

Prayer: Lord, we worship You for Your New Testament economy. How we thank You for the book of Revelation that conveys to us the picture of Your economy. Lord, we also thank You that You have opened Your Word to us. Thank You that You are speaking among us. Thank You that You do have an oracle here on earth for You to speak Your Word into all our hearts. Lord, we trust in Your cleansing blood that we may enjoy You and that we may enjoy Your anointing. Grant us the abundant and rich anointing. Anoint our mouth and our ears. Anoint our speaking and our listening. Lord, we are looking to You that You would move on and on among us in Your recovery until You reach Your goal. Lord, do cover us with Your prevailing blood against all the attacks, the frustrations, and the disturbances from the evil one. Lord, in these days of fighting destroy the power of darkness. We claim Your victory that You have gained on the cross over the enemy. We pray that You would shame Your enemy. May we all be filled with Yourself, filled with Your glory, filled with Your anointing, and filled with Your rich grace to meet every need. We bring every need to You. Lord, speak a particular word to meet every need. Thank You, Lord Jesus. Amen.

A VIEW OF REVELATION

The book of Revelation is very complicated. It covers many fields and many aspects. Unless you have a thorough study of this book, it will be hard for you to have a bird's eye view. In this chapter I would like to present a very simple and brief picture or view of the book of Revelation. You may have picked up many points in your reading of this book, yet I would ask you, at least temporarily, to drop all the impressions you have received in order to receive a fresh, clear view of this book.

The All-inclusive One

First, Revelation is a book revealing Christ as the all-inclusive One, and this all-inclusive One is the focus of God's New Testament economy in this book. This book of consummation is focused on Christ as the all-inclusive, excellent, marvelous, mysterious, and wonderful One. We also must see, on the other hand, that this book not only presents us with a focus but also with a view. A view is different from a focus. The focus is the central point of a view. In the past three chapters we mainly covered the focus of the book of Revelation, and the focus is a Person. We need to see the view that has this wonderful Person as its focus.

The Throne

The book of Revelation presents us a view of God's universal administration. In this view, there is a center. The center is not the focus. The focus is a Person, but the center is the throne. The throne in this book is a great item. The first three chapters in the book of Revelation are on the churches. Immediately after this section on the churches, John saw a throne at the beginning of chapter four. John was in his spirit and he saw a view in the heavens concerning the earth. The heavens were opened to him and he saw that there is a throne in the heavens. This throne is the throne of God for His administration and is the center of God's universal administration. Revelation 4:2 says, "Immediately I was in spirit; and behold, there was a throne set in heaven, and One sitting upon the throne." Of course, the One sitting on the throne is God, "and He Who was sitting was like in appearance to a jasper stone and a sardius" (4:3). Remember that the view that John had is a heavenly view, but it is concerning the earth.

The Seven Lamps of Fire
Burning before the Throne

In the center of such a view there is a throne with One sitting on the throne. There are also seven lamps of fire burning before the throne (4:5). The seven lamps of fire burning before the throne are burning horizontally. These seven lamps are the seven Spirits of God. They are sent forth into all the earth (Rev. 5:6) to carry out God's administration by their burning. In the Bible fire first implies judging. The fire came down upon Sodom to judge it (Gen. 19:24). Also, fire implies purifying and refining. There are many oil refineries in Texas to burn out the dross of the oil. Finally, the burning of fire also implies bringing forth.

The seven Spirits of God burning before God's throne as a flame of fire are judging the entire world, both the believers and the unbelievers. According to 1 Peter 4:17 this judgment begins from the house of God and will spread to the unbelievers, the entire earth. The seven Spirits are sent forth unto all the earth to judge the earth, to purify the earth, to refine the earth, and to bring forth the pure golden lampstands, shining in this dark age as the testimony of Jesus. The seven Spirits do not burn without a goal. There is an intent, a purpose, for the burning of the seven Spirits, that is, to bring forth the golden lampstands, the churches. If we are shortsighted and do not have the foresight, we will be very much disappointed by today's world situation. Today's world is full of darkness, corruption, and immorality. Thank the Lord, however, that His Word is like a lamp shining in a dark place (2 Pet. 1:19), and His Word is as a lamp unto our feet and a light unto our path (Psa. 119:105). Because we have the foresight, we would not be disappointed. Many Christians and all the people of the world do not know what is going on behind the scenes in today's world situation. We realize, however, according to His enlightening Word, that the seven Spirits today are burning to judge, to purify, and to refine with a purpose. The burning of the seven Spirits of God before God's administrative throne has a purpose to bring forth the golden lampstands, the churches, for the fulfillment of God's New Testament economy.

The Standing Lamb

Thus far, we have seen three items: the throne, the One sitting on the throne, and the seven Spirits of God burning as a flame before the throne. The fourth item is "a Lamb standing" (5:6). Around the throne are the twenty-four elders and the four living creatures. The twenty-four elders represent the angels. In God's creation, angels are the most ancient ones. The four living creatures represent all other living creatures. Among these are the lampstands, and the Lamb is the focus. The throne is the center and the Lamb is the focus. The Lamb is not only in the scene but in the center of the scene. He becomes the role at the center as the focus, and the seven lamps burning before the throne, which are the seven Spirits before the throne (Rev. 1:4), are His seven eyes (Rev. 5:6). Therefore, their location must be His face. The seven Spirits have also been sent forth into all the earth, running "to and fro through the whole earth" (Zech. 4:10). This gives us a heavenly view concerning the earth with the churches.

Some believers consider the book of Revelation even as "a fairy tale," so they put this book aside. We, however, should consider the book of Revelation in a serious way, since this concerns our destiny. Furthermore, to add something to the book of Revelation or to take away something is also quite serious. If anyone adds to the words of Revelation, "God shall add to him the plagues which are written in this book" (22:18). Also, if you cut off any of the words of this book, you will be cut off from the tree of life and from the New Jerusalem (22:19). The view which I have presented to you is something which we need to see since this concerns our eternal destiny. We have seen the Father sitting on the throne, God the Spirit burning before the throne, and God the Son as the slain Lamb standing there. We have also seen that the seven lamps burning before the throne of God, which are the seven Spirits of God, are actually the seven eyes of the Lamb.

The Seven Eyes of the Lamb

This view is economical because this is not a matter of the Triune God's existence, but something related to His move. Economically speaking, the seven Spirits are the eyes of the Son. Essentially speaking, the Father is the Father, the Son is the Son, and the Spirit is the Spirit for existence. Functionally speaking, however, the essential Spirit becomes the functional eyes of the Son. The key to define the Divine Trinity is to see both the essential and the economical Trinity. Revelation touches God's administration and the entire divine administration is a matter of God's economy. Therefore, whatever this book reveals to us concerning the Divine Trinity is economical, not essential. The traditional teaching of the Divine Trinity stresses that the Father, the Son, and the Spirit are three separate Persons. The last book of the Bible, however, shows us that the Spirit has become the eyes of the Son. We cannot say that the eyes of a person are another person. This shows us that the traditional teaching of the Divine Trinity is short of the adequate and full knowledge of the Bible. Economically speaking, the Spirit of God in God's administration is the eyes of the administrating Son. This is for function, not for existence. In order for us to do anything we need our eyes. This shows us that, in the divine administration, Christ needs the Spirit to be His eyes.

The view we have seen shows us how God is going to carry out His universal administration. In order to carry out His administration God needs an executor and this Executor is this wonderful Person, the slain Lamb. The all-inclusive, excellent, marvelous, mysterious, and wonderful One is the Executor of God's administration. John saw the view that in the entire universe no one was qualified or worthy to carry out God's administration except this One (Rev. 5:4-6). Because He is qualified and worthy, the seven seals were handed over to Him. This One is qualified to open the seven seals, to carry out God's economy. The way He carries out God's economy is by the seven Spirits as His eyes. Without the seven Spirits, Christ does not have the eyes. Christ is the very focal Executor of God's economy, yet He needs the seven

Spirits as His eyes to carry out God's economy. This view leads us eventually to the focus and to the eyes of the focus, Christ and the Spirit.

OUR "DICTIONARY" CONCERNING CHRIST AND THE SPIRIT

Many of us have a "dictionary" concerning Christ which is quite small. Christ, however, needs a universally great dictionary to define and describe Him. The entire sixty-six books of the Bible are needed to describe and define such a Christ. This is also true concerning the Spirit. In some people's dictionary, the Spirit is merely the "Holy Ghost." The full revelation of the Holy Scriptures, however, reveals that the Spirit is the all-inclusive, compound, processed, life-giving, indwelling, sevenfold Spirit. I must testify that every time I speak concerning the Triune God, Christ, and the church, I have the sense that there is always something more to speak. My "dictionary" concerning these items has been getting bigger and bigger throughout the years.

THE BURNING OF THE SEVEN SPIRITS DIRECTING THE WORLD SITUATION

Christ and the Spirit are revealed in Revelation to carry out God's economy. First, this carrying out of God's economy involves administrating the entire situation in this universe and mainly administrating the world situation. All the international affairs are neither in the hands of the diplomats nor in the hands of the United Nations. The deciding place is on the throne. Everything in today's situation is decided on the throne. By my reading and studying of the world situation over the past sixty years, I fully realize that the throne of God in the heavens is the deciding factor of the world situation. Neither Hitler, Mussolini, Stalin, nor any of the world governments were the deciding factors of the world situation. They all failed. The deciding factor is the throne of God. All of the world leaders are under the flaming of the seven Spirits. The seven Spirits are burning on this earth today for the carrying out of God's administration. Christ carries out His mission as the Ruler of the kings of the earth by the seven burning Spirits. We must realize that today the seven Spirits of God are burning not only concerning the churches but also concerning the world situation for the churches. The entire world situation is under the flame of the burning of the seven Spirits. The seven Spirits today are carrying out God's administration on this earth. The world situation, the international affairs, are all under the direction of this flame. I have seen the flame of the seven burning Spirits before the throne of God sovereignly controlling the world situation. When Hitler took over Belgium in World War II, it would have been possible for him to go straight into England. England was unprepared to face that situation and was ready to be taken over by Hitler, but Hitler made the decision to turn to attack Russia. The flame of the seven Spirits turned him away from England at that time. History tells us that this was a great mistake made by Hitler, and this was under the sovereign control of the seven burning Spirits before the throne of God.

Bringing Forth the Golden Lampstands

The purpose of the burning flame in carrying out God's economy is to bring forth the golden lampstands, the churches. Burning implies judging, purifying, refining, and producing. Never be disappointed by the rottenness, corruption, and immorality of today's human society. Do not be disappointed or so concerned for the world situation. Also, do not be disappointed by the weakness of the local churches. I do not believe in the seemingly disappointing condition in the world or in the churches. I believe in the flame of the burning seven Spirits which control and direct the world and which also judge, purify, and refine the church to produce a pure golden lampstand. We are here endeavoring to afford the Lord a chance and an entrance to judge us, purify us, and refine us to produce a pure golden lampstand. We are open wide to the flaming of the seven Spirits of God. We all need to pray, "Dear divine Flame, come! Come and judge! Come and purify! Come and refine that You may produce the golden lampstand." Nearly all the doors are closed to Christ in today's situation. By His mercy, though, we are open to Him.

Every day, every morning, and every evening, we need to pray, "Lord, come; we are open to You! We open every avenue of our being to You." I do not know how much you pray or how you pray, but I can testify that nearly every day I pray, "Lord, enlighten me; search me within and expose me, Lord. I like to be enlightened by You and exposed in Your light." Are you like this or do you shut yourself up and hide something from Him? We all need to pray, "Lord, we are open. Come and shine upon us and shine from within us and enlighten every avenue and every corner of our being. I like to be exposed, purged, and purified." Then the Lord has a way to produce a pure golden lampstand. The burning is going on not only in the entire world situation, but also in the churches. The more I read the newspapers, the more I get confirmed that the flaming Spirits direct the world situation, and also this flaming purifies the church to produce the golden lampstands.

The seven Spirits, who are out from the eternal One and of the redeeming One, are the seven lamps of fire burning before God's throne, executing God's economy in the universe, and the seven eyes of the slain Lamb, searching and infusing the churches (4:5; 5:6b). The twofold mission of the seven Spirits is to carry out God's administration and to search and infuse the churches. The seven Spirits search out our sinfulness and infuse us with the riches of Christ. While a person is speaking to you, his two eyes are also infusing you with his burden. In like manner, the seven Spirits of God as the eyes of the Lamb infuse us with this wonderful One's burden and essence.

THE EXECUTOR OF GOD'S NEW TESTAMENT ECONOMY

Furthermore, in Revelation the redeeming Lamb becomes the Executor of God's New Testament economy (5:7-10).

As Another Angel

As another Angel He cares for God's chosen people, the Israelites, executes the prayer of the saints concerning God's economy, possesses the earth in the future, and appears in glory to make the whole earth the kingdom of God (7:2-8; 8:3-5; 10:1-5; 18:1; 11:15). The all-inclusive One has another title—another Angel. The book of Revelation mentions this Angel four times. Revelation 7:2-8 indicates that this Angel takes care of God's chosen people, Israel. On this earth God has two peoples—the chosen people of Israel and the redeemed people, the saints, the church. In Revelation 8:3-5 Christ is mentioned again as another Angel to present the prayers of the church to God and to carry out the answers to these prayers. God is taking care of His two peoples, Israel and the church. Israel has been and still is under persecution. The entire world has been trying to diminish Israel, so Israel needs special care in order to be preserved. The little nation of Israel is surrounded by many Arab countries, yet it still survives. This is because another Angel is taking care of Israel.

God also has another people, the church. The church's function mainly is to pray, call on the Lord's name, and cry out to the throne; then the other Angel offers all the church's prayer to God and brings down the answer to these prayers (Rev. 8:3-5). His way to bring down the answer is to scatter the answer upon the earth. Christ offers the prayer to God, He adds Himself as the incense, then He receives the answer and pours the answer out upon the earth. Today the entire earth is under the answers of the saints' prayers.

The third time the book of Revelation mentions Christ as another Angel is in 10:1-5. As the strong Angel coming down out of heaven, Christ, the universal Person, places His right foot on the sea and His left foot on the land. To place His feet on the sea and upon the land is to tread upon them, and to tread upon them is to take possession of them (Deut. 11:24; Josh. 1:3; Psa. 8:6). This indicates that Christ is coming down to take possession of the earth. Only He is worthy to open the scroll of God's economy, and only He is qualified to possess the earth. Eventually, all the peoples of the earth who are fighting in order to claim more territory will discover that they have done this in vain. The earth is the Lord's (Psa. 24:1) and by the time of Revelation 10 He will come to take possession of it. All the waters and the lands will be under the feet of Christ! He will be the universal One coming to tread on the sea and the land. The land and the sea are His, not the rulers' of this earth. All the nations who are seeking to possess and dominate other countries are working in vain.

Finally, Revelation 18:1 shows us that as another Angel of God He appears in glory to make the whole earth the kingdom of God (11:15). He comes to take over the entire earth and make it His kingdom and God's kingdom. The kingdom of the world becomes the kingdom of Christ at His coming back after His judgment upon the nations (Dan. 7:13-14; 2:44-45). This is the wonderful One to be the Executor of God's administration to take care of His people, to present His people's prayer to God, and to possess the earth to make the earth His kingdom.

As the Lamb of God and as the Word of God

Also, the redeeming Lamb as the Executor of God's New Testament economy marries the Bride (19:7-9), and as the Word of God judges and wars against Antichrist and his armies (19:11-21). The church eventually will be the Bride for the Lamb to marry, and the worldly people will consummate in Antichrist with his army against God. This wonderful Executor as the Lamb of God will marry the positive people, the Bride. Then as the Word of God He will slay the negative ones. To us He is the Lamb of God. To the worldly people who are in rebellion against Him He is the Word of God. The Bible tells us that God judges, condemns, and puts people to death by His Word (2 Thes. 2:8). The totality of God's Word is Christ. The Christ in John 1:1 and 14 is the Word for incarnation and redeeming, but in Revelation 19 Christ as the Word is for judging. Both the Lamb and the Word are aspects of this wonderful Executor. As the Executor of God's New Testament economy He is another Angel, the Lamb of God, and the Word of God.

THE SEVEN EYES OF THE LAMB AS
THE SEVEN SHINING LAMPS

The seven eyes of the Lamb as the Executor of God's New Testament economy are the seven lamps upheld by the seven lampstands, the seven churches, shining and enlightening as the testimony of Jesus (Rev. 1:9b, 11-12). This burning, judging, purifying, refining, and producing Spirit is the lamps upheld by the lampstands, the churches. This means the churches shine through the lamps and these lamps are the Spirit, the real testimony. We have stressed very much that the seven Spirits today are judging, purifying, refining, and bringing forth the churches. We must realize, though, that the extent to which the seven Spirits refine is the extent to which they shine. If we do not allow the seven Spirits to refine us, the seven Spirits have no way to shine and there is no testimony. The shining of the seven Spirits is the testimony. The more we let the Spirit purify us and refine us, the more He shines through us and this shining is the testimony of the churches. This is why we have to open ourselves every day to welcome Him to enter into our being to refine, to judge, to purge, and to purify us. Then He will shine through us and this shining is the very testimony of the church, the testimony of Jesus. The testimony of Jesus is the shining of the seven Spirits from within all the believers in the churches.

THE SEVEN SPIRITS AS THE SEVEN LAMPS OF FIRE BECOMING THE RIVER OF WATER

The seven Spirits who are the lamps of fire in this age, executing God's New Testament economy (4:5), will become the river of water, saturating the holy city of God, the New Jerusalem (22:1-2). First, the seven Spirits are the lamps of fire and eventually the seven Spirits will be the river of water. Fire and water both refer to the same Spirit. Fire is to purge, refine, and produce, and water is to saturate and to supply. The Spirit is the refining fire in this age, and the Spirit is also the saturating, supplying water, first in this age and then in the coming age and eternity. The refining fire produces the lampstands, the churches, in this age with the saturating water, which will consummate in the New Jerusalem. Both the lampstand and the New Jerusalem are the full expression of God and the testimony of Jesus, in this age and in eternity.

CHAPTER TWENTY-FOUR

THE SEVEN SPIRITS

(5)

Scripture Reading: Rev. 1:9, 11-12

ISSUING IN THE GOLDEN LAMPSTANDS

God's New Testament economy consummates in the golden lampstands and in the New Jerusalem. In this chapter we want to see that the searching and infusing by the seven Spirits as the seven eyes of the redeeming Lamb issue in this age in the golden lampstands (1:11-12). As we have seen, the book of Revelation is the conclusion of the entire Scripture. In this book we see things both new and old. Some things revealed in this book are altogether new and other things were already revealed in the Old Testament. Genesis is a field where the seeds of nearly all the divine truths were sown. All these seeds grow in the following books until we reach the last book of the Bible, Revelation. In this book is the reaping, the harvest, of all the divine truths which were sown as seeds in the book of Genesis.

THE LAMPSTAND IN THE OLD TESTAMENT

The first issue of God's New Testament economy is the golden lampstands which are signs or symbols of the churches. The lampstand is not a new item because in Exodus 25 we see the lampstand in the Holy Place of the tabernacle (vv. 31-40). In Exodus 25 we see that in the tabernacle, which was God's dwelling place on this earth, there is neither light made by God from the heavens nor light made by man in a secular way. There is no natural light, but a particular light was there shining and enlightening the entire Holy Place. That light was the light of the lampstand. The lampstand in Exodus 25 was a type of Christ being the light from God to us. The second instance of the lampstand in the Scriptures is in the building of the temple in 1 Kings 7:49. The third instance had very much to do with the rebuilding of God's temple in Zechariah 4:2-10. The lampstand in Zechariah 4 does not signify Christ, but it symbolizes the children of Israel. The children of Israel should be a lampstand shining out God.

THE MULTIPLICATION OF CHRIST

In the book of Revelation we see that the lampstand is repeated again, but this time the lampstands are plural (1:11-12) because these seven lampstands are the figures, the signs, the symbols, of seven local churches. This shows us that in the eyes of God every local church is a lampstand, and by this we can see that a local church is a reproduction or a duplication of Christ. When all the lampstands or local churches are added together, they are a multiplication of Christ. In Exodus 25 Christ was the unique lampstand, but in Revelation this lampstand has been reproduced, duplicated, and thus multiplied. Actually, there were more than seven local churches on the earth at the time of Revelation so the number seven is a representative number. Every lampstand is a reproduction of the lampstand revealed in Exodus 25. The lampstand is an old item, yet it bears a number of new characteristics. In Exodus there was only one lampstand, but in Revelation there are seven. The lampstand was there in Exodus, but the sevenfold aspect of the lampstand was not there. The new aspect of the lampstand is its multiplication.

PAUL'S REVELATION CONCERNING THE CHURCH

One of the great teachers in the Bible concerning the church was the Apostle Paul. In the book of Ephesians which is on the church, he tells us that the church is the Body of Christ (1:22-23), the fullness of the One who fills all in all (1:23), the new man to fulfill God's purpose on this earth (2:15), the kingdom of God, God's household, which is God's family (2:19), God's dwelling place in our spirit (2:22), the wife, the bride, to satisfy Christ (5:23-32), and finally, the warrior fighting the battle for God's kingdom (6:10-20). Seven items are clearly revealed in this great teacher's Epistle on the church. When John spoke concerning the church he brought in something new which Paul never touched, and this new item is the lampstand. Paul unveiled seven wonderful items of the church in Ephesians, but in my opinion John exceeded Paul with his revelation of the church as a lampstand.

The most mysterious aspect of the church which Paul gives us is the Body as the fullness of the One that fills all in all. In Ephesians 1 the fullness is the fullness of Christ as the One who fills all in all, but the same fullness in chapter three of Ephesians is the fullness of the infinite God (v. 19). In Ephesians 3 Paul prays that Christ may make His home in our hearts that we may know His dimensions, the breadth, length, height, and depth, that we may be filled unto the fullness of the infinite God. The fullness is firstly of the unlimited Christ, the very Christ that fills all in all, and then the fullness of the infinite God. This fullness is a mystery which has been wrongly interpreted by many teachers as the riches of Christ. Fullness, however, in the book of Ephesians is not the riches, but the issue of our enjoyment of the riches of Christ. Our enjoyment of the riches of Christ issues in this mysterious fullness.

THE SIGNIFICANCE OF THE LAMPSTAND
BEING GOLDEN

The church as the fullness is mysterious and abstract, but the lampstands are very concrete. A lampstand is not mysterious, but very solid. When you pray much and get into this item in the holy Word, you will realize that the sign, the symbol, of the lampstand is not mysterious, but its significance is far beyond our understanding. From my youth, I have paid much attention to this item in the New Testament. I read a certain spiritual paper published in London, and the front cover always had a picture of a lampstand on it. As I was reading that paper I always wondered what the lampstand was. The writer of this paper gave a number of messages on the pure, golden lampstand and he mostly stressed one point—the pureness of the gold of the lampstand. This was very helpful in the spiritual life, but I still did not know what the main significance of the lampstand was. Later, I received some help to see that the lampstand is for shining in the night, to enlighten in the dark age. In the dark night there is the need of the light, and the churches are the lampstands holding the lamps to shine and enlighten. Although this is a correct understanding, I still felt that this was too superficial. Even little children know that a lampstand is for enlightening. I still wanted to see why it was a golden lampstand. Why are the lampstands not made of glass or some other material?

The lampstands as signs signifying the churches are made of pure gold. When reading this, some of the saints may feel that they have never seen a church so golden. They may feel that the churches they have seen are "muddy" or at best "wooden." Is the church in your locality muddy, wooden, or golden? On the night of a glorious meeting of the church you may feel that the church is golden, but the next day something will happen to make you feel that the church is altogether muddy. We must realize that we have our perspective of the church, and God has His. We think that our perspective is very smart, sharp, and to the point, but God's perspective is absolutely different from ours.

I still remember an incident that happened in a prayer meeting in Shanghai nearly forty years ago. A very elderly sister prayed in a very genuine way, crying to the Lord. Her prayer was long, earnest, and you may say that it was even powerful. She was lamenting the fact that the church was so weak with many shortcomings. According to her prayer, the church in Shanghai was muddy. Immediately after her prayer, Brother Nee prayed with praise for the church. He praised the Lord for the fact that His church was wonderful and he quoted Balaam's prayer concerning Israel in Numbers 23 where Balaam said that God "hath not beheld iniquity in Jacob, neither hath He seen perverseness in Israel" (v. 21). Balaam also went on to say concerning Israel, "Blessed is he that blesseth thee, and cursed is he that curseth thee" (24:9). This incident shocked all the saints. There were two kinds of prayers. One prayer described the church there as being weak, and another prayer uplifted the church to the heavens. Of these two prayers, which would you say was right? Actually, one prayer was right from the human perspective, and the other prayer was right from the heavenly angle. I was told that the elderly sister who prayed her prayer went back home weeping and regretting for her natural concept concerning the church.

Many times my feeling concerning myself was that I was worse than muddy. When Moses was called by God, he told the Lord that the Egyptians would not believe that the Lord had appeared unto him (Exo. 4:1). One of the signs which the Lord gave Moses to perform is in Exodus 4:6-7. The Lord told Moses to put his hand into his bosom. Moses did this and when he took it out, his hand was leprous. When Moses put his hand back into his bosom again and took it out, his hand became as it once was. Moses discovered through this sign that his inward nature was leprous. How could a leprous person be called by God? In God's heavenly perspective, however, Moses was a great vessel for God's use. God had already given Moses a vision of a flame of fire burning in a bush and yet the bush was not consumed (Exo. 3:2). God does not use what we have as the burning fuel. God Himself is the fuel, the fire, burning within us. We should not look at ourselves since we are not worth looking at. If any brothers were to stay with one another for approximately one week, they would discover that none of them are "golden brothers." On the other hand, we all need to realize that because we have received the Lord, we have something golden in us. We all need to praise the Lord that we do have some amount of gold in us.

Many of us have been in the church life for years and we do not have much realization that we have grown that much. According to our human perspective, there is too much waste of time. We must remember that to the Lord one thousand years is as one day (2 Pet. 3:8). According to God's perspective even fifty years is not such a long time. None of us should be disappointed concerning our growth in life.

I am not encouraging you not to grow, but our growth in life is not up to us. Paul says in 1 Corinthians 3:6, "I planted, Apollos watered, but God made to grow." Last night in the meeting you all may have shouted that the church in your locality is golden. The next morning, however, a phone call may have been made which was full of gossip, discrediting the church. Of course, we all should hate gossip in the church life, but sometimes matters such as this may be of the Lord's sovereignty. I do not encourage people to gossip, but we must realize that the Lord is sovereign over everything that happens in the church life.

We must realize that even during Paul's time there was not a church which was that good. I once heard a sermon many years ago telling the people in the congregation that the church in Philippi was the best church. When I studied the book of Philippians, however, I discovered that even the church in Philippi was not good because among them there were dissenting ones (4:2; 2:2). No church, humanly speaking, is not muddy. Also, from the human point of view no church is golden. God, however, knows that in you and in me there is an amount of gold (2 Cor. 4:7).

THE MULTIPLIED EMBODIMENT
OF THE TRIUNE GOD

After many years of study, I came to the realization that in Exodus the golden lampstand was not only a type of Christ as the light from God to man. The lampstand is also the embodiment of the Triune God. This corresponds with Colossians 2:9 which says, "For in Him dwells all the fullness of the Godhead bodily." As the embodiment of God, the lampstand has three crucial aspects. First, the substance of the lampstand is gold. Second, this gold is not merely a lump of gold but it has a shape, a form. Third, the lampstand has seven lamps shining. Three crucial aspects of the lampstand are the element, the shape, and the expression. When I considered these three aspects of the lampstand, I began to realize that this is a picture of the embodiment of the Triune God. The golden element according to typology always typifies the divine nature of God the Father. The shape of the lampstand signifies

Christ as the embodiment of the invisible God. The form of the lampstand undoubtedly signifies God the Son as the very embodiment of God (Col. 2:9). The seven lamps of the lampstand are the seven Spirits shining in the dark age. Therefore, the expression is God the Spirit. The element refers to God the Father, the shape signifies God the Son, and the expression is God the Spirit. The lampstand which typifies Christ is also the embodiment of the Triune God.

This embodiment, which was unique in Exodus 25, has been multiplied by the local churches which are composed of all the believers. All the believers are also the multiplication of Christ. In John 12:24 the Lord Jesus indicated that He was as a grain of wheat falling into the ground to die and that when He died He would bear much fruit. When the Lord died on the cross many grains were produced in His resurrection, and the many grains are the multiplication of that one grain. Also, Paul said in Philippians 1:21a, "For to me to live is Christ." This is another indication of the multiplication of Christ. Furthermore, 1 Corinthians 12:12 tells us that Christ is not only the Head but also the Body. In Exodus the lampstand was Christ and in Revelation the lampstands are the churches. This indicates that not only Christ Himself is a lampstand but every local church is also a lampstand; therefore, the lampstands as the local churches are the multiplication of that unique lampstand.

With God the Father's Nature
as the Divine Element

We have mentioned already that all of us have some amount of gold in us, and gold signifies God in His nature. When we believed in the Lord Jesus, we received God into us (1 John 4:15). All the believers have been born of God (John 1:13). This matter of being born indicates that something substantial of God enters into the children whom He begets. When a father begets a child something of the father is imparted into that child. As those who have been begotten of God we have to believe and realize that the divine substance has been born into our being.

In John 4:24 the Lord told us that God is Spirit. This

means that God is Spirit in substance. To say that a table is wood means the table's substance is wood. The Lord also went on to say that since God is Spirit, those that worship Him must worship Him in their spirit. Many of us think that to worship means to kneel down or bow down to God. However, the entire context of John 4 does not give us this kind of concept. Rather, in John 4 to worship is to drink (vv. 13-14). When you drink the Lord as the living water, this is your real worship to God. To worship God is to contact God in your spirit. The very God whom you worship in John 4 is the living water. It would not be logical to contact the living water by kneeling down to it. The living water is here for us to drink, and our drinking of the living water is a real worship to God who is the living water. When we drink the living water we receive something as a kind of element into us. Furthermore, in John 6 the Lord told us that He was the bread of life (v. 35). Life is very abstract, but bread is solid. When you eat bread, surely some element gets into your being. The New Testament shows us that we believers have received something of God substantially into our being and after believing we should drink of Him and eat of Him, continually receiving some substance of Him into our being.

When I was young, I was taught and encouraged to pray every day and to tell God what I needed and wanted. Eventually, however, I learned that the first thing in prayer is not to ask for what you want. To pray is to drink of God and to eat of God (John 6:57). The more you pray, the more you eat and the more you drink, and the more you drink and eat, the more of God you will substantially receive. Paul said that he planted and that Apollos watered but God is the One who makes to grow. Growth comes out of something substantial. If plants are not fertilized, they will not grow that much. If your children are not fed, they will not grow. Many of the American children grow substantially because of eating the rich food of America. After eating the riches of America and being constituted with them, they become "the fullness of America." We can only grow in Christ by receiving additionally and continually the divine substance into our being. The divine nature of which we partake (2 Pet. 1:4) is typified by gold. As believers, we need to eat (John 6:57), drink (John 7:37; 1 Cor. 12:13), and breathe the Lord (John 20:22; Lam. 3:55-56). When we do this, we are drinking "golden" water, eating "golden" bread, and breathing "golden" breath. Whatever we are drinking, eating, or breathing is gold because it is divine.

Although, humanly speaking, I can see many weaknesses in the church, I must testify that I see the increase of God in all the saints. Undoubtedly, our growth is very slow in the same way that our physical growth is also slow. From day to day the parents notice little growth in their children. After five years, however, a noticeable amount of growth has actually taken place. After twenty-two years, some children may grow up to be taller than their parents. After planting, watering, and fertilizing the plants, we can go home to rest because God gives the growth. This also applies to our growth in life, in Christ. All the churches are growing in the Lord.

With God the Son as the Embodiment of the Triune God

While we are growing with the divine element, we are being shaped. Life always has the life essence, the life power, and the life shape. We do not need to worry about an apple tree producing bananas. There is no need to make a mold so that the fruit on the apple tree will take the shape of an apple. The apple life has the apple shape in the same way that the divine life has its divine shape. The divine shape is Christ. Christ is the mold, the form, and the likeness, and the New Testament tells us that as His many brethren we will be conformed to His image (Rom. 8:29). In Philippians 3:10 Paul also tells us that as we experience Christ we are being conformed to His death. The more we grow, the more we are in the shape of Christ. According to my experience the shape of Christ is mainly in the mold of His death and resurrection. The more we grow in the divine life, the more we do not live the natural life. We do not move, act, or work in the natural life, but we move, act, and live in the resurrection life. People can see that in our daily life we do not live the natural life because the natural life is under the cross. We live another life, the resurrection life. As a result, in our daily life there is a form, a shape, of Christ's death and resurrection. All the saints in the churches are being shaped into the image of Christ, so all the churches are being molded into a form. When I was a young man studying the Bible, I was taught by some teachers that in the church life there should be no disorder. This teaching is right, but actually it is not a matter of order, but a matter of shape. We all have to be shaped by the divine life into its form, and the form of the divine life is Christ. We all need to let Christ be formed in us (Gal. 4:19).

With God the Spirit
as the Seven Shining Spirits

The golden lampstands are also filled with God the Spirit as the seven shining Spirits—the full expression of the Triune God. In the New Testament we are told to be filled with the Spirit (Eph. 5:18), to walk according to Spirit (Rom. 8:4; Gal. 5:16), and to bear the fruit of the Spirit (Gal. 5:22-23). In our service and in our ministry we need to have the manifestation of the Spirit, so in our daily life we need to have the fruit of the Spirit as our expression. In our church service we can only have the manifestation of the Spirit as our expression by praying in our spirit (Eph. 6:18). We all need to pray unceasingly (1 Thes. 5:17) that we may be filled in our spirit. Ephesians 5:18 charges us not to be filled with wine in our body, but to be filled with the divine element and riches in our spirit. As a result, the Spirit will spontaneously shine out of us. In our daily life we will have the fruit of the Spirit. In our work, service, and ministry, the Spirit will be the manifestation. The fruit of the Spirit and the manifestation of the Spirit are both the expression, the shining, of the lampstands.

Eventually, the church should be the lampstand with God the Father's nature as the element, with God the Son's mold as a shape, and with God the Spirit's expression as the shining. This shining is just the testimony of Jesus. This is the church life and this is what the Lord is after in His recovery today. God's New Testament economy, which is focused on one wonderful Person who has passed through all the processes, issues in this age in the golden lampstand to shine forth the testimony of Jesus. Eventually, in the coming eternity the issue will be the New Jerusalem and that issue will be much richer than the golden lampstand.

CHAPTER TWENTY-FIVE

THE SEVEN SPIRITS

(6)

Scripture Reading: Rev. 1:9, 11-12; Rom. 8:9-11; 1 John 3:9; 5:1-4; Titus 3:5; Eph. 4:23; 2 Cor. 3:18; Rom. 12:2; 8:29; Phil. 3:21

THE SIGN OF THE LAMPSTAND

We have seen that every single local church as a lampstand is an embodiment of the Triune God. When all the local churches are put together they are the multiplication of the lampstand as revealed in Exodus 25; therefore, in this age the lampstands are the multiplied embodiment of the Triune God as the testimony of Jesus. In Paul's fourteen Epistles he mainly taught the mystery of God which is Christ (Col. 2:2) and the mystery of Christ which is the church (Eph. 3:4). Christ and the church are a great mystery (Eph. 5:32). Christ is the embodiment of God and the church as the Body of Christ is the embodiment of Christ; the embodiment of Christ simply means the embodiment of the Triune God. This again shows us that the book of Revelation is the conclusion of all the books of the Bible, especially of all the books of the New Testament, which reveal to us Christ and the church. The conclusion of all the aspects of the church revealed in the foregoing twenty-six books of the Bible is that the church in this age is signified by the lampstand.

Revelation is a book of signs which are symbols with spiritual significance. The first sign of this book is the lampstand, a sign of the church. A sign is a picture, and a picture is always better than one thousand words. It would be hard to describe the lampstand without a picture of it. For example, it is very difficult to describe a person's face. How can one give the dimensions of a person's nose, ears, or cheeks? By looking at a picture of a person's face, though, we are able to see exactly what that person looks like. This is why the end of the New Testament gives us a conclusion of all the definitions of the church in the sign of the lampstand.

THE THREE ASPECTS OF THE LAMPSTAND

The three aspects of the lampstand are the element, the shape, and the expression. The golden element signifies God's divine nature. Also, Christ is described in the New Testament as the embodiment of the invisible God (Col. 2:9). He has a form and a likeness and He is a mold for us to be conformed into (Rom. 8:29). Christ desires to be formed in us (Gal. 4:19). This shows us that Christ is the shape of the lampstand. The Bible does not tell us that the Father has an image or a form, nor does it say that the Spirit has a likeness. The words image, form, likeness, and mold are ascribed to the second of the Trinity, so He is the shape of the lampstand. The expression of the lampstand is the Spirit. In our daily life we have the fruit of the Spirit, and the fruit of any tree is its expression. Then in our ministry, in our service in the church, we have the manifestation of the Spirit. The fruit of the Spirit is mentioned in Galatians 5 where our daily walk is revealed, and the manifestation of the Spirit is mentioned in 1 Corinthians 12 where our ministry or service in the church is mentioned. In our life we have the fruit as the expression, and in our ministry we have the manifestation as the expression. According to the entire revelation of the Bible, God the Father is the element, God the Son is the shape, and God the Spirit is the expression. When these three aspects are put together, we see the lampstand which is the embodiment of the Father, of the Son, and of the Spirit.

A local church is a lampstand, signifying the Triune God embodied in human beings. This is the great mystery of godliness revealed in 1 Timothy 3:16—God manifested in the flesh. This not only transpired in Jesus Christ as an individual person, but this also transpires in all the local churches.

Jesus Christ Himself was a lampstand, and today every single local church is also a lampstand. In element or in nature, in shape or in type, in expression or in manifestation, a local church is exactly the same as Jesus Christ. The local churches are the testimony of Jesus.

By the time we reach the book of Revelation, everything has been covered already in the Old and New Testaments. There is nearly nothing new in the book of Revelation. Not only the holy writings but also all the secular writings, after talking about so many things and covering so many aspects, have a conclusion. In the conclusion they repeat and confirm what has already been spoken. The Bible is the same. After sixty-five books everything has been revealed and now there is the need of a conclusion.

THE TRIUNE GOD WROUGHT INTO HIS REDEEMED

In the lampstand there is the crucial and vital concept that the Triune God is being wrought into His redeemed (Rom. 8:9-11). In the last chapter we saw that the lampstand is the embodiment of the Triune God which means the Triune God has been wrought into His redeemed. Without such an explanation, we cannot understand the lampstand thoroughly. We are now looking at the lampstand from another angle, another perspective. The lampstand signifies that the Triune God has been wrought into His redeemed, but now we need to ask how this takes place. We have already seen that in order for the Triune God to be wrought into us we all need to eat (John 6:57), drink (John 4:14; 1 Cor. 12:13), and breathe (John 20:22) of the Lord. We want to see how this takes place, though, from another perspective.

By the Divine Birth

First, the Triune God is wrought into His redeemed by the divine birth (1 John 3:9; 5:1-4). At the time I believed in the Lord Jesus I was very clear that I was born of God. I was taught by the Brethren that he who has been begotten of God does not practice sin (1 John 3:9), and that he who is born of God overcomes the world and Satan (1 John 5:4). For years, however, I was not clear that by the divine birth something divine had been born into my being. We all need to have the deep realization that through the divine birth, at the time we believed in the Lord Jesus, the divine element was born into us. Birth is not something vain, but always brings some element into the one born. A Chinese boy who is born of a Chinese father has the Chinese life and the Chinese nature. His eyes, nose, hair, face, color, and blood are all Chinese. The Chinese element has been born into that little baby. The more the little baby boy grows, the more the Chinese things come out. Everything that is Chinese is in the Chinese gene. In the Scandinavian countries most of the people have blonde hair. A Danish boy does not need to worry about having black hair. Someone who is born black does not need to worry about having blonde hair. The black birth brings the black hair genes into the baby's being.

Since we have been born of God, we must realize that everything of God has been born into us. In "God's gene" there are holiness, righteousness, love, and the highest morality. Through our growth in life, everything in the gene which we have received will come out. When we grow, eventually the divine holiness, the divine righteousness, and the divine love grow out of us. What a wonderful thing that we all have been born of God! What birth can exceed this birth? No birth is so high or so supreme as the birth of God. We have received a supreme birth, the birth of God, and by this birth something divine has been born in us, into our being.

Many of the teachings in today's Christianity turn people away from the divine gene to endeavoring and striving for self improvement. These teachings are off from God's economy. We all must realize that we have been born of God and all the divine attributes have been born into our being. In this divine gene are included all the divine attributes. We do not need teachings concerning self improvement or concerning how to be a better Christian. We need the scientific teaching of the divine life to find out how to water this life and nourish this life to cause this life to grow. We do not need the teaching which teaches people to improve their behavior and to try, endeavor, strive, and struggle to do good. This teaching is the same as the teaching of Confucius.

In the fall of 1964 I came to Dallas, Texas for the ministry of the Word. In one of these meetings I shared that today we do not need the teachings, but our desperate need is for the living Christ. After this meeting a group of people surrounded me and contended with me that we do need the teachings. They used 2 Timothy 3:16 as their basis in saying that all Scripture is profitable for teaching. The teaching Paul was talking about here, of course, was the healthy teaching (1 Tim. 1:10). Healthy implies the matter of life. Anything that is healthy refers to the health of life. The sound teaching of the apostles, which is according to the gospel of the glory of God, ministers healthy teaching as the supply of life to people, either nourishing them or healing them. Any teaching that distracts people from the center and goal of God's New Testament economy is not healthy. When these ones surrounded me after the meeting and told me this, I still insisted that they did not need teachings but the living Christ. Many Christians today have received many teachings, yet they are still so poor because the teachings they received were not the healthy teaching. Teachings which are not healthy do not help us. We need the watering and the "fertilizing" which help us to grow in life. We need the kind of teaching which teaches us how to fertilize and water for the growth in life. I have been teaching this way in the United States for the last twenty-two years. Our burden in the ministry is to minister the Lord as the healthy food to all His children. Many of us can testify that when we read the Life-study messages, we do not get mere teachings but we enjoy the Lord Himself as our food, our nourishment.

We all must see the tremendous significance of the divine birth. The divine gene has been born into us! We need to be those who are taking care of the divine gene within us, and our minds need to be renewed to have such a proper understanding of the divine birth. Even though I am older than many of you, I am actually very young because I have the divine gene within me. We need to tell our relatives, friends, neighbors, and colleagues that the divine gene, which includes the divine life and the divine nature, has been born into us. This is our capital and there is no mathematical

figure adequate to describe it. God Himself has been born
into us. Even if someone has been recently saved we need to
tell him that God has been born into him and that he has God
in him (1 John 4:15). The new birth is that God has been born
into me and into you. The Triune God has been wrought into
our being by the way of being born into us. We need the
scientific teaching, the scientific study, of the Bible concerning God being in us. We need to find out how God is in us and
what He is doing in us.

Paul did this kind of scientific teaching in Romans 8:9-11:
"But you are not in the flesh, but in the spirit, if indeed the
Spirit of God dwells in you. But if anyone has not the Spirit of
Christ, he is not of Him. And if Christ is in you, though the
body is dead because of sin, yet the spirit is life because of
righteousness. But if the Spirit of Him who raised Jesus from
among the dead dwells in you, He who raised Christ Jesus
from among the dead will also give life to your mortal bodies
through His Spirit who indwells you." In these verses, Paul
talks about Christ being in us and indwelling us in a very scientific, thorough, and detailed way. We all need this kind of
scientific study and teaching concerning the very God who
has been born into our being. We need this teaching to tell us
how this God is living in us and working in us.

By the Renewing of the Spirit

The Triune God is also wrought into His redeemed by
the renewing of the Spirit (Titus 3:5; Eph. 4:23). We all need
the practical knowledge and experience of the renewing of the
Spirit. The lampstand as the embodiment of the Triune God
is altogether a doctrine if we do not have the adequate experiential knowledge. This is why we need the fellowship in this
chapter in order to get into the experiential knowledge. The
renewing of the Spirit is the Spirit applying all the divine
things, of which we have been born, into our being in our
practical life. You have been born of a certain set of parents
and you have your disposition, your view, your thinking, and
your likes and dislikes. Now, however, you have been born of
God and God has been born into you to be your everything.
How could this God who is everything be applied to you? The

Spirit is here to apply all the divine things into your being in your daily life—this is the renewing of the Spirit. To renew simply means to replace. The Spirit replaces our old being with the divine being. We were born of our parents as the old being and we have been born of God as the new divine being. Now the Spirit is replacing our old being every day with His new being, and this is the renewing of the Spirit.

God is wrought into our being first by being born into us and second by Himself as the Spirit working in us to replace our old being with Himself as the new being, which is the renewing of the Spirit. Our birth is once for all but the renewing is lifelong. After God begot us, He came into us to dwell in us as the life-giving Spirit to replace our old being with Himself as the new being. This is not merely a matter of renewing our mind, but a matter of God replacing our entire being with Himself. The renewing of the Spirit is God Himself indwelling us as the Spirit to replace us with God Himself.

In Titus 3:5 Paul tells us that God saved us through the washing of regeneration and renewing of the Holy Spirit. We all need to be saved from our old being into God Himself as the new being. This kind of saving is the renewing of the Spirit, through which God works Himself into our being. This renewing is carried out by the indwelling Spirit. We need this kind of teaching. We do not need the kind of teaching that tells us how to be humble or kind. This is like the teaching of Confucius and this is not Christ. We have to see that all the divine things have been born into us and now we need God Himself in us as the indwelling Spirit to apply all the divine things into our being to replace our old being with God Himself as the new being. This is the renewing of the Spirit.

By the Transformation with the Divine Life

Furthermore, the Triune God is wrought into us by the transformation with the divine life (2 Cor. 3:18; Rom. 12:2). The renewing of the Spirit and the transformation with the divine life are very close. Transformation is not merely change but a kind of metabolic change. The Greek word for transformation is the source of the English word metamorphosis. The literal meaning of the Greek word is "a change in

form." In the metabolic process some new element is brought
in to replace the old element and to discharge it. The resul-
tant metabolic change that takes place is transformation. The
new element comes in, the old element is replaced and dis-
charged, and the new element becomes prevailing. One of the
best illustrations of this is the process of petrification. A current of water brings in the new element of minerals into the
wood and deposits them there; this current also carries away
the old element of the wood until the very cell structure of the
wood is entirely replaced with stone. This piece of wood
becomes a piece of precious stone, and this is transformation.

The Greek word for transformed is used in Romans 12:2
where we are told that we need to be transformed by the
renewing of the mind. It is also used in 2 Corinthians 3:18
which tells us that as we behold and reflect the glory of the
Lord we are being transformed into the same image. Philippians 3:21 also tells us that the Lord Jesus will transfigure
or transform our body. Romans 12:2 and 2 Corinthians 3:18
refer to the transformation of our soul, our inner being, and
Philippians 3:21 refers to the transformation of our body,
our outward being. The word for transformation conveys the
thought that the divine element is being brought into our
being by the current of the Spirit to replace our old element,
to discharge it, and to make the divine element so prevailing
in our life and in our living. Transformation takes place first
in our soul and last in our body at His coming back. By this
way God is wrought into our being. He is wrought into us not
merely by birth, but also by the renewing of the Spirit and by
the transformation with the divine life.

Suppose that a person's face is very pale. The cosmetic
way to change his appearance is for him to put some makeup
on his face. This is like the work of the morticians in the mor-
tuary. The work of the mortician is to make the appearance
of a corpse look as pleasant as possible. This, of course, has
nothing to do with the metabolic change of transformation. If
a person eats healthy food and sleeps well, his complexion
will look very healthy. When the nourishing, healthy food is
digested and assimilated by us, the issue is transformation.
God has begotten us with Himself and He Himself has been

born into our being. He now indwells us as the Spirit to apply all that He has put into us to replace our old being with Himself as the new being. This is the renewing of the Spirit. While He is doing this kind of renewing, He transforms us metabolically with the divine life as the element to make us "pieces of petrified wood." We are all now under God's divine petrification. A piece of petrified wood is a compound of the deposit of the mineral elements which all have been wrought into the wood. We are like the pieces of wood and God Himself is the heavenly mineral elements. Through the years and day by day the heavenly minerals have been deposited into our being to make us pieces of precious stone. This is transformation and this is the way God works Himself into our being. Then we become the lampstand in reality.

By the Conformation to the Image
of the Firstborn Son of God

Our becoming the golden lampstand is also by the conformation to the image of the firstborn Son of God (Rom. 8:29; Phil. 3:21). Conformation refers to the image, the shape. Every life has its own essence, its own power, its own shape, and its own expression. For example, the apple life has its essence, its life power to grow, and its shape. An apple spontaneously grows into the appropriate shape. It is the same way with a peach or a banana. Life grows into its own shape and life has its own expression. The life of an apple or a banana has its own particular expression as the issue of its growth. We also have the divine life which is the life of God's firstborn Son, and this life has its essence, power, and shape. This life grows into its own shape. As we grow we are being conformed, shaped, into the image of the firstborn Son of God. We are not imitating Christ, but we are being conformed to His image by growing. Washington apples are conformed to their particular form by their full growth. They are not imitators but they are growers. They grow in the apple life unto the conformity of a Washington apple. In like manner, we are not imitating Christ, but we are growing by Christ as our life and eventually we grow unto the conformity of Christ. Then at His coming back He will transform our body of humiliation metabolically by His great power and with His divine element, conforming it to the body of His glory. By that time we will be fully and thoroughly wrought with all the attributes of God. We have not reached that point yet, but today we are in the process, and today we can be the golden lampstand.

The Mingling of Divinity with Humanity

By the new birth, the renewing, the transformation, and the conformation, God has been gradually working Himself into us and by this we all become part of the golden lampstand. This is the church. This is more than holy, more than righteous, and more than mere learning. This is something divine and golden. This is the mingling of divinity with humanity for the fulfillment of God's divine economy.

Chapter Twenty-Six

THE NEW JERUSALEM—
THE ULTIMATE CONSUMMATION

Scripture Reading: Rev. 21:1-2, 9-11

We have seen that the third section of God's New Testament economy is in the book of Revelation. In Revelation are the seven Spirits as the intensification of the Triune God in the overcoming church consummating in the golden lampstands in this age and in the New Jerusalem in eternity. This is the finalization of God's New Testament economy. The New Jerusalem is the ultimate consummation of seven main things: of the entire divine revelation in the Holy Scriptures; of the eternal purpose of God; of God's purpose in man; of the mingling of the Triune God with His redeemed, regenerated, and transformed people; of the positive types, figures, and signs of the Scriptures; of the lampstands in the Scriptures; and of all the buildings of the Scriptures.

THE TRADITIONAL TEACHINGS
VERSUS THE ULTIMATE CONSUMMATION

By reading the Bible we can see God. Although God is a mystery, the Bible reveals Him to us in a great and clear way. The Bible also shows us the source of the universe. We do not need to grope like blind men to know the source of the universe, and we do not need Darwin to tell us anything. When we open the Bible, the first verse tells us that God created the heavens and the earth. The Bible also tells us where man came from. Man came from God and was created by God. As a young man reading the Bible, I received much knowledge and revelation, but I was always trying to know the result, the issue, of the sixty-six books of the Bible. According to the black and white letters, we all can see that the last item of the sixty-six books of the Bible is the New Jerusalem.

All of us, however, have been somewhat influenced by the traditional teachings in Christianity, which say that the New Jerusalem is a heavenly mansion. When I was a young believer, there was a gospel song on the New Jerusalem which told people how good heaven was. According to this song the streets in heaven were golden, and the gates were made of pearl. According to the traditional teachings, the New Jerusalem is such a physical, heavenly mansion. This concept occupied my thought, so I believed that the Bible ended with a heavenly mansion. With our mentality occupied with such a concept, we would never think that the New Jerusalem is the ultimate consummation of the entire divine revelation. Since this item is the conclusion of the Bible, logically speaking it should be the ultimate consummation of the Bible, but the traditional teachings poisoned our understanding.

The thought I adopted as a young believer was that the New Jerusalem was simply a wonderful mansion, and I never gave any room for another thought to come in concerning the New Jerusalem. One of the teachers I was under in the Brethren assembly told us that in John 14 the Lord Jesus said that He was going to prepare a heavenly mansion. After preparing this mansion, He would come back. Since He had not come back yet, this meant that He had not finished His preparation work. This teacher then said that since the Lord Jesus took nearly two thousand years to prepare such a place, how wonderful, marvelous, and excellent that place would be. I received this teaching and I believed it. I was happy and I praised and thanked the Lord that He was preparing a wonderful and excellent place for me. This concept occupied my mind concerning the New Jerusalem, but on the other hand I questioned, "What is the result, what is the ultimate consummation, of these sixty-six wonderful books of the Bible?" By that time I had learned many of the types and prophecies of the Scriptures, but I did not know what the result of the divine revelation was. The reason for this is because this result, this ultimate consummation, was taken away by the traditional teachings of Christianity. There are hardly any Bible readers who understand the last two chapters of the Bible in a proper and adequate way. Many Christians do not spend much time on these two chapters because they think that these two chapters are a record of the heavenly mansion.

The writings of two brothers in particular gave me much help and opened up a little door or a little window for me to get into the real significance of the New Jerusalem. Gerhardt Tersteegen, in some of his hymns, referred to the New Jerusalem in a deeper way. Brother T. Austin-Sparks also mentioned something concerning the spiritual and divine significance of the New Jerusalem. It was not until approximately forty years ago, though, that I really began to get into the significance of the New Jerusalem. In 1963 I wrote a number of hymns concerning the New Jerusalem which are presently in our hymnal (*Hymns*, #971, 972, 975, 976, 978-980). By 1963 the Lord had given me nearly a full understanding of this last great sign in the Bible. By this time I dropped any thought that the New Jerusalem is a physical thing. If you consider the New Jerusalem as a physical thing, you make the Bible low, meaningless, and insignificant. We know the Bible contains the divine revelation; the conclusion of such a revelation, therefore, should be very high and very significant. By 1963 I can testify that I was fully clear that the New Jerusalem is altogether a spiritual, heavenly, and divine sign and not something physical.

If you are a thoughtful person, you may ask why God created man, saved man, and chose and predestinated man. If you are thoughtful, you also have to think about why God is Triune, the Father, the Son, and the Spirit. Why does man have a body, a soul, and a spirit? What is the purpose and what will be the ultimate consummation of all these things? In principle, we have to realize that our God is a God of purpose. He is not a God of meaninglessness, but He is quite thoughtful and purposeful. We need to see and realize what the ultimate consummation of His purpose is, not only in the universe but especially in man. The answer to all these questions is at the end of the Bible, and the answer is the New Jerusalem.

The New Jerusalem is the consummation of every positive thing. It has nothing to do with the negative things such as Satan, the fallen angels, the demons, death, sin, darkness, the grave, Hades, or the lake of fire. It has nothing to do with all these negative things. On the positive side, however, the New Jerusalem is the ultimate consummation of God, of God's salvation, of Christ's redemption, of the Spirit's transformation, and of every positive thing in the Bible. All the positive things in the Bible consummate in the New Jerusalem, which is covered in the last two chapters of the entire Bible. God, the Trinity, the Lamb, the lamp, the tree of life, the living water, the throne, and the Spirit are among the many positive items composed together to make one universal, eternal, divine, spiritual, and heavenly unit. The New Jerusalem is surely not a physical city. The New Jerusalem is something divine, spiritual, and heavenly.

The New Jerusalem is first a sign and eventually a consummation. The entire universe needs a consummation. Even God Himself needs a consummation. You must also realize that even you need a consummation. Many sisters who are mothers have the desire to consummate in good children. Most mothers are always thinking about having good children, better children, or the best children. According to their thought, their future, their joy, their fortune, and their fate will be their children. All the mothers, however, need a change of mind in this matter. All of us need to consider the real consummation—the New Jerusalem. We all need to testify that the New Jerusalem is our consummation. I surely will consummate there, and I hope all of my children and grandchildren will consummate in the New Jerusalem. The New Jerusalem is the ultimate consummation.

THE ULTIMATE CONSUMMATION

Of the Entire Divine Revelation
in the Holy Scriptures

The New Jerusalem is the ultimate consummation of the entire divine revelation in the Holy Scriptures. The conclusion of the sixty-six books of the Bible is contained in its last two chapters which are on the New Jerusalem. The New Jerusalem is the ultimate "coming out" of the sixty-six books. The sixty-six books of the Bible cover many, many things which will consummate in one item—the New Jerusalem. Every positive thing in the Bible will have one outcome—the New Jerusalem. Some of us need to study the New Jerusalem to find out all the items of the divine revelation that can be seen there.

Of the Eternal Purpose of God

The New Jerusalem is also the ultimate consummation of the eternal purpose of God. The Bible reveals God to us, and this God whom we possess is a God of purpose. He is not meaningless but purposeful, and the consummation of His eternal purpose is in the New Jerusalem. You could only see the result, the coming out, of God's eternal purpose in the New Jerusalem. In the New Jerusalem we see that the very God who sits on the throne is our redeeming God, from whose throne proceeds the river of water of life for our supply and satisfaction. This depicts how the Triune God—God, the Lamb, and the Spirit symbolized by the water of life—dispenses Himself to His redeemed under His headship (implied in the authority of the throne) for eternity.

Of God's Purpose in Man

The New Jerusalem is also the ultimate consummation of God's purpose in man. God became incarnate to redeem us, and He became a life-giving Spirit to enter into us, to saturate us, to soak us, for His ultimate purpose in man. We must go along with His saturation so that He could fulfill His purpose in the creation of man.

It would be good if we could be transformed forever by one great saturation of the Spirit. However, God does it in the way of life, and He will have it consummated in the New Jerusalem. Our salvation, our spiritual experiences, and our transformation will consummate in the New Jerusalem.

The seven Spirits as the intensification of the Triune God are in the overcoming church. It is hard for us to see the overcoming church today, but for eternity the New Jerusalem will be the overcoming consummation of the church, and all of us, the believers, will be its constituents.

Without the New Jerusalem there is no answer to any question in this universe. Once you see the New Jerusalem, you have the answer to every question. Why did God create man, redeem man, transform man, perfect man, and glorify man? For the New Jerusalem. God wants Himself to consummate in the New Jerusalem and He wants you to be with Him in this consummation. This is the answer. The New Jerusalem is the answer. It is the ultimate consummation of God's purpose in man.

Of the Mingling of the Triune God with Man

Furthermore, the New Jerusalem is the ultimate consummation of the mingling of the Triune God with man. If God did not have a purpose, He would be foolish to mingle with us. We think that God bothers us frequently, but consider how much bothering we give Him. For example, certain parents may have three children, and there is no way for them to handle one of them. This one is the naughty one. As our Father, God has billions of children. Among these billions of children many of them are naughty. Is it easy for God to handle you as His child? I must testify that it is not so easy for my God to handle me. We may think that a certain Christian is a very good child of God. Actually, however, we do not know the real situation. There is a proverb which says, "Only the fathers know the children." Only our God, the Father, knows us. If God did not have a purpose to accomplish, it would be foolish for Him to suffer so much. He went to so much trouble not only to save us, but also to join Himself to us and to mingle with us.

When we all get there in the new heaven and the new earth as the New Jerusalem, we will be in ecstasy. We will be crazy to the uttermost! The New Jerusalem is much better than a physical, heavenly mansion. It is the full mingling of the Triune God with His redeemed, regenerated, and transformed people. The mingling of God with man can be seen in typology in Leviticus 2:4 with the meal offering, composed of fine flour mingled with oil. The entire New Jerusalem will be the fine flour mingled with the oil. The chorus of *Hymns,* #976 says that the holy city is God's complete expression in humanity. Humanity is the fine flour and God is the oil. The coming New Jerusalem will be a great meal offering, a big cake, made of fine flour mingled with oil. The Triune God is being mingled with us today, and this mingling will consummate in the New Jerusalem.

Of the Positive Types, Figures, and Signs of the Scriptures

The New Jerusalem is also the ultimate consummation of the positive types, figures, and signs of the Scriptures. In Genesis 2 we see the tree of life, a river, gold, bdellium, and onyx stone, and a couple—Adam and Eve. In the New Jerusalem we also see the tree of life, the river of water of life, gold, pearl, and precious stone, and a divine couple with the Lamb as the Husband and His redeemed people as His wife. Also, in the New Testament Jesus performed many signs. His incarnation, death, and resurrection were all signs. The bread of life, the living water, the door for the sheep, and the Shepherd, are all signs. All these signs will consummate in the New Jerusalem.

Of the Lampstands in the Scriptures

The New Jerusalem is the ultimate consummation of the lampstands in the Scriptures. The lampstand in the tabernacle signifies Christ Himself (Exo. 25:31-37). The lampstand in the temple signifies the enlarged Christ (1 Kings 7:49). The lampstand in Zechariah 4:2 signifies the people of Israel. Finally, the lampstands in Revelation 1 signify the churches (vv. 12-13, 20). Christ in His incarnation was a lampstand, and He was enlarged in His resurrection. The children of Israel as God's people were also a lampstand, and the churches as God's chosen people are the lampstands. The one aggregate of all the lampstands will be the New Jerusalem. The New Jerusalem in figure is a gold mountain (Rev. 21:18) like a stand. Christ is the lamp on the stand (Rev. 21:23) and God is the light within Him (Rev. 22:5). In the first chapter of Revelation are the seven lampstands, the churches, and in the last two chapters is the one unique lampstand—the New Jerusalem, which is the consummation of all the lampstands.

Of All the Buildings in the Scriptures

Finally, the New Jerusalem is the ultimate consummation of all the buildings of the Scriptures. In the Bible are the building of the tabernacle (Exo. 25:8-9), the building of the temple (1 Kings 6:1-2), the building of Jerusalem (Psalm 122:3), the rebuilding of the temple (Ezra 3:8-9), the rebuilding of Jerusalem (Neh. 2:17), and in the New Testament the building of the church. The Lord Jesus told us in Matthew 16:18 that He would build His church upon this rock and Peter indicated to us in his Epistle that we are all living stones for God's building (1 Pet. 2:5). Paul, furthermore, told us that he was a wise master builder who had laid the foundation of Christ, and all of us need to build on this foundation with gold, silver, and precious stone (1 Cor. 3:9-12). The New Jerusalem is the ultimate consummation of building work throughout the ages.

CHAPTER TWENTY-SEVEN

THE NEW JERUSALEM—ITS DESIGNATIONS

(1)

Scripture Reading: Rev. 21:2-3a; 2 Cor. 5:17; Col. 3:10-11; Heb. 11:10; 1 Cor. 3:12; Rev. 21:19, 20; Heb. 11:11-16; 12:22; John 1:14a; Exo. 26:15, 29a

We have seen that the New Jerusalem is the ultimate consummation of all the divine, spiritual things in the Bible. We need to have a thorough study of the New Jerusalem since it has never been thoroughly studied and properly interpreted. One point concerning the New Jerusalem which we will be unable to touch or to cover is the twelve foundation stones. To study these stones there is the need of much scholarship. My hope is that the younger generation would continue to study these twelve stones. In order for us to understand the real significance of the New Jerusalem we have to get into the real significance of its designations. According to my study of the Scriptures, there are five designations: the New Jerusalem, the holy city, the tabernacle of God, the wife of the Lamb, and the mother of the believers.

THE NEW JERUSALEM

New

We need to consider what the designation *New Jerusalem* means. We believers have a bad habit of taking the Bible for granted. Why does the Spirit use the word *new* in the designation *New Jerusalem*? The Bible reveals to us two creations—the old creation and the new creation. There is nothing of God's nature involved with any item in the old creation. In other words, God is not in the old creation. In everything of the new creation, however, God's divine nature is in it. The old man has nothing of God in it, but the new man is not only born of God but also created and constituted with God. None of the new items in the New Testament refers to anything material or physical. Our new heart is something of God (Ezek. 36:26). For our mind to be renewed means that God has been wrought into our mind (Eph. 4:23). Everything that is designated new in the New Testament indicates or implies that God has been wrought into these items. If you do not have God, you do not have a new heart. The new wineskins, the new wine, the new garment, and the New Testament all are designated new because God is in them. The Old Testament was something of the dead letters, but the New Testament has God in it. The New Testament is altogether something of God. It is a testament not only of life but of God. God is revealed in the New Testament, and the New Testament conveys God to us.

By this principle we can see that the old Jerusalem was a physical city. In its constituents there was nothing of God's nature. However, the New Jerusalem, just like the new man, has God wrought into it. It is new because God has been added in. Anything that is without God is old, but anything in which God is added is new. A piece of furniture is old because it does not have God, but as a believer you are new because you have God wrought into you. Those who have not believed in the Lord Jesus are old because they do not have God. God is newness, and newness is God. Oldness is the old creation, the old I, the old you. When you have God, however, you have the newness. You become new, and you become newness. All the new items in the New Testament such as the new heart, the new mind, the new man, and the new creation are new because God has been wrought into these items.

Possessing the Divine Nature and the Divine Life

The New Jerusalem as a new creation has God in Christ, possessing the divine nature and the divine life. We cannot have God outside of Christ. Also, Revelation 21 and 22 provide us with many indications that the New Jerusalem possesses the divine nature and the divine life. In the New Jerusalem there are the tree of life and the river of water of life. Besides the divine life, the New Jerusalem does not display any other life. Also, the city itself and the street of the New Jerusalem are pure gold like transparent glass (Rev. 21:18b, 21b). In typology gold signifies the divine nature. Thus, the New Jerusalem possesses the divine nature and the divine life.

The New Creation

Also, the New Jerusalem is created in Christ as the new creation with the divine element (2 Cor. 5:17). Some may think that the new creation refers to us believers and not the New Jerusalem. To say this, though, indicates that we do not have the sight to see that the New Jerusalem is a living composition of all of God's redeemed people, including the New Testament believers and the Old Testament saints. All the redeemed ones composed together are a new creation in Christ, and this new creation has the divine element. The divine element has been wrought into the new creation. Second Corinthians 5:17 says, "If anyone is in Christ, there is a new creation; the old things have passed away; behold, they have become new." It would be helpful if we could spend some time to pray-read this verse. To say that all things have become new means that they have become divine. Furthermore, to say that all things have become new means that all things have become God since God is new and since God is newness.

The New Man

Furthermore, the New Jerusalem is constituted with Christ as the new man with the divine nature and the divine life (Col. 3:10-11). According to Colossians 3:11, the new man is constituted with Christ because in the new man there cannot be any natural man. Not only is there no natural person in the new man, but there is no possibility, no room, for any natural person. In the new man there is only room for Christ. He is all the members of the new man and in all the members. He is everything in the new man. Actually He is the new man, His Body (1 Cor. 12:12). In the new man He is the centrality and universality. In the new man "there cannot be Greek and Jew, circumcision and uncircumcision, barbarian, Scythian, slave, freeman, but Christ is all and in all" (Col. 3:11). Although the church as the new man is composed with people from many different cultures and races, Christ is actually everything in the new man. This is a matter of constitution. Christ was born into you at your new birth, and from that time Christ is being constituted into your very being to transform you into Christ. Because a certain piece of furniture is made with wood and constituted with wood, we can say that it is wood or wooden. In like manner, because we have been born of Christ and constituted with Christ, we can say that we are Christ (in life and in nature). The Bible tells us that the new man, the church, cannot have the natural man and that what is in this new man is just Christ, not Christ by Himself, in Himself, or with Himself, but Christ in you and with you. Due to the influence and restriction of today's traditional teaching, we have been very much limited and even we do not dare to say that we are Christ. However, I hope we would receive a heavenly vision to see that since we have been born of Christ and constituted with Christ, we are Christ.

We like to say that we live Christ, but many times we dare not say this because we have some realization that we do not live Christ all the time. The reason why we do not live Christ is that we are void of Christ's constitution. What we are constituted with is what we live. Some saints told me, "To live Christ is wonderful, but I forget to live Him all the time. When I lost my temper, I remembered that I should have lived Christ, and by then it was too late!" The reason why you forget to live Christ is because Christ has never been constituted into you that much. To live Christ does not need you to remember that you have to live Christ. If He has been so much constituted into you, you cannot forget to live Him. Our bad temper is "quicker than electricity." If we do not have the constitution of Christ for us to remember that we need to live Christ, it is impossible to live Him. How much we live Christ depends upon how much Christ has been constituted into our being. According to our fellowship thus far, we can see that to say the New Jerusalem is a physical city prepared by God is

Life → Body
Person → New man

absolutely absurd. There is no way to interpret the consummation of the Bible in this way. Because this city is new, it has been wrought with God and has God as its contents.

Jerusalem—the Foundation of Peace

The title *Jerusalem* is composed of two Hebrew words—*Jeru* means "foundation," and *Salem* means "peace." Paul tells us in Hebrews 7 that the King of Salem is the King of Peace (v. 2). *Salem* is peace, and *Jeru* is something founded, something built, something laid as a foundation. Thus, *Jerusalem* means "the foundation of peace." Jerusalem is something grounded, founded, and safeguarded in peace. The Bible indicates that peace is God Himself. In the New Testament are two titles—*the God of peace* (Phil. 4:9; 1 Thes. 5:23) and *the peace of God* (Phil. 4:7). Both of these titles indicate that God Himself is our peace. Also, Ephesians 2:14 indicates that Christ Himself is our peace. This peace is God into whom we have been grounded. This is not an outward peace, but an inward peace in which we are safeguarded. In eternity we will enjoy peace forever.

The Lord Jesus told us, "Peace I leave with you; My peace I give to you; not as the world gives do I give to you" (John 14:27). Our Lord also said in John 16:33, "These things I have spoken to you that in Me you may have peace. In the world you have affliction, but be of good courage, I have overcome the world." Since the Lord has given us His peace and left us His peace, today we should live in His peace. Actually, the Lord Himself is still here as our peace. Jerusalem is the Triune God to be our peace, to be our safety. The whole New Jerusalem will be an entity of peace. When we consummate in the New Jerusalem, we will be in peace, that is, in the Triune God. The New Jerusalem will be solidly grounded and safeguarded in the Triune God as peace and safety, and we will enjoy the Triune God as peace forever.

2. THE HOLY CITY

Holy—Separated unto God and Saturated with God

The New Jerusalem is also designated as the holy city

(Rev. 21:2a). In the New Testament the word holy does not only mean separated unto God but also saturated with God. In the Old Testament to be made holy is to be separated unto God. There is no saturation of God in the Old Testament, and the holiness or sanctification there is only positional, not dispositional. In the New Testament, though, we see both the objective, positional holiness and sanctification and the subjective, dispositional holiness and sanctification. Romans 6:19 and 22 indicate that sanctification is something subjective and dispositional. In the Old Testament a piece of gold could be made holy and sanctified by changing its position, by putting it in the temple. The church today is made holy not only positionally, though, but also dispositionally.

In 1 Thessalonians 5:23 Paul prays that our whole being, spirit and soul and body, may be sanctified wholly. This is dispositional sanctification where the very holy God is saturating us with His holy nature. In positional sanctification there is only a change of position, but in dispositional sanctification there is the transformation in nature and in element. Therefore, the New Jerusalem is not merely holy in the sense of the Old Testament but in the sense of the New Testament. Based upon this principle, we can see that the holy city, the New Jerusalem, could never be a physical city since a physical city could never be saturated with God. This city is composed with living persons who can be and who are saturated with God. The New Jerusalem is not merely a city separated unto God, but it is also a city saturated with God. In the old Jerusalem and in the old temple we can see the separation but not the saturation with God. In the New Testament, however, the church is God's temple (1 Cor. 3:16) and this temple is not only separated unto God but also saturated with God. The New Jerusalem is not the Old Testament city but the New Testament city—a city saturated with God.

A City to Which We Have Come

When I studied Hebrews 11:14-16 as a young believer, I thought that these verses indicated that the New Jerusalem was a physical city. These verses tell us that the Old Testament saints longed after a better country, a heavenly country, and that God had prepared for them a city. In Hebrews 12:22, however, the writer tells us that we have come to Mount Zion and to the city of the living God, heavenly Jerusalem. This verse does not say that we will come but that we have come to the heavenly Jerusalem. If Mount Zion and the city of the living God were something physical, how could we have come to them even today? Also, this verse does not say that Jerusalem is in the heavens but that it is the heavenly Jerusalem. This city is heavenly in nature. We have received a heavenly call (Heb. 3:1), have tasted the heavenly gift (Heb. 6:4), and can live a heavenly life on earth today (Col. 3:1-2).

Hebrews 12:22 clearly indicates that the heavenly Jerusalem is not a physical city because we have already come to this heavenly Jerusalem. Many Christians are waiting to go to the New Jerusalem, but we must realize that we have come to the New Jerusalem already. The fact that we have already come to the New Jerusalem and the fact that the New Jerusalem is called the heavenly Jerusalem rescued me from my old concept. The church is the house of the living God so it is God's home and it is also our home today. When the church is enlarged to be a city, it becomes a heavenly country. Our heavenly country is a city to which we have already come.

Designed and Built by God

This city was designed and built by God (Heb. 11:10). Hebrews 11:10 tells us that the Architect and Maker of this city is God. The Greek word for architect in this verse can also be translated as either builder or artificer. This means that God is a skillful designer and a top craftsman. It is not logical to think that our living God designed a physical city.

Ephesians 2:10 tells us that the church is God's masterpiece. The Greek word for masterpiece is *poiema* which means something which has been written or composed as a poem. The church is a poem written by God. Poetry expresses the writer's wisdom. God makes known through the church His multifarious wisdom (Eph. 3:10). The New Jerusalem, as the ultimate consummation of the church, is full of wisdom. God designed the New Jerusalem with His wisdom and this city displays His wisdom. To say that the New Jerusalem is a physical city depreciates God's wisdom and belittles this eternal, wise Architect. If we have the realization that the New Jerusalem is a sign which signifies many spiritual, divine things, then we begin to see the wisdom of God in this city. God is a wise designer and artificer who designed such a city to be a full manifestation of His multifarious wisdom.

Built with the Divine Materials

Furthermore, this city is built with the divine materials. First Corinthians 3:12 tells us that in this age, the church age, we should build the church with gold, silver, and precious stones. In the coming age, silver becomes pearl, and the materials in the New Jerusalem are gold, pearl, and precious stones. Paul surely does not mean for us to build the church with actual, literal pieces of gold. If this were the case, no one could afford to build the church. Paul had laid the unique foundation of Christ and now we need to build on the foundation, not with wood, hay, or stubble, but with gold, silver, and precious stones. These are signs, not physical materials. Gold signifies God's nature, silver signifies Christ's redemption, and the precious stones signify the transforming work of the Holy Spirit. These signs signify the divine work of the Divine Trinity who is being wrought into our being through His divine work. We are now building the church with God the Father's nature, with God the Son's redemption, and with God the Spirit's transforming work. Again, by this we can see that the New Jerusalem should not be a physical city.

Built with Solid Foundations

This city is also built with solid foundations which are unshakable. (Heb. 11:10; Rev. 21:19-20). These foundations are composed of twelve kinds of precious stones. These twelve pieces of precious stones are represented by the twelve apostles. All the apostles were created pieces of clay (John 1:42), but they were regenerated and transformed into precious stones for God's eternal building. Ephesians 2:20 tells us that the church is built upon the foundation of the apostles and prophets. Hebrews 11:10 tells us that the city has foundations and in Revelation 21:19-20 we see the twelve foundations of the city.

A Heavenly and Better Country

This city is also a heavenly and better country (Heb. 11:14-16; 12:22). Our country is not a wilderness but a builded city. Although Abraham was expecting and waiting for a city, he may not have received a vision that the city he was expecting would be something divine and spiritual. By the help of the book of Revelation we can see that the very heavenly Jerusalem, the city of the living God, is not a physical city but absolutely a spiritual and divine entity. What God has actually prepared for Abraham is far better than what Abraham expected. Together with Abraham we all will enjoy this spiritual and divine city. This is really a better country.

3 THE TABERNACLE OF GOD

As a Person, Not as a Material Building

Revelation also tells us that the New Jerusalem is the tabernacle of God (21:3a). In the New Testament the tabernacle is firstly Christ and then Christ enlarged. John 1:14 tells us that the Word who became flesh tabernacled among us. When Jesus Christ was incarnated, He was a tabernacle. The tabernacle in the Old Testament was a material building, but the tabernacle in the New Testament is a Person. Furthermore, the temple in the Old Testament was a material building, but in John 2 the Lord Jesus indicates that He Himself is the temple (vv. 19-21). The temple is now a Person in the New Testament. In the Old Testament the tabernacle and the temple were both material buildings, but in the New Testament both the tabernacle and the temple are a Person. After His resurrection, this Person was enlarged, multiplied, and propagated, so this Person became a corporate Person. This is why Paul calls the church the temple of God (1 Cor. 3:16). In the Gospels Christ is called the temple and in the Epistles the church is called the temple. Both are a Person, not physical things. Since this is the case, how could the consummation of the New Testament be a physical building?

This is altogether illogical. The tabernacle and the temple in the Gospels are a Person, the temple in the Epistles is a corporate Person, the church, and the New Jerusalem in Revelation as a consummation of the New Testament is a corporate Person, not a material building.

Built with Humanity and Divinity

The New Jerusalem as the tabernacle of God is built with humanity and divinity combined together as typified by the acacia wood overlaid with gold (Exo. 26:15, 29). Without the type of the tabernacle in Exodus, we could not realize so clearly that the New Testament tabernacle is a combination of humanity with divinity. The standing boards in the tabernacle are made of acacia wood, which is hard, strong, and fine wood, overlaid with gold. The wood and the gold are combined together to be one entity—the standing boards. Gold always signifies God's divinity and wood signifies man's humanity. This shows us clearly that Christ as the tabernacle is composed with His divinity plus His humanity. He is the God-man in whom humanity and divinity are combined together.

In the tabernacle, of course, we cannot see the mingling of divinity with humanity so there is another wonderful type in the Scriptures to reveal this matter to us—the meal offering. The meal offering shows us two elements not merely added together but mingled one with the other. In this offering we see the fine flour mingled with oil (Lev. 2:4). In the tabernacle we can only see the combination or addition of gold with wood. In God's incarnation divinity came into humanity and was added to humanity. In this God-man's resurrection humanity was brought into divinity and added to divinity. This is a wonderful two-way traffic. These two natures, the human and divine, are not only added together but also mingled together as one entity, as one Person, without a third nature being produced.

A Dwelling for Both God and His Serving Ones

Eventually, the New Jerusalem will be a dwelling for both God and His serving ones. In the Old Testament the picture is

very clear. The tabernacle was God's dwelling and at the
same time it was also the priests' dwelling in which they
served. Both God and His serving priests dwell in the same
tabernacle. To God the New Jerusalem is His dwelling and to
us God is our dwelling because Revelation tells us that in the
New Jerusalem there is no temple "for its temple is the Lord
God the Almighty and the Lamb" (21:22). This means that
we are those serving God in God. God is the object of our service and of our worship, yet God is also our temple in which
we serve God. The holy city is God's dwelling and the holy
city as the temple is God Himself as our dwelling. The New
Jerusalem could never be a physical city because the temple
in the city is the Triune God. Actually, the entire city is a mingling of God with His redeemed people and this mingling is a
mutual dwelling for God and His redeemed. God lives in us
and we live in Him. He and we become one mingled entity for
eternity. The New Jerusalem is a spiritual, divine, and corporate Person and we are in Him because we have come to the
city of the living God, the heavenly Jerusalem!

CHAPTER TWENTY-EIGHT

THE NEW JERUSALEM—ITS DESIGNATIONS

(2)

Scripture Reading: Rev. 21:2, 9-14; 12:1-6, 13-17; 19:7-9; John 3:3, 5-6, 14, 29-30; Gal. 4:22-28, 31

As we have seen, the New Jerusalem is the ultimate consummation of all the revelations in the Bible. The five designations of the New Jerusalem are: the New Jerusalem, the holy city, the tabernacle of God, the wife of the Lamb, and the mother of the believers. The name by which a person or thing is designated always implies the constituents, the components, the elements, of that certain person or that certain thing. The word "dog" designates an animal whose elements, composition, and constitution are that of a dog. In the same way all the designations of the New Jerusalem imply its constituents, elements, composition, and constitution. This is why it is important for us to find out the significances of all these designations.

As we have pointed out, the word *new*, especially in the New Testament, denotes that the divine element has been wrought into God's creation. There was no divine element wrought into the old creation. However, the church as the new man and the new creation means that the divine element has been wrought into the man created by God. This shows us that the New Jerusalem is the old creation with the divine element wrought into it. Furthermore, we have seen that the designation "the holy city" denotes that God's holy nature has been wrought into the New Jerusalem. This is not merely positional holiness, but dispositional holiness, which is God's nature wrought into His creature. The New Jerusalem is also

Summary of last chapter

the tabernacle of God. According to the revelation of the New and Old Testaments, the word *tabernacle* is used to denote a building composed of two natures—the gold and the acacia wood. The gold signifies the divine nature, the acacia wood signifies the human nature, and these two are added together to become the basic elements for the building up of the tabernacle. Because this is a building of the divine nature and the human nature, it is a building for both God and man, a mutual building. The New Jerusalem is a mutual abode of God and of man.

Based upon these first three titles or designations, it is impossible to say that the New Jerusalem is a physical, material city. How could a physical, material city have the divine element? It is impossible. How could a physical, material city be wrought with God's holy nature? It is impossible. How could a physical city be built with the divine nature and the human nature and become a mutual abode for God and man? It is impossible. I must admit that my understanding concerning the New Jerusalem was poisoned and occupied by the traditional teachings. These traditional teachings keep us from going further or deeper into the depths of the Holy Bible. In this chapter we want to see the last two designations of the New Jerusalem—the wife of the Lamb and the mother of the believers. The significance of these two designations is much deeper than the first three.

THE WIFE OF THE LAMB

Revelation 21:2 tells us that the New Jerusalem is prepared as a bride adorned for her husband and Revelation 21:9 refers to the New Jerusalem as the bride, the wife of the Lamb. The first wife in the whole universe was Eve. In Ezekiel 23 the children of Israel are referred to as the wife of Jehovah (vv. 1-4). In John 3 all the regenerated believers are the bride of Christ to be His increase, His enlargement (vv. 29-30). In Ephesians 5 is the church as the wife of Christ and in 2 Corinthians 11:2 the believers have been engaged or betrothed to Christ as their husband. In Revelation 19:7-9 is a universal wedding day, the marriage of the Lamb. Finally, in the last two chapters of the Bible is the wife of the Lamb.

The Lamb is the embodiment of the Triune God and the wife
is the consummation of all the saints. The Bible concludes
and consummates with a divine couple living a married life in
eternity.

Composed of the Old and New Testament Saints

The New Jerusalem as the wife of the Lamb is composed
of the Old Testament saints represented by the twelve tribes,
and the New Testament saints represented by the twelve
Apostles (Rev. 21:9-14). The twelve gates of the New Jerusalem are inscribed with the names of the twelve tribes of the
sons of Israel. This indicates that the New Jerusalem is composed of all the redeemed saints of the Old Testament. Also,
"the wall of the city had twelve foundations, and on them
twelve names of the twelve apostles of the Lamb" (21:14).
"Apostles" here also indicates that the New Jerusalem is not
only composed of the Old Testament saints, represented by
Israel, but also of the New Testament saints, represented
by the Apostles.

The Children of Israel—the Wife of Jehovah

In Ezekiel 23:1-4 we see that the old Jerusalem symbolized the children of Israel as the wife of Jehovah. In these
verses, Ezekiel talks about Samaria and Jerusalem. In this
passage, Jerusalem does not denote a physical city, but the
people represented by the city. The old Jerusalem did not
merely denote a physical city, but a living people who were a
wife to Jehovah.

The Believers—the Wife of Their Redeemer

Also, the New Jerusalem symbolizes the believers as the
wife of their Redeemer. In 2 Corinthians 11:2, Paul says, "I
betrothed you to one Husband, to present a pure virgin to
Christ." "You" in this verse is a corporate you. Many saints
have been betrothed to Christ as one corporate virgin. There
is one church with many members and Paul betrothed the
believers in a corporate way as one corporate virgin to one
husband—Christ.

One with Her Redeemer

The wife of the Lamb is one with her Redeemer, as Eve taken out of Adam and attached back to him to be one flesh, two as one in one nature and one life (Gen. 2:21-24; Eph. 5:25-27, 29-32). Eve was originally a piece of bone, a rib, taken out of Adam. This bone was taken out of Adam, builded into a woman, a wife for Adam, and attached back to Adam to be one flesh. These two, Adam and Eve, were as one in one nature and one life. A wife is one that is one nature and one life with her husband. Based upon this significance we must again ask how the New Jerusalem could be a physical city. A physical, material city could never be one with Christ in one life and in one nature. The New Jerusalem is not only something with the divine element added to it and with the holy nature wrought into it, but also it is one with the Redeemer in one nature and in one life.

The Universal and Heavenly Woman

The wife of the Lamb as symbolized by the universal and heavenly woman in Revelation 12:1-6, 13-17, is composed of all the Old Testament and the New Testament saints. According to Revelation 12:1, this woman is "clothed with the sun, and the moon underneath her feet, and on her head a crown of twelve stars" (see Message 34 of the *Life-study of Revelation*). This universal and heavenly woman is the total composition of God's people on the earth. The sun signifies God's people in the New Testament age (Luke 1:78), the moon signifies God's people in the Old Testament time, and the stars signify the patriarchs (Gen. 37:9). We know that this woman is composed of both the Old and New Testament saints because among the sun, the moon, and the stars are the brothers who overcome Satan because of the blood of the Lamb (Rev. 12:11). We also see that the rest of the woman's seed are those who keep the commandments of God and have the testimony of Jesus (Rev. 12:17). Those who keep the commandments of God are the Jews, and those who have the testimony of Jesus are the New Testament believers. When I was a young believer I read some books which said that this woman was Mary and that the man-child was Jesus. When I studied this woman with her man-child, though, I discovered that this kind of teaching was unscriptural and illogical. After the man-child is brought to the throne of God there is a period of 1,260 days, which is the period of the great tribulation (Rev. 12:6). This very universal and heavenly woman in Revelation 12 is the wife of the Lamb. This woman is a universal composition of all the saints and this woman consummates in the New Jerusalem.

The Consummation of the Wife as the Church

The wife of the Lamb is also the consummation of the wife as the church in Ephesians 5:25-27 and 29-32. An example may help to illustrate what we mean by the wife in Ephesians 5 consummating in the New Jerusalem. When a certain man's wife was only ten years old, she was his wife, but she was not consummated to be his wife. As she was growing up, she was consummating. When she finally reached the age of twenty-three to become this man's bride, that was the consummation of this ten-year-old girl. The bride on that wedding day was the consummation of that little girl. The church in Ephesians 5 is like that little girl who is ten years old, and the New Jerusalem will be the consummated bride. The bride in Revelation 21 can never be improved. She will live forever but she will not grow. The wife in Ephesians 5, however, is still growing. The church in Ephesians 5 still has wrinkles and spots, but the bride in Revelation 21 has no wrinkles or spots. The New Jerusalem is the consummation of the wife in Ephesians 5. The Lord is still working in the church to cause her to grow.

His Increase (Enlargement)

All the regenerated believers constitute the bride of their Redeemer as His increase, His enlargement (John 3:3,5-6,14, 29-30). As a young believer I was taught in a thorough way concerning regeneration, but no one told me that the regenerated believers constitute the bride. Many believed in the Lord Jesus by the time of John 3. They had been regenerated and had received the eternal life. As a result, the disciples of John became jealous and told John that all were coming to Jesus (John 3:26). John then told his disciples that He who has the bride is the Bridegroom and he indicated that everyone who was regenerated should go to Him since He was the Bridegroom. This indicates that all the regenerated believers are composed together to be the bride to match the Bridegroom as His increase. Following this John said, "He must increase, but I must decrease" (John 3:30). Many of those in inner life circles interpret this verse wrongly to mean that we all have to be decreased and that Christ has to increase. The increase in John 3:30, however, is the bride in verse 29, which is a living composition of all the regenerated people. All the believers regenerated by the Triune God should be attached to Him as the Bridegroom. The believers should not have been detached from their Bridegroom to form a religion, taking John as the head. For many years I could not understand why God was seemingly so cruel in allowing John to be put into prison after using him. Then I began to see that John had to be put into prison; otherwise, there would have been two bridegrooms— Jesus Christ and John the Baptist. Since John the Baptist had carried out his ministry to introduce Jesus Christ, it was necessary that he must decrease. All the regenerated ones should not have come to John to attach themselves to him. They all needed to go and attach themselves to Jesus, the Bridegroom.

The Millennium and Eternity

The millennium will be the wedding day in which the overcoming saints will participate (Rev. 19:7-9). To the Lord a thousand years are as one day (2 Pet. 3:8), so the millennium will be the wedding day of the Lamb with the church as His bride. A wife is a bride for one day, but after the wedding day she is no longer the bride. The millennium of one thousand years will be one day for the Lamb to marry His bride. In the new heaven and new earth, all the saints of both the Old Testament and the New Testament will be the New Jerusalem, enjoying the divine married life with the Triune God for eternity.

THE MOTHER OF THE BELIEVERS,
THE NEW COVENANT OF GRACE

Galatians 4:26-28 and 31 reveal the New Jerusalem as the mother of the believers. This mother is the Jerusalem above, the heavenly Jerusalem (4:26). It is impossible for a physical city to be a mother bringing forth children. The New Jerusalem, the heavenly Jerusalem, the Jerusalem above, is our mother. In Galatians 4 Hagar symbolizes the old covenant of law that condemns and brings in death, bringing forth the children unto slavery (vv. 24-25) while Sarah symbolizes the new covenant of grace that justifies and brings in life, bringing forth children unto freedom (vv. 26-28, 31). The New Jerusalem, the heavenly Jerusalem, the Jerusalem above, is our mother and this mother is the new covenant of grace. This new covenant is our mother because it brought us forth as children of freedom.

By grace you have been saved.

The children brought forth by the old covenant of the law were the children of Hagar, but the new covenant of grace brings forth children of freedom by God as grace to enjoy the Triune God, not by human effort to keep the law. Also, her children become her components. This is a great mystery in the Bible that the children of the mother become the components of the mother.

The Triune God as the Center, Substance,
Element, and Essence

The center of the New Jerusalem, who is the mother of the believers, is God and the Lamb on the throne (Rev. 22:1). This is the Triune God as the center and the element of the mother of the believers. The element of the new covenant of grace is also the Triune God. Grace is nothing less than God Himself for our enjoyment. When God is revealed, this is truth, and when God is enjoyed by us, this is grace. The new covenant brings us God for our enjoyment, so it is called the new covenant of grace. Furthermore, the real element, essence, and nature of the children of freedom is the Triune God. The element and substance of the components of the mother is also the Triune God. Finally, the center, substance, element, and essence of the ultimate consummation of the Scriptures, the

New Jerusalem, is the Triune God. This shows us that the mother of the believers, the new covenant of grace, the components of the mother, and the New Jerusalem are all one. Throughout the entire Bible from Genesis to Revelation we see one divine wonderful Person—the Triune God. The ultimate consummation of the divine revelation in the Holy Scriptures and of everything the Triune God has done and achieved is the New Jerusalem, which is the composition of the Triune God mingling Himself with the tripartite man. The New Jerusalem as the divine composition of the Triune God mingling Himself with His redeemed, transformed, tripartite man is the ultimate, universal consummation of all of God's divine revelation and His divine doing.

The Triune God firstly created everything including man, and He permitted Satan to be there as the troublemaker in the universe. God's enemy Satan caused man to fall. Then God became incarnated to be a man to redeem His fallen creature and He lived with man as a man. This Triune God-man then went to the cross, dying an all-inclusive death. On the cross He was our substitute, bearing our sins to redeem us from our sins back to God. After His death in the flesh, Christ made a tour of Hades and proclaimed His victory to the rebellious angels (1 Pet. 3:19-20). This wonderful One came out of death and entered into resurrection to become a life-giving Spirit to enter into all the believers. He regenerated us and He is now transforming and conforming us to His image by making us a divine composition which is today's church, tomorrow's kingdom, and eternity's New Jerusalem. The history of the entire universe is focused on the Triune God dispensing Himself into His chosen and redeemed people and mingling Himself with them to produce a universal fullness to express Himself. Our eyes need to be opened in order to see such a vision.

The New Covenant, the Heavenly Jerusalem, and the Church

To take the new covenant and to keep it is to come to the heavenly Jerusalem and to the church (Heb. 8:7-13; 12:22-23). The new covenant, the heavenly Jerusalem, and the church are one. In order to understand this we must see the link between Galatians and Hebrews. Galatians deals with Judaism, warning the believers not to backslide into Judaism but to stay in grace. Hebrews charges us not to drift into the old covenant but to remain in the new covenant. Chapters seven through ten of Hebrews are on the better covenant, the new covenant. Hebrews 8 indicates that the old covenant is over and the new covenant has come in to replace it. Then in Hebrews 12 Paul tells us that we have come to Mount Zion, to the city of the living God, and to the church (vv. 22-23).

Based upon our fellowship thus far, we can understand that to come to the new covenant is just to come to the New Jerusalem. Without Galatians 4 as a background, it would be hard to understand this. Galatians 4 clearly shows us that the mother of the believers, which is the Jerusalem above, the New Jerusalem, is also the new covenant of grace as symbolized by Sarah. To come to the new covenant is not only to come to the New Jerusalem but also to come to the church (Heb. 12:23). To keep the new covenant is to remain in the New Jerusalem. We need to realize that we are not going to the New Jerusalem but we are in the New Jerusalem already. We have come! The tense of the verb in Hebrews 12:22 is the perfect tense, "have come," not the future tense. We know that we have come to the New Jerusalem because the New Jerusalem is the new covenant. Because we have taken the new covenant, we have entered into the New Jerusalem. The taking of the new covenant is the entering into the New Jerusalem.

The New Jerusalem is the ultimate consummation of the Triune God passing through the long process of His new covenant. Without the Triune God, the new covenant is just an empty shell. The Triune God in His new covenant is imparting and dispensing Himself into all of us all the time, making us His components, the components of His ultimate consummation. The ultimate consummation will not be the Triune God Himself alone, but it will be the mingling of the Triune God with His redeemed, tripartite man—this is the New Jerusalem. We all have to be wrought with God and by God that we might be fully transformed, saturated, and conformed to Himself. Then we will be participating in that ultimate consummation. Thank Him that today we are in this mingling of God with man, which is today's church life. We should remain here and should not be distracted by anything.

CHAPTER TWENTY-NINE

THE NEW JERUSALEM—
THE BASIC ELEMENTS OF ITS STRUCTURE

(1)

Scripture Reading: Rev. 21:11, 18-21; Gen. 2:11-12; 1 Cor. 3:12a; 1 Pet. 2:4-5; Matt. 13:45-46; 2 Pet. 1:4; 2 Cor. 3:18

GOLD, PEARLS, AND PRECIOUS STONES

The basic elements of the structure of the New Jerusalem are gold, pearls, and precious stones (Rev. 21:11, 18-21). Gold is an element created by God and characterized by its unchangeableness. Pearls are produced by oysters. When an oyster is wounded by a particle of sand, it secretes its life-juice around the sand and makes it a precious pearl. The particle of sand is something created by God, yet the life-juice of the oyster is added to this particle by secretion and a pearl is produced in a marvelous way. Precious stones are not created, but transformed from things created. Due to intense heat and pressure these stones were transformed from their original form and nature to a transformed form and nature.

GENESIS 1—2

Gold in typology in the Bible refers to the divine, uncreated nature of God. If we would pay our attention to this matter of gold when we study the Bible, we would realize that gold is a special item in the Bible. In Genesis 1 and 2 we see God's creation of man, the tree of life, the flow of the river, and the gold. Genesis 1 and 2 are very economical and these two chapters cover a great span of the creation of the universe and unveil to us God's eternal purpose, His original

intention in man. Following the gold in Genesis 2 we see
bdellium. Bdellium is a kind of pearl produced from a tree's
secretion. When the resin of the tree, the tree's life secretion,
the tree's sap, congeals into gum, this gum is considered as a
kind of pearl. Following the bdellium in Genesis 2 is the onyx
stone, the precious stone (v. 12b). Finally, we see a woman
named Eve who was Adam's counterpart. The Lord God took
a rib from Adam's side and built it into a woman. Actually, in
Genesis 1 and 2 we see ten significant items—God, creation,
man, the tree of life, the river that flows, gold, bdellium, onyx
stone, a wife, and a couple who became one flesh. If you
understand these ten items you know the real significance of
God's creation, especially of man, recorded in the first two
chapters of His divine revelation.

REVELATION 21—22

At the conclusion of the divine revelation in the last two
chapters of the Bible, Revelation 21 and 22, we see a city
built with gold, pearls, and precious stone. In the real structure of a building the first item is the base or foundation. On
the base the doors are set up and the wall is built up to fit the
doors. In any building you need the base, the doors, and
the wall. In the New Jerusalem the gold is for the base, pearls
are for the gates, and the precious stones are for the wall. The
record of these three materials in Genesis 2:12 is in this
sequence because this is the sequence of building.

GOLD, SILVER, AND PRECIOUS STONES

In 1 Corinthians 3:12 Paul refers to the building up of
the church. For the proper building up of the church Paul
mentions three kinds of materials—gold, silver, and precious
stones. Instead of the bdellium or pearl Paul mentions silver
in 1 Corinthians 3. In Genesis 2, in 1 Corinthians 3, and in
Revelation 21 we see the materials for God's building. In
these three portions of the Scriptures the first item is gold
and the last item is precious stone. The second items in these
three portions are all somewhat different. In Genesis there is
bdellium, in 1 Corinthians there is silver, and in Revelation
there are pearls. It is quite marvelous to see the consistency

of the divine revelation. In Genesis 2:12 we see three materials in typology for God's building and in 1 Corinthians 3 we also see three materials for the actual building of the church. Paul says that he laid the unique foundation and that we should build on this foundation with gold, silver, and precious stones. Paul, of course, is not talking about a material building but about the building up of the Body of Christ. To say that the Body of Christ can be built with gold, silver, and precious stones indicates that these three materials are signs which signify something.

Gold, silver, and precious stones signify the various experiences of Christ in the virtues and attributes of the Triune God. It is with these the apostles and all spiritual believers build the church on the unique foundation of Christ. Silver in typology according to Exodus 30 always typifies redemption (vv. 11-16; cf. 38:25-28). The building materials of the church are first the gold referring to God with His divine nature, and second the silver referring to the Redeemer with His redemption.

We also must look into the significance of precious stones. According to John 1, Andrew went and found his brother Simon Peter and brought him to Jesus (vv. 41-42). By that time Peter was a "muddy" person. When Jesus saw Peter, He said, "You are Simon the son of John; you shall be called Cephas (which translated means a stone)" (John 1:42). Peter (Gk.) means a stone. At that time Simon was not a piece of stone, but a piece of mud. When he came to the Lord, however, the Lord immediately changed his name. When we reach the book of Revelation we see that on the twelve foundation stones of the holy city there are twelve names (21:14). Undoubtedly, Peter is the first foundation stone—jasper.

All the Apostles were created pieces of clay, but they were regenerated and transformed into precious stones for God's eternal building. In the Gospel of John, Peter was named "a stone" by the Lord and in John's Revelation this same Peter is one of the twelve foundation stones. The Lord's word in John 1 concerning Peter being a stone was a prophecy which was fully fulfilled in Revelation 21. Even at the time when the Lord was going to be crucified, Peter was still a piece of

mud and not a stone. He first boasted that he would never
deny the Lord and eventually in the same night he denied the
Lord three times. At that time none of us could recognize or
acknowledge Peter as the first layer of the foundation of the
New Jerusalem, God's eternal habitation. He was still quite
muddy.

In between John's Gospel and his Revelation are Peter's
Epistles. In his first Epistle Peter tells us that the Lord is the
living stone and that we all need to come to Him as living
stones for God's building of His habitation (2:4-5; Eph. 2:22).
All of us believers including Peter are the living stones for
God's building. After he experienced Christ in His resurrection and ascension, Peter declared that he was one of the
precious stones for the building up of a spiritual house. John 1,
1 Peter 2, and Revelation 21 all refer to Peter. He was predicted to be a stone in John 1, he became a stone in 1 Peter 2,
and he is a foundation stone in the New Jerusalem. Peter was
a piece of mud or clay transformed into a piece of stone and
transformed further to be a piece of precious stone for the
building of God's dwelling in the entire universe.

BDELLIUM, SILVER, AND PEARLS

In type in Genesis, in the actual building in 1 Corinthians,
and in the fulfillment in Revelation there are only three categories of materials for God's building. Also, their sequences
are the same. Gold is first and precious stones are last. In
between these two items we see bdellium in Genesis, silver
in 1 Corinthians, and pearls in Revelation. Bdellium is not
something of the animal life but of the plant life. In the Bible
the animal life with the blood is for redemption. Without the
shedding of blood there is no forgiveness (Heb. 9:22). Also,
in the Bible the plant life signifies the producing, multiply-
ing, and propagating life. Bdellium is out of the plant life in
Genesis 2 and pearl is out of the oyster, the animal life
in Revelation 21. The reason for this is because in Genesis 2
sin had not come in yet. The producing of bdellium out of the
plant life means that at this time there was no need of
redemption. After Genesis 3 when sin came in, God still
wanted to produce the pearls but now there is the need of

redemption. Therefore, in the process of the actual building in 1 Corinthians 3 the second item is silver which signifies redemption. Then in the conclusion or the fulfillment of the divine revelation, a sign of God's redemptive work will remain forever as the pearls, signifying the produce of Christ in His redemptive work with His secreting life for the entry into God's building.

In Genesis 2 there was only the tree of life without the Lamb. But in Revelation 22 is the tree of life with the Lamb. The tree of life grows in the river of water of life, which flows out of the throne, not only of God but also of the Lamb. The Lamb is not implied until Genesis 3 when Jehovah God made coats of skins to clothe Adam and Eve after man's fall. In eternity the pearl will not be a kind of bdellium produced out of the plant life, the producing life, but a pearl produced out of the animal life, the redeeming and producing life, a pearl produced by and out of the crucified and resurrected Christ.

THE TRIUNE GOD AS THE BUILDING MATERIAL

In all three sections concerning God's eternal building, the materials are always three in number and are in a unique sequence—gold, pearls, and precious stones. These materials are three in number because the actual material for God's building is the processed Triune God—God the Father, God the Son, and God the Spirit. God would never use anything other than Himself in His processed Trinity to build up His dwelling. It would be impossible for a man to build a house for himself with himself. The only way that a contractor could build a house with himself as the material would be to "kill himself."

Now we must ask the question—who killed Jesus? For Jesus' martyrdom, the Jews killed Him, but for Jesus' redemption, God killed Him. Pilate sentenced Jesus to death but this sentence was a persecution for martyrdom. Isaiah 53 tells us that God judged Jesus, that God condemned Him, and that God gave the verdict of death (vv. 4, 6, 10). It was God Himself who killed Jesus. The One who was killed on the cross was the Man Jesus, but He was not merely a man but a Triune God-man. On the cross, the very God killed the Triune

God-man for the purpose of redeeming us and secreting Himself as the life-juice around His redeemed ones to make them into pearls for the building up of His dwelling place. Thus, we may say that God killed Himself in man in order to be the building material for His eternal dwelling place.

LIVING STONES
AND PARTAKERS OF THE DIVINE NATURE

The Apostle Peter was an uneducated and unlearned person. As a Galilean fisherman he had very little schooling. In spite of this, Peter in his first Epistle told us that Jesus Christ his Lord is the living stone. He also told us that we who come to this Jesus are also living stones. To speak such a word needs much realization which comes from the proper knowledge. In Peter's second Epistle he furthermore told us that we all are partakers of the divine nature (1:4). We not only inherit the divine nature in the future but we are partakers of the divine nature, partaking of, enjoying the divine nature, today. Although Peter was an uneducated fisherman, he could tell us that the Lord is the living stone, that he also was a living stone, that we all are living stones, and that we partake of, enjoy, the divine nature. This is the pure Biblical teaching, not the ethical or philosophical teachings of Confucius or other philosophers. There is no comparison between the philosophical books and the Bible. The Bible teaches people in a divine way showing us that we believers have God's divine nature. This is not a doctrine but a reality.

THE BASE OF GOD'S BUILDING

Gold signifies the divine nature of God for the base of God's building. This divine nature is the golden base within us for God's building. The more we partake of the divine nature, the more we have the base for God's building. I do not care for people's humility or for people's pride. Human pride and human humility are the same. Both human pride and human humility are useless for God's building. I only care how much God you have, how much divine nature you have partaken of, and how much divine nature you are partaking of day by day. It is possible to be a very good wife and a very nice husband and still not have much of God's divine nature. We all need to ask how much God we possess. This is the base for the building up of the church. According to my realization, the Lord has done much in these last twenty-three years in the United States. Many of the saints have really partaken of the divine nature and have a substantial amount of the divine nature within them. This is the base for God's building and this is the base in which I put my trust for the work. Man's humility can never be the base for the building up of the church. Only God's nature, God Himself, can be such a base. Neither a proud nor a humble person is good for the building up of the church. Only those who are partaking of the divine nature daily are good for the building up of the church. The basic thing in the Lord's recovery is not a great number of people, but how much divine nature is here as a base for the building up of His Body.

We must realize that we are not simply allegorizing the Bible, but pointing out the real things in the Biblical allegories. The entire New Jerusalem is an allegory. Even in human language there is the need of allegory because some things cannot be expressed or described by mere plain and direct words. Because this building up of God's eternal dwelling place is altogether mysterious, spiritual, heavenly, and divine, there is the need of an allegory to express and describe it. Gold, pearls, and precious stones are all part of this allegory to express and describe the divine reality.

From the time I was a young believer I realized that I was regenerated, born again. However, I never realized that within me there was something divine. It was not until a number of years after I had received the Lord that I began to realize in a small way that through regeneration God had come into me. As a human being regenerated by God, you not only have the human nature but also the divine nature. Nature always denotes a certain kind of essence. Any element or substance has its essence. God is the divine gold as the element, and in this element is the essence with its nature. Today we believers have this divine nature.

We all have to fight the battle, showing people that the Bible unveils to us that we believers have God within us as the divine nature. We are not merely studying the New Jerusalem. We are here to dig out all the divine truths that we may realize what we are today, where we are today, where we are heading, and what we should be. We have to realize that we are the people who have the divine nature, the divine element, the divine substance, and the divine essence, in our being. As a believer you are "a golden man." You are not a muddy man. All the sisters need to realize that they are not muddy women but "golden women." Because we are so golden, we cannot go dancing. Do you think a golden man would quarrel with his wife? Gold never changes. Despite what you do to it, it remains the same. We the believers in Christ today are golden! We are divine! We have the divine nature! We all have to declare that we are not muddy but golden. Gold is the base for the building up of the dwelling place of God for eternity.

The Lord Jesus told Peter that he was a stone (John 1:42) and reminded him in Matthew 16 that he was a stone (v. 18). He also said that He would build His church. Today the Lord is doing a building work. From the day of Pentecost the Lord began to build the church with you and me as stones based upon God's divine nature. The stones are built upon the golden base, which is the site. All the materials are built upon this site and the site is the base. The base for the Lord's building today is God's divine nature. It is not your knowledge, your education, your good character, your kindness, your humility, or even your love. The base is the nature of God. I have the assurance and the confidence to say that in the Lord's recovery there is a strong base of the divine nature within so many of us who are loving the Lord.

What we have seen in this chapter is according to the divine revelation. The base for God's eternal building and for His present building work is His divine nature. We all should say, "Lord Jesus, thank You. Through Your redemption I have the position, the standing, and the right to take my God as my divine nature. Thank You, Lord, that I have taken and am still taking and enjoying You as my divine nature." The basic elements of the structure of the New Jerusalem are the gold as the base of God's building (Rev. 21:18b, 21b),

the pearls which signify the produce of Christ in His redemptive work with His secreting life for the entry (Rev. 21:21a)
into God's building (1 Cor. 3:12a; John 3:5), and the precious
stones (Rev. 21:11, 18a, 19-20) signifying the produce of
the Spirit in His transforming work (2 Cor. 3:18) with His
divine element for the building up of God's building. All these
three precious materials are built together and built up to
be a universal wife, the wife of the Lamb (Rev. 21:2, 9),
the redeeming God, which corresponds with and reflects the
wife in Genesis 2, who was a type of this universal wife of
the redeeming God.

M29.33-34

CHAPTER THIRTY

THE NEW JERUSALEM—
THE BASIC ELEMENTS OF ITS STRUCTURE

(2)

Scripture Reading: Rom. 1:20; Col. 2:9; Gen. 1:26a, 27; John 1:13; 1 John 3:9; 1 Pet. 1:3; 2 Pet. 1:4; John 4:24; 1 John 4:8, 16; 1:5; John 1:4; Rom. 8:2

THE DEFINITION OF THE DIVINE NATURE

In all the messages we have given, we have never touched in a thorough and adequate way the definition of the divine nature. This term "the divine nature" is only mentioned once in the entire Bible—in 2 Peter 1:4. This verse mentions the divine nature in a very particular way in that it says that we have become partakers of the divine nature. A partaker is different from a receiver. We have received the divine nature, but there is a question as to whether or not we are partaking of the divine nature. This is why Peter in his second Epistle told us how to partake of the divine nature in the first chapter. We need to be the partakers of the divine nature in the same way that we are partakers of food every day. Not many of us have ever paid an adequate amount of attention to the matter of how to become an enjoyer of the divine nature.

It is not an easy task to define the divine nature. It would even be hard for any of us to give an adequate definition of the human nature. From our fellowship, I hope we all will be able to see the definition of the divine nature, how to partake of and enjoy the divine nature which we have already received through our divine birth, and the issue of our partaking of the divine nature. In this chapter we will focus our attention on the definition of the divine nature.

When many Christians study the Bible, their first concern is for their welfare or for what blessing or profit they can get from the Bible. Their second concern is how to worship God, how to fear Him, how to please Him, and how to do things to glorify Him. Not many Christians even think concerning how to fellowship with God. They mostly would be concerned with how to have a time with God. The third real concern for many Bible readers is how to improve or better themselves. We all have the realization that we are not that good. Therefore, to many of us the Bible is a divine, heavenly book telling us how to improve ourselves. Finally, many Bible readers hope that the Bible could be an instruction book telling them what to do. Not many have really seen something concerning God's interest, really realizing that God intends to work Himself into us to be our life and to be our nature. A few persons whom I met talked a lot about how God is to be our life, but they spoke very little concerning how God's nature could be our nature. For God to be our life is a deep subject, but for God's nature to be our nature is an even deeper matter.

There are three verses in the Bible which puzzle many Bible students and translators—Romans 1:20, Colossians 2:9, and 2 Peter 1:4. Romans 1:20 refers to God's eternal power and divinity. Some translators translate the word "divinity" wrongly into "divine nature." The King James Version translates this word into "Godhead." In Colossians 2:9 we are told that all the fullness of the Godhead dwells in Christ bodily. The word for Godhead in Colossians 2:9 and the word for divinity in Romans 1:20 denote different things concerning God and are two different Greek words. Then in 2 Peter 1:4 we see the divine nature. In the past, we may have felt that these verses referred to the same thing, but we need a clear understanding in order to differentiate among them. Since gold signifies the divine nature of God for the base of God's building, we need to have a clear vision concerning the definition of the divine nature.

DIVINITY

In a note on Romans 1:20 Darby says that the Greek word for divinity means "what is characteristic of God." In

Romans 1:20 "divinity," Gk. *theiotes,* denotes the characteristics of the divine nature. For example, the nature of a piece of furniture may be wood and the grain of the wood is a characteristic of the nature. According to Romans 1:20 the creation only shows the characteristics, the expressions, of God's divine nature. In the creation you cannot see God's divine nature itself.

GODHEAD

The creation cannot show or exhibit the Person of God. The Person of God was exhibited and expressed by Jesus Christ. Colossians 2:9 says that in Christ dwells all the fullness of the Godhead, not the fullness of divinity but the Godhead, the Person. Because the creation is not a person it can only show God's characteristics, not God's Person. Only a person can exhibit or express a person, and the Person that exhibits God's Person is Jesus Christ. The word "Godhead" in Colossians 2:9 refers to God's Person. The creation only shows the characteristics of God but not God's Person. Christ, as the embodiment of God, shows the Godhead, God's Person, and shows Him in full bodily.

THE CHARACTERISTICS OF GOD
SHOWN IN CREATION

We all need to see what characteristics of God are shown in creation. The universe as a whole is not dark but very bright. Because it is bright it is very pleasant. If God had created a universe full of darkness, it would not be a very pleasant place in which to live. Light makes us pleasant and makes everything pleasant to us. The entire universe being so bright and full of light denotes that the Creator is also like this. Brightness is one of God's characteristics. The entire universe is also full of beauty. No one can say that the universe is something ugly. This indicates that beauty is also one of the divine characteristics.

In addition to this, the universe is in a good order. Everything in the universe is orderly. Orderliness is another characteristic of God. Our God as the Creator is not One of confusion, but One of orderliness. He keeps everything in order.

When the Lord Jesus was going to feed the five thousand, we can see the orderliness of God. He firstly ordered the crowd "to recline by companies on the green grass. And they sat down in groups, by hundreds and by fifties" (Mark 6:39-40). After the feeding of the five thousand, there were many leftovers. Our thought might have been to forget about the fragments of bread and the pieces of fish which were left over. But when the crowds were fully satisfied, the Lord said to His disciples, "Gather the broken pieces left over that nothing may be lost" (John 6:12). The Scriptures record that the disciples took up twelve baskets full of broken pieces of bread and of the fish (Mark 6:43). This shows us that the Lord performed a marvelous miracle which signified the bountiful and inexhaustible supply of His divine life, but this miracle also shows us that one of the major characteristics of God is orderliness.

Also, in His creation we see the characteristic of love. "He makes His sun to rise on the evil and the good, and sends rain on the just and the unjust" (Matt. 5:45).

Light, orderliness, and love are some of the characteristics of God, and actually they are characteristics of God's divine nature. Characteristics always come out from the nature. If there is no nature, no characteristics will be shown or exhibited. Romans 1:20 refers to the characteristics of the divine nature shown in God's creation.

In Colossians 2:9 the Greek word for "Godhead" is *theotes*. The only difference between the Greek word for divinity in Romans 1:20 and the Greek word for Godhead in Colossians 2:9 is the letter *I*. Divinity in Greek in Romans 1:20 is *theiotes*. *Theotes*, however, in Colossians 2:9 refers to the Godhead, God the Person. What dwelt in Jesus Christ was not merely the divine characteristics but God the divine Person, the Godhead. As believers we should have the divine characteristics of the divine nature and even the divine nature itself, but we cannot have the Godhead. In the Godhead, though, the divine nature is implied. In Colossians 2:9 the

Godhead implies the divine nature because the divine nature is one of the constituents of God.

MAN IN GOD'S CREATION

In God's creation, man was made only in the image of God, without the divine nature (Gen. 1:26a, 27). If you read the Bible carefully, you will see that the ten commandments were called God's testimony (Exo. 16:34; 25:16, 21). God's testimony simply means God's description. The ten commandments were a description of God. The law that a person makes reflects the kind of person he is. If you were a bank robber, you might make a law legalizing bank robbing. When we read the ten commandments, we can see that God is love, that God is light, that God is holy, and that God is righteous. This describes the very Lawgiver, the Legislator in the universe, who made the ten commandments. Man was made in the image of God, in the image of love, light, holiness, and righteousness. Unless God comes into man and becomes man's contents, of course, man has merely the image with no reality. Love, light, holiness, and righteousness are the virtues of human morality. Every human being has a natural love and a natural tendency to seek after light; every human being is seeking to be something higher, something uncommon, which is holiness; and every human being seeks to be right and to do the right things with others. This proves that man was made in such a way.

As we have seen, God created man in such a morality of love, of light, of righteousness, and of holiness. These are the virtues of the human morality created by God, but in God's created man there was no divine nature. Man only had the image, the form, of God. When we believed in the Lord Jesus, however, we received a Person as our content and reality. Most Christian teachers would say that we received salvation, forgiveness, justification, reconciliation, and many other items, but very few Christian teachers stress that when we received the Lord Jesus we received a Person. After Peter preached the gospel at Pentecost he told the ones to whom he was preaching to repent and be baptized upon the name of Jesus Christ for the forgiveness of their sins, that they might receive the gift of the Holy Spirit (Acts 2:38). This gift is the Holy Spirit Himself, as the realization of Christ, given by God to the believers in Christ. When we believed in the Lord Jesus we received Him, the Person, as our salvation.

THE DIVINE NATURE— RECEIVED THROUGH THE DIVINE BIRTH

When this Person entered into us, regeneration transpired and we were born "not of blood, nor of the will of the flesh, nor of the will of man, but of God" (John 1:13). We all should praise the Lord for the divine fact that we have been born of God! The Apostle John also tells us in his first Epistle that when we were begotten of God, a divine seed entered into our being (1 John 3:9). As believers in the Lord, God's seed is now in us. This Person we have received is the divine seed which has been planted into our inner being. This is not superstition but a marvelous divine fact.

With any seed there is life and in that life there is the nature which is going to be developed. A grain of wheat is a seed of wheat. When this seed is sown into the earth it develops in life with its nature. The full development of the life of the seed with its nature issues in a stalk with many grains, many seeds. The development of the grain of wheat comes out of the nature of that grain or seed. The same thing is true of a carnation seed. If a carnation seed is sown into the earth, it develops with its nature into a beautiful carnation blossom.

We have received the divine life through the divine birth and this divine life has a nature which is the divine nature of God. John 1:13 tells us that we have been born of God, 1 John 3:9 says that since we have been born of God we have the divine seed in us, 1 Peter 1:3 says we have been regenerated by God through the resurrection of Jesus Christ, and 2 Peter 1:4 indicates that since we have received the divine life we are now partakers of the divine nature. We are not receiving the divine nature, but partaking of, enjoying, what we have already received.

The problem is this—we all have received the divine nature, but we do not regularly enjoy what we have received. Not many of us can testify that all day long we are those who are partaking of the divine nature and that all day long we are enjoying the divine nature within us. We neglect this divine nature because we are wrapped up with four things: our welfare, how to please God, how to improve ourselves, and how to do things in a right way. We need to forget about these things and to pick up one thing—how to enjoy the divine nature and how to partake of the divine nature. In order to partake of and enjoy the divine nature we first need to see what the divine nature is.

THE DIVINE NATURE—WHAT GOD IS

Spirit, Love, and Light

The divine nature is what God is. The nature of a piece of furniture is what the furniture is. If the furniture is wooden, the nature of the furniture is wood. The Bible tells us emphatically and directly that God is Spirit (John 4:24), God is love (1 John 4:8, 16), and God is light (1 John 1:5). All these items concerning what God is were written by the Apostle John. The divine nature is a constitution of these three items—Spirit, love, and light. To be a partaker of the divine nature is to be one partaking of God as Spirit, as love, and as light. Spirit denotes the nature of God's Person, and love denotes the nature of God's essence. God is a divine Being with a divine essence. The essence is more intrinsic than the element of something. Within the element is the essence, and this divine essence has love as its nature. Furthermore, the divine light is the nature of God's expression.

God is a Person who has His essence and His expression. The divine nature is the nature of God's Person, the nature of God's essence, and the nature of God's expression. God is a divine Being, a Person, and the nature of His Person is Spirit. This Person also has an essence and the nature of His essence is love. God is a constitution of love. Also, light is the nature of God's expression, so Spirit, love, and light are the constituents of the divine nature. To partake of the divine nature is to partake of the divine Spirit, divine love, and divine light.

John tells us that the divine birth brought into us a seed (1 John 3:9). In this seed is the divine nature. Peter, furthermore, tells us that God has given us all things relating to life (2 Pet. 1:3). Based upon this fact God gave us exceedingly great and precious promises that through these we might become partakers, enjoyers, of the divine nature. Now we all have to learn how to taste the constituents of the divine nature which are Spirit, love, and light. In other words, when you partake of the divine nature, you enjoy God as the Spirit, as love, and as light.

To illustrate this, let us consider our set apart time to fellowship with the Lord. In such a fellowship you realize and enjoy the Lord as the Spirit, and simultaneously you enjoy the nature of God's essence, which is love. Love then saturates you and even becomes you. Before this time, you may have been disgusted with many things. After this kind of fellowship, however, everything is lovable. You may have been disgusted with your wife before this fellowship, but afterwards you are filled with love for your wife. This love has not only filled you but saturated you. The reason why we Christians can love persons whom others cannot love is because we enjoy God as love. We enjoy the divine nature of this loving God. This is why John tells us in his first Epistle that if we love our brother this means we are born of God because God is love (4:7-8). When you love others you are enjoying the divine nature. One who does not have God or who does not partake of God's divine nature hates everything. Do not think that people love everything. They are just cultured and trained to be polite. Their kindness and loving is a kind of politics. The genuine love is the issue of the enjoyment of the divine nature. A supervisor or a boss may say something in a loving way to an employee. Unless what he has said is an enjoyment of the divine nature, he is actually playing politics. When the time comes for him to fire or lay off this employee, he will have no problem. Only those who partake of the divine nature love people genuinely. They are not taught to love others, but they have become love toward others. They are the partakers of the divine love, which is the very nature of the divine essence.

If we would spend an adequate amount of time in the morning with the Lord, we would be full of light inwardly and we would not do things nonsensically or say things foolishly. Whatever we do and whatever we say would be full of light. This is the issue of our enjoying of the divine nature. This is because one constituent in the divine nature is light. If we would all spend time to fellowship with the Lord, we would have the sensation that we are enjoying the Lord as the Spirit and we would become a person of love. Love would saturate us. Furthermore, whatever we would say would be light, and whatever we would do would be transparent as crystal. This is an evidence or proof that we are partaking of the divine nature.

Love and Light Related to God as Life

The Bible also tells us that God is life. Love and light are related to God as life (John 1:4), and life is of the Spirit (Romans 8:2). God is life to us mainly in love and light. If you are not saturated with love, you are not living the life of God. If you are not so transparently bright, you are not enjoying God as life. When you are enjoying God as life, you are full of love and full of light. Therefore, love and light are both related to God as life, and life is of the Spirit. God, the Spirit, and life are actually one. God is Spirit, and Spirit is life. Within such a life are love and light. In John's Epistle we come to the Father to participate in His love and light in the fellowship of the Father's life. This is further and deeper in the experience of the divine life. Love and light are God the Father Himself for our deeper and finer enjoyment in the fellowship of the divine life with the Father in the Son (1 John 1:3-7) by our abiding in Him (1 John 2:5, 27-28; 3:6, 24).

Chapter Thirty-One

THE NEW JERUSALEM—
THE BASIC ELEMENTS OF ITS STRUCTURE

(3)

Scripture Reading: John 1:13; 1 John 3:9; 1:2-3; 4:8, 16; 1:5-7;
2 Pet. 1:3a, 4-7

We all need to remember that the New Jerusalem has a base and this base is pure gold, which in typology refers to God's divine nature. We believers have all been made partakers of this divine nature (2 Pet. 1:4). It is a very hard task to define the divine nature. Simply speaking, the divine nature is what God is, just as the nature of anything is what that thing is. We have seen that the Bible tells us that God is Spirit (John 4:24), that God is love (1 John 4:8, 16), and that God is light (1 John 1:5). Then in a total way the Bible tells us that God is life (John 1:4; 5:26; 14:6). These four items of what God is are very basic. Spirit, love, and light are the very constituents of God's being and life is God Himself. God Himself, God's being, is our life and He is constituted with Spirit, love, and light. Spirit is the nature of God's Person, love is the nature of God's essence, and light is the nature of God's expression.

God is Spirit in person, God is love in essence, God is light in expression, and God is life in love as its essence and in light as its expression. When we touch God, we touch Him as Spirit in His Person, as love in His essence, and as light in His expression. After touching God, we walk, we live, we have our being, in His Spirit as our person, in His love as our essence, and in His light as our expression.

THE PARTAKING AND ENJOYING
OF THE DIVINE NATURE

Since we have defined the divine nature we need to see how to partake of it. Second Peter 1:4 is the only verse in the Bible which tells us directly that we are partakers of the divine nature. We do not merely partake of the divine nature, but need to be the partakers. We do not merely eat, but we are the eaters. The Christian life is a life of enjoying the divine nature.

We may have had some experiences of enjoying the divine nature without realizing it. Two hundred years ago people enjoyed vitamins without having any knowledge concerning them. Today, however, even many little children know what vitamins are. My hope is that one day even our children would know what the divine nature is and that this would be common knowledge. This is why we are burdened to see the basic element of gold in the New Jerusalem. The New Jerusalem is God's building and gold, which is the very symbol of His divine nature, is the base of His building. In fact, the divine nature is the base of all God's building through all the generations.

We can see the partaking and enjoying of the divine nature in John's line and in Peter's line. These are the two lines of writings concerning the enjoyment of the divine nature. In Paul's fourteen Epistles there are some implications concerning the enjoyment of the divine nature, but there is no clear word because Paul's ministry is not centered on the enjoyment of the divine nature but is altogether concentrated on the law of life. The divine nature, which mainly refers to the constitution of the divine life, the constitution of God, is constituted with Spirit, love, and light. Paul's burden, however, is to show us the working principle of the divine life which is the law of life. The law of a certain life is deeper than the element of that life. John and Peter deal with the nature, but Paul deals with the law. In Romans 8:2 he tells us that the law of the Spirit of life sets us free from the law of sin and of death. This law is the natural principle of the divine working.

In John's Line

In 1 John we first see the eternal life, whom John had heard, seen, beheld, and handled as the Word of life. Then John testified and reported to us the eternal life that we may have fellowship (1:1-3). John's first Epistle mainly is to keep us living in the divine fellowship of the divine life. As believers we have the divine life, and this life brings us into the divine fellowship. We all need to remain in the fellowship. If we remain in the fellowship, we touch God as light (1 John 1:5), and as love (1 John 4:8-16). This is our enjoyment of God as light and love in our fellowship with Him. We have seen that love and light are the constituents of God's divine nature. When we remain in the divine fellowship with God, we enjoy God directly as light and love, which is the enjoyment of the divine nature. To partake of the divine nature is to fellowship with God, to enjoy God as love and as light, because love and light are two constituents of God's nature.

In John's Gospel we see that Christ came with grace and truth (1:17). When we believed in Christ, we received Him as grace and truth. Grace is God in the Son as our enjoyment; truth, reality, is God realized by us in the Son. In John's first Epistle we see that the divine love is the source of grace and the divine light is the source of truth. When this divine love appears to us, it becomes grace, and when this divine light shines upon us, it becomes truth. John's Gospel reveals that the Lord Jesus has brought grace and truth to us that we may have the divine life (3:14-16); whereas his Epistle unveils that the fellowship of the divine life brings us to the very sources of grace and truth, which are the divine love and the divine light. In his Gospel it was God in the Son coming to us as grace and truth that we might become His children (1:12-13); in his Epistle it is we the children, in the fellowship of the Father's life, coming to the Father to participate in His love and light. John's Gospel is Christ coming to us bringing grace and truth to us, and John's Epistle is that we go back in Christ to the source in our fellowship and we touch God as love and as light. Love and light are deeper than grace and truth because they are the sources. This is a divine two-way traffic between God and us. To partake of the divine nature is to touch the source of grace and truth since the divine nature is the source of grace and of truth.

The way to touch this source is to remain in the fellowship with the source. We are in the fellowship already, but we need to remain, to abide, in the fellowship. Once electricity is installed into a building, there is an electrical current flowing, and that current is a good illustration of the divine fellowship. The divine fellowship is a heavenly electrical current. If the electric appliances remain in the current, they function. If they do not remain in the current, they actually are cut off from the enjoyment of the electricity. As believers we do have a heavenly current of the heavenly electricity and we need to remain in this current, to remain in the fellowship. When we remain in the fellowship, we touch God as the source; we touch Him as Spirit, as love, and as light. To touch God as Spirit, love, and light is to partake of the divine nature. This is not a vain theory or a mere teaching but something in our experience.

All of us have experienced partaking of the divine nature in different degrees. If you spend ten or fifteen minutes to contact the Lord and stay with Him and pray honestly and sincerely, confessing your failures, mistakes, shortcomings, defects, wrongdoings, and sinfulness, you touch God as the Spirit in His Person. Deep within your being you sense the Spirit. At this juncture everything in your home, in your yard, on the street, in the heavens, and on the earth is so pleasant and lovely. This is the issue of partaking of love as the nature of God's essence.

Before I received the Lord, I was easily disgusted with people. After I was saved, no one taught me but I knew that I had to go to God in prayer and fellowship. After praying for a few minutes and repenting of and confessing my sins, I was joyful, and everyone and everything were pleasant and lovely to me. The reason for this is because I was partaking of the divine nature. Even though I did not have the knowledge concerning this, this was still my experience.

Once when I was at my son's home, I saw my three

grandchildren working on their homework at the table. The two girls were seven and nine years old respectively and the boy was eleven years old. When I saw them I asked, "Have you children all prayed today?" The two girls told me that they had not prayed yet because their way was to pray before bedtime. Then the oldest girl told me that she saw her older brother praying and that while he was praying he was weeping. These two young girls are always watching their older brother to find some fault with him, but instead they found their older brother praying and weeping. If this young boy continues to contact the Lord in such a way, everyone and everything will be lovely to him. There will be no need to teach him to love his sisters because love will be within him. In his prayer and fellowship with the Lord he is partaking of the divine nature.

All of us can testify, at least to some degree, that we have enjoyed the Lord in such a way. This is our partaking of the divine nature, which is constituted with the divine love in essence and with the divine light in expression. I believe that after my young grandson prayed in such a way, he was transparent and he was in light. Just by contacting God for ten to fifteen minutes, after we rise up from our knees, we become a person who is transparent and no longer in darkness or opaqueness. What we should say or do also becomes transparent to us. You may not even have the utterance or know how to explain a matter, yet within you there is the light. You know where you should be, and you know where you are. This is the issue of the partaking of the divine nature.

After having a time with the Lord, you sense that One is within you, living, acting, leading, and guiding you. This One is the divine Person, who is the Spirit and this Spirit is also one of the constituents of the divine nature. Everyone who has been genuinely regenerated has had this kind of experience at least once or twice. You touch the source of grace, which is the divine love, and the source of reality, which is the divine light, in your fellowship with the Lord, and both of these sources are the constituents of the divine nature for your enjoyment.

In Peter's Line

We all need to realize that God is with His divine nature for our enjoyment. Beef can never be your enjoyment unless you enjoy the nature of the beef. When you enjoy fish, you enjoy the nature of fish. This is why Peter according to his own experience tells us that we partake of the divine nature. To say that we merely partake of God is too general, but to say that we partake of the divine nature is particular.

Peter, who was an unlearned fisherman from Galilee, wrote this according to his experience. Even though he was unlearned, Peter could write such a marvelous Epistle which included many wonderful divine points. He said that we all have been allotted like precious faith and that the divine power has granted us all things related to life and godliness. Based upon this, Peter tells us that God has given us precious and exceedingly great promises that we might become the partakers of the divine nature. Furthermore, he tells us that in our allotted faith we have to develop virtue, in virtue knowledge, in knowledge self-control, in self-control endurance, in endurance godliness, in godliness brotherly love, and in brotherly love, love (2 Pet. 1:1, 5-7). What Peter's writing implies is much higher, even a thousand times higher than the highest philosophy. Peter wrote this because he experienced this. When he was writing, undoubtedly, the Spirit was within him giving him the utterance and the proper expressions.

According to his experience, Peter told us that God's divine power has imparted to the believers all things related to life (2 Pet. 1:3a). Furthermore, he told us that God has given to the believers precious and exceedingly great promises that the believers might become partakers and enjoyers of the divine nature through its development (2 Pet. 1:4-7). First, God by His divine power has imparted into us all the things pertaining to life and godliness. Second, based upon this He gave us His promises. The first part of 2 Peter 1:4 says, "Through which He has granted to us precious and exceedingly great promises." "Which" refers to glory and virtue in verse 3. Through and on the basis of the Lord's glory and virtue by and to which we have been called, He has given us His precious and exceedingly great promises, such as in Matthew 28:20; John 6:57; 7:38-39; 10:28-29; 14:19-20, 23; 15:5; and 16:13-15. All these are being carried out in His believers by His life-power, as the excellent virtue, unto His glory.

Based upon what He has imparted into us, God gives us His promises. By these promises we can be partakers of the divine nature. This means we can enjoy and know God in what He is, in Spirit, in love, and in light. Peter goes on according to his experience to tell us that there is a process of development. We all have the allotted faith and from this faith we have to develop the virtues.

Faith is the substantiation of the substance of the truth (Heb. 11:1), which is the reality of the contents of God's New Testament economy. The contents of God's New Testament economy are composed of the "all things which relate to life and godliness" (2 Pet. 1:3), that is, the Triune God dispensing Himself into us as life within and godliness without (see points 1, 2, 5, and the last paragraph of note 1[1] in 1 Tim. 1— Recovery Version). The like precious faith allotted to us by God through the word of God's New Testament economy and the Spirit, responds to the reality of such contents and ushers us into the reality, making its substance the very element of our Christian life and experience. Such a faith is allotted to all the believers in Christ as their portion, which is equally precious to all who have received it. As such a portion from God, this faith is objective to us in the divine truth. But it brings all the contents of its substantiation into us, thus making them all with itself (faith) subjective to us in our experience. It is like the scenery (truth) and the seeing (faith) being objective to the camera (us). But when the light (the Spirit) brings the scenery to the film (our spirit) within the camera, both the seeing and the scenery become subjective to it.

This allotted faith is the substantiation, the response, of the divine seed, the Triune God dispensed into us, which has been sown into our being, referred to in 1 John 3:9. We have to cooperate with this seed in order for it to have some development. In our faith, in the substantiation of the divine seed, virtue needs to be supplied and developed. Virtue denotes the energy of the divine life issuing in vigorous action to overcome all obstacles and to carry out all excellent attributes. This virtue with all things relating to life has been given to us by the divine power, but it needs to be developed on the way to glory. When you contact the Lord, you have the sensation that something within you is energizing, stirring up, and rising up. This is the virtue, the life energy. Then in this life energy there is more development and we begin to know the Lord much more, in knowledge.

Furthermore, in this knowledge, just by contacting the Lord, there is a realization that you need to restrict yourself. You begin to realize that you are too wild, too free, especially in the passions, desires, lusts, and in the self. This restricting of yourself is self-control. This is a kind of temperance. Then you develop further from self-control to endurance. Self-control is to restrict yourself and endurance is to bear with others and with circumstances. Without contacting the Lord, you would be so wild and so free in doing things and you would not endure anything or anybody. You may even feel that the entire earth is your world and your empire, and you might get angry with everybody. However, when you stay with the Lord in fellowship the divine nature within you develops and you restrict yourself, tolerate others, and endure any kind of environment.

Then in endurance godliness is developed. As the divine nature develops within you, you will spontaneously be a person that is like God and expresses God. When we exercise control over ourselves and bear with others, godliness needs to be and is developed in our spiritual life that we may be like God and express Him. In this godliness, the divine nature develops further in a love for the brothers. The consummation of this development is that in brotherly love the nobler love is developed.

Some sisters who live together may love one another when they contact the Lord. In this kind of love, however, one of the sisters will still complain. She might say, "Why is it that I have to do all the dishes and that sister would never help me." This proves that there is the need of further development. Our brotherly love needs to be developed further into a nobler, higher, and even super love which in Greek is *agape,* used in the New Testament for the divine love, which God is in His nature (1 John 4:8, 16). By the time the divine nature within us has been developed to such an extent, we love everyone. We become like our heavenly Father who loves the ones who love Him and even loves the ones who hate Him. If we were God, we would send the rain only on the lovers and keep the rain from all the haters. God, however, "makes His sun to rise on the evil and the good, and sends rain on the just and the unjust" (Matt. 5:45). This is the super and nobler love, and this nobler love is the very basic constituent of God's divine nature.

I hope that we all have seen that there are two lines which unveil to us the partaking and enjoying of the divine nature. John's line is to remain in the fellowship and Peter's line is to develop the divine seed sown within us, until it reaches its consummation in the nobler love, *agape,* which is one of the constituents of God's divine nature. We need to remain in the divine fellowship, and for the divine seed to develop itself, we need to cooperate. We should not resist or keep obstacles in the way of this development. We have to cooperate with the development of this basic divine blessing which is the divine seed sown into us and substantiated by the allotted faith. Then we will reach to the top of the enjoyment of the divine nature which is to partake of the nobler love. At this point, we not only love those who behave themselves in the brothers house but also love those who do not behave.

Ephesians 5:25 charges the husbands to love their wives. A certain husband may feel that since his wife is not so lovable, he could not love her. Furthermore, he may think that if his wife were like another sister, he would love her. Even if another sister were married to this brother, however, he would still not be satisfied. What he needs to experience is the nobler love. Our poor human love is always short. To say or to think that you cannot love your wife proves that you have not partaken of the divine nature to the extent that you are experiencing and enjoying the divine love. If you have partaken of the divine nature to such an extent, you would love any kind of wife. A nobler love does not exercise any kind of choice.

When we remain in the fellowship, we touch the source, and we enjoy the divine love as the essence and the divine light as the expression. This means we partake of the divine nature. In this enjoyment we let the divine seed of the allotted faith develop to its consummation—the divine nobler love.

CHAPTER THIRTY-TWO

THE NEW JERUSALEM—
THE BASIC ELEMENTS OF ITS STRUCTURE

(4)

Scripture Reading: 1 Pet. 1:15-16, 22; 2 Pet. 1:7; 3:11; 1 John
1:5-9; 2:29; 3:7

THE ISSUE OF PARTAKING OF
AND ENJOYING THE DIVINE NATURE

In the last two chapters, we have seen what the divine
nature is and we have also seen how to partake of this
divine nature. The way to enjoy the divine nature is to
remain in the divine fellowship and to cooperate with the
development of the divine nature. In this chapter we want to
see the issue of our partaking of and enjoying the divine
nature.

We have mentioned that Paul's writings in the New Testament do not touch the divine nature that much. His writings
imply the divine nature, but they are mainly concentrated on
the law of life. In Romans 8:2 Paul refers emphatically to "the
law of the Spirit of life" which has set us free from the law of
sin and of death. Paul also stressed the inner law of life in
Hebrews 8:10 and 10:16. Paul stressed this inner law because
he was an apostle through whom God's dispensation, God's
economy, was unveiled to the uttermost. God's dispensation
or economy depends upon two laws—the law of letters and
the law of life. The New Testament is altogether dependent
on the law of life, while the entire Old Testament economy
depended upon the law of letters.

Without the law of letters, there would be no Old Testament. The law of letters is a description of what God is. We can compare the law of letters to a photograph of a real person. The law of letters is a photograph of God, which gives us the image of God. Genesis 1:26 tells us that God made man in His image, and God's image is the expression of four items: love, light, holiness, and righteousness. The ten commandments were established and given based upon these four divine attributes, which are a description of what God is. The ten commandments testify and show forth that God is love, light, holy, and righteous. This is the image of God, the description of God, the photograph of God.

The New Testament is the new economy or new dispensation, and this dispensation depends upon the law of life. The law of life is actually God Himself. In the Old Testament we see a photograph of God, but in the New Testament we see the actual Person of God. The Old Testament was a photograph, a description of God, not the real Person. The law, the photograph, was given in the Old Testament, but the real Person, as embodied in Jesus came in the New Testament (John 1:17). This Person came to be life, the life supply, and the law of life to His people. The law of the Spirit of life is the Triune God working in us. The law of life in the New Testament is a living Person, of whom a photograph was given in the Old Testament, which was the law of letters. Paul's line was to unveil the new dispensational working of God as the law of life. Paul was occupied with this and would not be distracted from this. His writings imply the divine nature, but in Peter's writings the divine nature is clearly mentioned, and we are shown how we can become the partakers of the divine nature.

God is surely sovereign in His choice of the writers of the New Testament. Both Peter and John were uneducated and unlearned fishermen. If God had charged them to write about the law of life in the New Testament economy, they probably would not have been able to do it since they did not have an adequate education. This is why I encourage all the young ones to get a better education. If you are a fisherman like John and Peter, you can be used by the Lord only according to that particular measure. You could never be used like the

Apostle Paul. Paul was educated as a young boy in Tarsus, celebrated for its learning, and brought up in Jerusalem at the feet of Gamaliel with the highest education (Acts 22:3). His writings, therefore, are the writings of a scholar. He wrote his Epistles not only according to his own experiences, but also according to the divine revelation. To unveil the divine revelation in the way Paul did there is the need of a higher education. To write what Peter and John wrote, however, there is no need of a higher education. John's writings, for example, are quite simple—"In the beginning was the Word, and the Word was with God, and the Word was God" (John 1:1). "In Him was life, and the life was the light of men" (John 1:4). "I am the light of the world" (John 8:12). Paul's writings, however, were the writings of a "top professor." To write something concerning God's eternal plan, His eternal economy, needs a higher education. To merely tell your experience, however, does not need that much education. Even Peter told us that in Paul's letters "some things are hard to understand, which the unlearned and unstable twist, as also the rest of the Scriptures, to their own destruction" (2 Pet. 3:16). John and Peter wrote things mainly according to their experiences. This matter of enjoying the divine nature and remaining in the divine fellowship to cooperate with the development of the divine nature is the highest experience of both Peter and John. Only in these two apostles' writings can we see clearly and emphatically the enjoyment and partaking of the divine nature.

In Peter's Line

Holiness with Love

We have seen that when we enjoy the divine nature, we mainly enjoy God as Spirit, love, and light because these are the three main constituents of the divine nature. Spirit is the nature of God's Person, love is the nature of God's essence, and light is the nature of God's expression. To partake of the divine nature is to partake of the divine Spirit, the divine love, and the divine light. When we touch the Spirit this issues in the Person of God. When we touch God as the super, nobler, and higher love the issue is that we are made distinct and different. If we never touch the love of God, we are all people who have "the same feathers." The human community can be described by the saying, "Birds of a feather flock together." Human society has been "darkened" by sin. In this respect, everyone in the human race is basically the same. The high officials, the professors, the people from different cultures, the modern people, and the backward people are all the same, of the same feathers. When someone gets saved, however, and they contact the Lord daily, remaining in the fellowship and cooperating with the inward divine operation, they are filled with God as love. This inward love makes them different. They become distinct in their school, in their homes, and among their relatives, colleagues, and classmates.

The real meaning of the word holiness is separation and distinction. Among billions of material things in the universe there is one item that is distinct and uncommon—gold. Gold typifies God in His divine nature. God is distinct, which means that God is holy. The opposite of the word holy is common. Gold signifies the "golden God" or the holy God, the very God of separation. Our God is separated and is a God of separation. To be holy is to be set aside, to be separated, to be made distinct, just as God is.

After reading this, do not make up your mind to be distinct or to make yourself different. If you remain in the divine fellowship to enjoy not only what God gives or what God does for you but also what God is as love in His essence and as light in His expression, you will be bathed in the love of God. You will become not only a man of love, but you will become love itself. This love makes you distinct. If you are a married brother, the first one to realize that you are different and distinct is your wife. If you would remain in fellowship with the Lord for a length of time, both your wife and your children will have the realization that you are different after this fellowship. The issue of remaining in the fellowship is that you become someone who is not common but holy. In your office all your colleagues realize that you are different. In your school the teachers realize that you are different. Among your relatives you are a different person and they realize it. You are holy, which means that you are different from all the others. You are different, separated, and uncommon. God is distinct and separate from all the material things in the universe, and the New Jerusalem is a golden mountain, a distinct entity in the entire universe. Also, every local church as a golden lampstand is distinct and different.

First Peter 1:15 and 16 indicate that we must have a holy manner of life because our God is holy. He is called "the Holy One." This means that since our God is golden, we have to be golden. Our God is a big piece of gold, so we have to be small pieces of gold. First Peter 1 also refers us to love. Verse 22 of chapter one tells us that we have to love the brothers with an unfeigned love. Our experiences tell us that the genuine holiness, the consummation of the Christian holiness, is the issue of the enjoyment of God as love. This love makes you holy, makes you different, makes you distinct, and makes you separated from being common. In Peter's first Epistle, we see holiness with love.

Love is the nature of the divine essence. Note 10^1 of Hebrews 12 (Recovery Version) tells us that holiness is God's nature. We must realize, however, that holiness is God's nature in its separation and distinction. Holiness is not an element but a condition, a manner. Love is God's nature in His essence, light is God's nature in His expression, Spirit is God's nature in His Person, but holiness is not God's nature in some element. It is God's nature in its condition, and the condition is separation and distinction.

Love in Holiness

In Peter's second Epistle we also see love in holiness. Love is the ultimate development of the divine nature (2 Pet. 1:7). Holiness is the manner of the life partaking of the divine nature (2 Pet. 3:11). Love issues in holiness. When you partake of the divine nature to the uttermost, you will be filled with God as love. This issues in a manner of life, and this manner of life is a separated and distinct life, making you no more common but holy. Holiness is the manner of this life that enjoys the divine nature to the uttermost. When we enjoy God as love, we even become love, and this issues in holiness. Holiness is the manner. When we become love, we become different and distinct from the common people. The divine love sanctifies us, separates us, and makes us different. We are a people who are so holy, so golden. We are no longer pieces of clay but pieces of gold, and when we come together, all the pieces put together become a golden lampstand, bearing a testimony of the "golden" Jesus. This is the central lane, the central thought, of Peter's writing.

The consummation of our enjoying the divine nature is *agape,* the divine love. Love is the ultimate development in the divine nature (2 Pet. 1:7) and the consummation of the development of the divine nature. In his second Epistle Peter tells us that we have the allotted faith within us as the divine portion and that God has given us exceedingly great and precious promises that we might become partakers of the divine nature. As we cooperate with this divine nature, it will have the opportunity to develop itself to its consummation, which is love.

In 2 Peter 3, Peter tells us that one day "the heavens will pass away with a roar, and the elements burning with intense heat will be dissolved, and the earth and the works in it will be burned up. All these things being thus dissolved, what kind of persons ought you to be in holy manner of life and godliness" (vv. 10-11). Peter's second Epistle begins in chapter one with the development of the divine nature which consummates in love, and it ends in chapter three with a holy manner of life and godliness. In the development of the divine nature, love is developed in brotherly love, and brotherly love is developed in godliness. This means that at the beginning of 2 Peter godliness consummates in love, and at the end of 2 Peter we see that the holy manner of life goes with godliness. The consummation of the enjoyment of the divine nature is love, and the consummation of 2 Peter is holiness. Love is the essence of this holy life, and holiness is the manner of such a life of love. Holiness is the manner, the expression, of the life partaking of the divine nature.

If you have been born of God, you have received His divine life with His divine nature. Now for you to enjoy God is to enjoy the divine nature, which is constituted mainly with love as the essence and light as the expression. When you enjoy God in His divine nature, you enjoy Him as love and as light. Love is the consummation of your enjoyment of God's divine nature. As you enjoy and partake of the divine nature you live a life of love, and this life has a manner. This is a life fully separated from the common life, a life that is distinct and different. In our community, our neighborhood, and among our relatives, colleagues, and classmates, we must give people an impression of distinction. They should realize that we are not common. This distinction comes from your being a person of love. Because you are a person of love, you do not quarrel, argue, or fight with anyone. You do not hate anyone and would never be mad with anyone. (First Corinthians 13 is a wonderful chapter showing us the virtues of love and the definition of love.)

Because you are a person enjoying the divine nature, you are a person of love. The people around you would notice that you are different and distinct. This is not a matter of behavior, but it is a matter of our being. Because you are a person remaining in the fellowship and cooperating with the inner operation of the divine nature, this makes you "a bit of love, a bit of God." The others around you are "muddy," but you are golden; you are a piece of gold. Among all the muddy people, you are different. You are holy.

In conclusion, the central thought of Peter's writing is this: we believers have received the divine life and with this divine life we have the divine nature which is God Himself for us to enjoy. When we enjoy this divine nature to the uttermost, love will be the consummation. Then we become a loving being, a being of love. This love makes us different, just as Jesus was different and distinct when He was on this earth. He was altogether distinct, different, and separated from the others. He was a piece of gold among the "muddy" people. Even the twelve disciples in the Gospels were "twelve pieces of mud." Only Jesus Christ was golden. He was a Person of love. The divine love, the noble love, *agape,* made Jesus Christ distinct among all the people, which means He was holy. Peter saw this in the Gospels and after Pentecost he experienced this. In his two Epistles we see that love is the consummation of the enjoyment of the divine nature and that this love has an expression—holiness. Therefore, love is the essence of the divine life and holiness is the manner of this life.

In John's Line

Righteousness with Light

The enjoyment of the divine nature is mainly to enjoy the divine love and the divine life. Peter did not stress the divine life but the divine love. The ultimate development of the divine nature is love, *agape,* and this love issues in holiness. John mentions that God is love, but he does not stress love that much. Rather, he stresses light which is the nature of the divine expression. John tells us in his first Epistle that he preached the eternal life to others that they might be brought into the divine fellowship (1:2-3). Through this life, you have received the divine fellowship and if you remain in the divine fellowship, you will enjoy God as light (1:5-7). The message which John heard from God and announced to others was that God is light. John stressed that when we enjoy the divine nature, God becomes light to us and we enjoy God as light.

This light issues in righteousness. Righteousness is the expression of the life partaking of the divine nature. In Peter's line love issues in holiness and in John's line light issues in righteousness. Peter stresses holiness; John stresses righteousness. In his first Epistle he calls the Lord the Righteous One (2:1). Righteousness is the issue of light. When you are in the light, you do everything right. If you do everything wrongly and foolishly, this means that you are in darkness. You do not know where you are going, what you are doing, or what you are speaking because you are in darkness. However, when you are in the light, everything becomes crystal clear to you. You know where you are, what you are doing, where you should go, what you should do, and what you should speak.

In John's writing, he was trying to inoculate the believers against a heresy which taught that the believers did not have sin and that they did not need to make any confession of their sins. John proved in his Epistle that even though we have been regenerated, we still have sin within us and there is the possibility that we will commit sins (1 John 1:8—2:1). John indicates that if we remain in the fellowship and enjoy God as light there is no way that we can say that we are not sinful anymore. We still have a sinful nature and there is still some possibility that we may fall into sin. Therefore, we need to confess our sins. John then goes on to talk about righteousness which is the opposite of sin. Anything that is unrighteous is sin. He says that "If we confess our sins, He is faithful and righteous that He may forgive us our sins and cleanse us from all unrighteousness" (1 John 1:9). To cleanse us from all unrighteousness is to make us right.

Light in Righteousness

First John 2:29 says, "If you have known that He is righteous, you know also that everyone who practices righteousness has been begotten of Him." Then 1 John 3:7 tells us that "he who practices righteousness is righteous, even as that One is righteous." Verses like these indicate clearly that enjoying God as light issues in righteousness. Love separates us from being common, and light makes us right in everything.

When we are in darkness, we do everything wrong. Light regulates us. If the place in which we are is in darkness, our walk is not regulated since we cannot see where we are going. Light always regulates us and keeps us in order. Righteousness comes out of the enjoyment of God as light. Light is the nature of the divine expression and righteousness is the expression of the life partaking of the divine nature, the expression of the life that enjoys God. If you are in the light and are enjoying God as light, you will have an expression that you are right in everything and with everyone. When you do things wrongly and when you do wrong things to others, this is a strong indication that you are not in the light.

We can prove this by our experiences. Nothing else tests or proves our Christian life as much as the marriage life. How good or how bad a husband is is always proved in the eyes of his wife. No one knows a brother as thoroughly as his wife does. Whether or not he has stayed with the Lord and remained in fellowship with the Lord is known by her. Whenever a husband loses his temper with his wife, he knows nothing, he is the most foolish person, and he speaks nonsense. He is absolutely not right because he is in darkness. However, when a brother stays with the Lord, remaining in His fellowship and enjoying Him as love and as light, he becomes holy and righteous in the sight of his wife. As an issue of being in the light the husband does everything right and says everything right. It is possible for one to pretend to be something in others' eyes, but you cannot pretend to be anything in the eyes of your spouse. He or she knows the real situation. When you stay in the divine fellowship, however, the other party of your marriage knows and can testify that you are different. The enjoyment of God as love makes us holy and the enjoyment of God as light makes us right. Light is the essence of righteousness, and righteousness is the shining of light.

In conclusion, holiness is the issue of the enjoyment of the divine love and righteousness is the issue of the enjoyment of the divine light. The ultimate consummation of holiness is the enjoyment of God as love, and the ultimate consummation of righteousness is the enjoyment of God as light. The issue of our partaking of and enjoying the divine nature is holiness and righteousness.

CHAPTER THIRTY-THREE

THE NEW JERUSALEM—
THE BASIC ELEMENTS OF ITS STRUCTURE

(5)

Scripture Reading: Rev. 21:11, 18-21; John 19:34; Matt. 13:45-46; John 3:5; Gen. 2:12b; 1 Cor. 3:12a

THE GREATEST ALLEGORY IN THE BIBLE

The Bible is not a book of religion, philosophy, or something invented by the human mentality, but it is God's revelation of the divine life. The Bible, of course, covers many things but its focus and very central thought is the divine life. Our human life is a mystery, and the divine life is even more abstract and mysterious. No human words in human language can fully utter the mystery of this divine life. Therefore, God exercised His wisdom to reveal such a mystery concerning His divine life by many allegories.

Many Bible students and teachers are insistent upon not using too many allegories. Paul, however, in Galatians 4 said that Sarah and Hagar and each of their sons were an allegory. Sarah and Hagar represented two covenants (vv. 22-24). Without Paul's writing in Galatians 4 none of us would dream that these two women were an allegory of the two covenants. Paul, though, received this revelation probably with the realization that it would be hard for us to understand the two covenants in such a marvelous way without the allegory of these two women. Also, the Lord Jesus and the other apostles pointed out items in the Old Testament, which were allegories to reveal the unutterable revelations of the divine life. The greatest allegory in the Bible is in its last two chapters, and this allegory is the ultimate consummation of the divine revelation—the New Jerusalem. Throughout the centuries, the New Jerusalem has been a puzzle to all the students and teachers of the Bible. However, in the last thirty years by the Lord's mercy, this puzzle has been brought into a fuller light. In order for us to receive a vision of the holy city we need to be uplifted to a "high mountain" that we may see God's dwelling place for the fulfilling of His eternal purpose (Rev. 21:10).

THE DIVINE TRINITY

In this one allegory it is possible for one to see nearly every single divine point revealed in the Bible. If we know the Bible, we can see that the most central and most mysterious point in it is the Divine Trinity. The main and basic structure of this allegory of the New Jerusalem is the Divine Trinity. It is not possible to understand the structure of this allegory unless you enter into the entire Bible to see all the points revealed concerning the Divine Trinity. The Divine Trinity is the most basic and chief attribute of God's divine Person. Love, light, and life are a few of the many attributes of God's divine Person, but the most basic attribute of God is the Trinity. It is easier to explain what love, light, and grace are as attributes of God, but it is really hard for anyone to define what the Divine Trinity is. The Divine Trinity is the greatest and the basic attribute of God.

The first divine title revealed in the Bible implies God in His Trinity. The word for God in Genesis 1:1 is *Elohim* which is plural in number. Then in Genesis 1:26, God refers to Himself as "Us." In the Bible there is one God, but this one God is the Father, the Son, and the Spirit, the Trinity. By studying the sixty-six books of the Bible, we can conclude that the Divine Trinity is for His dispensing. As the Father, the Son, and the Spirit, He dispenses Himself into His chosen people, and this dispensing is the main operation, the main goal, of God's being triune. The Divine Trinity is for the divine dispensing, and this dispensing consummates in the New Jerusalem.

In the New Jerusalem there are three gates on four sides, and the New Jerusalem is constructed with three basic elements—gold, pearls, and precious stones. The reason why the number three is so prevalent in the New Jerusalem is that this number represents the Divine Trinity. In this chapter and in the remaining chapters we will see that every aspect of the New Jerusalem is triune. Without such an allegory, it would be impossible to understand such a divine mystery of God dispensing Himself to consummate in a wonderful, divine building—the New Jerusalem.

THE SIGNIFICANCE OF THE PEARLS

In this chapter we want to see the significance of the pearls in the New Jerusalem. Revelation 21:21 tells us that the twelve gates of the New Jerusalem are twelve pearls. A pearl is not created or manufactured but produced by an oyster. A pearl is something produced organically just as a piece of fruit is not something manufactured or created but is the produce of an organic tree. The fact that an oyster produces a pearl is quite significant. Pearls are produced by oysters in the waters of death. When the oyster is wounded by a particle of sand, a little rock, it secretes its life-juice around the sand and makes it a precious pearl.

Since the Bible says that in the New Jerusalem there are twelve gates and that every gate is a pearl, we have to study every aspect of this pearl. Especially, we need to see how the pearl comes into existence. This is the purpose of God's wisdom in using an allegory. Without such an allegory of the oyster producing a pearl, how could we imagine that the gates as the pearls signify the produce of Christ in His redemptive work with His secreting life for the entry into God's building? As Christians we have heard repeatedly that Christ died and resurrected for our redemption. Merely by using the words death, resurrection, and redemption, however, our understanding is somewhat limited. In one of Charles Wesley's hymns he refers to the five bleeding wounds which the Lord bore when He was being crucified on the cross (see *Hymns,* #300). This, however, is a "physical teaching" concerning the divine truth. This is not an allegorization.

Without such an allegory of the oyster producing a pearl, we cannot adequately understand the significance of Christ's death and resurrection to redeem and transform us.

In this allegory, we need to see the illustration of Christ's death. The oyster depicts Christ as the living One coming into the death waters, being wounded by us, and secreting His life over us to make us precious pearls for the building of God's eternal habitation and expression. That the twelve gates of the holy city are twelve pearls signifies that regeneration through the death-overcoming and life-secreting Christ is the entrance into the city.

REMAINING IN THE DEATH OF CHRIST

The oyster's wound is an inward wound caused by a little rock. This rock can remain in this wound or, we may say, in this death. In like manner, we can remain in Christ's death. Where are you staying today? You should say, "Praise the Lord! I am staying in Christ's death. The Lord's death is my abode, my dwelling." You are a "little rock" that wounded Christ. After being wounded, He keeps you in His wound. Now you need to stay in His wound, in His death. I have been a Christian for over fifty-nine years and I must testify that His death is my best residence.

Are you not staying in the Lord's death? If you are not staying in His death, you have nowhere to stay or to remain. We all need to realize that every moment we need to stay in the all-inclusive death of Christ. The reason why we lose our temper is because we move out of the death of Christ. Because you "left home" and did not remain in His death, you lost your temper. As long as you remain and stay in the death of Christ, you will never lose your temper. Where can you get the victory over sin, over your temperament, over the world, and over Satan? Nowhere but in the death of Christ.

You may have been a Christian for many years, and yet you have never been told that you need to remain in the death of Christ. You may have been remaining in your kind of endeavor to behave properly. This means that you have been a wanderer. You have been homeless with no place to stay. However, if you stay in the death of Christ, you do not need to try to be nice. Not many of us realize that the Lord's all-inclusive death should be our residence, our home, in which we must stay. After the little rock wounds the oyster, it stays in the wound, and the oyster will not let it go. It grasps the rock in the very wound it made, so the wound becomes its residence, its home, its dwelling place. In like manner, the very death which Christ accomplished on the cross becomes our dwelling place. We have to stay in the death of Christ.

If we stay away from the wound, we cannot enjoy the secretion of the resurrection life. If the rock stays away from the wound of the oyster, it is not in the position to enjoy the secretion of the life-sap of that oyster. The secretion symbolizes the move of the resurrection life. Because an oyster is living and organic, it immediately reacts to being wounded by a rock by secreting its life-sap around the rock to keep it and even imprison it in its wound. This picture or allegory shows us that we are imprisoned in the death of Christ by His secreting power and that this secretion is the move of His resurrection life.

The wound signifies the death of Christ in which we sinners who wounded Christ are captured, kept, and imprisoned. The only place that one can be a normal, proper Christian is in the wound, the death, of Christ. We all need to say, "Lord, I have no choice; my unique residence today is Your death." Hallelujah for the death of Christ! This death is our rest, our residence, our home, and our unique place of protection. As long as I am staying in His wound, His life reacts, and this reaction is a secretion of His resurrection life. The death of Christ and the resurrection of Christ have been taught mostly as objective items, which have nothing to do with our daily Christian life. Actually, the death of Christ is not merely objective but very subjective. We have to be conformed to His death (Phil. 3:10). His death has to be our daily dwelling place, and His resurrection should be our daily experience. We should be one with Him all the time in His death and resurrection. Our oneness with Him is in the Spirit. Hence, the secretion of His resurrection is in the Spirit—the reality of His resurrection.

Day by day I enjoy the secretion of Christ's resurrection life. A kind of secretion is around me all the time because I am always imprisoned in His death. Where death is, resurrection is. Resurrection works in death and through death. This resurrection is the secretion of the life-sap of the resurrected Christ around your entire being in the way that oysters produce pearls.

The oyster is an allegory of the wonderful Christ. He is the unique One that can live in the death waters. As One who is living and organic, He was wounded by us, and He reacted by resurrecting to secrete His life-sap around the wounding ones. What a mercy! We wounded Him, and He will not let us go. Because of His great love with which He loved us, His wound caused by us became our prison. His desire is to imprison us in His death that we might enjoy His life-secreting resurrection. Even though you may have never heard this before, you should have had some experiences of this. After you believed that the Lord died for you and that He is in resurrection, you enjoyed staying with Him. When you aspired to be in the Lord, you were abiding in His death, and within you there was a life secretion. Even though you had not heard this fellowship, you did have this kind of experience. Christ makes us pearls by being wounded by us, by keeping us in His wound, and by secreting Himself around us in His death through resurrection in the Spirit, who is His reality.

The pearls are the gates, and this point of the allegory means that the more we are made pearls, the more we are in the New Jerusalem. When we believed in the Lord Jesus, we were regenerated, and this was the initiation of our entering into the New Jerusalem. At that time, though, we were barely in the New Jerusalem in our experience. As we stay in the Lord's death and enjoy His life-secreting resurrection, there is a further entering into the New Jerusalem. Our experience of the Lord's death and resurrection becomes our entry into the New Jerusalem. We can enjoy being in the New Jerusalem to a great extent by staying in the death of Christ to enjoy His secretion of Himself as the resurrection life-sap around us. We all need to ask ourselves how much we are in the New Jerusalem and how much we are still outside the gates. The only way for a further entering into the holy city is by a further staying in the death of Christ. The death of Christ is the right place for you to receive and experience the secretion of life by the resurrected Christ. What I am telling you is not an objective teaching concerning the resurrection, but is altogether concerning our daily experience of the subjective, resurrection life of Christ. We need this kind of subjective experience.

I hope that after reading this chapter, all of us would pray, "Lord, imprison me and keep me always in Your death. I do not want to leave Your death but to make Your death my sweet and wonderful dwelling place. Lord, I want to stay with You in Your death." His death is the place where He has the position to secrete Himself around you, and this is the only place where you can enjoy and experience His resurrection life as a kind of life-sap secreting itself around your being, making you a wonderful piece of pearl. We need to see that the pearls signify the believers produced of Christ in His redemptive work with His secreting life for the entry into God's building.

BLOOD AND WATER

The producing of the believers as the pearls by Christ in His redemptive work is allegorized in the blood and water which came out of His side (John 19:34). When He was dying on the cross, a soldier pierced His side and immediately there came out blood and water. Blood and water are two allegories to describe the redemptive work of Christ. Blood is for redemption and water is for regeneration. We need redemption because we are sinful, and we need regeneration which is the initiation of the secretion of Christ's resurrection life, because we are merely human and do not have the divine life. We need the blood to wash away our sins, and we need the water as the flow of the divine life to germinate us, to bring the divine life into our being, that we may have the life power to overcome so many things. The first stanza of *Hymns,* #1058 says:

Rock of Ages, cleft for me,
Let me hide myself in Thee;
Let the water and the blood,
From Thy riven side which flowed,
Be of sin the double cure,
Save me from its guilt and power.

The writer of this hymn refers to the "double cure." His redemption gives us a double cure. First He washes away our sins, and second He regenerates us. His blood saves us from the guilt of sin and His life saves us from the power of sin. In His redemption Christ can give us a double cure—He washes away our filthiness and He keeps away our death. This double cure is His redemptive work, yet for us to enjoy His redemptive work, we must be willing to be imprisoned in His death. While we are in His death, He has the position to secrete Himself around our being. Then we will surely receive the double cure, and we will be produced as pearls for the entry into God's building.

THE DIVINE ELEMENT
BEING ADDED TO OUR HUMAN ELEMENT

To produce pearls the main thing needed is that another element has to be added to the wounding rock. The rock is one element and the oyster's secretion brings the element of the oyster life to this rock. Two elements are mingled together to produce a pearl. Your human life, your human being, with your natural element is the rock. After we wounded Christ, He captured us and He is now keeping us in His death to secrete Himself around us, which is the adding of His divine element to our human element. This shows us how marvelous the allegories in the Bible are. No plain word could explain this divine mystery to such an extent. All the unseen, invisible mysteries are unveiled in this allegory. The divine element is being added to our human element making us pearls for the building of God's eternal expression.

At the time a certain brother was married, he may have been very rough. But after years of abiding in the Lord's death and enjoying His life-secreting resurrection, even his wife can testify that a great part of her husband has become pearl. Before we came into the enjoyment of Christ in His death and resurrection in the church life, we were very rough, but we can all testify that at least some part of our being has become pearl and that we are in the process of becoming pearls. We are under the secretion of the resurrection life of Christ through His imprisoning death. His death is imprisoning us to keep us in the position of enjoying the secretion of Christ around our entire being.

All the meetings of the church help us to stay in the death of Christ, and they keep us in the death of Christ. Do not get away. Stay home. Where is your home and what is your home? Your home is the death of Christ, and He is here secreting and moving in His resurrection life. This secretion is His resurrection which is fully realized in His life-giving Spirit. The secretion is the operation of His life-giving Spirit; if you do not have His Spirit, you do not have His resurrection. Also, the way to enjoy His Spirit is to stay in His death. The more you stay in His death, the more you have His Spirit moving in you. This moving of His life-giving Spirit is the secreting of His divine life.

A COLLECTIVE PEARL

We also must realize that although every gate is a single pearl, this pearl is collectively singular. It is a collective piece of pearl, not just you yourself. It is a group of believers. After this fellowship, I believe that we understand in a more thorough way one more of the basic elements of the New Jerusalem—the pearls.

THE ENTRY INTO GOD'S BUILDING

Christ was wounded for us in order to have us imprisoned in His wound that He might carry out His secretion over us again and again throughout our entire life to make us pearls for the building of God's eternal habitation. This is for the entry (Matt. 13:45-46; John 3:5). The more we are made pearls, the more we are in the New Jerusalem, and the more we are in the kingdom. We were regenerated to enter into the kingdom of God. To use the allegory of a pearl, however, to illustrate the entering into the kingdom of God by regeneration is much more significant.

I hope that we could follow the Spirit to fully enter into the denotation and significance of the pearls. Then we will no longer be shallow in our understanding of Christ's death, resurrection, and redemption. We will not be "skating on the ice of the truth" in this matter. We want to get into the depths of this truth to enjoy the riches of Christ.

CHAPTER THIRTY-FOUR

THE NEW JERUSALEM—
THE BASIC ELEMENTS OF ITS STRUCTURE

(6)

Scripture Reading: Rev. 21:11, 18a, 19-20; 2 Cor. 3:18; Phil. 1:19; Gen. 2:12b; 1 Cor. 3:12a; 1 Pet. 2:4-5; Rev. 4:3a

GOLD, PEARLS, AND PRECIOUS STONES

We all have seen that the basic elements of the structure of the New Jerusalem are gold, pearls, and precious stones. Gold refers to the divine nature of God the Father, and pearls refer to the produce of Christ in His overcoming death and life-secreting resurrection. In this chapter we want to see the third item of the basic elements of the structure of the New Jerusalem—precious stones. Precious stones (Rev. 21:11, 18a, 19-20) signify the produce of the Spirit in His transforming work with His divine element for the building up of God's building (Gen. 2:12b; 1 Cor. 3:12a; 1 Pet. 2:4-5; 2 Cor. 3:18).

Gold only refers to the nature of God the Father, not to any of His work. Gold is God Himself as the divine nature given to us as a gift of which we may partake and which we may enjoy. Pearls, however, do not refer to Christ Himself directly, but to the produce of His work of redemption through His death and resurrection. The work of the Son is His redemptive work, of which there are mainly two aspects— one aspect is to wash away all our negative things through His death and the other aspect is to germinate us, to make us alive, with the divine life through His resurrection. This work produces the pearls. The precious stones are also a kind of produce. The work of Christ produces pearls and the work of the Spirit of Christ produces precious stones. It is difficult to differentiate between these two kinds of works. Christ's work is to secrete His life over us, and the Spirit's work is to transform us into precious stones.

THE LESSON OF GAMALIEL

Even though Christianity has been on the earth for nearly two thousand years and the Bible has been given to God's children, the depth of the divine revelation has been missed, lost, and even buried by the traditional concept, teaching, and knowledge. It is not easy for us to stay away from the traditional teaching and knowledge which we picked up in the past. In Acts 5 we see a great teacher of the law named Gamaliel (v. 34), under whom the Apostle Paul received his education (Acts 22:3). Gamaliel was a great teacher among the Jews and was respected by them. Do you believe, however, that Gamaliel had any concept or any share in God's New Testament economy? God's economy in the New Testament began on the day of Pentecost under the leadership of a Galilean fisherman named Peter. God's economy was being carried out in a marvelous way, but all the Pharisees, including Gamaliel, did not have any idea that this was God's move on the earth. Gamaliel was a godly man who feared God, yet he did not know anything concerning God's economy and had no share in God's economy. This godly man was fully blinded by his Judaic, traditional theology and actually he was in darkness. Gamaliel and the other Pharisees were content with the knowledge of God that they had received according to their traditional teaching. When the Pharisees were intending to do away with the apostles, Gamaliel advised them not to do this but to leave them and the entire situation in God's hands (Acts 5:38-39). His advice was very good, godly, and wise, yet he did not have any share in God's New Testament economy.

Today there are many Gamaliels who are godly and prayerful and yet hold on to their traditional theology. Actually, the Judaic theology is not wrong, but it is short. In the same way, many people today who have doctor's degrees in theology and many theological professors in today's seminaries are just like Gamaliel. They are short of the knowledge and vision of God's New Testament economy. We may be "Galilean fishermen," yet we must testify that we know what God's New Testament economy is. We do not have the burden to minister the "Judaic theology," which is so fundamental and scriptural, yet has nothing to do with God's New Testament economy.

The situation of Gamaliel is a warning to us. We may be godly and even respected and revered by other people, and yet have no share in or knowledge of God's New Testament economy. The Lord Jesus promised us that He would come quickly and yet nearly two thousand years have passed since His ascension because very few of His believers throughout the centuries entered into God's New Testament economy. Rather, they all were "caught" and occupied by traditional theology. Today's seminaries teach the traditional theology and yet they know nearly nothing concerning God's New Testament economy. In today's theological teaching there is not such a term as God's New Testament economy. Gamaliel did not know anything about Jesus Christ moving as the very embodiment of the Triune God to dispense the Divine Trinity into God's chosen people and how this dispensing produces a corporate vessel which is the church, the Body of Christ, the fullness of the One who fills all in all, to express God in a corporate way consummating in the New Jerusalem.

THE DIVINE NATURE AND ITS DEVELOPMENT

The New Jerusalem is a golden mountain. Revelation 21 tells us that the city was pure gold and also that the street of the city was pure gold (v. 21). When we were regenerated, we received the nature of God and a part of this golden mountain entered into our being. We all have a part of the golden mountain, the New Jerusalem. We need to realize that something within us is divine. A part of our regenerated being is gold, and this divine gold is God's nature. As the children of God we have God's divine nature which means we have a part of the golden mountain. Your part, my part, and the parts of billions of believers in Christ including Paul, Peter, and John, when added together, equal the golden mountain.

The gold within us does not need any further work, but it needs some development. A small tree develops, which means that it grows, but the tree does not work. When trees grow, they develop. As we have seen, 2 Peter 1 tells us that we are partakers of the divine nature and shows us the development of the divine nature. Although trees grow or develop, they still need a suitable environment for their development. The divine nature within us as symbolized by the gold does not work but it grows or develops, and its development needs a good environment. Otherwise, the development will be frustrated, limited, or restricted. In order for the divine nature to develop within us to its fullest extent, we need to give it the best environment.

As a young believer I heard that Christians have to grow, but when I asked how we grow no one knew the answer. Some said that to grow is to acquire more knowledge from the Bible. I knew one particular older brother who had a tremendous amount of Bible knowledge. Although he gave sermons on the Bible and was one of the best teachers I was under, he still smoked. Although he had a great amount of the knowledge of the Bible, he was short of life. Today the Lord has opened our eyes to see that God the Father's nature is in us as the ground, the site, of God's building and that this nature is developing. Now we need to let this divine nature have the best cooperation and the best environment that it may grow and develop within us.

THE SON'S SECRETING WORK

The redemptive work of God the Son is all-inclusive. His desire is for us to stay in His death so that He might secrete His "life-juice" over us. This is the life-secreting work of Christ. Because this work is hard for us to realize, we need such an allegory. Without this allegory, we would not be able to see that Christ's resurrection life is actually the divine life element secreted over us to make us pearls.

If we check with our experience, we will be able to understand more fully Christ's secreting work. Whenever you remain in the all-inclusive death of Christ, whenever you take the cross, the resurrection life of Christ secretes over you. It may be that a certain young brother feels that his father is wrong in a certain matter. He may feel that he needs to complain or rebel, but if he does this, he is running away from the death of Christ. However, if this brother stays under the cross in the death of Christ and says, "Lord, I praise You that You have kept me in Your death; I praise You that I am now residing in Your all-inclusive death," immediately something within him will be secreting around his inner being, and he will sense the inner supply. As he experiences this inner secretion time after time, he will become a pearl more and more. This is the secretion of the resurrected Christ in His resurrection life.

Even in our marriage life we must remember that in order to enjoy the secreting work of Christ in His resurrection through His death, we must remain and stay in His death. Do not run away. Many married sisters run away from the death of Christ in their relationship with their husbands. When a wife is nagging, or scolding her husband, she has moved out of the death of Christ. We all need to see that the marvelous, all-inclusive death of Christ is our "home sweet home." Regardless of what a sister's husband would say to her, she needs to stay, to remain, in Christ's death. If she would do this, she would sense the secreting of Christ's resurrection life. The more trouble her husband would give her, the more enjoyment she would have as long as she remains in the death of Christ. This fellowship is not a doctrine or a teaching but an explanation of our subjective experience of Christ. Thank the Lord that today He has opened the veils and has shown us the way to be victorious and to be an overcomer. We do not need to "gnash our teeth" to endeavor or to struggle. We only need to stay home, to remain in the death of Christ. Then we enjoy the secreting of the divine life in resurrection.

THE SPIRIT'S TRANSFORMING WORK

The Spirit's transforming work is different from Christ's secreting work. Without Christ's secretion of life, the Spirit has nothing as an element with which to transform us. Christ secretes His resurrection life over you and following this the Spirit works to transform you with the life element. In other words, the transforming work of the Spirit continues the secreting work of Christ. When we received Christ, we received God the Father as the divine nature into us. Then as we remain in the death of Christ, we enjoy His life secretion in us. The Spirit then uses this secreting life to transform us. The secreting work is only an addition to add more of the divine life to our natural life, but the transforming work is to change our being metabolically. In order to change any living being metabolically, there is the need of some new element. This new element is the very life which has been secreted into our being. After Christ's secretion, the Spirit comes and continues to transform our being with this secreted life. Then our entire being will be gradually transformed not only in form but also in essence.

Second Corinthians 3:17-18 shows us the transforming work of the Spirit. Verse 17 tells us that the Lord is the Spirit. The One who died on the cross was Christ the Lord and the One who proceeded out of Him was the Spirit. Now we see, however, that the Lord is the very Spirit who proceeded out of Himself. This is a mysterious fact, which is beyond our understanding. Verse 17 goes on to tell us that where the Spirit of the Lord is, there is freedom. The Spirit of the Lord is the Lord Himself, with whom is the freedom from the letter of the law.

Verse 18 indicates that we need to behold the Lord with an unveiled face. Originally our face was veiled, but many of us today have unveiled faces. This means that our heart has turned to the Lord so that the veil has been taken away, and the Lord as the Spirit has freed us from the bondage, the veiling, of the law, so that there is no more insulation between us and the Lord. Now with an unveiled face we look at the Lord. The more we look at the Lord, the more He secretes the resurrected life over our being. While we are looking at the Lord, we are being transformed. Verse 18 tells us that we "are being transformed into the same image from glory to glory, even as from the Lord Spirit." Eventually, the transforming work is done by the Lord Spirit. The Spirit who transforms us is "the Lord Spirit." The Lord is the One who secretes life into you,

and the Spirit is the One who transforms you with the life
secreted into your being by the Lord.

TRANSFORMATION FOR GOD'S BUILDING

The Spirit's transforming work is with His bountiful supply of the divine element (Phil. 1:19) for the building up of
God's building (Gen. 2:12b; 1 Cor. 3:12a; 1 Pet. 2:4-5). Consum-
mately, the transforming work of the Spirit issues in the New
Jerusalem, which bears the image of God for His expression.
God appears like a jasper stone in Revelation 4:3, and the
New Jerusalem, having the glory of God, shines like a jasper
stone (Rev. 21:11). Also, the first layer of the wall's foundation, as well as the entire wall of the New Jerusalem, is built
with jasper (Rev. 21:18-19). This indicates that the main material in the building of the holy city is jasper. Since jasper signifies God expressed in His communicable glory (Rev. 4:3),
the main function of the holy city is to express God in bearing
His glory.

The transforming work of the Spirit produces the precious
stones for God's building. Pearls which are used for the gates
of the holy city bear an attractive appearance. Pearls are
good for attracting, but they are not good for the building of
the wall. To build the wall there is the need of some solid
material. Pearls are good material for the gates since they
are for attraction, but precious stones are the solid material
for God's building of the wall. The transforming work is an
advancement of the secreting work. The secreting work is the
initiation and the entrance into the holy city, but the transforming work is for the building of the wall. Life secreting
makes us into pearls, but for us to be precious stone there is
the need of a further step—the transforming work of the
Spirit.

First, we have the golden nature as a gift from God the
Father; second, we are enjoying the secreting work of Christ
to make us pearls; and third, we are experiencing the transforming work of God the Spirit to make us precious stones.
God the Father imparted His divine nature into you as a
piece of gold and this gold is a part of the city proper of the
New Jerusalem, the holy mountain. Then if you stay in the

death of Christ, you enjoy His secreting work to add more and more of the divine life with the divine element into your being. Finally, God the Spirit will continue by using the secreted life to transform your entire being from a piece of rock to a jasper stone, which is good for the building of God's eternal dwelling place. This dwelling place has been initiated today in the church life, and we are proceeding toward the ultimate consummation, the New Jerusalem.

CHAPTER THIRTY-FIVE

THE NEW JERUSALEM—
ITS TRIUNE ENTRANCE

Scripture Reading: Rev. 21:12-13, 21a; Eph. 2:18; Luke 15:4, 8, 20; Matt. 8:11; Gal 3:24; Rev. 5:9; Luke 15:7; Heb. 1:14

Prayer: Lord, how we worship You for Your New Testament economy. Lord, we thank You for the revelation conveyed in Your written Word. How we thank You that You have opened up this Word to us in these last days. Lord, we even thank You for all the churches with so many seeking saints to be Your audience. Lord, this is the best oracle for You to speak Your word. We are waiting on You. We thank You for Your cleansing blood that cleanses all of us all the time and has brought us into Yourself. Lord, grant us Your rich anointing. Visit everyone, Lord. We bring all the needs to You. Lord, give us the instant word that meets our need. Grant us a word to everybody that all our need might be fully met by Yourself. Lord, do anoint us. O Lord Jesus—glorify the Father that the Father may glorify You. Lord, give us the understanding. Remove all the veils. Lord, take away all the covering. Give us liberty, freedom, and the full release that we may have the insight to look into Your Word and to get into its depths. Lord, have mercy upon us that we all may receive new grace. Lord, we need You in a new way, in a refreshing way, and in every way. Defeat the enemy and shame him. Grant Your rich blessing upon everyone who is seeking You. Lord, we trust in You. How we love Your dear Name, and in this Name we look unto You. Amen.

In this chapter we will focus our attention on the gates of the New Jerusalem. In order to enter into the full significance of the New Jerusalem we need to be unveiled to see the meaning of the three gates on the four sides of the holy city. To see the significance of the gates we need an adequate understanding of nearly the entire Bible. We have seen that in the first verse of the first chapter of the Bible, the first divine title for God is *Elohim,* and according to Hebrew *Elohim* is a noun in plural number. Also, in Genesis 1:26 God said, "Let us make man in our image." In this verse the plural pronoun "us" is ascribed to the unique God. This implies that the Triune God, from eternity past, is Triune in order to bring His created man into Himself. Actually, Triune does not mean three in one, but three-one. God is one and yet three, and He is three yet still one. He is the three-one God, the Triune God. Verse 26 of Genesis 1 is actually a direct continuation of verse 1, as far as we human beings are concerned. The Triune God, *Elohim,* had a conference with Himself to make man in His own image with the purpose that one day He would bring this man into Himself. At the conclusion of the Bible, we see that the Triune God Himself is the very entrance for man to enter into Him.

THE SON'S OUTER SEEKING, THE SPIRIT'S INNER SEARCHING, AND THE FATHER'S RECEIVING

In the New Testament, the Triune God is our entrance into Himself. Luke 15 unveils the love of the Triune God toward sinners by the parable of a good shepherd (vv. 1-7), by the parable of a seeking woman (vv. 8-10), and by the parable of a loving father (vv. 11-32). The shepherd refers to the Son who came to seek the fallen sinners, the woman refers to the Holy Spirit who is searching the sinners within themselves, and the Father receives the repenting and returned sinner as a certain man receives his prodigal son. In these three parables we see the Trinity—the Son as the seeking shepherd, the Spirit as the searching woman, and the Father as the loving and receiving father.

In these three parables the sinner is illustrated as a lost sheep, a lost coin, and a prodigal son who gives up the father and the rich inheritance in the father's house. Eventually, the sheep was brought back, the coin was found, and the prodigal son was brought back to the father and to the father's house to enjoy a feast. This is the entrance into the kingdom of God which consummates in the New Jerusalem. These three parables portray a complete triune entrance. It is one entrance, but in three steps. If the Son had never come to die on the cross, there would be no basis for us to enter into the kingdom of God. By dying on the cross, He laid the foundation to open up the gates. Following the Son's redemption, the Spirit came, not to find us outwardly, but to search us inwardly. The Son died on the cross to find us outwardly, but the Spirit came to seek us by searching within our being. All of us who have been regenerated have had this experience. Due to the Spirit's inner searching, we repented and came to our senses. We realized that we were foolish to be a prodigal son eating the husks. Through the searching of the Spirit, we woke up and repented and came back to the Father. Based upon the Son's redemption and through the Spirit's searching, the Father was ready to receive us back into His house to enjoy Him and to enjoy His rich inheritance. This is our triune entrance.

THROUGH THE SON, IN THE SPIRIT, UNTO THE FATHER

Without such an allegory of a city at the end of the Bible with three gates on each of its four sides, it would be difficult to understand and to see the triune entrance. Ephesians 2:18 covers all three aspects of the triune entrance. This verse says, "For through Him we both have access in one Spirit unto the Father." We were sinners who were far away from the Father, far away from the commonwealth of Israel, far away from God's interest, far away from the kingdom of God, and far away from the ultimate consummation of God's economy, the New Jerusalem. But, hallelujah! The Son came to be our channel and through this channel we get into the Spirit, and the Spirit brings us unto the Father. We may also say that through Christ we have access in one Spirit into the Father. We do not only come unto the Father but we also come into Him. Through the Son as a channel and by the Spirit as a sphere, we have been brought not only unto the Father but also into the Father. The three persons of the Godhead are the three gates which form one complete entrance.

THE FATHER'S CHOOSING, THE SPIRIT'S SANCTIFYING, AND THE SPRINKLING OF THE SON'S BLOOD

First Peter 1:1-2 tells us that we have been chosen "according to the foreknowledge of God the Father, in sanctification of the Spirit, unto obedience and sprinkling of the blood of Jesus Christ." The foreknowledge of God the Father was exercised in eternity past. The span of this entrance began from eternity past. Then in time the Spirit came to sanctify us, and the Spirit's sanctification is based upon the Father's choosing. The Spirit came to you based upon the Father's selection of you. Your obedience unto faith in Christ resulted from the Spirit's sanctifying work. You may have been very busy in many other things, but the Spirit sanctified and separated you. This sanctifying and separating work resulted in our receiving the sprinkling of the blood of Jesus Christ and we were redeemed. In 1 Peter 1:1-2 we see the Father's choosing, the Spirit's sanctifying, and the sprinkling of the Son's blood. Again we see that God is triune in one entrance to bring us into God, into God's interest, into the kingdom of God, and into the economy of God, which will consummate in the New Jerusalem. The Bible reveals that the Triune God is our Triune entrance.

TOWARD ALL THE INHABITED EARTH

The twelve gates as the entrance of the New Jerusalem are on four sides of the earth (Rev. 21:13), signifying that the entrance of the New Jerusalem is toward all the inhabited earth (Matt. 8:11). It is available to all the peoples on the earth (Rev. 5:9).

THE TRIUNE ENTRY

In our fellowship concerning the gates of the New Jerusalem, we will use the words *entrance* and *entry*. *Entrance* will be used to denote the gates, and *entry* will be used to denote the entering in. We need to consider how we entered into the kingdom of God in our experience. When we heard the preaching of the gospel the Spirit worked within us. We then believed in Jesus Christ and were touched by the Spirit to call on the name of the Lord Jesus, the Son of God who became incarnated to be our Redeemer. Eventually we reached the Father and were brought into the Father. This is the triune entry.

No one can enter into God without the inspiration of the Spirit and without the redemption of the Son. In order to enter into the Father there is the need of the Spirit and the Son. We entered into the Father through the Son as a channel and in the Spirit as a sphere. In the ultimate consummation of the entire revelation of the sixty-six books of the Bible there is an allegory, a picture, showing us how to enter into God through three gates. We enter into God through the triune entrance. The Son is the channel, the Spirit is the sphere, and the Father is the very destination. Now we are in the Father, in His kingdom, in His interest, and in the church. Eventually we will be in the New Jerusalem.

TWELVE GATES

In the New Jerusalem are the twelve foundations with the names of the twelve apostles, twelve gates which are twelve pearls with the names of the twelve tribes, and twelve fruits of the tree of life. Spacewise the city proper is twelve thousand stadia, one thousand times twelve, in three dimensions, and its wall is one hundred forty-four cubits, which is twelve times twelve. Timewise, in the new heaven and new earth, there are twelve months yearly, twelve hours daily, and twelve hours nightly. Twelve is the number of the New Jerusalem.

There are three gates on each of the four sides of the holy city. Three multiplied by four is twelve; therefore, there are a total of twelve gates on four sides. The number four refers to God's creation. In Revelation 4:6 we see that the four living creatures represent all other living creatures (cf. Ezek. 1:5-14). Four refers to us as God's creatures and three refers to the Triune God. The number twelve in the New Jerusalem is not arrived at by an addition but by multiplication.

Multiplication is a blending or a mingling. The number twelve is mingled or blended by three times four. This means that the entire New Jerusalem is a blending, a mingling, of the Triune God with us human beings. God is mingled with His creature man in His eternal administration in the New Jerusalem.

Twelve is the number of absolute perfection and eternal completion in God's administration. In the Old Testament, God administrated His government through the twelve tribes. The twelve tribes were for God's administration. In the New Testament the twelve apostles' preaching was for the producing of the churches, and the churches are God's government for God's administration. Thus, both the twelve tribes in the Old Testament and the twelve apostles in the New Testament are for God's governmental administration. The number twelve indicates God's governmental administration and the entire New Jerusalem will be the consummation of God's administration. This is why the center of the New Jerusalem is God's throne, which is mainly for God's governmental administration.

This administration has twelve gates. The gates are for communication, coming in and going out. Hence, "twelve gates" indicate that the communication in the New Jerusalem is absolutely perfect and eternally complete for God's administration.

TWELVE PEARLS

The twelve gates are twelve pearls (Rev. 21:21a), signifying that the entrance is the produce of Christ in His redemptive and secreting work. We have seen that the produce of Christ's all-inclusive death and all-inclusive resurrection are the pearls. The produce of such a Christ becomes the very communication of the city, and this communication constitutes an entrance and fellowship that we may enjoy all the riches of the Triune God in every way. This is our marvelous portion even today. Today we are the pearls and we are the gates. Praise the Lord for the triune gates and the triune entrance, which are the communication of God's administrative business.

THE NAMES OF THE TWELVE TRIBES

Also, the twelve gates are inscribed with the names of the twelve tribes of Israel (Rev. 21:12) who were the representatives of the law of the Old Testament, signifying the requirement of the law at the entrance into the kingdom of God. The gates bear the names of the twelve tribes. Because the twelve tribes in the Old Testament were for God's administration, this indicates that the twelve gates are for God's administration. Also, the twelve tribes are representatives of the Old Testament law. Therefore, the names of the twelve tribes inscribed on the twelve gates indicate that the law is watching over the twelve gates. With the law there is nothing that supplies or nourishes. The law only requires something of us. The law is watching over the gates. If a sinner is to come into the holy city, the requirement of the law must be fulfilled. The law is the gate watcher or the guard at the gate to insure that you have fulfilled its requirement. As you are "walking through the gate" and you call on the name of the Lord Jesus, the law says that you are okay. As long as you are in Jesus Christ, every part of the requirement of the law is fulfilled and you are okay. You can now get into the holy city.

Without such a picture, I do not think that any of us would imagine that when we called on the name of the Lord Jesus the law was watching over us. This picture shows us, though, that we entered through the gates with the names of the representatives of the law inscribed on them. This means that when we entered into the gate, the law was satisfied since the requirement of the law had been fully fulfilled. When we came to the triune entrance we had a "free ticket" because Christ paid the price for us, and the guard at the gate (the law) honors Christ.

THE LAW—A CHILD-CONDUCTOR

In addition, we must realize that the law is not only a watcher at the gate but also the child-conductor of the entry (Gal 3:24). The law is not only at the gate, but the law also brings all God's chosen people to the gate. If the law could speak to a chosen one it would say, "I will bring you to the gate and I will meet you there." The law was not given for us to keep, but the law was given to conduct us to Christ. The law is the conductor to bring you to the gate, the law is also the guard to "okay" your entry.

TWELVE ANGELS

Furthermore, we see twelve angels at the twelve gates (Rev. 21:12), signifying that the angels watch over the entry into the New Jerusalem (Luke 15:7, 10; Heb. 1:14). Each gate not only bears one of the names of the twelve tribes, but also has an angel. The law requires and the angel watches. The angels are spectators. The entire realm of God's New Testament economy is actually "a big show." To enter into this show you need a free ticket and in this show there are spectators. These spectators are the angels. If you do not confess the name of Christ, you cannot get a free ticket. However, if you call on the name of the Lord Jesus you get a free ticket into the holy city, and the angelic spectators will rejoice and welcome you in. One angel at the gate actually represents the entire angelic realm. In Luke 15:10 the Lord Jesus says, "There is joy in the presence of the angels of God over one sinner repenting." When we believed in the Lord Jesus, when we repented and called on His precious name, we probably did not realize that there was a myriad of angels in heaven "clapping their hands" and rejoicing.

It was not a small thing for us to enter into the realm of God's interest on this earth. The Triune God, the Father, the Son, and the Spirit, the twelve tribes, the law, and all the angels were involved in our entrance into the kingdom of God. Our entrance began from eternity past since God exercised His foreknowledge to choose us. Without such a picture, none of us would realize that our entering into God's interest involved so much. Our entering into the New Jerusalem involved God the Father in eternity, God the Son coming to die on the cross for us to accomplish redemption, and also God the Spirit reaching us and searching within us in order to sanctify us and bring us unto the obedience of Christ. Our entrance into the holy city furthermore involved the law and the entire angelic realm. If we have this view, our realization of our all-inclusive salvation will be strengthened. God the Father, God the Son, and God the Spirit are in this salvation, the law works for this salvation, and the angels are expecting something to happen in this salvation.

The Triune God, the twelve tribes, the law, and all the angels were working together for our entering into the New Jerusalem. We all have to say, "Praise the Lord" for our all-inclusive salvation. We may not have rejoiced that much when we were saved because we did not see the vision concerning all that the Triune God went through to be our entrance. We all need to celebrate our birth in Christ. According to the vision the Lord has shown us in this chapter, I would say, "Happy birthday to you." Rejoice in the salvation of God which involves the Triune God, the twelve tribes, the law, and all the angels.

CHAPTER THIRTY-SIX

THE NEW JERUSALEM—
ITS WALL, ITS FOUNDATION, AND ITS STREET

Scripture Reading: Rev. 21:12a, 14, 17-20, 21b; 22:1-2; 4:3a; Matt. 22:30

In order to enter into the full significance of the divine allegory of the New Jerusalem, we must have a revelation of its wall, its foundation, and its street.

ITS WALL

Revelation 21:18a tells us that the wall was built with jasper, signifying the appearance of God (4:3a) for His expression. God sitting on His throne looks like jasper and the entire wall, a great and high wall, is built with jasper. Also, the first foundation of the wall is jasper. Jasper, according to Revelation 21:11, is "a most precious stone...clear as crystal." Its color must be dark green, which signifies life in its richness. God's appearance being like jasper means that His very appearance is life in its richness. Jasper is the appearance of God, which will also be the appearance of the holy city, New Jerusalem (Rev. 21:11). The entire city, in appearance, looks the same as God is. We all need to see the wonderful picture portrayed in this city. The center of the city is God on the throne who appears as jasper and the circumference of the city is its wall which is built with jasper. This means that the entire city from its center to its circumference is an expression of the very God of life in His richness.

Revelation 21:12 tells us that the wall is great and high for separation unto God and for protection of God's interest. The height of the wall is one hundred forty-four cubits. A

cubit is approximately eighteen inches, so on that basis the
wall would be two hundred sixteen feet high. Also, Revelation
tells us that the wall is twelve thousand stadia long. Since
one stadion is approximately 600 feet, the wall is approximately one thousand three hundred and sixty-four miles long.
This is approximately the distance from Los Angeles to Dallas.
China boasts of its Great Wall, but the Great Wall of China is
not as high as the wall of the New Jerusalem. The wall of the
New Jerusalem is at least seven times higher than the great
wall of China. We need to boast concerning our great wall
which is in the book of Revelation. The Great Wall of China is
built with old bricks, but our great wall is built with jasper,
and this jasper is clear as crystal (Rev. 21:11). The Great Wall
of China is opaque, but our great wall is transparent. No wall
on earth can compare with the wall of the New Jerusalem.

Seven Implications

With the wall of the New Jerusalem there are seven implications. The wall implies transformation, building, the image
of God, the expression of God, the testimony of Jesus, separation, and protection. A wall always separates a particular
piece of space from all the other spaces. A wall also protects
what is in it from all sorts of negative and evil things.
In order to fully understand this allegory of the New Jerusalem, we need to get into these seven implications. We can
never exhaust all the significances and all the meaningful
and crucial points of this allegory since it is the ultimate
consummation and conclusion of the sixty-six divine books of
the Bible.

Transformation

The foundations of the wall bear the names of the twelve
apostles. Each apostle is signified by a precious stone. Peter
should be the first of the twelve apostles, and he was named
by the Lord Jesus in a "renewing way." The name Peter
means a stone. A stone is something created by God but not
transformed. All the precious stones are transformed entities.
Peter was originally a stone, but eventually he became jasper,
the first foundation of the New Jerusalem. The wall itself is

jasper, and the first foundation of the wall is also jasper. Peter was merely a stone, but in the New Jerusalem he is a jasper stone, the first layer of the wall's foundation. This implies transformation.

Paul tells us in 1 Corinthians 3 that he had laid a foundation as a wise master builder and that we believers needed to build upon this foundation with gold, silver, and precious stones (vv. 10-12). Our building of the church needs to be not merely with stones but with precious stones. These are not natural stones but transformed stones which became precious. Peter could never forget the Lord's changing of his name, so in his first Epistle he indicated that the Lord was a living stone and that we also as living stones are being built up into a spiritual house (2:4-5). Peter's word implies that once he was dead, but the Lord changed him into a living stone. As a living stone, Peter was always under the transforming work of the Spirit. Transformation is a metabolic change. With such a change, there is always the need of some new element to discharge and replace the old elements. From the day the Lord Jesus changed Simon's name to Peter, He was doing His best to add Himself into Peter. As a result of being under the Lord's transforming work, eventually Peter became jasper, a precious stone, the first layer of the foundation of the New Jerusalem.

The wall is not built with natural materials merely created by God, but the wall is built with transformed items. We all are God's old creation, but God put us into Christ to make us His new creation. We all were natural beings, but we have been transformed from the old creation into the new creation in Christ (2 Cor. 5:17). In the New Jerusalem there will be no Chinese, American, Spanish, Mexican, Japanese, Korean, French, Italian, German or any other culture or race. All of us will be fully transformed. I believe that even our color will be transformed. In that day we will all be "green." We will all be jasper! We will be one people in one color— "green"! All the different colors and all the different cultures will be swallowed up by the rich divine life of the Triune God. This is transformation.

All of us must realize that the church life is a transformed life, a life under transformation. The church life is not a life of a good, natural life, but the church life must be a transformed life. This is why Colossians 3:11 tells us that in the new man there cannot be Greek, Jew, circumcision, uncircumcision, Barbarian, or Scythian, because all of us are under transformation. We are not practicing the church life according to our natural status, but according to the transformed life. Transformation is implied in the wall. In the wall of the New Jerusalem there is no piece of natural material. The entire wall is built with jasper, transformed material.

Building

The second implication in the wall is building. To be transformed is one matter and to be built up is another matter. It is wonderful that you have been transformed, but you have to learn how to be built together with others. When masons are building something with stone, they may need to cut some sharp edges off the stone to make it fit in the wall they are building. In like manner, our "sharpness" has to be cut off. Do not be so sharp in the church life. If you are too sharp, it will be hard for you to be built up with others. All of our sharp corners need to be cut off in order to get along with others.

According to my experience being transformed is easier than being built up with others. To be transformed is glorious, but to be cut off is a kind of humiliation. Why do I "cut" you and why do you "cut" me? The reason why is for us to fit into the building. Without being cut, you could never fit into the building. You may like to be in the building, but you may not like to be cut. However, as long as you will not agree to being cut, you cannot be built in. We all need to realize that we are under the transformation, but do not forget that following transformation is cutting. Thank the Lord that He is transforming us and cutting us that we may fit in the building of the wall of His eternal habitation.

The Image of God

The entire great and high wall of the city bears one image. In today's Christendom each denomination bears a particular and different image from the others. Today, in the Lord's recovery there are over six hundred churches in thirty-nine nations. I thank the Lord that all the churches bear one image. We do not have different images or flavors, but we are one in appearance and one in flavor. The entire wall of the great city bears one unique image—God's image. The appearance of the city is the same as the One sitting on the throne.

The jasper wall signifies that the whole city, as the corporate expression of God in eternity, bears the appearance of God. Sometimes in our meetings, however, we hear testimonies that convey a little different flavor. Also, we may have seen some activities that bore some other kind of appearance. This signifies a lack of transformation and building. Argument or adjustment does not work in cases like these. You have to pray for the dear ones who voice different flavors and who express a different appearance that they may have the mercy and grace to experience more and more of transformation and building. Only transformation and building can bring all the saints into one image with one flavor. All of us need to have God's image and God's flavor. In the church there should not be the European, Asian, American, Mexican, Chinese, or any other flavor, but only the flavor of the Triune God expressed in His unique image.

The Expression of God

The wall of the New Jerusalem also implies the expression of God. The great wall is the unique expression of the jasper God, and the jasper God is expressed in the jasper city through the jasper wall. A picture such as this is better than one thousand words. When we look at this city which is in the appearance of God for His expression, we can see that today's Christianity does not match this. With the denominations there are too many different kinds of expressions, but in the church life, which will consummate in the coming New Jerusalem, there is only one expression—the expression of the divine image through transformation and building.

The Testimony of Jesus

This expression of God in the New Jerusalem will be a testimony of Jesus. On the one hand, the book of Revelation gives us the revelation of Christ (1:1), and on the other hand, it shows us the testimony of Jesus (1:9; 12:17; 19:10; 20:4). The expression of the greenish wall is the testimony of Jesus. Jesus was the embodiment of the Triune God. While He was on this earth He expressed the Triune God. The New Jerusalem will be His enlargement, His increase, and His expansion to express Him as God's embodiment, and this is the testimony of Jesus. Today every local church must be such a testimony, but it depends upon the degree of transformation and building. The transformation and the building are the basic factors to have the testimony of Jesus expressing the Triune God.

Separation

Such a testimony is also for separation unto God. The surrounding wall separates what is in it from all other things. This separation in the New Jerusalem is the absolute sanctification. The designation "the holy city" means the separated city, a city that is separated from anything other than God. The city as the very embodiment of the Triune God is a separated, sanctified, holy city. No other city is as holy or as sanctified as this one because this city is the embodiment, the increase, and the expansion of God.

Protection

The seventh implication of the wall is that it protects God's interest. It is the circumference of the interest of God, which is the kingdom of God. Whatever is protected within this wall is the very kingdom of God, and this kingdom of God is the economy of God to carry out God's eternal purpose, which is made according to His desire. The church in every locality today should be such a separated and protected entity. There should be nothing in the church but God's desire. Only what God wants is within the wall and nothing else.

In Resurrection

The wall is also measured in "a measure of a man, that is, of an angel" (Rev. 21:17). It is in resurrection that man will be like the angels (Matt. 22:30). Hence, "a measure of a man, that is, of an angel" signifies that the wall of the city is not natural but in resurrection. The entire wall is something transformed and built up in resurrection. In this sense, all of us in the church life should be like angels. In our natural life we are not like angels, but in resurrection we are. Many of the sisters would like to be angels, but we must remember that if we want to be like an angel, we have to be in resurrection. In the natural life, everyone is a "scorpion, gopher, or turtle." But hallelujah, there is a hope that in resurrection we could be transformed to be like angels.

The wall is something transformed and built up in resurrection, so its measurement is one hundred and forty-four cubits, signifying absolute perfection and eternal completion of absolute perfections and eternal completions. A hundred forty-four is twelve times twelve. Twelve signifies absolute perfection and eternal completion in God's administration. The wall refers to God's administration because it encircles, sanctifies, and protects the city. Within this protected city is God's throne to carry out His administration, which is absolutely perfect and eternally complete. No other number should be ascribed to the church life but twelve. In the New Jerusalem everything is perfect and complete for God's complete and eternal administration.

ITS FOUNDATION

Built with Twelve Kinds of Precious Stones

Twelve foundations (Rev. 21:14a) signify the foundation of absolute perfection and eternal completion in God's administration. The twelve precious stones of the foundation indicate the unsearchable riches of the all-inclusive Christ. Every foundation expresses a certain amount of Christ's riches. The colors of the twelve precious stones of the foundations, which signify the twelve apostles, are as follows: the first is green, the second and third are blue, the fourth is green, the fifth and sixth are red, the seventh is yellow, the eighth is bluish-green, the ninth is yellow, the tenth is apple-green, the eleventh and twelfth are purple. The twelve layers of the foundation in the above colors give the appearance of a rainbow, signifying that the city is built upon and secured by God's faithfulness in keeping His covenant (Gen. 9:8-17). The entire city is built upon the eternal faithfulness of the faithful God.

Built upon the Grace of God

The names of the twelve apostles are inscribed on the twelve foundations (Rev. 21:14). As we have seen, the twelve names of the twelve tribes inscribed on the twelve gates of the city indicate that the twelve gates are there to fulfill the requirement of the law and to satisfy the law's demand upon sinners. The twelve foundations bearing the twelve names of the apostles, who are the representatives of the grace of the New Testament, signify that the New Jerusalem is built upon the grace of God according to the New Testament. The entrance of the city answers the requirements of the Old Testament law, and the foundations of the city show us the grace of the New Testament. The law is for the entry, and the grace is for the foundation. We enter into the New Jerusalem according to the requirement of the law, and we are in the New Jerusalem according to and based on the grace of the New Testament.

ITS STREET

God's Nature

The street of the city is gold (Rev. 21:21b), signifying God's nature. The street is a part of the city proper, and every part of the city proper is gold. The street being gold means that God's nature is the way in the city and the way in the church life. We must do everything according to God's nature since His nature is the way. For a man to divorce his wife is not according to God's nature, so he should never take this way. In everything we do in the church life, we have to check with God's nature. Even the way we dress and what we buy should be according to God's nature. As brothers in the Lord we should buy our ties according to God's nature and wear our shoes according to His nature. Some Christians who are concerned about being holy have regulations, but in the New Jerusalem there is only one regulation—the golden street. God's divine nature is the unique regulation, and this is the way we have to take and the street we have to walk on. God's divine nature is our way and our strength. I praise the Lord that in all the churches so many saints are not regulated by a written code but by the one golden street which is the divine nature of God. Revelation 21:21 tells us that "the street of the city was pure gold as transparent glass." If we take God's nature as our unique way, we will be pure, without mixture, and transparent, without opaqueness.

With the River of Water of Life and the Tree of Life

In the middle of this street is the river of water of life (Rev. 22:1-2), which indicates that when you take the way according to God's nature, the life of God flows within you. The divine life flows in the divine nature as the unique way for the daily life of God's redeemed people. If I do not buy a tie according to God's nature, there is no flow of life within me. However, if I buy a tie according to God's nature, I sense the flow of life. If a husband is going to divorce his wife, this is against God's nature, and this will lead to spiritual death. However, if this husband would live with his wife and love her according to God's nature, the river of life would flow within him. Whatever we do according to God's nature, we immediately have the deep sensation of the flow of life watering us.

The one tree of life growing on the two sides of the river (Rev. 22:2) signifies that the tree of life is a vine, spreading and proceeding along the flow of the water of life for God's people to receive and enjoy. The fruits of the tree of life will be the food of God's redeemed for eternity. They will be continually fresh, produced every month, twelve fruits yearly. This means that when we walk and move in the divine nature of God, we not only sense the flow of life within us but also sense the supply of life, the nourishment of life, the spiritual food. When you take the divine way, the street of God's divine nature, you have the life flowing in you, and you also have the life supply nourishing you. Day by day, as we are living such a life and walking according to God's divine nature, we enjoy the water of life and the tree of life as our supply. We all need a day-by-day experience of the divine street of gold with the river of water of life and the tree of life in its middle, signifying that the life water and the life supply flow in the divine way.

CHAPTER THIRTY-SEVEN

THE NEW JERUSALEM—
ITS DIMENSIONS, ITS TEMPLE, AND ITS LIGHT

Scripture Reading: Rev. 21:15-16, 22-24a; 22:5; Deut. 33:27;
Psa. 90:1

ITS DIMENSIONS
The Number Twelve

The dimensions of the New Jerusalem are stressed in Revelation 21:15-16. We have seen that twelve is the number of the New Jerusalem and that the height of the wall is one hundred forty-four cubits, which is twelve times twelve. Revelation 21:16 tells us that the length, breadth, and height of the city are twelve thousand stadia. Twelve thousand, of course, is one thousand times twelve. Ten is a number of completion in the Scriptures, but it is not as complete as a hundred or even one thousand. The Psalmist tells us that a day in the Lord's courts is better than a thousand (Psa. 84:10). The number one thousand is a complete unit, and in God's eyes one thousand years is equal to one day (2 Pet. 3:8). This indicates that one thousand is the ultimate completion in God's figuration. Since twelve signifies absolute perfection and eternal completion in God's administration, twelve thousand signifies a thousand times this.

The Holy of Holies

The measurement of the New Jerusalem shows us that it is a cube with three equal dimensions. This means that the entire New Jerusalem is straight, perfect, and complete, without any defect, bias, obliqueness, or shortage. The dimensions of the Holy of Holies, both in the tabernacle and the temple, are equal in length, breadth, and height (Exo. 26:2-8; 1 Kings 6:20). Hence, that the length, the breadth, and the height of the New Jerusalem are equal signifies that the entire New Jerusalem will be the Holy of Holies.

Measured with a Golden Reed

The city is also measured with a golden reed. The reed is for measuring, and measuring signifies to take possession (Ezek. 40:5; Zech. 2:1-2; Rev. 11:1). Since gold signifies the divine nature of God, the golden reed signifies that the measuring of the city, its gates and its wall, is according to God's divine nature. Anything that does not match the divine nature of God does not belong to the New Jerusalem. The whole city, with its gates and wall, can pass the measuring and testing of the divine nature of God; hence, it is fitting for God's possession. A reed is not that strong, but the nature of the measuring reed for the New Jerusalem is golden. The holy city is not measured according to man's concept, idea, philosophy, or qualification, but according to God's divine nature.

A Square City

The city lying foursquare (Rev. 21:16a), signifies that the New Jerusalem is perfect and complete in every way, absolutely straight, without any obliqueness. God's divine nature is absolutely perfect and eternally complete for God's divine administration. On this earth today there is no government which is perfect. Every government is full of defects, bias, and crookedness. In God's eternal, divine administration, however, there is nothing but perfection and completion. The governments of this earth are full of politicians, but in the church we have to learn one thing—do not play politics. In the church, when we say yes we mean yes, and when we say no we mean no (2 Cor. 1:17-20). When we say black we mean black, and when we say white we mean white. In the church there is no "gray color." The holy city is not a round city but a square city. To be "round" means to play politics. If you told me that I was a round person, I would feel ashamed. We all need to be "square persons" who are so frank, straight, and open. The city's being equal in three dimensions as a cube means that the city is perfect to the uttermost with no defects, bias, or obliqueness. The city's being square has a very spiritual significance. Here there is no politics, no crookedness, and here is God's frankness, faithfulness, and openness.

ITS TEMPLE

The Redeeming Triune God

In Revelation 21:22 John says, "And I saw no temple in it, for its temple is the Lord God the Almighty and the Lamb." This verse shows us that the temple is not something physical or material, but the temple is a personal temple, even the Triune God Himself. The Lord God the Almighty and the Lamb indicate the redeeming Triune God. The Lamb, who is the second of the Trinity, is also the temple. We have seen thus far that the entire New Jerusalem is a cube just like the Holy of Holies in the tabernacle (Exo. 26:2-8) and in the temple (1 Kings 6:20), but here it says that John saw no temple. The temple is a Person, and this Person is the Triune God, the Lord God the Almighty and the Lamb. Our God today is the very Redeemer as well as the Triune God, so the redeeming Triune God is our temple. Since our redeeming Triune God is our temple, how could He be a literal cube? Again, we cannot understand this city in a physical way. If we try to understand the city in a physical way, we cannot get through in any direction. The fact that the New Jerusalem is a cube of twelve thousand stadia in three dimensions shows the absolute perfection and eternal completeness of our redeeming Triune God who is the temple and who is the Holy of Holies. With Him there is nothing wrong and there is no bias, obliqueness, or crookedness.

A Mutual Dwelling Place

The city is not a physical thing, but a personal entity, and we must understand the New Jerusalem in a personal way. Revelation 21:3 indicates that the city is the tabernacle of God. John saw no temple in the New Jerusalem, because the entire New Jerusalem is the tabernacle of God, a precursor of the temple of God, and it is even the Holy of Holies. We may understand the word "tabernacle" as a physical thing, but Revelation 21:2 tells us that this city is a bride. The term "bride" proves that the city is something personal. On the one hand, the New Jerusalem is a tabernacle for God's dwelling, and on the other hand, the city is a temple for us to dwell in. The tabernacle is good for God to dwell in, and the temple is good for us to dwell in. God being the temple is not for Himself to dwell in but for us to dwell in. The New Jerusalem will be a mutual dwelling place. To God it is a tabernacle and to us it is a temple in which we dwell and in which we serve God.

The Building Material of the Temple

This temple, in which we are serving God in this New Testament age, is built with His Trinity, with all His attributes plus all His accomplishments. All that He has obtained and attained are the materials for the building up of this wonderful temple that we have today. The designation "the Lord God the Almighty and the Lamb" signifies the many attributes and accomplishments of the Triune God. We are in such a temple built with the Lord, with God, with the Almighty, with the Lamb, and with all His attributes and accomplishments.

God Himself as the Spirit Reaching Us

The temple being the Lord God the Almighty and the Lamb signifies that the Triune God is our dwelling place in eternity (Deut. 33:27; Psa. 90:1), in which we serve Him. Many people feel that we serve God in the sanctuaries, in the chapels, and in the cathedrals. However, we must realize that the Bible reveals that we serve God in God Himself. We may also say that we serve God in the Spirit. The New Testament shows us that the Spirit is the processed Triune God reaching us. When God went to the cross to die for our sins and to accomplish redemption, He was the Lamb of God taking away the sin of the world (John 1:29). When God reaches us, however, He is the Spirit.

Actually, we serve God in God Himself as the Spirit reaching us. When we pray, we pray in God Himself as the Spirit reaching us. The proper prayer and the proper service we render to God must be in God Himself. If we pray in ourselves, that prayer is not genuine. The genuine prayer must be to God and in God. God is our dwelling in the New Testament, and even the Old Testament saints had the same consideration. In Deuteronomy 33:27 Moses says, "The eternal God is thy dwelling place" (ASV), and in Psalm 90:1 Moses says, "Lord, thou hast been our dwelling place in all generations." This indicates that while Moses was traveling in the wilderness with the children of Israel for forty years, in his deep feeling he was dwelling in God. God was his dwelling place.

When we get into eternity, we shall dwell, serve, worship, and pray in the processed Triune God as the Spirit reaching us. The entire New Jerusalem is a great reaching of God to us. We all need to ask ourselves where we pray and where we are staying while we are worshipping God. A great number of times when I was praying and worshipping in my home, I did not have the feeling that I was in my home. Instead, I had the feeling that I was in my redeeming, processed God who was reaching me as the Spirit. In my home I was in the Spirit, praying, worshipping, and enjoying Him.

It is very poor for you to feel that God is far away from you when you pray. You may feel that He is sitting on the throne as the Almighty One, and you are so pitiful on the earth, praying in a "poor cottage." Do you worship God with such a feeling? Do you have the feeling that you are praying in a poor cottage or that you are praying in the Triune, processed, redeeming God reaching you as the Spirit? If you are praying with the sense that you are in a poor cottage, your prayer is cold and pitiful. Your feeling may be that you are begging a very hard God who is sitting on the throne and does not care for you. You are like a poor beggar in your prayer, begging a rich man for help. Today in God's New Testament economy, however, we do not pray that way.

Whenever I pray, I have the deep thought that I am in the Triune God, the Father, the Son, and the Spirit, the processed God, the redeeming God, the God who is now the all-inclusive Spirit reaching me. I am praying to God in God Himself. Whether He answers my prayers or not is secondary. When I pray in this way, I enjoy Him in an excellent way. This kind of prayer makes me ecstatic.

Today we do not have any physical temple, but our temple is our Triune, processed, redeeming God, reaching us as the Spirit. Such a Spirit is our temple. We worship and serve God in this temple, and day and night God is our dwelling place. When I was traveling in a plane, I told the Lord, "This plane is not my dwelling place. You are my dwelling place. I am not actually in this plane, but I am in You." Sometimes when people asked me where my home was, I was hesitant to answer them. It was hard for me to tell them where my home was, because my home is a "floating home." My floating home which always is with me is my Triune, processed, redeeming God reaching me as the Spirit. This is my home, my dwelling place.

Even today our God is our temple. It is not reasonable to think that when we enter into eternity, we will have another temple. We will not get out of God and enter into another temple. When we get into eternity, God will be our temple, and this should not be a surprise to us. We should be able to say that while we were living on the earth, we remained in this temple all the time, in our God who is Triune, processed, redeeming, and reaching us as the Spirit. The New Jerusalem, this allegory, is the ultimate consummation of the entire divine revelation, and this is a practical application of God being our temple.

Today we are dwelling in this temple. This is our habitation, this is the place where we serve and worship God, and this is the place where we meet. In the church meetings we need to have the realization that we are actually meeting in the Triune, processed, redeeming, and reaching God. In eternity the New Jerusalem will be a consummation of today's reality. The New Jerusalem shows us that we are God's dwelling place as the tabernacle and that He is our dwelling place as the temple. This is not something physical but something altogether personal.

The New Jerusalem as the tabernacle to God and the temple to us indicates a marvelous mingling in that God's dwelling is our dwelling and our dwelling is God's dwelling.

We are here to be God's dwelling, and God is here to be our dwelling. God dwells in us and we dwell in Him—a mutual indwelling. This corresponds with John 15:4. In eternity future the New Jerusalem will be the tabernacle for God's dwelling and the temple for our dwelling.

The dimensions of the New Jerusalem indicate that it is the Holy of Holies, and this Holy of Holies is not a physical thing but the divine Person. How could the divine Person be measured? Is not God immeasurable and unlimited? God is the Holy of Holies, and it has been measured to be twelve thousand stadia in three dimensions. God is immeasurable, but He has some measurements. These measurements show the perfection and completion of our wonderful God. Even today we are in our perfect and complete God as our Holy of Holies, our temple. In eternity the New Jerusalem should not be a new building or a new temple to us. All of us should be able to say that we have been enjoying remaining in this temple for our whole lives.

In John 4 the Lord told us that God is seeking the proper worshippers who have to worship Him in spirit (v. 23). In Revelation, however, John tells us that the temple in which we worship is the Lord God the Almighty and the Lamb. John 4:24 also tells us that God is Spirit whom we worship. This is the Triune God reaching us as the Spirit, and this is our temple. Here in this temple, we worship and dwell with God in our spirit. In our human spirit He dwells in us who are His tabernacle, and in the divine Spirit we dwell in Him who is our temple. In our spirit we enjoy our Triune, processed, redeeming, and reaching God as our habitation. What an enjoyment! After reading this chapter, we all need to exercise our spirit to get used to enjoying God as our temple.

ITS LIGHT

The Glory of God, the Lord God Himself

The New Jerusalem has no need of the sun nor of the moon, neither of the light of a lamp (Rev. 21:23a; 22:5a). The fact that there is no need of the sun nor of the moon indicates that in the New Jerusalem there is no natural light, and the fact that there is no need of the light of a lamp means that there is no man-made light. God Himself, the very divine Person, is the light. The glory of God, the Lord God Himself, illumines the city (Rev. 21:23b; 22:5b). God is both the light within and the glory without. He is the inner light and the outer expression of the light, the glory.

The Lamb Being the Lamp

Such a light needs a lamp and the Lamb is the lamp of the city (Rev. 21:23c). We need to ask why God, being the light, needs a lamp. Every electrical light needs a holder or a bulb. Without the bulb, your touching of the electricity may electrify and kill you. In like manner, without the Lamb being the lamp, God's shining over us would "kill" all of us. However, the divine light shines through our Redeemer. This light has become so lovable and touchable, and we even walk in this light (1 John 1:7). Without the Lamb's redemption, God's shining over us could only kill us. God as the light, though, has a holder, and this holder is the Redeemer, the Lamb. The Lamb as the lamp expresses the light in a very approachable and lovable way.

Without the Lamb being the lamp, when the divine light shines we would all run away. Through the redeeming One, however, the killing light becomes the real shining for us to enjoy. This is again the Triune God. The Triune God, on the one hand, is the light, and the Triune God, on the other hand, is the holder as our Redeemer. He shines and He also holds Himself.

This lamp also has a stand. In Revelation 1 this stand is the golden lampstand, but in Revelation 21 the stand for the lamp is the golden mountain, the city proper of the New Jerusalem. The ultimate consummation of the divine revelation shows us God as the light; the Lamb, the Redeemer, as the lamp; and the New Jerusalem as the stand. Furthermore, the nations will walk by the light of the city (Rev. 21:24a).

OUR PRESENT EXPERIENCE

Our Triune God is our lamp, our light, and our temple in whom we serve. We dwell in Him and He shines within us.

We are His tabernacle in whom He dwells, and He is our temple in whom we dwell. He is also our lamp and our light who shines from within us through the lamp. He is in us and we are in Him. This is a mingling of the divine Spirit with our human spirit. In our human spirit He dwells in us, the tabernacle, and we dwell in Him, the divine Spirit reaching us, the temple. We take Him as our temple, our abode, and then He as the divine light shines from within us. This is the mingling of divinity with humanity, which is our present experience and which will be the coming New Jerusalem.

We are experiencing the New Jerusalem today. I have to testify that I experience being a part of His tabernacle today, and I experience that He is my temple today. I experience that I dwell in Him and that while I am dwelling in Him, He is shining from within me. The New Jerusalem will be the consummation of all that we have experienced for so many years. It will be an intensification and a consummation of our present experience. The New Jerusalem will not be something new to us in eternity future if we are now experiencing it.

Chapter Thirty-Eight

THE NEW JERUSALEM—ITS THRONE

Scripture Reading: Rev. 22:1-3, 5c; 2:7; 22:14, 17; John 7:38-39

THE THRONE OF GOD AND OF THE LAMB

The last item that is recorded in the section concerning the New Jerusalem is the throne of God and of the Lamb (Rev. 22:1). The throne, of course, is for God's administration. God is the One who had a purpose and who made a plan in eternity past and who created all things for the fulfillment of His plan. The Lamb is the One who redeemed us, the One who has accomplished a full redemption to fulfill God's plan. Thus, the throne of God and of the Lamb denotes that this throne is to carry out God's plan through Christ's redemption. Both God's plan and Christ's redemption are being carried out through this throne. The throne is the very source from which the river of water of life flows, and it flows with the tree of life growing in it (22:2). The throne for the accomplishment of God's eternal purpose is to flow out God Himself that by this flow of life His purpose could be accomplished.

"A LITTLE NEW JERUSALEM"

When we get into the full record concerning the New Jerusalem, we will spontaneously understand that this is fully related to our personal experiences of the Triune God. Do not think that the New Jerusalem is merely something objective in the future for a certain group of people. We have to realize that what is recorded in Revelation 21 and 22 should be experienced by us today in a very personal way. Experientially speaking, every proper and normal Christian is "a little

New Jerusalem." Whatever is ascribed to the New Jerusalem corporately should be experienced by us individually and personally. With and in each one of us are the three gates of the Divine Trinity. Furthermore, in each one of us there must be the throne of God and of the Lamb. We must enthrone Him in our heart and in our spirit. In other words, in the very center of our being there should be the throne of God and of the Lamb. At the end of the record of the New Jerusalem the unique item is the throne.

THE CENTER OF OUR CHRISTIAN LIFE

In our Christian experience the unique item should be the throne of the One who purposed and of the One who redeemed. Such a throne must be set up in our entire being, and this should be the center of our Christian life. This means that we would accept the God who purposed and the Christ who redeemed us as our Head, Lord, and authority. We should be willing to subject ourselves to such a headship. We adore Him as the Lord, and we take Him as our authority. We enthrone Him in our being and in our Christian life.

In our Christian life the center is the throne of God and of the Lamb. We are not here living for ourselves. We are living and existing for the accomplishment of God's purpose, to carry out what Christ has accomplished. Therefore, we experience the One on the throne in His headship and lordship, and we submit ourselves to such an authority. In our daily life, in our family life, in our marriage life, in our business life, and in our church life the center must be God's throne. Everything should be subjected to His headship.

All of us have experienced that whenever we would subject ourselves to this headship, we immediately sense something full of God's riches flowing within us. This is the flow of the Triune God as life, life supply, and everything to our being. Within us we sense such a flow, and this flow is from the throne of God and of the Lamb as the water of life.

THE FLOW OF THE DIVINE TRINITY

In Revelation 22:1 we see the flow of the Divine Trinity— God, the Lamb, and the water of life (the Spirit). According to

John 7:38-39, the water of life refers to the Spirit. God was the One who purposed, He became the Lamb who redeemed (John 1:14, 29), and finally became the life-giving, flowing Spirit (1 Cor. 15:45b). God flows in the water of life, the Lamb flows in the water of life, and the Spirit flows as the water of life. Thus, this is the triune flow, the flow of the Divine Trinity as the very life supply.

This should not be taken as a theological teaching. According to our daily experiences, we Christians should experience the flow of the Divine Trinity every day. Every morning after rising up we need to say, "Lord, thank You for a new day for me to take You as my Lord. I subject myself under Your headship for the whole day. Lord, set up Your throne in my life. Set up Your throne in the center of my being. Lord, bring my whole day with my daily life under Your throne." If you would offer such a prayer to the Triune God every morning, from that moment you would have the living water flowing within you. This living water flowing is the flow of the Triune God. It is not a small thing that the Triune God flows in you today. He flows in you as the One who purposed, as the One who redeemed, and as the One who is the life-giving Spirit. This One is the very consummation of the Triune God reaching us as the living water.

Such a subjective revelation has been missed by many of today's Christians. I hope we all would realize in our experience that whenever we subject ourselves to the Triune God, taking Him as our Head, we enjoy a flow within us. Thank the Lord that in the Lord's recovery, day after day, month after month, year after year, and time after time, what is stressed is the unique flow. We have given message after message which tells us that the Triune God is flowing. There are also many hymns in our hymnal concerning this subject. The first two stanzas of *Hymns,* #12 say:

> O God, Thou art the source of life,
>   Divine, and rich, and free!
> As living water flowing out
>   Unto eternity!

In love Thou in the Son didst flow
Among the human race;
Thou dost as Spirit also flow
Within us through Thy grace.

Many times in the Lord's table meeting, we all sense the flow of the Father, the Son, and the Spirit. Our Father is the very God who had a purpose and who purposed to accomplish His eternal plan. The Son as the very Lamb is also flowing to dispense what He has accomplished on the cross. Whatever was accomplished on the cross was objective, and this has to become subjective to us by the flow of the Lamb. Even the Lamb is flowing in this divine flow because this flow proceeds out of the throne of God and of the Lamb. This means that the water of life flows out of God and out of the Lamb. We do not only have such a vision and revelation, but we have this experience day by day and even moment by moment. I can testify that without such a divine flow I cannot live, I cannot minister, and I have nothing to minister. But praise the Lord, this divine flow is always availing in our life and in our being.

THE SOURCE OF LIFE WITHIN US

Do not say the source of the divine life flowing within us is in the heavens. We have to say the source is within us. Some may argue that John saw the throne in the heavens, but we must realize that according to Ephesians 2:6 we are now seated together in the heavenlies in Christ Jesus. The source is in us because the source is in the heavens, and we are in the heavens. God is in the heavens and we are in the heavens, so God is in us. Some may feel, however, that though God and we are in the heavens, we are in the heavens separately. We should not forget, however, that when we believed, we believed into the Triune God. We were also baptized into the name of the Father, of the Son, and of the Holy Spirit, and the name denotes the person (Matt. 28:19). We were baptized into the person of the Father, the Son, and the Spirit, so after being baptized we are in the Triune God. God and we are in the heavens, but also we are in Him and He is in us. We and God are coinhering. We should enjoy this wonderful coinherence with the Triune God.

The Jews only believe God, but we believe "in" God. The difference between the Jews believing and our believing depends on the small preposition *in*. We believe in God, and actually in Greek the preposition for *in* is *into*. We believe into God. When we believed in the Lord Jesus, we believed into the Triune God, and at the same time the Triune God came into us. There is no way to demonstrate the fact that we are in God and God is in us. We are not on this earth, but we are in the heavens, on the one hand, and in God, on the other hand.

This very God who is in us is the source of life. The throne of God and of the Lamb should be the center of our being. In the meeting we may say the throne is in us, but many times when the sisters go shopping, the throne is thrown away to the heavens. The brothers also need to ask themselves if they have the throne of God in them in doing business. Who is our Lord, Head, and authority in our daily life? Many times even in small things such as buying a tie or a pair of shoes, we would not let the throne in our heart.

We must realize that whenever the throne is gone, there is no source of the flow. This is why many times we have the feeling that we are dry and even dried up. There is not the flow of the living water because we do not accept or recognize the lordship, the headship, and the authority of the Triune God in the very center of our being. This is why the throne is the last item revealed concerning the New Jerusalem. Without the throne, the New Jerusalem does not have a center, and without the throne, there is no flow of life. As a result, the entire New Jerusalem would be dried up and even starved to death. The water of life flows out of the throne, and the tree of life grows in the water of life and on the two sides of the river of the water of life as a vine producing timely fruits for the food of God's redeemed for eternity. Both the water of life and the tree of life are the issue of the throne. If there were no throne in you, what would be the issue? Many Christians are dried up, starved to death, and there is no growth in life because the throne is put away to the heavens and is not in their experience.

The tree of life also has leaves for the healing of the nations, symbolizing the deeds of Christ guiding and regulating the nations outwardly that they may live the human life forever. This indicates that when we enjoy Christ as the tree of life, the unbelievers are regulated by our conduct, which we live out of Christ.

Every single saint is a "little New Jerusalem." Within you in the center of your being there should be the throne of God and of the Lamb. Whenever you would take the Triune God as your Head, that will be the time when something begins to flow in your being. We have to apply this to our daily life in every instance and in every small thing. Even in our talk to our children and in our talk to our spouse, we have to practice submitting ourselves to the inner throne. Do not look into the heavens, but look to the center of your entire being where there should be a throne. The throne should be prevailing in the center of your being. Then the water of life will be proceeding out of the throne to supply you and to bring to you the tree of life, which nourishes you all day long.

OUR DAILY LIFE—
A LIFE OF THE NEW JERUSALEM

Our daily life must be a life of the New Jerusalem. In that day when we arrive at the ultimate consummation of the divine revelation, we should not be surprised, because today we are experiencing the same thing. What will be in the New Jerusalem will be an intensification and a consummation of our present experience. We are now experiencing the same thing day by day in our family life, in our marriage life, in our school life, in our business life, and in our church life. We are experiencing the throne of God and of the Lamb out of which flows the Triune God for our enjoyment. The water of life, the flow of the Spirit of life, is the divine life in resurrection for the drink of God's redeemed (Rev. 22:17b; John 7:38-40). This river of water of life proceeding out of the throne is bright as crystal with no dimness or opaqueness, purifying God's redeemed and making them transparent.

In the last forty years of my ministry, I have not had a heart to speak concerning anything else. What burdens me in my ministry is to tell people that the Triune God is flowing Himself into their being. I have spoken this one thing from many directions and with many messages. The last pages of the New Testament are on the throne, out of which flows the Triune God. The river flows with the God who purposed, with the Lamb who redeemed, and with the Spirit who is now the all-inclusive, processed, triune, life-giving Spirit. I do not want to merely teach you concerning the throne in Revelation 22, but I believe that while you are reading this chapter, the throne of God and of the Lamb, out of which the Triune God flows, is being spoken into you. The Triune God is now flowing into you as the water of life with the tree of life growing in it.

EATING AND DRINKING GOD

In the place where the Triune God flows, we serve Him (Rev. 22:3). Not only do we serve Him but also we see His face (Rev. 22:4). His face is in the water of life and in the fruit of the tree of life. When you drink the water of life, you see His face. When you eat the fruit of the tree of life, you receive His face. You serve Him by drinking and eating Him. Do not do anything for Him. He can do everything, but He cannot drink Himself nor can He eat Himself. He depends on you to eat Him and to drink Him. I say again, do not think you can work for Him. He can do everything for Himself and He does not need you. He needs you only to eat Him. He needs you only to drink Him. He needs you only to enjoy Him. Do not say, "I will go to the mission field to be a missionary." God can do everything, but He needs someone to eat Him and to drink Him. He needs many eaters and drinkers.

Revelation 22:14 is on eating God as the tree of life, and verse 17 of the same chapter is on drinking God as the water of life. Since God is flowing as the water of life, who will drink Him? Not only the sinners who do not believe in God but also many Christians do not know how to eat God. Our robes have been washed in His precious blood for the purpose of giving us the right to eat Him. But many of us do not enjoy this right. We thank Him for the washing of the precious blood, yet we do not come to eat Him. We all need to exercise our right to come and eat Him. Revelation 22:17 tells us that whosoever will may come to drink of the water of life freely. Verse 14 of Revelation 22 may be considered a promise for the enjoyment of the tree of life, which is Christ with all the riches of life; and the second half of verse 17 may be considered a call to take the water of life, which is the life-giving Spirit. Thus, this book ends in a promise and a call, both of which are for eating and drinking the all-inclusive Christ as the life-giving Spirit.

Even in the Gospel of John the Lord said that He was the bread of life (6:35) and that "he who eats Me shall also live because of Me" (6:57). The thought of eating God is in John 6. God was incarnated not only to be the Redeemer but also to be the bread of life. He is the bread of life that came down out of heaven for us to feed on. This is the greatest blessing. Then John says that on the last day of the feast Jesus stood and cried out, "If anyone thirst, let him come to Me and drink" (7:37). When we drink of Him we receive the water of life, and as a result rivers of living water flow out of our innermost being (John 7:38). In the Gospel of John there is the concept of eating and drinking God.

The last book of the Bible, John's Revelation, presents us a picture of the New Jerusalem. The heart of the picture is the throne out of which flows the drinking water, in which grows the tree of life. Both the water of life and the tree of life are God Himself. When the Triune God flows, He becomes the water of life for us to drink, and He grows the tree of life for us to eat. In order to experience the New Jerusalem we all should say, "Lord, I receive You as my Head and I take Your headship, lordship, and authority. Lord, I enthrone You in my heart. I put You on Your throne." Once you put Him on His throne, immediately the water flows and the tree grows, and you have something to drink and to eat. This is our Christian life.

SERVING HIM, SEEING HIM, AND REIGNING WITH HIM

It is here in this flow from the throne that we serve Him

and that we see His face. Also, in this flow we reign as kings (Rev. 22:5). If you do go to the mission field, you must go by taking God's throne in the center of your being. Then every day out of the throne the water flows and the tree grows. When you drink the water of life and eat the tree of life, you will serve Him, you will see His face, and you will be a king. On the mission field you will not be a poor missionary, but you will go and be there as a king. The Lord Jesus told us that all authority had been given to Him in heaven and on earth and that now we need to go with His authority to disciple the nations (Matt. 28:18-19). We need to go with the authority of the heavenly King who is now enthroned in our being. We all have to realize that here is the power and the impact of the preaching of the gospel—we have One who is the Lord of all, the Head of the entire universe, enthroned in the center of our being. When He is enthroned in our being, the water flows and the tree grows, and our service will be an enjoyment. When you enjoy Him you serve Him, you see Him, and you reign with Him to be kings with Him.

THE THRONE, THE WATER OF LIFE, AND THE TREE OF LIFE

May the Lord grant us three things in our experience— the throne, the water of life, and the tree of life. This is why I say to the sisters not to go shopping apart from the throne, without the water of life and the tree of life. Go shopping with the throne in the center of your being and under the flow of the water of life, in which grows the tree of life for you to eat. There is absolutely nothing wrong with going shopping, but go shopping with the throne. When you get into the door of the department store, do not leave the throne outside the door. Enter the door with the throne. When you pick up an article, pick it up with the throne. Many times when the sisters go shopping, they leave the throne at home. At other times, the throne went with them to the entrance of the department store, and they left the throne outside the door when they entered the department store. However, none of us should put the throne aside. Go shopping with the throne and enter the department store with the throne. The Christian life is a life centered with the throne. As long as you have the throne as the center of your daily life, you are okay because you will have the water of life to drink and the tree of life to eat. Then you are "a small New Jerusalem." In the flow of the water of life you serve Him, you see Him, and you reign with Him. The flow of the Divine Trinity saturates and nourishes the entire New Jerusalem. This indicates that the carrying out of God's administration for the fulfillment of His purpose, His desire, is by the flow of Himself as life and life supply, not by any work. May this be quite an enlightenment to all of us.

Chapter Thirty-Nine

THE NEW JERUSALEM'S APPLICATION TO THE BELIEVERS— THE TRIUNE ENTRY

Scripture Reading: John 3:36a; Matt. 28:19; John 15:4a; 14:17, 23; Col. 2:7a; Eph. 3:16-19

We have already pointed out that the New Jerusalem is the greatest allegory in the Bible since it is the ultimate consummation of the divine revelation in the entire Scripture. In order to interpret the significance of this allegory, we need the proper understanding of the spiritual revelation in the entire Bible and also the experience of all the crucial points of God's revelation in the New and Old Testaments. We all need to see how the allegory of the New Jerusalem is applied to us. The New Jerusalem is not merely objective, nor is it merely something for the future, but it should be subjective in our daily experience.

THE APPLICATION OF THE NEW JERUSALEM

In these final six chapters we will cover the six aspects of the application of the New Jerusalem to the believers. The first application is the triune entry. We are using "entry" in the denotation of entering in, not in the denotation of an entrance or a door. The entering into the New Jerusalem is triune because it is an entry through the Divine Trinity, through the Son, with the Father, and by the Spirit.

After we enter into the Triune God, we experience Him as the triune constitution, the second application. We are now being constituted with the Father's divine nature, the gold; with the Son's produce in His redemptive work, the pearl; and with the Spirit's produce in His transforming work, the precious stones. The New Jerusalem is built with these three basic materials, which are the three basic elements for our spiritual constitution.

Through the entering in we have the constitution, and in the constitution we have the triune existence. Our spiritual existence is totally dependent upon the Triune God. Second Corinthians 13:14 says, "The grace of the Lord Jesus Christ, and the love of God, and the fellowship of the Holy Spirit be with you all." Such a "benediction" does not only bear a sense of enjoyment but also denotes the way we Christians are existing today. We are existing by the grace of Christ, by the love of God, and by the fellowship, the flow, of the Spirit. In other words, we are existing by what the Triune God is. He is grace and love to us, and this grace with love is carried on within us in the fellowship of the Holy Spirit. We exist spiritually by and with the very Triune God.

The way that we exist is the way that we live, so the fourth aspect of the application is the Triune God as our living. We are living by, with, and in the Triune God. We are living by the Son, with the Father, through the Spirit. We live in the same way that we entered into the Triune God. We live by the Triune God, with the Triune God, and in the Triune God. This living is on the highest plane. How marvelous it is that human beings could live in such a way! We do not live by ourselves, with ourselves, and in ourselves. Rather, we admit the accomplished fact of what Christ has done for us on the cross, and we admit that we ourselves have been crucified with Him. "It is no longer I who live, but Christ lives in me" (Gal. 2:20). We live by Christ (John 6:57), and we even live Christ (Phil. 1:21a). Since Christ is the very embodiment of the Father and realized in the Spirit, when we live by Christ, we live by the Triune God, and when we live Christ, we live the Triune God.

The fifth application is the triune enjoyment. Everything related to our spiritual life is triune. The word triune is a good adjective to describe our spiritual condition, situation, existence, living, and enjoyment. We are those who are enjoying the Triune God. We enjoy the Son's grace, the Father's love, and the Spirit's fellowship. Christ is grace, God is love, and the Holy Spirit is fellowship. Therefore, we enjoy a triune blessing—the blessing of the Son as grace, the blessing of the Father as love, and the blessing of the Spirit as the fellowship. This is our threefold enjoyment; our enjoyment is triune.

Finally, the New Jerusalem expresses the Triune God so its expression is triune. All of us individually should express the Triune God. People should be able to see God's golden nature in us and that we are the pearls. We are not rocky, but we are "pearly." The rock wounded the oyster, stayed in this wound, and the oyster secreted its life-juice around the rock making it a pearl. Thus, we were changed from being rocky, and we became pearly. Not only the sisters but also the brothers are pearls. We must be found by others in Christ (Phil. 3:9). Paul was pursuing Christ to be found in Christ. He did not want others to find him as Saul of Tarsus, a natural, "rocky" man, but he wanted others to find him in Christ. He desired to be wrapped up with the secretion of Christ's resurrection life in order that others could see him as a pearl, full of Christ's life.

Also, we express the sevenfold Spirit. The lampstand has seven lamps which are the seven Spirits of God shining to express all that the Triune God is. We must be persons who are expressing God by shining with the sevenfold intensified Spirit. This is the triune expression. Thus, the six applications of the New Jerusalem to the believers are its triune entry, triune constitution, triune existence, triune living, triune enjoyment, and triune expression.

THE ENTERABLE GOD

In this chapter we want to specifically look at the triune entry. According to the divine revelation in the sixty-six books of the Bible our God is enterable. That God is righteous, holy, merciful, and faithful has been preached and taught for centuries. We must also realize, though, that the righteous, holy, merciful, faithful God is enterable.

Noah's ark is a type of our God being enterable. The ark typifies Christ, the embodiment of God, and that ark was enterable. Noah, his wife, his three sons, and three daughters-in-law all entered into the ark. The ark was not only trustworthy but also enterable. Because the ark was enterable, the eight people who entered into it were saved from the flood. In like manner, every airplane is enterable. If a 747 were only trustworthy and not enterable, we could not go anywhere with it. When we enter into the 747, however, we are saved from the wind and the storm, and we are on our way to our destination. Our enterable God is the real ark and the real 747.

BELIEVING INTO THE SON
AND BAPTIZED INTO THE TRIUNE GOD

The second type which shows that our God is enterable is the tabernacle. The tabernacle is also a type of Christ. John 1:14 tells us that the Word who was God Himself became flesh and tabernacled among men. Christ was a tabernacle for people to enter into. When we believed in Him, we entered into Him. John 3:36 says, "He who believes *into* the Son has eternal life" (lit.). The same Greek preposition for "into" is used in Romans 6:3 which tells us that we have been baptized into Christ Jesus. Just to say that you were baptized in Christ is not adequate. You were once outside of Christ, but when you were baptized into the water, that signified that you were baptized into Christ.

Furthermore, Matthew 28:19 indicates that we need to baptize people into the name of the Father, of the Son, and of the Holy Spirit. We were once outside of the Triune God, but when we were baptized, we were baptized into the Triune God. Vincent indicates in his word study that the preposition "into" denotes a kind of spiritual and mystical union with the Triune God. In other words, an organic union transpired at the time we were baptized into the Triune God. When we were baptized into the Triune God, we were baptized into the very Spirit, who is the ultimate consummation of the Triune God. The Spirit is just the Triune God reaching us. Because He is the Spirit, we all can be baptized into Him.

This matter of our entering into the Triune God is a crucial aspect of the divine revelation which has been missed among most Christians. When we baptize people, it should not just be a ceremony or a religious form to accept people into Christianity. When we baptize them, we must tell them to exercise their faith to be immersed into the sum total of the divine Being, equivalent to His Person. We need to tell the ones being baptized that we are not only baptizing them into the water, but also into all that the Triune God is.

The Jews believe God, but they believe in an objective God that exists in the universe but has nothing to do with them experientially. Our believing, however, is very subjective because we believe into God. Our believing creates an organic union between us and the Triune God. "Into" means entering in. No one told me when I was baptized that I was being immersed into the Triune God. We all have to realize this wonderful fact of our baptism, that is, when we were baptized, we entered into the Triune God.

BEING IN GOD

We have seen that the three gates of the New Jerusalem portray the Triune God as our entrance. Also, the three parables in Luke 15 with the Son as the shepherd, the Spirit as the seeking woman, and the Father as the loving father, show us that the Triune God is receiving sinners, not only back to His home but also back into Himself. We all have entered into the Triune God, and now we are in the Triune God! I always consider myself as a person in God. While I am living in my home, I am actually in God. While I am taking a plane, my sensation is that I am in God. While I am walking on the street, I am in God. I am altogether in my Triune God, in the Father, in the Son, and in the Spirit.

This one realization of being in God will preserve you from many evil things. If you realize that you are in God, can you go dancing? Whenever you realize that you are in God, you would never fly to Las Vegas to gamble. Also, this realization will stop your gossip. We Christians gossip frequently nearly every day. However, whenever you begin to gossip and you realize that you are in God, this realization will stop you from gossiping. Do not "jump out" of God. To gossip is to jump out of God. We should not take a leave of absence from our dwelling place in God. We may feel that we could gossip a little bit and then come back into God. Many times, however, after we gossip, it is hard for us to get back into God. We have to make a strong confession and let the blood wash us. Then our conscience would be cleansed to allow us to be in God experientially.

ABIDING IN THE SON

Furthermore, we need to abide in the Son that the Father, the Son, and the Spirit may abide in us (John 15:4a; 14:17, 23). Once you get into God, do not get out. You need to abide in Him. To abide implies to enter in further. The depths of God are unfathomable, so we need a further entering into Him. After entering into Him, we have to stay in Him. To stay in Him actually is to enter in further and further. John 15:4a says, "Abide in Me and I in you." Our abiding becomes a term or condition for His abiding in us.

John 14:17 and 23 indicate that when we abide in the Lord, the Spirit of reality abides in us and the Father comes with the Son to make an abode with us. This indicates that the Father, the Son, and the Spirit abide in you because of your abiding in Him. Your abiding is a term or a condition for His abiding in you, and the fulfilling of this condition furthers your entering into Him. This can be fully proven by your experience. We all need to pray, "Lord, thank You that I am now in You. Lord, thank You that hour after hour I abide in You." When you abide in Him, you realize He is abiding in you and that His abiding is becoming deeper and deeper in you. This shows us that our entering in is triune and our abiding is also triune. While we are abiding in the Lord, the Father, the Son, and the Spirit are abiding in us. This is a kind of triune abiding which brings in a triune entering in further into the Triune God.

Not many Christians are for the proper experience of the Triune God. They know the Trinity in doctrine, and they talk and teach about the Trinity as theology. However, in the Bible the Triune God is revealed to us for our experience. The grace of Christ, the love of God, and the fellowship of the Holy Spirit referred to in 2 Corinthians 13:14 are not for doctrine but for our enjoyment. To be baptized into the name of the Father, and of the Son, and of the Holy Spirit is not for doctrine but for bringing us into an organic union with the Triune God. The Father, the Son, and the Spirit are not for us merely to know about, but for us to experience. We need to be born of the Father, joined to the Son, and one with the Spirit. The experience of the Triune God begins with our entering into Him and continues with our abiding in Him. When we abide in Him, He abides in us in His Divine Trinity.

ROOTED IN CHRIST

Colossians 2:7a indicates that we have been rooted in Christ. This indicates that we believers are like plants and Christ is likened to the soil. We believers, the plants, need to be rooted into the soil, Christ. A tree does not only grow upward but also downward. The root system of a tree grows downward deeply. Quite often, we Christians do not pay attention to our roots or to our being rooted in Christ. We only talk about our growing, but we have to realize that our growing depends upon our rooting. Colossians indicates that we have received Christ as the mystery of God (2:2) and that now we have to be rooted in Him. To be rooted in Christ simply means to enter into Him. When the tree is rooted into the soil, it enters into the soil. When we are rooted in Christ we will enjoy a further entry into the Triune God.

CHRIST MAKING HIS HOME IN OUR HEARTS

We are rooted in Christ that He may make His home in our hearts (Eph. 3:16-19). In Ephesians 3 the apostle prays that God the Father would grant the believers to be strengthened through God the Spirit into their inner man, that Christ, God the Son, may make His home in their hearts, that is, to occupy their entire being, that they might be filled unto all the fullness of God (vv. 14-19). The phrase "make His home" is only one word in the Greek, *katoikeo*. This Greek word basically means to settle down in a dwelling, to make a dwelling place. The prefix of this word *kata* means "down." This means that Christ is making His home, not upward but downward. In many of today's cities we see parking lots which are built downward, and in some big cities there is an "underground city" with all types of shops and eating establishments. In the same way, Christ likes to make a home downward or "underground." Christ is not superficial like many of today's Christians who "skate on the ice" of the truth contained in the Bible. The Father, according to His wisdom, is exercising His sovereignty to strengthen you through His Spirit into the inner man that Christ may make His home in your heart.

In Ephesians, Paul's writing is long and redundant. Verses 14 through 19 of chapter three are one long sentence. Verses 3 through 14 of Ephesians 1 are also part of one long sentence. Paul did not care for language, but he only cared for the divine revelation. (For a full explanation of all the details of the apostle's prayer for the church in Ephesians 3:14-19, it would be profitable to read all the notes on these verses in the Recovery Version.) The reason why Paul writes in such a redundant and seemingly complicated way is because our God is not that simple. He is not merely God, but He is the Triune God, the Father, the Son, and the Spirit. The divine mystery of the Trinity is beyond explanation. Martin Luther indicated that if a person can explain the mystery of the Triune God, then that person must be the teacher of God. We do know, however, that our God is the Father, the Son, and the Spirit, not for us to know doctrinally, but for us to experience. We all need to say, "Thank You, Father! You are the One granting us to be strengthened. You have a plan, You have a purpose, and You are wise. Praise You that You are exercising Your sovereignty to cause us to be strong. Thank You, Father, that You do this through the Spirit. Thank You we are being strengthened into the inner man that Christ may make His home in our heart."

God the Father is exercising His authority through God the Spirit to strengthen us into the inner man that God the Son may make His home deep down in our hearts. I am sorry to say that some Christians even argue that Christ is not in us. They say that Christ is merely on the throne. They argue that Christ is too great to enter into us small human beings. We all need to declare, however, that the Bible teaches that Christ is not only in us (Col. 1:27) but that He is also making

His home downward in our heart. He is housing Himself in our heart.

We all have entered into the Triune God, and we are now abiding in Him. Our abiding in Him affords Him a way to abide in us triunely. The Triune God is now abiding in us, so we have been rooted into Him. While we are rooted into Him, the Father works to strengthen us through God the Spirit that God the Son, Christ, may make His home deep down in our heart which is composed of our mind (Heb. 4:12), will (Acts 11:23), emotion (John 16:6, 22), and conscience (Heb. 10:22). Before He began to make His home in our heart, our mind, emotion, will, and conscience were devoid of Him. However, since we began to pray that God the Father would strengthen us into the inner man, Christ gradually began to occupy our mind, take over our emotion and will, and possess our entire conscience.

Our heart is like a house that has four rooms, and these rooms are the mind, the emotion, the will, and the conscience. Christ has the desire to occupy every room of our heart and every corner of every room. As He makes His home downward in our heart we become strong to apprehend with all the saints the breadth, length, height, and depth of Christ (Eph. 3:18). These are the dimensions of the universe. No one knows how wide the breadth is, how long the length is, how high the height is, or how deep the depth is. All these dimensions describe the immeasurable Christ, whose dimensions are the dimensions of the universe. He is the breadth, length, height, and depth. We can only apprehend His universal dimensions with all the saints. Eventually, we know the knowledge-surpassing love of Christ that we may be filled unto all the fullness of God (Eph. 3:19). When we are filled unto all the fullness of God, this is the complete entering into this wonderful, marvelous, all-inclusive Triune God. When we enter into the Triune God completely, we have entered into the entire constitution of the New Jerusalem. This is the triune entry.

We have seen that our baptism into the Father, the Son, and the Spirit is triune, that we abide in the Son that the Father, the Son, and the Spirit may abide in us, and that the

Father grants us through His Spirit to be strengthened into the inner man that Christ may make His home in our heart. We enjoy a triune entering in, a triune abiding, and a triune making home in our hearts. This is not the teaching of ethics, morality, or character improvement, but the pure teaching according to the pure, divine revelation. We are being filled with the Triune God unto or resulting in the fullness of God, which is the expression of the Triune God as the New Jerusalem. This is our enjoyment and experience in today's church life.

Today many Christians do not like to talk about the church, but in Matthew 16:18 the Lord Jesus promised that He would build His church. In order for this to be realized, the church has to enter into a state where so many saints will have Christ making His home deep down in their heart that their entire being would be saturated within with Christ as the embodiment of the Triune God, possessing and occupying every corner and every avenue of their entire being. This is the subjective experience of the Triune God and is the very mingling of the Triune God with His chosen and redeemed people. This is divinity mingled with humanity, the composition of the divine God with His redeemed people which is termed the New Jerusalem in this great allegory. We have entered into the Triune God and we are still entering. We are entering, and He is making His home deep down in our heart. The more we enter, the more He deepens. Eventually, He gets into our inward being to such an extent that He has housed Himself in every corner and avenue of our entire being.

CHAPTER FORTY

THE NEW JERUSALEM'S APPLICATION TO THE BELIEVERS— THE TRIUNE CONSTITUTION

Scripture Reading: Rev. 21:18-20, 3, 11, 22

I love this allegory of the New Jerusalem because it speaks about or depicts our experiences of Christ. There is not another type or allegory in the Scriptures which speaks so much about Christ according to our Christian experience. In this chapter we will see the second aspect of the application of the New Jerusalem to us—the triune constitution.

We partook of the triune constitution at the very beginning of our Christian life. Our faith in Christ, our baptism into Christ (Gal. 3:27) or into the Triune God, (Matt. 28:19), and our regeneration in the Spirit (John 3:6b) were the very initiation, the very beginning, of our Christian life and of our spiritual constitution. Regeneration made us another kind of being. By being born of Adam, we were born into the old creation, but we had a second birth, a new birth, a birth from on high, a birth of, in, and with the Spirit. Through this birth, we became another kind of being. In one sense, all of us have "two faces." We have the face of our old being and the face of our new being. According to the New Testament revelation, we believers have two lives—the Adamic life and God's life, the divine life. Regretfully, many of us also have two kinds of living. Our coming to the church meetings, pray-reading the Word, fellowshipping with the saints, and meeting in the homes is a heavenly, spiritual, and divine living. Many times, however, when the sisters go shopping, this is another living which is something different in nature from God's nature.

As believers we do have the realization that, on the one hand, we possess the divine nature and that, on the other hand, we have a nature that is rotten and full of corruption—our natural, human nature. The Adamic nature can easily be seen even in our children. We may have the feeling that our children are loving and innocent, but at times we all have to admit that our children are "ugly." The reason why they are ugly is because all of us human beings have an ugly nature which we inherited from Adam. Our natural nature is ugly, but thank the Lord that through the second birth, regeneration, we received another nature, the divine nature. We have an excellent nature, which is the very nature of God Himself.

Since we were regenerated, a constituting work began to take place in our being. When I was a young believer, I frequently heard the word edification. I was told that all the believers needed to be edified. As a young Christian, the word edification became a very popular and strong word to me. Actually, the New Testament speaks about edification, but this word denotes the building. The natural understanding concerning edification is that we need to be educated or taught. The very Greek word for edification in the New Testament (King James Version) is the very word for building up. Many Christians feel that they need to be edified, which to them means that they need to be taught, trained, disciplined, regulated, adjusted, improved, and educated. Not many understand this word in the New Testament in the sense of being built up. The New Testament denotation, however, is mainly on the aspect of being built up, and to build up is to constitute. We all need to be constituted, to be built up. To be educated is altogether a matter of knowledge in the mentality and not a matter of being built up with some element. To be built up is to receive more and more of the divine element which becomes your constituent to constitute you.

Today's Christianity is mostly a religion of knowledge, theology, biblical teaching, regulation, adjustment, and character improvement. Because of this, the basic thought in the Holy Word of constitution has been altogether lost. Not many Christians have the thought that they need to be constituted with the Triune God and not merely taught. All the mothers know that they have to teach their children, but the main thing that they do is feed their children. If a mother would merely teach her children day and night for two weeks without feeding them, the children would not be able to live. Mere teaching does not constitute a child, but feeding does. Mothers are not so bothered by their child being naughty, but they are really bothered when their child does not eat. Eating is not to receive knowledge but to receive some nourishing, constituting element to enable one to grow.

When we look at the New Jerusalem we cannot see any doctrine or anything concerning the theology of the Trinity. What we see is gold, pearls, and precious stones. These elements signify the Triune God, but they do not indicate a theology of the Trinity. Gold, pearls, and precious stones are not doctrines but elements.

THE TRIUNE GOD AS OUR INTRINSIC ELEMENTS

The triune constitution is with the Triune God wrought into the believers as their intrinsic elements. Intrinsic means something that is inward and hidden. Even our physical body receives some nourishing element into it every day, which eventually becomes our body's intrinsic element. For example, every morning I eat a big breakfast, and this breakfast becomes my intrinsic element. As this food is assimilated within me, it supports, sustains, and strengthens me to live. My strength comes from this intrinsic element. The food is taken into my being and becomes the intrinsic element in my physical body.

The allegory of the New Jerusalem is quite marvelous because it shows us what we could not see outwardly— the intrinsic elements. The city is not organized but constituted with gold, pearls, and precious stones. The city is not only constituted with these three elements, but also its constitution becomes a building. The constitution is the building up. Also, we need to remember that this city is a composition of God blended with all His redeemed people. This composition is arrived at by constitution. When we receive the Triune God into us, the Father is given to us as the gold, the Son is secreting over us to produce the pearls, and the Spirit is transforming us to make us precious stones. These three elements are in our being working in us, and they are the very intrinsic elements which constitute our spiritual being. In a corporate sense, our spiritual being is the church today and the New Jerusalem in the coming ages.

GOLD—GIVEN BY THE FATHER
AS THE BASIC ELEMENT

The first intrinsic element of the triune constitution is gold, given by the Father as the basic element (Rev. 21:18b). We have seen that gold in typology always refers to God's divine nature, and Peter told us that we are partakers of the divine nature (2 Pet. 1:4). When we were born physically, we all inherited our father's nature by being born of him. We all have been given our human nature by our begetting father. In like manner, when we were born of God, as the begetting Father He imparted His own nature into our being, which is the gold of the "golden mountain," the New Jerusalem. The city proper is like a mountain with the height of twelve thousand stadia, and Revelation 21:18 tells us that the city was pure gold. Also, Revelation 21:21 tells us that the street of the city was pure gold. All of this denotes that the divine nature is the basic element of our spiritual constitution, just like our human nature is the basic element of our human being.

The divine nature becomes the golden street on which we walk and in which we behave. As a human being, you behave in your human nature. In the same way, a dog has a "doggie nature" and he always behaves in this nature. A dog does not need anyone to teach it to bark. The dog's barking is because of his nature. The dog nature becomes the "street" for the dog to walk on. Since we as the children of God have the divine nature, this divine nature should spontaneously be our street and our walkway. The reason why we do not go dancing is because this is against the divine nature. The divine nature regulates us, not by a written regulation, but by being a street in our inner being. Our driving a car is not only regulated by a street but also by the lines painted on the street. Our Christian life should not be regulated by a church code or by a written regulation, but by the divine nature as our unique street.

In the New Jerusalem there is one, unique street—God's divine nature. Why do we Christians not gamble? There is not a code which says that the members of the church should not gamble, but the divine nature within us will not allow us to gamble. We are walking on the divine street, which means we are walking in the divine nature. The divine nature has been given to us, and 2 Peter 1:3-4 says that God has granted to us all things which relate to life and godliness and that we may be those partaking of the divine nature. To partake of the divine nature means that you have received the divine nature already. Partaking of the divine nature means enjoying the divine nature. All of us have a share of the golden mountain within us since we have received God's divine nature. We do not need to receive His nature again, but we have to enjoy it every day.

Peter tells us in his second Epistle that through the precious and exceedingly great promises, the believers might become partakers of the divine nature (v. 4). We all need to praise the Lord that we have God's divine nature as the gold within us. His divine nature is rich, high, excellent and brilliant! He has also given us great promises in both the Old and New Testaments to enable us to partake of this golden nature.

In order to illustrate how we partake of the divine nature through the great promises of God, we need to consider something which plagues every human being—anxiety. Everyone has anxiety and worry; no one can avoid this. We all must admit that anxiety is a "killer." There are some wonderful promises in the Bible, however, concerning anxiety. In Matthew 6 the Lord Jesus tells us not to be anxious concerning our life, which involves what we eat, what we drink, and what we put on (v. 25). The Lord then goes on to tell us to look at the birds of the heaven. Although the birds do not sow or reap or gather into barns, our heavenly Father nourishes them (v. 26). Finally, the Lord charges us to "seek first His kingdom and His righteousness, and all these things shall be added to you" (v. 33).

Upon graduating from college, a certain young man may aspire to get the best job. If he does not get a job after three months, however, he probably will become anxious. He will begin to wonder where he will get the money to feed and clothe himself. The Lord Jesus, however, promised us that if we seek His kingdom and His righteousness, He will take care of our needs. If we take His promise, we will enjoy the divine nature.

In 2 Peter 1:4-11 there is a record of the divine nature and its development. The development of the divine nature is the growth of the divine nature. The divine nature has been given to us for us to partake of and enjoy. Through the promises of God we can enjoy the divine nature, and by this the divine nature develops and grows from one state to another. While we are enjoying God's nature, we are being constituted with it. In the physical realm, what I eat and enjoy becomes my intrinsic element to constitute me. My healthy facial color and my strength are from the inner constituting by the intrinsic element.

Through the promises of God, we can enjoy the divine nature wrought into our being as our intrinsic element. Philippians 4:6-7 says, "In nothing be anxious, but in everything, by prayer and petition with thanksgiving, let your requests be made known to God; and the peace of God, which surpasses all understanding, will guard your hearts and your thoughts in Christ Jesus." These verses also contain a promise through which we can deal with anxiety and partake of the divine nature. When you have anxiety, the enjoyment of the gold within you is annulled. This means that when you are in anxiety, you need the enjoyment of the divine nature in you. When you keep or take the promises concerning anxiety, you will enjoy the divine nature. Whenever anxiety threatened to take me over, I said, "Lord Jesus, Philippians 4:6!" Sometimes I shout—"Philippians 4:6!" To let your requests be made known to God means to tell God what you need. If you are anxious about your children, tell God, and the peace of God will guard your heart and your thoughts. In nothing be anxious, but in everything tell God what you need. Once we tell the Lord what we need and that we do not like this anxiety, from that time the thing that is causing us the anxiety becomes His business and His job. Therefore, we enjoy Him and we enjoy His golden nature.

He has granted us all things pertaining to life, and He has also given us the great promises that we may partake of, that we may enjoy, the divine nature. While we are enjoying this divine nature, it constitutes us. When we are in anxiety, we cannot enjoy God's nature constituting us in any way. However, when we appropriate and apply God's promises, the divine nature has a way to constitute our being and grow within us. This is the first aspect of the triune constitution.

PEARLS THROUGH THE SECRETION
OF CHRIST'S RESURRECTION LIFE

The second aspect of the triune constitution is the pearls which are produced through the secretion of Christ's resurrection life (Rev. 21:21a). The divine nature was given to us by God, but pearls are produced through the secretion of Christ's resurrection life from the time that we entered into Christ. When we stay in the death of Christ, Christ's resurrection life secretes itself over us, making all of us pearls. In Galatians 2:20 Paul says, "I have been crucified with Christ." When we say this, we stay in the death of Christ. When you say that you have been crucified with Christ, this means that you admit that you have been crucified on the cross. When you recognize this divine fact, you stay in His death. When you declare, "I have been crucified with Christ," this means that you are staying in His death, that you would not go away from His death, and that His death is your dwelling place. When you stay, remain, and abide in Christ's death, then it is no longer you that live but Christ that lives in you. His living and moving in you is the secretion of His resurrection life over you to make you a pearl. This secreting is a constituting. When you get up in the morning, you should stay in the death of Christ for ten or fifteen minutes; while you are staying in His death, the Lord is moving in you. This moving is His secreting of His resurrection life around you. After fifteen minutes of abiding in His death in morning watch, you will look like a pearl to your spouse. If you do not have a morning watch to stay in the death of Christ, Christ has no chance to secrete His life over you, and your appearance may be "ugly" instead of "pearly."

If we stay in the death of Christ every day for five to ten years, we will eventually become a "big round pearl." Sometimes because our stay in the death of Christ was a little short, His secretion of His resurrection life over us was not complete. Therefore, when others looked at us, they saw that we were pearls, but they also could still see "the rock" of our fallen nature. Also, because the secretion of the resurrection life is not that thick in us, there are still parts of our being which the resurrection life has not touched. As pieces of rock, we need to abide in the death of Christ and enjoy the rich, thick secretion of His resurrection life to make us pearls. The rock is not made into a pearl by being taught, but by being constituted with the resurrection life of Christ through His death.

I thank the Lord for encouraging me with all the saints and with all the churches. When I go back to visit a church after having been there before, I can see that the saints have enjoyed more secretion and that Christ has been constituted more and more into their very being. We have not only been taught by the ministry, but we have been ministered to with the indwelling Christ secreting His resurrection life over us all the time to make us pearly. When a mother notices that her son is growing, this encourages her. This growth comes from the mother's feeding him with nourishing food, and this food constitutes him, becoming his intrinsic element to make him grow. Her son then becomes not only knowledgeable but also constituted.

Today in the church life we need to be taught, but more importantly, we need to be constituted. Constitution means more than knowledge. This constitution is going on all the time in the Lord's recovery because we have heard and are hearing so many messages which minister Christ's resurrection life to us. We need to admit that we have been crucified with Christ. When you take this fact and stay in this fact, admitting that you are dead in Him, you will be staying in His death. As long as you stay here, the resurrected Christ will secrete His resurrection life around you to make you a pretty pearl. Many of us can testify that we have seen saints in the Lord's recovery who are not the same as they were before they came into the church life. This is because they have become constituted and not merely taught. I do not like to teach, but I love to minister some element of the Triune God into your being.

PRECIOUS STONES THROUGH THE TRANSFORMATION OF THE SPIRIT

The third item of the triune constitution is the precious stones through the transformation of the Spirit (Rev. 21:18a, 19-20), from the time that we began to look to the Lord. In the New Jerusalem we firstly see the base, the golden mountain, then there are the pearly gates, and finally, there is the building, mainly with jasper and other precious stones. The gold is given, the pearl is produced by Christ's resurrection life through His death, and the precious stones are produced by the transforming work of the Spirit.

In order to see the transforming work of the Spirit to make us precious stones we need to look at our experience. I have been practicing to remain in the death of Christ for approximately fifty years, and I am still practicing this every day. If I do not practice this, I lose the ground for Christ to secrete His resurrection life over me. When I remain in His death, spontaneously I look unto Him with an unveiled face. If you are not remaining in His death, even if you would look unto Him, your face would be fully veiled. The more you stay in His death, however, the more the veils are taken away. Then you see Him with an unveiled face. When we stay in the death of Christ, not only does Christ secrete His resurrection life around us, but also we behold Him, we look at His face, we appreciate Him, and we love Him. This affords the Spirit within us a great opportunity to move and to bring in more riches of the Divine Trinity into our being to transform us (2 Cor. 3:18). Transformation is a metabolic work. The divine element is added to us, and this element replaces our old nature metabolically.

The secretion of the resurrection life of Christ is good for our entering into the Triune God, but transformation is good for building. The wall is not built with pearls but with precious stone. You not only have the experience of Christ secreting His resurrection life over you, but also the experience of the Spirit supplying you with the rich element of the Divine Trinity which transforms you into His image. Through this transforming work, you become not only pearls but also precious stones good for God's building. This is constitution by the Father's nature as the gold, by the Son's secretion to produce pearls, and by the Spirit's transformation to produce stones. We are not separate pieces of precious stone, but we are pieces fitted in together to become God's building. The building up of the church is not a kind of arrangement or organization but a constitution. We are being constituted with the Father's divine nature, with Christ's resurrection life, and with the bountiful supply of the riches of the Divine Trinity. This constitution not only changes our being, but builds all of us together in the intrinsic elements of the Divine Trinity.

GOD'S DWELLING PLACE
AND CORPORATE EXPRESSION

As God's building, today we are the church and tomorrow we will be the New Jerusalem. The triune constitution is for the building up of the New Jerusalem to be God's dwelling place (Rev. 21:3). God dwells in this constitution. The church today and then the New Jerusalem in the future, being the house of God, has to be a spiritual constitution with the element of the Divine Trinity. This constitution is God's dwelling place. Secondly, this constitution is God's corporate expression (Rev. 21:11). God dwells in such a constitution and this constitution expresses God in a corporate way as a corporate Body. The function of the church today is to express God corporately, and in eternity in the New Jerusalem we will be such a corporate expression forever. This corporate expression is also a constitution with the intrinsic element of the Triune God.

GOD'S EXPANSION

Finally, the triune constitution is God's expansion—the temple to be our dwelling place (Rev. 21:22). If God had never been expanded, how could He be the temple? John was looking for the temple in the New Jerusalem, but he saw no temple because the temple is the Lord God the Almighty and the Lamb. This means that the Triune God has been expanded to be a temple. To us God is the temple for us to dwell in, to serve Him, and to stay with Him. To God, however, we are His tabernacle for Him to dwell in. The New Jerusalem is the tabernacle, and in another sense it is a temple. This is a strong proof that the New Jerusalem is not a physical city but a personal entity. The New Jerusalem is the believers, God's tabernacle, and God, the believers' temple. He dwells in us, the tabernacle, and we dwell in Him, the temple. We serve God in God. This is God's expansion. The New Jerusalem as a spiritual, divine constitution is God's dwelling place, God's corporate expression, and God's expansion to be our temple for us to live in and to serve Him. Praise the Lord for the triune constitution.

CHAPTER FORTY-ONE

THE NEW JERUSALEM'S
APPLICATION TO THE BELIEVERS—
THE TRIUNE EXISTENCE

Scripture Reading: Eph. 4:4-6; Gal. 2:20a; John 6:57b; Phil. 1:20-21; 1 Cor. 12:13; John 3:6b; Rev. 1:4b

We need to be reminded of our need to realize that the New Jerusalem is not just an item of prophecy concerning something coming in the future, but the holy city is altogether applicable to us today. In this chapter we want to see the New Jerusalem's application to us as the triune existence. We have seen that the New Jerusalem is built with gold as its city proper, with pearls as its gates, and with precious stones for its foundation and wall. The standing of this city with its three basic elements is its existence. The New Jerusalem has a triune existence.

EXISTING IN THE BODY BY THE TRIUNE GOD

We need to see how this triune existence can be applied to us today. Since the New Jerusalem is the ultimate consummation of the entire divine revelation in the Holy Scriptures, its existence can be applied to us by going back to look at the church. In Ephesians 4:4 is the Body. The Body is the church, and the church is a miniature of the New Jerusalem. We can also say that the Body of Christ is a precursor of the New Jerusalem. The New Jerusalem is coming, and the church exists today as its precursor. The New Jerusalem will be a full consummation of this precursor, the Body of Christ.

We are not in the New Jerusalem yet, but we are surely in the Body. What is applied to the Body today will consummate in the New Jerusalem. As we have already seen, in the New

Jerusalem there are three materials for its existence: gold signifies God the Father in His divine nature, pearls signify the produce of Christ through His death and in His resurrection, and precious stones signify the produce of the Spirit's transforming work. According to Ephesians 4:4-6 we see the Spirit, the Lord, and God the Father for the existence of the Body of Christ today which will consummate in the existence of the New Jerusalem. In Ephesians 4 the existence of the New Jerusalem has been applied to us already and is still being applied to us. Day by day we who are in the church, in the Body, are enjoying this application of the existence of the New Jerusalem. We are existing in the Body by the Triune God.

Ephesians 4:4-6 says, "One Body and one Spirit, as also you were called in one hope of your calling; one Lord, one faith, one baptism; one God and Father of all, who is over all and through all and in all." In these verses are the Spirit, the Lord, and the Father. This, of course, refers to the Divine Trinity, yet the order of the Trinity in these verses is not the Father, the Lord, and the Spirit. We need to ask why Paul begins with the Spirit, goes on to the Lord, and ends with the Father. This is because Paul is touching a subjective matter, and in our experiences the Spirit is the Triune God reaching us. When the Trinity reaches us, He is the Spirit; therefore, Paul begins with the Spirit as the reaching aspect of the Divine Trinity. When you have the Spirit, you also have the Lord because the Lord is the Spirit (2 Cor. 3:17). When the Spirit reaches you, the Lord is with you since there is no separation between the three of the Divine Trinity. There is a definite distinction among the three yet no separation. You can never separate the Lord from the Spirit, nor can you separate the Father from the Lord. When the Lord is here, the Father is here. If you have one, you have all three. When the Spirit reaches you, the Lord is here, and when the Lord is here, you also enjoy the Father.

EXISTING WITH GOD THE FATHER

Firstly, in the triune existence we are existing with God the Father, who is over all, through all, and in all. You may think that it is easy to understand that God is over you and in you, but can you explain what it means for God to be through you? We Christians have a bad habit of taking things in the Bible for granted. Many of us have probably read Ephesians many times, but did we ever check what it means for God the Father to be over all, through all, and in all? How is this verse applied to our experience? Do we experience God being over us, through us, and in us?

Verse 6 uses the term "one God and Father." We all know that God is our Father, but in this verse Paul inserts the conjunction "and." We need to ask what the difference is between God and the Father. God is the originator of all things and the originator of His eternal purpose, His eternal economy. As the Father, God is the source of life for the Body. As the originator, He created us in the old creation, and as the source, He regenerated us in the new creation to be the church. Concerning the old creation, we were created by God. Concerning the new creation, we were regenerated by the Father. On the one hand, we are still the old creation, and on the other hand, we are the new creation. Ephesians 2:15 tells us that through the death of Christ in the flesh, one new man has been created, and this new man is the Body. This Body is of God the originator, and of the Father the source. The very originator and the source are over all of us, through all of us, and in all of us.

Over All

To say that God is over all of us signifies God's sovereign authority. In business corporations people are either over others or under others. God is over us and we are all under Him. This means that He is sovereign over us and that He has the authority over us. We have already seen in chapter thirty-eight that when we submit to the inner throne, we experience the flow of the divine life. When you go shopping, do not "throw the throne away." When you get into the department store, do not dethrone God. You have to enthrone Him. You have to realize that you are under God and that God is over you. God is sovereign and God is the authority over you. You must submit yourself to His authority.

The unbelievers do not have God over them or above them in their experience, but what about our experience? For God to be over us is not a doctrine. We should always be under God's sovereignty. Our home and our family must be under God's authority. If we are going to enjoy the triune existence applied to us today, we should be under God's authority, under His sovereignty. He is over us and we are under Him, so we need to submit ourselves to Him.

On this earth today everybody likes to have freedom. Also, everyone likes to be over everyone else. Today, however, we have to realize that God is our authority, and we have to submit ourselves under His authority. We should not be like the unbelievers who do not want to be under anybody, but we are the believers having God over us as our authority.

Through All

The one God and Father is also through all. We all should ask ourselves whether God was able to get through us today. Did He get through us or did we frustrate Him? On certain streets or lanes there is a sign which reads—"No Thorough-fare." This, of course, means that you cannot get through on this street. In my early days as a Christian, God was struggling to get through me quite often. Actually and outwardly, I was very ethical, moral, and good. However, God could not get through me easily as a young believer. At that time, on most of the lanes and on most of the streets within me there was a sign which read—"No Thoroughfare." God could not get through. The young saints among us especially need to ask themselves whether God has gotten through in them in certain matters. You may come to the meetings regularly, but this does not mean that you let God through. God must be over us, and He also must be through us. The question is—do we give Him the thoroughfare? Most of the time in us or with us God only sees a "dead end."

Many times all the avenues in our being are blocked, and God cannot get through in us. Do you believe that God can get through you all the time? Most of the time God does not have a freeway in us, but instead He runs into "many red lights." The basic problem that we have with God is that we do not give Him a thoroughfare. Your character may be excellent and there may be nothing wrong in your behavior morally speaking, yet all the avenues and streets within you are blocked to God. It is a very precious thing that we would give God a thoroughfare through us. Quite often, we do not let God get through in us for a whole day. This means that we do not have much enjoyment of God for our existence. We Christians have God, but because He could not get through us, we do not enjoy Him as our existence. He is over us and He is in us, yet He could not get through us. Paul's teaching here is altogether experiential.

In All

Paul then goes on to say that God is in all. Paul begins with over all, continues with through all, and ends with in all. First, you must be under God's sovereignty, and then you must give Him a thoroughfare all the time. As a result, He can abide in you. Paul is not talking about an objective God, but his description is altogether subjective. For God to be over us, through us, and in us is experiential and subjective that we may enjoy His presence as our existence. We exist by this God who is over us, through us, and in us.

Our Experience

All of us as believers have God, but do we have God in our experience that is over us, through us, and in us? Is God really over you, through you, and in you? Maybe your job, your business, your education, or a promotion is over you, but not God. Many things are getting through you daily. You may give a thoroughfare to many things, but not to God. A lot of things may be right now abiding in you, but not God. God may not be above you, through you, and in you. We may have a God who is merely in the third heavens, far away from us. Paul, however, unveils the very God of the Body of Christ who is over the Body, through the Body, and in the Body. This is the subjective God for our daily existence. We need to be honest before the Lord to allow this word to "check us out" so that we can see where we really are. If we would really open to the Lord, we may see that we are off and that we are not under Him, we are not letting Him through us, and we do not give Him the rule within us. He wants to be such a God to us, but we may not agree with Him.

What we have been fellowshipping is a preapplication of the New Jerusalem to us today in the church life. In the church life today we must have God existing with us in this way, applied to our daily experience. Daily we must be under Him, daily we must let Him go through us, and daily we must give Him our inner room that He may stay in us. Then we exist with Him. Most saints, however, do not exist with God over them, through them, and in them.

EXISTING WITH THE LORD CHRIST

We also need to be those existing with the Lord Christ (Eph. 4:5). Our existence today must be one with Christ in the way He lives in us. Many of us have heard message after message telling us that Christ lives in us, yet in our daily life we do not exist with Christ living in us. Christ living in us is a continuation of the Father being over us, and eventually in us. The Son's living in us is a continuation of the Father's being in us. When God is over us, through us, and in us, that is Christ living in us. When Christ lives in us (Gal. 2:20a), we live by Him (John 6:57b), which means we exist by Him. Furthermore, we even live Christ (Phil. 1:21). To live by Christ is not as high as to live Christ. We need to live Christ. The very Christ whom we live is the very substance with which we exist. We exist with Christ as the living substance.

The facade of the New Jerusalem is its twelve pearl gates. The front of a building is its facade. Today we must have Christ living out of us as our facade, our front. We exist not only with God the Father over us, through us, and in us, but also with Christ living in us, that we may live by Christ and that we may live Christ. Eventually, we magnify Christ (Phil. 1:20). The first thing that can be seen in the New Jerusalem is the pearl gates. These gates are the magnification of Christ, and today we must exist in a way that Christ is magnified in our existence. In order for us to enter into such a state, there is the need of much time for the divine nature within us to develop and for our growth in life, yet we have to realize that the existence of the New Jerusalem should be applied to our daily life. The New Jerusalem has the Father's nature as its city proper and the pearls as its gates. We must live by Christ, we must live Christ, and we must magnify Christ by His living in us. When He is living in us, He is surely secreting His resurrection life around us, making us pearls, and these pearls are His magnification.

EXISTING WITH THE SPIRIT

Finally, we should be those existing with the Spirit (Eph. 4:4). Ephesians 4:4 refers to the one Body and the one Spirit. This verse indicates that the very Spirit is the essence and the substance of the Body, the church. The church today must be substantially and essentially the Spirit Himself. If there is no Spirit, there is no Body, no church. Without the Spirit, all we have is a kind of human congregation. The church must be substantially and essentially the Spirit. When we sing a hymn, we sing it with the Spirit. When we speak, we speak with the Spirit. When we serve, we serve with the Spirit. When we testify, share, and function, we do it entirely with the Spirit. Without the Spirit, there is no substance of the church. Without the Spirit, the church is the same as any other social organization. The church must be one Body with the Spirit as its substance.

Some may wonder how we can say that the Spirit is the substance or the essence of the church. First, the New Testament tells us that we were regenerated by the Spirit (John 3:6b). Since the Spirit has regenerated us, this regenerating Spirit has become the very substance and the very essence of the church. The New Testament also tells us that we have been baptized in the Spirit (1 Cor. 12:13a). Now we are those drinking the Spirit (1 Cor. 12:13b). Day after day the Spirit is our drink, and whatever we drink becomes our intrinsic essence. Therefore, the Spirit must be the intrinsic essence of the church life. Furthermore, we are now being transformed by the Spirit (2 Cor. 3:18). He is now transforming us with the divine element, which is being added to us to replace and discharge the old element of our old nature. You and I have to exist with the Spirit as our spiritual essence. Finally, we are being strengthened and enriched by the sevenfold intensified Spirit (Rev. 1:4b) for the Body life, which will consummate in the New Jerusalem.

THE NEED OF A VISION

The application of the New Jerusalem in its triune existence is described in Ephesians 4:4-6. These verses show us how the church can exist with the Triune God, with the Father, with the Lord, and with the Spirit. I hope that we all have seen something concerning the triune existence. The Bible is a book full of revelations and full of visions. We should not limit our understanding of the Bible according to the ability of our mentality. Our mentality is too small. This is why Paul prays in Ephesians 1:17 that the Father would give us a spirit of wisdom and revelation, that He would open our inner eyes that we might see something. We need the vision to see how the Triune God can be our daily existence. We need a vision to see how we have to exist with God the Father over us, through us, and in us; with the Son living in us that we may take Him as our life to live by Him, to live Him, and to magnify Him; and we also have to see that the very consummation of the Triune God is the reaching Spirit who is right now within us. He has regenerated us, we have been baptized in Him, we are drinking Him, and He is transforming us. He is the very substance and the very essence of our church life. This is the existence of the New Jerusalem applied to us today. I am happy for this wonderful portion of the Scriptures where we can see the Spirit, the Lord, and God the Father being the substance of our daily existence. It is truly marvelous that today we can enjoy a foretaste of the existence of the New Jerusalem in eternity.

CHAPTER FORTY-TWO

THE NEW JERUSALEM'S APPLICATION TO THE BELIEVERS— THE TRIUNE LIVING

Scripture Reading: John 1:13; Eph. 4:18; 1 John 4:8, 16; 1:5, 2-3; Col. 2:9; 3:4; Rev. 2:7; Phil. 1:20; John 14:17a; 15:26; 16:13-15; Rom. 8:2; Rev. 22:17b; Phil. 1:19

THE PICTURE OF THE NEW JERUSALEM

I hope that we all have been impressed with the picture that we have seen concerning the New Jerusalem. The holy city is a golden mountain, and around this mountain is a wall built with jasper. The city itself lies "foursquare" (Rev. 21:16) with its length, breadth, and height equal. At the bottom of the wall are twelve layers of precious stone as the wall's foundation. On each of the four sides of the wall are three pearl gates. On the top of the city is a throne, and this throne is the throne of God and of the Lamb. The Lamb is the lamp of the city, and God is within the Lamb as the light. Out of the throne proceeds the river of water of life, and this river is in the middle of a golden street which goes down the mountain in a spiral fashion. On the two sides of the river grows the tree of life, which is a vine spreading and proceeding along the flow of the water of life, producing new fruit each month, for God's people to receive and enjoy.

THE LIVING OF THE NEW JERUSALEM

Such a picture has helped us to see the entry into the city, the constitution of the city with the divine element of the Triune God, and the existence of the city. Now we need to se the living of the New Jerusalem. The living of the city is al

triune. In the New Jerusalem we see that the One sitting on
the throne is the source of life. This refers to God the Father
who is within the Lamb as the light and who is the source of
life (John 5:26). Proceeding out of the throne is the river of
water of life. John 7:38-39 indicates that the river of water
of life denotes the Spirit of life. In this river grows the tree of
life which refers to the Son. Thus, we see the triune living
of the New Jerusalem—the Father sitting on the throne as
the source, the Spirit flowing out of the Father as a river, and
the Son as the tree of life growing in the Spirit to express
Himself for the life supply of the entire city. Actually, the
city's living is the Triune God's living. In eternity in the new
heaven and the new earth, the Triune God and His redeemed
people are one entity. The Triune God and His chosen,
redeemed, called, forgiven, regenerated, transformed, and
glorified people will be mingled together as one for eternity.

Some believers may feel that God is one entity and that
they are another entity. However, we must realize that God is
not only with us and in us but also mingled with us (1 Cor.
6:17). Many Christians do not believe in the truth of mingling. They contend that it is a heresy to say that a person is
mingled with God and that this is to make yourself God. They
feel that to say that God is mingled with man is to lower
down God by making Him a man. The Bible, however, tells us
that the Word became flesh (John 1:14). The Word is God and
flesh is man, which means that God made Himself man and
was a man. God became a man, and He lived on this earth for
thirty-three and a half years as a man. In the last three and a
half years of His earthly life, He traveled and ministered. He
was a genuine, perfect man with a stomach to digest food,
with tears to shed, and with blood to shed on the cross for our
sins. To say that God became a man is not to lower down God,
but to honor and respect Him. What a wonder it is that God
became a man, that the Creator became a creature! What a
glory that our God made Himself a man!

To say that we are mingled with God, though, does not
mean that we become God in His deity and that we are qualified to be the object of people's worship. This is a top
blasphemy and is utterly heretical. To say that we have been

born of God, though, and that we have the life of God and the nature of God is a divine, scriptural fact (John 1:13; 1 John 5:11-12; 2 Pet. 1:4). Since we all were born of a man, this makes us a man. Whatever is born of a dog is a dog. Because we were born of a man, we have a man's life and a man's nature. In like manner, the fact that we have been born of God means that we have God's life and God's nature and that we are the sons of God. If you say that you are God and that you are deified with His deity and Godhead to be an object of worship, this is heresy. However, if you say that you are like God in your being (1 John 3:2), having His life and nature, this is the truth according to the divine revelation.

The New Testament tells us that the Lord Jesus is God and the Son of God; also the Lord Jesus is man as well as the Son of Man. Some of the church fathers have used the term "deification" to describe the fact that we have been mingled with God and that we are partakers of God's life and nature. When you use the word deified, though, if you mean that you have been made God in His Godhead to be an object of worship, this is heresy. On the other hand, if your denotation is that through regeneration you have received God's life and nature and that now you are a son of God, this is altogether safe and scriptural. We all have to admit and boast of the wonderful fact that we have been born of God. We have received His life and His nature, and we are now partakers of the divine nature, enjoying the divine nature daily. We and our God are mingled together as one entity.

On the one hand, we are one with God, being mingled with Him. On the other hand, He is the object of our worship and we are His worshippers. First Corinthians 6:17 tells us that "he who is joined to the Lord is one spirit." The New Testament also tells us that God dwells in us and that we are dwelling in God (1 John 4:15). The fact that we are in God and God is in us is coinherence. Coinherence is even deeper than mingling. Even today we and God are not two entities but one. When eternity comes, we will not be an entity separate from God, but we will be one with God, thus one entity. This one divine entity is the New Jerusalem.

We can see God in the New Jerusalem in His Trinity, and we can see ourselves in the New Jerusalem in a triune way. Our entry into the New Jerusalem is triune, our constitution is triune, our existence is triune, and now we must see that our living is triune. We live triunely with the Father, with the Son, and with the Spirit. The church life today as a precursor of the New Jerusalem should be the same. The church life is a miniature of the New Jerusalem, but in its nature and in the intrinsic element of the triune living, the church today should be exactly the same as its full consummation. Individually we are a small New Jerusalem and corporately as the church life we are also a miniature New Jerusalem.

Living with the Father

We should be those living with the Father as the source of life (John 1:13; Eph. 4:18; John 5:26) on the throne. The first striking point of the New Jerusalem is that God is sitting on the throne. This God is the Lamb-God, the redeeming God, God the Redeemer. Genesis 1:1 does not tell us that in the beginning God and the Lamb created the heavens and the earth. The first verse of the book of Genesis tells us that God only created. In Revelation 22:1, however, we see God and the Lamb which signifies that God is now the redeeming God, no longer merely the creating God. In Genesis 1:1 He was the creating God, but in Revelation 22:1 we see the redeeming God.

Revelation 22:1 tells us that the throne is the throne of God and the Lamb. Here it indicates that two are sitting on one throne. How can two sit on one throne? Actually, God and the Lamb are not two, but they are coinhering. The Father is in the Son and the Son is in the Father (John 14:10-11). For eternity they are the redeeming God. The "green," jasper God is within the "red," sardius Lamb (Rev. 4:3). This redeeming God is the source of life. We all need to look at this marvelous picture. Here is a golden mountain twelve thousand stadia or approximately thirteen hundred and sixty-four miles high. On the top of this high mountain is a throne and One is sitting on this throne who is both God and man, the redeeming

God. He is the source from which flows the river of water of life.

In 1977 a few of us brothers went to see the Holy Land. One day we drove to the north, to Caesarea Philippi. At the foot of Mt. Hermon, there is a fountain which is one of the three sources of the Jordan River. There is a big spring that comes out of this fountain, and the Jordan River flows out from this spring. The flow of the Jordan River comes from the spring, and the spring comes from the fountain. This is a picture of the Triune God flowing Himself into His redeemed people. The redeeming God is sitting on the throne with His sovereign authority as the very source of life. God the Father is the source, God the Son is the redeeming element, and the throne of God is the element of the divine authority. From this source flows the Spirit as the living water throughout the entire city. Today we should have a living with the Father as the source of life on the throne. We must take the Godhead as our very source and as our very authority. We have already seen that we cannot "throw the throne away" and still enjoy the flow of life. We must take the throne and be under the throne in order to have the enjoyment of the flowing life. Today we must see that we need to take God as our source with His redeeming element and with the element of His divine authority. When we do this, we have the flow of life.

We must have a living with the Father as the source of life. What is the source of our daily living, of our marriage life, of our home life, and of our church life? We should be able to tell ourselves, "Amen, Lord. The source of my family life, marriage life, business life, and church life is God the Father with His redeeming element and with the element of His divine authority." We also live with the Father as love (1 John 4:8, 16), the nature of God's essence, and as light (1 John 1:5), the nature of God's expression. In the very divine life which flows from the divine source is love and light.

The only way that we could have such a living, taking God as the source of life, as love, the nature of His essence, and as light, the nature of His expression, is in the fellowship of His divine life (1 John 1:2-3). We must remain and keep ourselves in the fellowship of the divine life. In order to do this, we must have a definite, set-aside time every day to stay with the Father in fellowship. This time should be at least five minutes long. The longer your time is for this fellowship, though, the better. During this time, do not care for anything and lay aside every other burden. Just have a time absolutely for you to contact the source of the divine life to remain in the divine fellowship.

In order to have such a time, you first have to practice to get everything done. Then gradually, you have to learn that you can still have this time of fellowship with many things undone. At first, if you have anything undone, your heart is always there. During your time of fellowship, your mind may wander to think about the things you have to do or bear. You have to improve yourself in this practice of remaining in the fellowship, however, until you advance into a state where you can be so free to remain with the Father for a set time with many things still undone. Even though there are many things around me that I see undone and that I feel compelled to do, I still set aside some time to enjoy the fellowship of the Father's divine life.

You must also learn during this set aside time to keep yourself in the fellowship of the divine life. After three or four minutes of having a time with the Lord, the telephone may ring. Let it ring. You do not need to answer it. Learn to free yourself from outside disturbances to keep yourself in the fellowship of the divine life. Finally, you must learn to stop anything that you sense interrupts your fellowship. Always try your best to keep yourself in the divine fellowship. Then you will enjoy God the Father as the source of life, as love, the nature of His essence, and as light, the nature of His expression.

Living with the Son

We also need to be those living with the Son as the embodiment of God (Col. 2:9). When you have the Father, you have the Son, and when you have the Son, you have the Father. The Son as the embodiment of God is life (Col. 3:4). We live with the Father as the source of life, but we live with the Son as life. The New Testament does not tell us that the Father is life, but it always says that the Son is life (Col. 3:4; John 14:6). The life comes out of the source, of course, just as the flow comes out of the fountain. We live with the Father as the fountain, and we live with the Son as life and as the life supply, the tree of life (Rev. 22:2; 2:7). Even today in the church life, as indicated by Revelation 2:7, we can eat the tree of life.

The Lord Jesus is our daily life supply, and every day we must call upon His name to enjoy this supply (Rom. 10:12). Day after day we need to be those who call upon the name of the Lord again and again. When we call, "O Lord," this is very good, but it is not as sweet as when we call, "O Lord Jesus." In our experience, our calling becomes sweeter when we add the name Jesus. If we call by saying, "O Lord Jesus Christ," this makes our calling richer. At times our praying for many things frustrates us from the enjoyment of the Son as our life and as our life supply. If we would come to the Lord and call upon His dear name, praising and worshipping Him for who He is and for what He has done, our enjoyment and fellowship with Him would be quite rich.

We all have to learn how to take our Lord individually and extensively as our enjoyment for His magnification (Phil. 1:20). When we enjoy the Lord in such a way, we magnify Him. Sometimes our prayer to the Lord is in a "pitiful way," where we complain about our negative situation or environment. If this is the case, we are not magnifying Christ. Despite our environment or negative situation, we need to learn to enjoy Christ to a great extent. Then we will be able to say, like Paul did, that our expectation and hope is that Christ will be magnified in our bodies, whether through life or through death (Phil. 1:20). Paul enjoyed Christ even in prison because he was enjoying the bountiful supply of the Spirit of Jesus Christ for his daily salvation (Phil. 1:19). Through this all-inclusive bountiful supply, Paul was saved to magnify Christ in his body. He was living in prison with Christ as the embodiment of the Triune God, as the life, and as the life supply. This means that he was eating Jesus as the tree of life all the time.

Living with the Spirit

We also need to be those living triunely with the Spirit as the realization of Christ the Son (John 14:17a; 15:26; 16:13-15). When you call, "O Lord Jesus Christ," you enjoy the Lord. When you enjoy the Lord, immediately the Lord within you is the Spirit. The Lord is realized as the Spirit. The more you call on the Lord, the more you have the Spirit within you as the realization of Christ, the Spirit of reality. The reality mainly denotes the very Being in the divine essence of the Triune God. The Spirit is the reality of the Triune God.

This Spirit is also the Spirit of life (Rom. 8:2). The Father is the source of life, the Son is life, and the Spirit is the Spirit of life. The power plant is the source of electricity, and the electricity itself is electricity. But in order for the electricity to be applied to us, there is the need of the flow or the current of electricity. The electrical current is actually the electricity itself, but if the electricity is not moving, it cannot be applied. Electricity can only be applied by its current. The current is the flowing of electricity. We may say that the Father is the power plant, the Son is the electricity, and the Spirit is the current of electricity. The Spirit of life simply means the current of life. When life moves, it is the Spirit of life. This corresponds to 2 Corinthians 13:14 which refers to the grace of Christ, the love of God, and the fellowship of the Holy Spirit. The fellowship of the Spirit is the flow of the Spirit. When we live with the Spirit, we enjoy the flow of life, and this life becomes our real supply. The Spirit of life is also the water of life (Rev. 22:17b), and we live with the Spirit as the water of life for the bountiful supply of the Triune God (Phil. 1:19).

OUR LIVING TODAY

Our living should be a triune living, in which we live with the Father in the fellowship of His divine life, live with the Son for His magnification, and live with the Spirit for the bountiful supply of the Triune God. The entire New Jerusalem lives by the Father on the throne, by the Spirit flowing as the river of water of life, and by the Son growing as the tree of life. The Son growing is the life supply, and the Spirit flowing is the bountiful supply of the Triune God to support the entire city. This should not be something merely in the future, but this must be our living today. We are living with the Father as the source, as love and as light, in His fellowship of the divine life; we are living with the Son as the embodiment of the Triune God as life and as life supply for His magnification; and we are living with the Spirit as the realization of this enjoyable Christ as the Spirit of life and as the water of life for the bountiful supply of the Triune God to nourish the entire church life. This should be our triune living.

CHAPTER FORTY-THREE

THE NEW JERUSALEM'S
APPLICATION TO THE BELIEVERS—
THE TRIUNE ENJOYMENT

Scripture Reading: Rev. 21:23; 22:5; John 1:4; 8:12; 1 John
1:5; Rev. 21:11; 22:2, 14; Gen. 2:9; Rev. 22:1, 14, 17

The fifth aspect of the New Jerusalem's application to
the believers is the triune enjoyment. This is the most crucial
aspect of the application of the New Jerusalem. According
to the record in Revelation 21 and 22 the main stress of the
New Jerusalem's application to us is the aspect of the triune
enjoyment. The enjoyment of the New Jerusalem is of the
Triune God, the very Godhead of the Trinity. The items of our
triune enjoyment are the divine light (Rev. 21:23a; 22:5), the
divine river (Rev. 22:1), and the divine tree (Rev. 22:2a, 14;
Gen. 2:9).

Any type of beautiful scenery needs light, a river, and
trees. The earth lives by these three items. If there were no
light, no water, and no trees, there would be no life. Also, we
ourselves live by light, by water, and by food. These three
items are necessities to the earth and to us human beings. In
the same way, the New Jerusalem will live by God as light, by
God as water, and by God as food.

IN THE DIVINE LIGHT

Light refers to God the Father. First John 1:5 tells us that
God is light, and according to the context of this verse, God
mainly refers to God the Father. While love is the nature of
God's intrinsic essence, light is the nature of God's outward
expression. In the New Jerusalem light refers to God Himself
to illuminate the entire city for His expression. Revelation

21:23 tells us that the city has no need of the sun or of the moon. This indicates that in the new heaven and the new earth the sun and moon will still be there. The fact that the tree of life in the New Jerusalem yields its fruit each month also indicates that in the new heaven and new earth the moon will still be there to divide the twelve months. The sun will also be there to separate day and night into periods of twelve hours each. Isaiah 30:26 tells us that in the coming days, "the light of the moon shall be as the light of the sun, and the light of the sun shall be sevenfold." In the New Jerusalem, however, there will be no need of the sun or of the moon. The light in the city will be God Himself as the light of life (John 1:4; 8:12). Since such a divine light will illumine the holy city, it has no need of any other light, whether created by God or made by man (Rev. 22:5). The God-created and man-made lights will not be needed in the New Jerusalem because we have God, who is much brighter than the sun and the moon and even more bright than the man-made lamps.

God as the divine light, the light of life, is contained in the Lamb as the lamp (Rev. 21:23b). An electrical light always needs a bulb or a lamp to contain it; otherwise, there is the possibility of a person being electrocuted. In the New Jerusalem, the redeeming Lamb is the lamp, and God is within Him as the light. This indicates that without the redeeming Christ to contain the divine light, the divine light would "kill" us. With the redeeming Christ as the lamp, however, the divine light does not kill us; it illumines us. The killing becomes a kind of enlightening through the redemption of Christ. First Timothy 6:16 tells us that God dwells in unapproachable light. In Christ, though, God becomes approachable. Outside of Christ, God's shining is a kind of killing, but inside of Christ, God's shining is a kind of illumination. Since the day we were saved, we began to enjoy God as the divine light in the redeeming Christ illumining us all the time. Even today we should enjoy God in this way.

Today we Christians actually have God Himself within Christ as our light. We do not need philosophy, the human-made light, and we do not need ethical teachings such as that of Confucius. We do not need any kind of religious teaching,

because we have God Himself within us. Do you need someone to tell you to love your parents? Do you not have a divine
light in you all day long shining within you to let you know
that you have to honor your parents? We have to realize,
though, that Paul still tells us to honor our father and mother
(Eph. 6:2). If all Christians have God as the light within
them, why does the New Testament still teach many things?
Beginning in Ephesians 5:22 through 6:9 Paul unveils the
kind of living needed in ethical relationships. He talks about
the relationship between wife and husband, between children
and parents, and between slaves and masters. These charges
are not given in the first chapter of Ephesians, but in the last
two chapters. Before giving us this kind of teaching, Paul
says in Ephesians 5:14, "Wherefore He says, Awake sleeper,
and arise from among the dead, and Christ shall shine on
you." The New Testament does not reveal the teaching to us
first, but the divine light. Because we are still in the old creation, we still need this teaching. When we get to the New
Jerusalem, however, there will be nothing old, and there will
be no teaching there. If we would care for the new creation
and the inner anointing all the time, there would be no need
of teaching. Because we are in the old creation, however,
many times we need some teaching to remind us to awake
from our sleep.

According to the principle of the new creation, we have
God in us as light. In Him there is no darkness at all (1 John
1:5). When you are fellowshipping with God, you do not need
any other light. As long as you have Him, He is the very light
to you, and you do not need any teaching or doctrine. As long
as you have the very God who is light to you in your fellowship with Him, there is no need of anything else.

In the New Jerusalem gold symbolizes God's divine
nature, and light refers to His divine shining. This shining is
in the redeeming Lamb as the lamp to hold the divine light
for our benefit that we may enjoy God as the shining One in
the redeeming Christ. Revelation 21:11 indicates that God as
the light shines through the New Jerusalem. This verse tells
us that "her light was like a most precious stone, as a jasper
stone, clear as crystal." The word for "light" in this verse is

"luminary" or "light-bearer" in the Greek. The entire wall of the New Jerusalem is built with jasper (Rev. 21:18), and the light of the New Jerusalem is like jasper stone, bearing the appearance of God (Rev. 4:3) to express God by her shining. God in the redeeming Lamb is the light, and the entire city is a luminary, a great light-bearer. This means that God as the divine light shines within and through the redeeming Christ, and this shining enlightens the entire city. Then the entire city becomes a light-bearer. This bearing of God's light becomes an expression, and this expression is God's goal. This is why Revelation 21:11 also tells us that the holy city has the glory of God. Glory is God expressed. In the New Jerusalem God is light, and His shining is His glory. The shining is the coming out of the light, so when God shines in the city, God is expressed in glory, first in Christ and through Christ and then in the city and through the saints. God is the light, Christ is the containing lamp, and the city's wall bears the divine light to express God.

We need to apply this picture to our daily life. Today we have God in the redeeming Christ shining within us, and we are being transformed to be transparent. In our old creation we are opaque, but in our new creation we are transparent. Second Corinthians 3:18 says we are being transformed into His image from one degree of glory to another degree of glory. Eventually we will have the appearance of jasper and will fully express the "jasper God" (Rev. 4:3).

A certain saint may be a very good person, but he may still be opaque and not transparent because he remains in the old creation so much. Because of this, not much transformation has transpired in his being. When you are with another saint, though, you may sense that with him everything is transparent since he has experienced much transformation in life. Many times when you come to a certain brother, you cannot get any light. Your coming to another brother, however, may bring you into the light. Even before he begins to talk to you, you are in the light. When you are home, you are in darkness. But when you come to this dear saint, your coming means light to you. When you come to him everything is clear, darkness is gone, and there is light. Opaqueness is over, and everything is transparent. We all need to be transformed to such an extent that we are full of light and transparent.

In the Bible darkness is a type of punishment. God punished the Egyptians with a thick darkness for three days (Exo. 10:22), and in the future God will punish the Antichrist and his kingdom with darkness (Rev. 16:10). Part of the enjoyment in the New Jerusalem is that there will be no night. The city will be full of light, and this light is God the Father. He will not only be the nature of the New Jerusalem, but He will also be the shining light as an enjoyment to the entire city. The first enjoyment in the New Jerusalem is God as our light. Our experience today is the same. When we are left in darkness, this is a real punishment. When we open our entire being to Him, however, we are in the light, and the light is God Himself enjoyed by us in our daily life. This is the first aspect of the triune enjoyment.

IN THE DIVINE RIVER

The second aspect of the triune enjoyment is the river of water of life (Rev. 22:1). This river refers to the Spirit as the consummation of the Triune God. John 7:38-39 indicates that the rivers of living water refer to the Spirit. In Revelation 22:1 is the throne of God (the Father) and of the Lamb (the Son) out of which flows the river of the water of life (the Spirit). God, the Lamb, and the water of life refer to the Trinity. The river is the flowing of the Triune God and the consummate coming out of God. When God flows out, He becomes the river of water of life. When the Triune God reaches you, He is the living water. (See notes 1^2—1^5 in Rev. 22—Recovery Version.)

This flowing river is the ultimate consummation of the Triune God reaching you. God on the throne in the Lamb reaches the entire city as the flowing river. Today God reaches us by being the life-giving Spirit (1 Cor. 15:45b). God the Father made an eternal plan (Eph. 3:11), He sent the Son, and the Son came with Him (John 8:29) to accomplish His plan on the cross. While He was accomplishing God's plan on the cross, blood and water issued out of His side (John 19:34). This was typified in the Old Testament by the cleft rock flowing out the living water (Exo. 17:6). The water signifies the ultimate consummation of the Triune God reaching His redeemed people. In Revelation 22 God in the Lamb flows as the living water to reach His redeemed people.

Revelation 22:1 says, "And he showed me a river of water of life, bright as crystal, proceeding out of the throne of God and of the Lamb in the middle of its street." Many Christians have never paid adequate attention to this last phrase—"in the middle of its street." The river flows out of the throne, but it flows in the middle of the street. Revelation 21:21 tells us that the street of the city is pure gold. Without the street, the river cannot flow. If there is no street, there is no river. The street in the New Jerusalem is the very riverbed of this flowing river. The street being gold indicates that the way in the New Jerusalem is God's divine nature. The Christian way for the Christian life is God's divine nature. We should dress according to God's divine nature, behave ourselves according to God's divine nature, talk to others according to God's divine nature, and deal with our spouse according to God's divine nature. The highway of our Christian life is God's divine nature, which is the street of the entire city.

If the street is there, in the middle of the street flows the river. According to our experience, if we do not behave and live according to God's divine nature, we feel dried up within, and we do not sense the flow of life within us. We have the flow of the water of life within us when we are living, behaving, and having our life according to God's divine nature. If you do not walk in the divine nature as the divine street, you are dried up because there is no riverbed for the flow of the street. There is the need of a riverbed so the river can flow in and through our inner being. This corresponds with our daily experience.

The light of the New Jerusalem is God the Father, and the river is God the Spirit. This Spirit can only flow in the middle of the divine nature. It cannot flow in the human nature. Obviously, God the Spirit cannot flow in anything sinful. Also, He cannot even flow in your natural, human nature. He can only flow in the divine nature. When you live the divine nature and have your daily life in the divine nature, that divine nature becomes an excellent riverbed for the Holy Spirit to flow through. This is a crucial matter. Sometimes you may wonder where the flow of life within you is. You may feel that every day you are a "dried up" Christian. The reason why you are dried up is that you do not know how to lead a life according to the divine nature. You must make a decision that from now on as a child of God with His divine nature, you will live, behave, and do everything according to this divine nature. If you do this, you will immediately have the sense that you are no longer dried up but that a river is flowing within you.

For God the Father to be our light, we need the redeeming Christ, and for God the Spirit to be our river, we need the divine nature. The divine light is contained in the redeeming Christ, and the divine river is flowing in the divine nature. Without the redeeming Christ, you cannot take and enjoy God as the shining light. Without the divine nature, there is no way for the Holy Spirit to flow in you. You need both the redeeming Christ and the divine nature. Praise the Lord that we are the partakers of the divine nature and that we also have the redeeming Christ. We have the full right and privilege to enjoy the divine light and to claim the divine flow. Both the divine light, God the Father, and the divine flow, God the Spirit, are our portion even today. We must apply God the Father as the divine light in the redeeming Christ, and we must apply God the Spirit as the flowing river in the divine nature. This kind of revelation is much higher than any kind of ethical teaching. By the Lord's mercy, we are here under this revelation. This river flows in the divine street, and the street spirals down the golden mountain until it reaches all twelve gates. This means that the river saturates the New Jerusalem, carrying the tree of life with its fruit to nourish the city (Rev. 22:2a, 14).

IN THE DIVINE TREE

Where the divine river goes, the tree of life grows (Rev. 22:2). The tree of life signifies God Himself in Christ as the life supply to us (Gen. 2:9; John 1:4; 14:6). God the Father is the divine light, God the Spirit is the divine river, and God the Son is the divine tree, the very embodiment of the Triune

God as life. After God created man, He prepared a garden and put the man whom He had formed into that garden. Many trees were there, and among these trees one particular tree stood out—the tree of life (Gen. 2:9). This tree is the very embodiment of life. According to the divine revelation, only God Himself is life in the entire universe. This God who is life is absolutely embodied in Christ (Col. 2:9). Christ is the tree of life, and in this tree of life is the full enjoyment of all the riches of life. Revelation 22:2 tells us that the tree of life yields its fruit each month. Every month there is a crop. The tree of life produces twelve fruits to be our life supply. This depicts that today our Triune God embodied in Christ is our enjoyment. The fruits of the tree of life, as our life supply, will be the food of God's redeemed for eternity. They will be continually fresh, produced every month, twelve fruits yearly.

The tree of life was closed to the fallen man by God's glory, righteousness, and holiness until Christ's death fulfilled all the divine requirements. Through Christ's death, the tree of life is open again and available to all the sinners who would believe in Him and take Him as their Savior and life. Then they, as the believers in Christ, have the privilege to drink His Spirit as the water of life. In Revelation 22:14 is a promise of the tree of life, and in Revelation 22:17 is a calling to the water of life. We have answered the calling and we are now enjoying the promise.

THE TRIUNE ENJOYMENT TODAY

We all need to be enjoying God the Father as the light, God the Spirit as the river, and God the Son as the tree in a daily way. When you enjoy the Triune God in this way, you become "the most beautiful scenery." When a sister sees her husband enjoying God the Father as light, God the Spirit as the flowing river, and God the Son as the tree of life, she can see that her husband is "beautiful scenery." Light is with him, the river is flowing in him, and the tree is growing in him. If there is no light, no river, and no tree, there is nothing but desolation. In some Christian homes that I visited, I saw this desolation. I could not see the light, the river, or the tree. Quite often, though, when I entered into a saint's home, I had the full realization that the light was there, the river was flowing, and Christ was growing there.

Many times when I visit a certain church, I can see that it is full of light, full of the flowing river, and full of the tree of life. If this is the case, the church is full of beautiful scenery. It is beautiful, comfortable, and enjoyable. If the church in a certain locality is not enjoyable, this is because the light is dim, and the river and the tree are absent. A kind of desolation may exist in a particular church. Our hope, though, is that every church in the Lord's recovery would be full of beautiful scenery with these three divine things—the divine light shining, the divine river flowing, and the divine tree growing. The divine light is shining to enlighten us, the river is flowing to saturate and supply us, and the tree is growing to be our life supply and meet our every need. Today we can enjoy such a Triune God, and this Triune God will be our triune enjoyment in full in the New Jerusalem.

THE NEW JERUSALEM'S
APPLICATION TO THE BELIEVERS—
THE TRIUNE EXPRESSION

Scripture Reading: Rev. 21:9-14, 18-21; 22:1-2

Thus far, we have seen five aspects of the application of the New Jerusalem to the believers: its triune entry, triune constitution, triune existence, triune living, and triune enjoyment. In this final chapter we want to see the triune expression. Since we have entered into the Triune God and are being constituted with Him, existing and living with Him, and enjoying Him, we will surely express Him. In the New Jerusalem the city is a mountain of gold with pearl gates and with a jasper wall built upon twelve layers of precious stones. Gold expresses God in His divine nature, pearls express Christ in His death and resurrection, and precious stones express the Spirit in His transforming work with all the unsearchable riches of Christ. In the New Jerusalem we see the triune expression of the Father as the source of all the divine riches, of the Son as the embodiment of all the divine riches, and of the Spirit as the realization of all the divine riches.

OF THE FATHER—
THE SOURCE OF ALL THE DIVINE RICHES

We have to see the very intrinsic contents of the Father as the source of all the divine riches. The expression of God the Father as the source of all the divine riches is based upon His nature typified by gold (Rev. 21:18b). The base of the entire New Jerusalem is gold since the city itself is a mountain of gold. God's divine nature is the very base, ground, and site of the city. The triune expression of the Father is not only based upon His nature but also is in His glory (Rev. 21:11). The New Jerusalem does not need any natural or man-made light because God Himself is the light of the city. Light is the nature of God's expression. God Himself is signified as gold in His intrinsic nature, and God being light denotes His nature in His expression. When this light shines, this shining becomes His glory. The first two striking things about the New Jerusalem are the gold and the shining glory. The triune expression of the Father as the source of all the divine riches is based upon His golden nature in His shining glory.

This vision should be applied to us today in our practical life. Revelation tells us that the city itself is gold (21:18) and that the street of the city is pure gold as transparent glass (21:21). This means that the golden mountain in our experience becomes our way or our street. The divine gold which is pure and transparent should be our walkway in our daily life. The walkway in today's church life is God's pure and transparent divine nature. In the church life, you must be pure, transparent, frank, straight, and open; you must be divine. Playing politics is not God's way, but God's golden nature is our walkway. If you walk, behave, and have your being in God's divine nature as your walkway, God's light will shine from within you and this shining is His glory. When others come to your home, they will have the realization that glory is there. In your daily life, family life, business life, and church life, others should be able to see the divine gold, the divine shining glory. If you behave yourself in a clever, human, and political way, people will not be able to sense any divine nature in your behavior. In your behavior there will not be the shining glory, but rather your entire behavior will be opaque. Nearly all the worldly people are behaving "politically." Most of the time, their politeness is actually politics. Who, however, is behaving, walking, and having their living in the nature of God? Even most of today's Christians do not live in the divine nature. In the world today there is no golden street. In the past fifty-five years some people advised me not to be that frank in my speaking. However, whenever I tried not to be frank, I had the sense that I was behaving myself in the serpentine nature. Many people are "backbiters," talking behind each other's backs, yet behaving politely in front of each other. This kind of behavior is not the gold walkway of the New Jerusalem. Today in the Lord's recovery, by His mercy, we can see a little bit of the golden street, and there is also some amount of the divine glory shining.

The Bible does not teach us ethical things in the natural way; the Bible is a revelation unveiling what kind of walk we should take. We should take a walk in the nature of God, and spontaneously the divine glory will shine in us. Then people will be able to see an expression of God the Father as the gold and as the light. What I am telling you is according to my daily experience of the Father as the source of all the divine riches.

OF THE SON—THE EMBODIMENT
OF ALL THE DIVINE RICHES

The second aspect of the triune expression is the expression of the Son as the embodiment of all the divine riches. Whatever the source is and has is embodied in the Son. This triune expression of the Son as the embodiment of all the divine riches is in His Person and with His work. In Revelation, the Lamb is the redeeming Person, and this Redeemer as a Person is the lamp (21:23). The Lamb as the lamp is altogether for expression. All the light bulbs are for expressing the light contained within them. The entire New Jerusalem is under the expression of Christ the Person as the lamp. The lamp is like a big bulb which is able to enlighten a city whose breadth, length, and height are approximately thirteen hundred sixty-four miles. Such a large entity has only one lamp, and this lamp is Christ. God the Father is the gold and He is also the light, but this light needs a lamp. Without an adequate lamp or bulb, an electrical light will not shine in an enlightening way. In like manner, without Christ, the Lamb, being the lamp, God could not shine in the enlightening way.

As we have seen, in any kind of scenery, the first thing needed is the light. If God did not shine, we would not be able to see His golden nature. But God shines within the redeeming Lamb as the lamp in the enlightening way. The Son, being the Lamb in His Person, is the lamp to express all that the Father is as the light and as the source of the divine riches. All the divine riches are embodied in this lamp. A light bulb is the embodiment of the electrical light, or you may say it is the embodiment of the electrical riches. Because we are under the shining of the Son as the embodiment of all the divine riches, we can enjoy these riches. The light establishes and confirms us in our experience of the Triune God.

In the lamp is the Person of the Son shining and expressing the Triune God, but in the pearls (Rev. 21:21) is the Son's work of death and resurrection. We have seen that pearls are produced by oysters in the waters of death. When the oyster is wounded by a particle of sand, it secretes its life-juice around the sand and makes it a precious pearl. The oyster's wound typifies the death of Christ, and the life secretion of the oyster signifies the secretion of Christ's resurrection life. His Person is in the lamp, and His work is in the pearl.

Paul tells us in Galatians 2:20 that he has been crucified with Christ, and it is no longer he that lives but Christ lives in him. When you would not live by yourself and live absolutely by the crucified and resurrected Christ, in your daily life Christ is there as the lamp. It is no longer you that live, but Christ lives in you. If a husband and wife would live according to themselves and not according to Christ, they may argue frequently. But if both of them would declare "it is no longer I who live, but Christ lives in me," Christ as the lamp would be shining in their marriage life. When you say "it is no longer I who live, but Christ lives in me," you also stay in the wound, the death, of Christ. At the same time, Christ secretes His resurrection life around you making you a pearl for His expression. When you deny yourself by staying in His death, and live by taking your Redeemer as your life, Christ as the lamp is shining from within you, and based upon His redemptive death, He is secreting His divine life over you to make you a pearl. This is our expression of Christ in His Person and with His work of death and resurrection.

The lamp refers to the Son's person, the pearls refer to His work of death and resurrection, and the tree refers to His nourishment. He is not only making you into a pearl through His work of death and resurrection, but He is also the tree of life (Rev. 22:2) to nourish you with all His unsearchable riches. The twelve fruits of the tree of life yielded each month from the divine tree are for your nourishment.

OF THE SPIRIT—THE REALIZATION OF ALL THE DIVINE RICHES

The triune expression of the Spirit as the realization of all the divine riches is in His all-inclusiveness as the consummation of the Triune God. In Revelation 22:1 is the river of water of life proceeding out of the throne of God and of the Lamb. The Triune God reaches us in this river, and this reaching of the Triune God is the realization of all the divine riches. This reaching river makes everything that the Father is and has and everything that the Son is and has so practically real. The Spirit as the realization of all the divine riches is all-inclusive. The throne of God and of the Lamb is in this river, this river flows in the golden street, the divine nature, and in this river and along its banks is the tree of life (Rev. 22:2). All the divine things are wrapped up with this one flow. Without this flow, we would not be able to touch the throne, we would not be able to enjoy the divine nature, and we would not be able to partake of the tree of life, the rich Christ with all His unsearchable riches. God, the Lamb, the throne, the divine nature as the divine way, and Christ with all His unsearchable riches are wrapped up with this flow. When this flow comes to you, all these wonderful divine items come with it. This flow is the ultimate consummation of the Triune God with all His divine riches.

I am grateful to the Lord that in these last days He has opened the veil for us to see this all-inclusive and ultimate Spirit. In Revelation we first see that this all-inclusive Spirit is the seven Spirits as the seven lamps of the golden lamp-stand (4:5). At the end of the book of Revelation, we see the flow of the water of life, which is the all-inclusive Spirit as the ultimate consummation of the Triune God. The last symbol of the all-inclusive Spirit is a river proceeding out of the throne of God and of the Lamb. In John 7:38-39 the Lord Jesus predicted that the Spirit would be such a flow out of our innermost being. The consummate flow is the universal river which flows with God, with the Lamb, with the throne, with the divine nature as the divine way, and with all the unsearchable riches of Christ.

The Christian life must be a life in the Spirit, by the Spirit, and with the Spirit. In our homes, in our daily life, and in our church life, there must be a river flowing all the time that brings with it God, the Lamb, the throne, the divine nature as the divine way, and Christ with all His unsearchable riches for our enjoyment. The wife's submission should be the Spirit, and the husband's love should be the Spirit. Every aspect of our virtues must be the Spirit. The fruit of the Spirit in Galatians 5:22-23 are the very characteristics of Christ becoming our virtues. These virtues are the fruit of the Spirit which issue from the all-inclusive flow of the Spirit. Even today in the church life there is such a marvelous, all-inclusive flow. As long as we have God and the Lamb on the throne flowing in His divine nature as the divine way with Christ as the rich supply, there is nothing else that we need.

TODAY'S CHURCH LIFE

Today's church life in the Lord's recovery must be a precursor and a miniature of the New Jerusalem. We should be those who are being constituted with the Triune God, existing with the Triune God, and living with the Triune God. Every day we need to enjoy the Triune God, and spontaneously we then express the Triune God. This should be our present experience, and this will be our future destiny in eternity. The book of Revelation ends with a promise and a call. Revelation 22:14 promises that those who wash their robes have the right to the tree of life. In 22:17 there is a call from the Spirit and the Bride to drink the water of life. The church life today is passing on the promise of the tree of life and the call to drink the water of life. We are enjoying the Triune God in such a way and calling others to participate in the same kind of enjoyment. While we are enjoying Him, we express Him in a triune way.

A WORD OF CONCLUSION

In the application of the New Jerusalem, we have three main categories of the divine items which we partake of, enjoy, and express:

1)   The light, the lamp, the light-bearer, and the glory of the New Jerusalem. The light is God (Rev. 21:23; 22:5), the lamp is the Lamb (Rev. 21:23), the light-bearer is the city (Rev. 21:11b), and the glory is God expressed (Rev. 21:11a). God as light shines from within the Lamb as the lamp through the city as the light-bearer to express Himself as the glory.

2)   The throne, the street, the river and the tree of the New Jerusalem. The throne is the center (Rev. 22:1b), the street is the way (Rev. 22:1c), the river is the river of the water of life (Rev. 22:1a), and the tree is the tree of life (Rev. 22:2). From the throne as the center spirals the street as the way to pass through the entire city and to reach all its twelve gates. In the middle of the street flows the river of water of life to saturate the entire city, and on the two sides of the river grows the tree of life producing fruits to nourish the entire city.

3)   The creating God, the redeeming God, the flowing God, and the nourishing God. The creating God is God the Father as the Creator (Rev. 22:1b), the redeeming God is God the Son in His death as the Lamb (Rev. 22:1b), the flowing God is God the Spirit as the river (Rev. 22:1a), and the nourishing God is God the Son in His resurrection as the tree (Rev. 22:2). God the Father as the creator created the heaven and the earth and all the things within them, God the Son in His death as the Lamb redeemed the fallen creation, God the Spirit as the river saturates the redeemed, and God the Son in His resurrection as the tree of life nourishes the redeemed.